AFRICAN CHRISTIAN THEOLOGY

The Quest for Selfhood

AFRICAN CHRISTIAN THEOLOGY

The Quest for Selfhood

K. Gordon Molyneux

Mellen Research University Press
San Francisco

Library of Congress Cataloging-in-Publication Data

Molyneux, K. Gordon, 1945-
    African Christian theology : the quest for selfhood : a study of
contrasting processes of theological reflection in Zaire with
special reference to examples selected from Roman Catholic,
Kimbanguist, and Protestant church bodies / K. Gordon Molyneux.
        p.   cm.
    Includes bibliographical refernces.
    ISBN 0-7734-1946-2
    1. Christianity--Zaire--20th century. 2. Zaire--Religious life
and customs. I. Title.
BR1443.Z28M65   1993
230' .096--dc20
                                                        93-16622
                                                        CIP

Copyright   ©1993 K. Gordon Molyneux.

Editorial Inquiries:

Mellen Research University Press
534 Pacific Avenue
San Francisco
CA 94133

Order Fulfillment:

The Edwin Mellen Press
P.O. Box 450
Lewiston, NY 14092
USA

Printed in the United States of America

*Dedicated to
my Parents*

TABLE OF CONTENT5

2

4

AFRICAN CHRISTIAN THEOLOGY

Dr Gordon Molyneux

The contribution which Dr Molyneux has made to an understanding of African theology in this book seems to me to be a very considerable one and particularly for English-language readers. An English missionary in Zaïre, he is interpreting for us a full range of Zaïrean theology. It is remarkably comprehensive and ecumenical, extending across Catholic, Protestant and Kimbanguist experience, across oral theology as well as written, vernacular theology as well as Francophone, the theology of hymns as well as that of doctoral theses. No other work I know of has attempted to understand African theology in this way as a living whole.

For many readers the most exciting part of the book may be its study of Kimbanguist hymns. This is likely to prove a major contribution to an understanding of the development of African vernacular hymnody but it is no less important for the light it throws on Kimbanguism itself at the popular level, demonstrating for instance a deeply Christ-centred devotion.

The relationship Dr Molyneux demonstrated to exist between Christ and Kimbangu across hundreds of hymns should show how dangerous it is to contrast simplistically a French-language Kambanguism centred upon Christ and a vernacular Kimbanguism centred upon Kambangu.

6

Chapter 4 on 'the Gospel and Culture' seminars in North-East Zaïre takes us into what may be an even less well-known area of modern African theological experience, the interaction between a sensitive post-Lausanne evangelical missionary and the grass-roots of a 'mission church'. Here as in the earlier chapters on the Catholic theological faculty of Kinshasa and the making of Kimbanguist hymns, it is less the final conclusions that matter to the author than the analysis of a functioning theological metholody.

As a well-researched description of African theology as it is actually practised today, Dr Molyneux's work should be of the greatest value to anyone concerned to understand its growth, its diversity and its sheer living importance for millions of modern Christians. I warmly recommend it.

Professor Adrian Hastings
University of Leeds

20 November 1992

AUTHOR'S PREFACE

My initial expectation upon leaving the shores of England to return to the land of my birth was that I would be teaching students at secondary and post-secondary level in residential theological establishments in north-eastern Zaïre. I saw my task as transmitting the fruits of my own theological studies to relatively educated young men who would enter leadership positions in the Church.

Over the ensuing twenty years and more, two major perceptual adjustments have had to be made. The first concerns the loci of theological reflection. I had naively assumed that the theological process was carried out almost exclusively in theological schools and Bible Schools. That it does take place there is obvious. However, my own concern that my students should become skilled in communicating with ordinary and often unschooled people in the rural areas meant that I accompanied them to outlying and sometimes remote villages for preaching and extension teaching. Listening to the discussions during the day and at night around the log fire impressed upon me that theological thinking in fact takes place at all levels and in all places. The quest for making sense of one's faith is going on just as much in the oral sector as in the educated, literary one. Its dynamics and methods may be different, but the search is the same.

The second adjustment came upon realising that since it is man that does theology, then theology will not be the same everywhere but will reflect the diversity of man in his particular context. Even if the notion of biblical revelation is taken very seriously as I believe it should, the questions, understanding and issues that are brought to interact with that revelation will mean that the parameters of theology will be to a greater or lesser degree different. Repeatedly in the classroom I have been reminded that my theological parameters and those of my students have not coincided, and I have been compelled not to abandon mine as necessarily incorrect, but to recognize theirs as legitimate.

For an outsider, an understanding of the 'different-ness' of a particular culture will come not so much in classroom discussions as through shared life-situations. For me, one such moment of understanding came when I joined a day-long hunt with Bangalema villagers deep in the forest 80 miles north of Kisangani. As the day wore on, their voiced perceptions as to why the hunt was not succeeding told me a lot about their very different world-view which I needed to penetrate and understand if I was going to communicate meaningfully with them. The measure in which the theological process refuses to acknowledge the legitimacy of these different contextual issues on the theological agenda will be the measure in which theology in that context will be irrelevant.

The subject of the research represented in this book started out as a comparative study of academic theology in three different church bodies in Zaïre (Catholic, Kimbanguist, and Protestant). The observations expressed above soon led me to prefer an approach which gives due prominence to the different range of places and types of theological thinking.

Although the methodologies and the forms are very different from each other, the three studies reflect a process of faith seeking authentic rather than borrowed understanding. In essence this is the quest for self-hood, without which African Christian Theology and indeed African Christianity would remain estranged from itself.

Gordon Molyneux

ACKNOWLEDGMENTS

It would be impossible to name all those in Africa and in England who have helped to bring to fruition this piece of research. The following paragraphs name but some whose contribution has been particularly appreciated. Responsibility for any shortcomings in the thesis, however, is mine alone.

First, I would like to acknowledge the encouragement and guidance of my supervisor at the School of Oriental and African Studies, Professor Richard Gray; his combination of personal friendliness and academic rigour has helped to make this period of research both enjoyable and rewarding.

I have been indebted to several for their willingness (despite very full time-tables) to read and comment on early drafts of various chapters; among such I particularly thank Dr John Mbiti, Bishop Kalilombe, Dr Paul Bowers, Dr W. J. Hollenweger and Dr Humphrey Fisher. Others have put their time and their resources at my disposal in other ways: Dr Harold Turner facilitated my use of the rich collection of articles in the Study Centre for New Religious Movements, in Birmingham; Fr François Bontinck in Kinshasa allowed me unhurried use of his personal library which must be one of the richest resource centres of historical material in Zaïre, if not in Africa; Dr Marie Louise Martin arranged a profitable and informative visit to the Kimbanguist Theology Faculty in Kinshasa; Pastor Heintze-Flad in Switzerland generously provided material on Kimbanguist hymns. I thank Miss Kathleen Brain (MBE) for her help in translating some Kimbanguist hymns from Kikongo into English. Dr John Gration (USA) kindly sent photocopied material, including copies of his field-notes of the 'Gospel and Culture Seminars'.

That my period of field research in Zaïre was as profitable as it turned out to be was largely due to the active assistance of people in each of the three areas of research. Revd David Langford who had been involved with the 'Gospel and Culture Seminars' in the North-East of Zaïre, helped me to establish contact quickly with nearly all of the Swahili-speaking participants in the Rethy area. His personal reminiscences of the seminars, and our stimulating exchanges of ideas, both in conversation and by letter, have been a valued contribution. The French-speaking participants, all personal friends from my several years of service with the CECA Church, each unhesitatingly spared time for unhurried conversation. For my time with the Faculty of Catholic Theology in Kinshasa, Cannon Alfred Vanneste arranged accommodation at the nearby Scheutist Guest Centre, and made the necessary introductions to the Faculty personnel. Almost daily during my three weeks with the Kimbanguists, Pastor Nsambu (the Director of Department of Hymns) put himself at my disposal, answering my questions and accompanying me to the different choir activities in Kinshasa that he had drawn up. The translation of many dozens of hymns from Kikongo to French would never have been accomplished without the loyal and untiring help of Cit Nziama. He became a true friend, and my debt to him is indeed great. To my generous Kimbanguist hosts, and to His Eminence Diangienda Kuntima, the 'Chef Spirituel' (without whose official approval little of my Kimbanguist research would have been possible) I offer grateful thanks.

I am also indebted to the Theology Project Fund of the Universities and Colleges Christian Fellowship and to the Research Fund of the School of Oriental and African Studies for their contributions towards university fees and field research expenses respectively.

Finally, I must thank my wife Christine. Her help with library searches, photocopying, and proof-reading, as well as her constant encouragement and interest in the subject, have all contributed significantly towards the completion of the thesis. This work is dedicated to the African Church which we are privileged to serve together.

INTRODUCTION

Thirty-five years ago the expression 'African Theology' was still unknown although many of the factors that have since promoted its emergence were already at work then, and had been, some of them, for many years, it was only in the later years of the 1950's that there emerged, hesitatingly at first, then with increasing insistence, the theological process or processes which came to be known by the name. It is a measure of 'African Theology's' recognition that the 'Revue Africaine de Théologie' has undertaken to publish, in instalments, a bibliography of works (books and articles) relating to the subject. By its April 1986 issue, the RAT catalogue was still listing works published before 1980, but already the inventory numbered well over 6,000 items. The mushrooming literature, divided into several different categories, testifies not only to its mounting importance, but also to its rich diversity.

The theology under examination is 'African' in the twin senses of authorship and context; it is done primarily by Africans and with Africa in mind. However, this statement needs qualification in two directions. First, closer inspection reveals that there have been and are a considerable number of non-African names involved in the theological process in Africa — names such as Edwin Smith, Bengt Sundkler and Aylward Shorter come to mind. Their writings rightly figure among the corpus of 'African Theology' because they have deliberately sought to address the African context and its bearing upon theology. The on-going debate of the subject will assess to what extent their contribution has been significant, but the fact that they have contributed cannot reasonably be denied. Thus in deciding what constitutes 'African Theology', the concerns of the theological reflection in question are more important than the colour or race of the theologian. For the same reason, not all theology done by Africans warrants the epithet 'African'; its 'African-ness' will depend rather on its discernible relevance to questions of African existence and perception.

Secondly, the term does not usually encompass all of the African continent. The areas to the north of the Sahara Desert which are dominated by Islamic religion and culture and where the Christian presence is a very small minority, are not normally included. Nor has it traditionally included South Africa where in the past black Christians have articulated their voice only with difficulty under the 'apartheid' regime. The increasingly clamant theological utterances by Church leaders in that part of the continent have usually been categorized separately as forming part of the 'Black Theology' corpus, a theology with a distinctly urgent political flavour to it. It is, however, becoming increasingly difficult to keep the two 'theologies' apart as if they had nothing to do with one another, and many theological works from Africa and many conferences of theologians in Africa have deliberately sought to include the South African voice, as one element of the whole complex picture. 'Black Theology' is no less contextualized than 'African Theology', but because political factors dominate that context its emphases are political rather than cultural. For this reason, Tutu has argued that 'Black Theology' and 'African Theology' might be regarded as concentric circles, with 'Black Theology' forming the smaller, inner circle[1]. The All Africa Conference of Churches has repeatedly included the South Africa situation within its parameters, and has frequently used language reminiscent of Latin American 'Liberation Theology'. Although the present thesis has chosen to concentrate on 'African Theology', the increasing interpenetration of

'Black Theology', 'Liberation Theology' and 'African Theology' is noted.

The theology under discussion in the thesis is deliberately qualified as Christian, because in the broad and complex subject of theology in Africa, some have argued that a true African Theology will be a careful systematization of traditional African concepts of God and religion. According to J. K. Agbeti (Ghana):

When we talk about 'African Theology', we should talk about the pre-Christian, pre-Muslim African people's experience of their God.[2]

There have been many distinguished works on the African religious heritage, and there is no doubt about the correctness of Mbiti's assertion: *'African peoples are not religiously illiterate'*.[3] However, while the 'African Theology' which is the subject of this thesis cannot be understood apart from this heritage of traditional religion, it seeks rather to examine theological reflection in Africa which relates to an understanding of the Christian Gospel in relation to life and existence in Africa.

As for theology itself, it will become clear from the thesis that what is envisioned by the term is reflection about God, salvation through Christ, and human existence; 'faith seeking understanding', to quote Aquinas' definition of theology. The breadth of this definition is important for the investigations and conclusions of the thesis, for it follows that theology as an academic study, performed by an elite in the classroom or lecture-room, is only part of a greater whole. While the 'specialists' in the University Departments of Theology and in theological and Bible schools with their technical terminology occupy a privileged place within theology, It is not the only place, nor is it necessarily the greater place. At all levels and in all places, African Christians of differing cultural and educational backgrounds are reflecting upon and expressing (in various ways) their beliefs about God and Christ and the meaning of life. The thesis seeks to explore some of these dimensions of theological reflection, their different dynamics, and their importance to the life and thought of the Church in Africa. To an extent, these 'lieux théologiques' correspond to educational levels. It is difficult to avoid conveying unintended value

judgments when speaking of 'higher' and 'lower' levels, and for this
reason I have preferred to use terminology such as 'the academic
dimension of theological reflection' or 'theology in the oral sector'.

Some scholars, in recognition of the rich diversity of the African
socio-religious context and the lack of theological consensus, have
argued that it is more accurate to speak of 'African Theologies' in the
plural. Tienou states:

> Those who choose the singular seem to do so on the
> assumption of a unified Christian theology (and an) essen-
> tial uniformity of traditional religion in Africa,[4]

and he quotes Fashole-Luke in support of the plural form:

> The way forward seems to be the recognition that 'African
> Theology' will never be a unified movement, but will take on
> different colours or emphases depending upon the local
> situations where attempts are being made to express Chris-
> tianity in meaningful African terms.[5]

I have deliberately chosen to retain the singular form, however. My
emphasis in the thesis is not upon the products but upon the process.
The process of faith in Christ seeking understanding is a complex one,
capable of being done in a bewildering variety of different languages,
at different levels, reflecting different contexts with their particular
emphases, and with different results. Yet all relate to the same quest.
In the same way as 'art' can encompass an extraordinary variety of
imaginative human skills (painting, sculpture, pottery, tapestry, etc.
— whether done by the Great Masters or by school children), so
'theology' can legitimately embrace the many and varied attempts to
articulate belief.

'African Christian Theology' is above all contextual; that is, it arises
from and in turn addresses the African context. Almost by definition,
therefore, it is not an isolated phenomenon; it jostles with other
discernible factors, like one in a crowd. The aim of the first chapter of
the thesis is to set the quest for theology done by Africans and for
Africans in its continent-wide setting. Other currents, distinct from
theology yet running broadly in the same direction, are examined, and

the sometimes controversial relations between the religio-theological and (for example) historical or political influences are studied. Within the complexity, a recurring 'leit-motif' can be discerned.

In the remaining chapters, the thesis turns from the general scene in Africa to the specific situation in the one Central African country of Zaïre. The 'case studies' chosen for consideration have been selected from three different confessions. Chapter Two is devoted to one example of theological reflection of an academic nature, Kinshasa's Faculty of Catholic Theology (FTCK). The Faculty played no small role in the debate about the legitimacy of the notion of 'African Christian Theology', and it continues to maintain a voice in the continuing articulation of it. The historical background to the FTCK's rigorous academic standards is examined. Particular attention is drawn to the Faculty's emphasis upon theological publication, which, the thesis argues, has helped in establishing the 'influence' of the Faculty in Africa and beyond.

Chapter Three examines an example from the other end of the theological spectrum, the area of 'oral theology'. The characteristics which differentiate orality from literacy are considered. Whereas literary theology both uses and can be assessed by accepted scholarly standards of verbal directness and logical argument, oral expression of beliefs is at the same time more concrete yet more allusive and symbolic. In examining one example of 'oral theology', the hymns of the 'Eglise de Jésus-Christ sur la Terre par le Prophète Simon Kimbangu' (the Kimbanguist Church) the importance of respecting the oral genre and not forcing it into rigid, speculative moulds is stressed. Nevertheless, the hymns afford access to the Kimbanguist world of popular beliefs that are sometimes not disclosed by the more measured statements of the official, literary sector, and yet which arguably echo more nearly the beliefs of the majority. Although hymns have been selected for examination in the chapter, they constitute but one of the avenues of oral theological expression; others include drama, sermons, prayers, liturgy and dance. The chapter reveals the important role that language plays in expressing certain beliefs.

The tendency of the two sectors, oral and literary, to diverge is one of the concerns of the thesis. The Gospel and Culture Seminars which took place in North-East Zaïre and which form the subject of the fourth and final chapter were a theological experiment situated part way between orality and literacy. Participants at the seminars had had some theological training either to diploma-level at the local Bunia Theological Seminary, or elsewhere to degree level or beyond, but almost all of them were pastors with considerable experience at the 'grassroots'. Their concern was to direct their attention to the real-life situation in their own geographical region and to effect an interrelation between traditional beliefs and practices on the one hand and the Christian Gospel on the other. The methodology at the seminars led the delegates to identify areas of recurring weakness in the Church where the Gospel seemed powerless. These were areas of traditional custom and belief which had met a response of unsympathetic denial or rejection by the missionary bearers of Christianity and by their African associates.

Consequently, these attitudes and practices were submerged yet nevertheless continue to persist, not only in traditional society but also to some extent within the Church. The agenda for theological instruction and reflection in the many Bible schools and theological establishments of the church-body in question, the 'Communauté Evangélique au Centre de l'Afrique' (CECA), is to a considerable extent the legacy of Western patterns, covering a spectrum of subjects reminiscent of Western equivalents. The Seminars deliberately sought to explore by discussion crucial areas of belief and behaviour not usually included in those curricula. The Zaïrian participants of the seminars thus shared with the oral sector a concern for real-life issues and problems. On the other hand, their educational background had equipped them with the necessary ability to conceptualize the practices and beliefs, and, having done so, to see if the Bible addressed these same issues directly or indirectly. The entire exercise was done, not for purposes of an academic debate, but for pastoral reasons, to permit an integrated Christianity where no cultural or social issues are left for the Zaïrian Christian 'outside' of the reach of the will of God as he understands it to be revealed in the Christian Scriptures. Further, the experiment was designed to self-reproduce in other places under the guidance of the delegates. The purpose of the research was not only to examine the methodology of the Seminars, but to explore to what extent they achieved their objectives.

It needs to be emphasised that the three 'case studies' selected for analysis in the thesis are in no way considered to characterize their respective confessions. The Roman Catholic Church in Zaïre has loci of theological reflection other than the 'Faculté'. It has its seminaries, its 'communautés de base' (local Christian communities); and its liturgy, hymns, sermons, etc. could have been explored for what they reveal about Catholic oral theology in Zaïre. In the same way, the Kimbanguists have a Theology Faculty and a growing theological literature emerging from it. So do the Protestants, with their Protestant Faculty of Theology in Kinshasa and almost ten diploma-level theological seminaries in different corners of the country. In other words, the full spectrum of the different 'types' of theology is to be found in each of the three confessions. A thesis could have been written on a comparative basis, comparing and contrasting, for instance, literary theology in each of the three confessions, or oral theology in each. The present thesis does not attempt to present a comparative study between confessions. It rather seeks to explore contrastive ways of doing theology, with selected case studies to illustrate the different sectors in which theologizing is going on.

The thesis concludes by considering the implications of the research. The broad-spectrum definition of theology as 'faith seeking understanding' necessarily has repercussions upon three areas of the theological scene in Zaïre and Africa. Firstly, it affects perception of what theology is, and therefore of who may do it. Secondly, and consequently, theological education in Africa needs to recognise the place and importance of the different sectors in which faith-reflection is done, and encourage the process not only at the academic end of the spectrum, but also at every level. It must be particularly concerned to relate its theological reflection to the African context. Finally, there are necessarily implications for theological educators at whatever level they may be working. If theological education is more than mere content-transmission and is rather facilitating faith-reflection (with its effects on praxis), it follows that the educator should be skilled at bringing about a dynamic encounter between context and Gospel. This will go at least part-way towards a Christian theology in Africa which is not mediated or imposed but truly 'owned'.

References

1. D. Tutu, 'Théologie Africaine et Théologie Noire; la quête de l'authenticité et la lutte pour la libération', in *Flambeau*, Vol. 49, 1976, p. 21.

2. J. K. Agbeti, 'African Theology; what is it?', *Presence.* No. 5, 1972, pp. 6ff. I owe this reference to B. Kato, 'Theological Issues in Africa', *Biblical Christianity in Africa.* p. 42.

3. J. Mbiti,'Concepts of God in Africa'. *S.P.C.K.,* London, 1970, p. xiii.

4. T. Tienou., 'The Problem of Methodology in African Christian Theologies', *unpublished PhD Thesis, Fuller Theological Seminary, School of World Mission,* 1984, pp. 19-20. (Permission to quote applied for.)

5. E. W. Fashole-Luke, 'Footpaths and signposts to African Christian Theologies', in *Bulletin de Théologie Africaine*, Vol. 3, No. 5, 1981. Quoted by Tienou, op cit, p. 20.

Chapter One
African Christian Theology: the quest for self-hood

The wider context

The process which we have chosen to call 'African Christian Theology' is but one expression of a much wider, more complex development that has taken place in the continent during the 20th Century. The transition from colonial status to independent nationhood received impetus from internal and external factors and promoted the quest for the discovery or re-discovery of an 'African identity'. It is against this background that our subject should be viewed.

The Colonial Experience

The meeting of the two worlds in the colonial era was a very unequal one, in which the European world was the actor and the African world the stage. The partition of Africa between the European powers of France, Britain, Portugal, Germany, and Belgium, (decided at the Berlin Conference of 1884-85), was essentially a projection into Africa of the internal politics of Europe,[1] and it neither consulted nor had regard for the people of the continent concerned. Decisions which were to affect the destinies of future generations of Africans were made by European statesmen poring over inaccurate maps in the comfort of country residences in France or Britain. Some of the frontiers could claim no rationale other than the convenience of lines of longitude and latitude. Ethnic and linguistic entities in Africa were thereby often severed in two. The lines drawn by European politicians across maps of Africa unwittingly dramatized the crossing out or cancelling of tribal and cultural identity.

The two principal colonial powers, Britain and France, developed divergent policies towards their fledgling African territories. Broadly speaking, the British approach was that of 'direct rule' which envisaged the internal progress of the country, building on traditional foundations, and providing local political institutions in which the Africans were represented. France, on the other hand, understood the development of its territories (boldly called 'France Outremer') in term of itself, as a political, cultural and linguistic extension of France; it opened its governmental doors in Paris to African participation, and Africans were elected to the prestigious 'Assemblé Nationale'.[2] Either way, however, deliberate planning towards increased responsibility and eventual independence was slow. While there were notable exceptions, there is much documented evidence of colonial paternalism and racial discrimination based on concepts of the evolutionary biological and mental inferiority of the Negro as compared with the Caucasian races, with Britain making perhaps a poorer show in these attitudes than France. And in the Belgian, Portuguese, and Spanish territories provision for eventual independence was even scantier.

After initial and often bloody resistance by African peoples to European intervention at the beginning of the colonial era, it appears that many later African leaders did not resent or see any alternative to the pattern established of development within the circle of their colonial patrons. Some were positively enthusiastic. Casely Hayford, prominent leader of the Gold Coast insisted to the Legislative Council in 1923 that

> loyalty and cooperation with His Majesty's Government is no mere matter of sentiment; for we feel and realise that our interests as a people are identical with those of the Empire, and we mean, as in the past, in the present and the future, to stand by the Empire through thick and thin in every circumstance.[3]

On the French side, Blaise Diagne, Senegalese deputy in the French National Assembly sharply rejected the overtures of Marcus Garvey, leader of a 'Back to Africa' movement, stating:

> We French natives wish to remain French since France has given us every liberty and since she has unreservedly accepted us upon the same basis as her own European children. None of us desires to see French Africa delivered exclusively to the Africans...[4]

and in this he was echoed as late as 1957 by Felix Houphouet Boigny of the Ivory Coast when he appealed:

> I am only asking you to be fair and consider the facts. Is there a single country in the world which would offer to an African of my colour, race, and stage of civilization the liberty, equality and fraternity we can find within the French community? [5]

The warmth of such remarks was understandable as the manifest benefits of the international links within the colonial framework were becoming visible, especially after the First World War. The newly constituted League of Nations described the territories as a '*sacred trust of civilization*' to be governed until such time as they were able '*to stand on their own feet*'. The internationally sanctioned philosophy of the colonial role, therefore, even if it was not always practiced, became one of tutelage and development. The outward symbols of educational, economic, and political development were increasingly evident as schools, hospitals, offices, factories, and communication facilities multiplied.

Less conspicuously, and less happily, a pattern was asserting itself in which the metropolitan powers were casting themselves in the active role while the territories were being cast in the passive. Society was experiencing rapid and profound changes, and these were not the consequence of internal evolution but imposition from without. In Western societies, too, there exist both traditional and progressive sectors typified by rural and urban groups respectively, but these are the results of dynamic evolution within the country and are largely complementary to one another; having a common origin, they are not mutually incompatible. The widely divergent traditional and modern sectors in Africa, however, are due to quite distinct forces which not only have little in common with each other but are even incompatible.[6] The social and cultural dislocation experienced by Africans as a result of the bewilderingly rapid changes brought about by the colonial experience is expressed by M. Assimeng:

> If the social collectivity is generally stable, with a very piecemeal and predictable rate of change, the individual's connection with such a collectivity which is a fundamental pillar of his identity, is assured of stability, continuity, and meaning. But if the collectivity begins to experience rapid and sudden change, then the question of meaning and structure becomes a major one... In brief, African social structures came to embrace, at various levels of congruence and disharmony, the modernizing features of monetized economy and its implications; individualism and economic and status competition; urbanization and the relatively permanent physical and psychological movement of people from their places of birth and nurturing to new centres of population aggregation; secondary relationships becoming dominant as an imperative of bureaucracy, new patterns of social stratification...[7]

The writer goes on to quote Ruch to show that the up-rooting was so profound as to do violence even to concepts of being and time:

> The cyclical time of myth gives way to lineal time of conscious and planned progress. The stability and perennity of mythical life, in which the individual was perfectly and harmoniously integrated with his physical and social surroundings disappears. Man is now torn between his own rapid individual becoming and the slow growth of society; two lineal times running at different speeds.[8]

Imperial western values and concepts, themselves profoundly influenced by Judaeo-Christian thinking, were at one and the same time opening to African societies the intellectual and economic means of nationhood and also creating a universe where their traditional world-view found no place. Education obviously played a major role in spreading the new ways of thinking. In this the Christian missionaries were the first and most important agents. Everywhere they went they opened schools as an effective means of evangelism, and the education thus acquired, however rudimental, granted the school-goers with '*at least some sense of mastery over the new conditions created by the colonial system.*'[9] Literacy was often Bible orientated, and this in itself, introduced a historical view of life that was different from the traditional one which was

> essentially static, looking along the lines of lineage and genealogy into the mythical past and finding there in common origins whatever unity there might be for present sections of society.[10]

The Biblical notion of progress towards a future which could be different from the past contrasted with the traditional conservative and repetitive society, and permitted the notion of national development and improvement. As Mbiti explains:

> To the African peoples, history moves backwards and cannot therefore head towards a goal, a climax, or termination... But a future dimension of Time is being born in (African) thinking and life as a result of the impact of Christianity with its eschatology and of Western type education with its emphasis on individualism and planning for and thinking about the future.[11]

The overall effect of these forces and changes was that extrinsic factors (in the form of colonial ideas, personnel, and values) acted the part of 'subject', while the African continent and its peoples were 'object'. There were, of course, administrative and missionary personnel who were culturally sensitive and who were anxious not to ignore or disdain African values and insights, but viewing the entire colonial experience as a whole, the impression was given that the African had little or nothing to contribute; religiously, as well as culturally, what he possessed before was to be relinquished; it was his privilege to receive, learn, accept. Thus came into being what Kwame Nkrumah called

> the central myth in the mythology surrounding Africa' namely, 'the denial that we are a historical people. Africa, it is said, entered history only as a result of European contact, its history is widely felt to be an extension of European history.[12]

Education, literature and 'negritude'

Education, the very factor which pushed traditional values and concepts into the background, contained within itself the seeds of the new quest for a rediscovery of African identity. The quest, at least in a deliberate, self-conscious form, was earliest expressed by a group of black French-speaking intellectuals in Paris. Although only one of three founder members was African, they shared a common African ancestry, and, being black, were personally aware of the social and political disadvantages of the Negro. In 1934 a cultural and literary movement articulated through the journal *L'Étudiant noir* was founded by Léopold Sedar Senghor (Senegal), Léon Damas (French Guiana), and Aimé Césaire (Martinique). It came to represent in literary form the notion of 'negritude' which Janheinz Jahn has described as

> The successful revolt in which Caliban broke out of the prison of Prospero's language, by converting that language to his own needs for self-expression[13]

The Negritude movement reached its apogee with the publication of Senghor's *Anthologie de la nouvelle poésie nègre et malagache de la langue francaise (Black Orpheus)* . Its preface was written by Sartre who recognised that this literature was struggling for emancipation, although he still interpreted this struggle in communist terms. While the movement was originally connected with the French Communist Party, its thrust was cultural rather than political, as Senghor himself insisted:

> Negritude is the sum total of cultural values of the Black
> world, such as are expressed in the life, institutions, and
> works of black people.[14]

The decades since the 1930s have seen a prolific literary activity by African writers. Much of what has been written has had in mind a readership outside of Africa, not only for economic reasons, but also because it is there that attitudes are deemed to need changing.

Increasingly in recent years the works of African authors and playwrights have been studied in secondary and higher institutions within Africa, and have undoubtedly been instrumental in shaping African ideas and values. Especially in the earlier works, African authors emphasised the past, insisting

> we must first set the scene which is authentically African;
> then what follows will be meaningful.[15]

In their 'retour aux sources' the African authors present often a magnificent past which answers and replaces the glories of Europe so long presented to them in class as the only ones worthy of a place in history. This alternative to a borrowed history is what Césaire meant when he said, 'ma négritude n'est ni une tour, ni une cathédrale'.[16] The contemporary influential Nigerian writer, Chinua Achebe, sees the role of the African author in terms of the dignity which the African once had, but which he lost during the colonial period:

> The writer's duty is to help regain this (dignity) by showing
> them (the African peoples) in human terms what has
> happened to them, what they lost... To help my society
> regain belief in itself, and to put away the complexes of years
> of denigration and self-abasement... I would be quite satis-
> fied if my novels (especially the ones I set in the past) did no
> more than teach my readers that their past, with all its
> imperfections was not one long night of savagery from which
> the first Europeans, acting on God's behalf, delivered them.[17]

Long condemned to be a people without history, the young

intellectuals of 'negritude' recalled their glorious past or their rural traditional values.[18]

'Negritude', therefore, was an attempt by African writers and thinkers *'to be truly ourselves'* (Césaire). it was a major 'prise de conscience' by black Africans; a negative reaction against the economic, cultural and political assimilation of the colonial period, and also a positive reassertion of black African values:

> To set our own and effective revolution, we had first to put
> off our borrowed dresses, those of assimilation, and affirm
> our being, that is, our negritude.[19]

The whole process undoubtedly received fresh impetus and wider dissemination from the various international forums which provided opportunities for cross-fertilization of ideas. Literary reviews enabled philosophical ideas to penetrate political concepts and vice-versa. Both Nyerere and Mboya were involved at one time or another with *Transition* a literary review which started in Kampala in 1961 and moved to Ghana in 1971. *Penpoint*, another review based in Kampala, was started in 1958. Francophone Africa had had, since 1947, the literary journal *Presence Africaine* founded and edited by Alioune Diop, and published both in Paris and Dakar. It was *Présence Africaine* which organised the 'Premier Congrès International des Ecrivains et Artistes Noirs', held in Paris in 1956. This Congress in turn gave birth to an anglophone equivalent of *Présence Africaine* published since 1957 in Nigeria, and called *Black Orpheus*.

The German Janheinz Jahn, himself instrumental in bringing about *Black Orpheus*, emphasizes the important function of the African writer as shaper of the new Africa and articulator on behalf of the people not only of the distant past, but also of a vaguely hoped-for future:

> He is word-magician and announcer, Africa's spokesman,
> sponsor, and interpreter to the outside world, Africa's
> educator within... Reality offers dormant subject matter
> which his word awakens, turns into images and projects
> towards the future. The function of this kind of writing is not

to describe things as they are for the sake of description. but to create prototypes; visions of what ought to be. Therefore the style is in the 'imperative'.[20]

This increasingly prescriptive (present and future orientated) rather than merely descriptive (backward looking) style of writing matches Senghor's own concern:

It is not a question of resurrecting the past, of living in some Negro-African Museum; it is rather a question of quickening this world 'hic et nunc' with the values of our past.[21]

Towards Independence

The literary contribution undoubtedly gave impetus to the political winds that began to blow with increasing strength towards the end of the colonial era, especially after the Second World War. Indeed many have pointed to the War itself as being part of the process that swept Africa to independence in the late 1950s and 1960s. The declared aim of the Allied Forces (in which many African soldiers served) was to save the Free World from the oppression of Hitler's Germany and from his uninvited domination of weaker countries like Poland. The virtues of freedom and the rights of nations to self-government were at stake. Now it was becoming increasingly difficult to justify the colonial overlordship which these same 'liberators' exercised in Africa. The very reasons which justified Britain and France's opposition to the Third Reich in Europe put into question their colonial role in Africa. Nnamdi Azikiwe, eventual President of independent Nigeria, wrote during the years of the Second World War:

Self-government we must have. Great Britain cannot deny us this birthright of ours. Britain cannot be fighting a war of liberation and yet keep millions of Nigerians in political bondage. Nigerian soldiers are now shedding their blood. In the deserts of the Middle East, in the jungles of Burma, in the wilds of North Africa, in the mountains of East Africa they are sacrificing in order to make the world safe for democracy. They fight and die so that Nigerians and the rest of the world may enjoy political freedom...Will their sacrifice be in vain?[22]

On the part of the colonial powers there was a noticeable shift in policies after the end of the War. Charles de Gaulle's provisional government convened a conference in Brazzaville early In 1944 to elaborate the French policy towards the African territories, and even if there was no thought then of eventual self-government, the first steps were taken towards a more just and equitable association. Britain, as has been noted, had encouraged all along the internal development of their African territories along their own lines, but the process of development was accelerated as Britain accepted a large measure of responsibility for welfare and education. African participation in local government was encouraged, and when this participation constituted an African majority it became almost impossible to check the growing demand for full self-government and independence.

The post-1945 world scene saw a shift in the centre of gravity of international politics away from the European powers now exhausted from two World Wars, and towards the new assertive influence of the United States and the Soviet Union. Both of these emerging super-powers were opposed to European colonization. Russia, increasingly antagonistic to the 'Free World' (including the colonial powers) and with its own history of the 1917 Bolshevik revolution, became ever more vociferous in its declamation of the imperialistic and colonial policies of the West and thereby encouraged, directly or indirectly, the African pursuit of independence.

The position of the two major powers on this issue was to a large extent echoed by the newly established (June 1945) United Nations Organisation, which was far more sensitive to the colonial situation than ever its predecessor (the League of Nations) had been. Its Universal Declaration of Human Rights proclaimed by the General Assembly on 10th December 1948 had to be signed by all members and affirmed faith in the human rights of all without distinction of race, language, sex or religion. Even if the UN proved unable always to achieve these goals, its stated and agreed objectives helped to create a changing ideological atmosphere where the perpetuation of colonial values was becoming increasingly difficult. And its words were certainly taken seriously by African leaders. It was to the 73rd Article of the UN Charter that Gabriel d'Arboussier, one of the founders of the 'Rassemblement Démocratique Africain', an inter-territorial nationalist party in French West and Equatorial Africa, appealed for

> the fundamental principle of the right of people to dispose of
> themselves as they wish, and as a corollary, the primacy of
> the interests of the people of each territory.[23]

African leaders thus had in the UN a respected supporting authority for their aspirations outside of themselves. By the time the first African states had gained their independence there could be no acceptable outcome short of full independence for all African territories. In 1960 the General Assembly of the UN was able (despite 9 abstentions, including the US, the UK, and France) to denounce colonialism as contrary to the Charter and to fundamental human rights and to assert the right of all peoples to self-determination.

The shift in international political climate coincided with (and certainly promoted) a proliferation within the African continent of institutions of higher learning. Before the Second World War the number of Black African universities south of the Sahara were few: only Fourah Bay College in Sierra Leone (founded by the Church Missionary Society in 1827) and Fort Hare in South Africa's Ciskei (founded in 1916 with a Free Church of Scotland tradition). Up until this time, it was assumed that the best and almost only higher education would be obtained outside of Africa, and most of Africa's emerging intellectual and political leaders such as Jomo Kenyatta, Nnamdi Azikiwe, Kwame Nkrumah, Hastings Banda, Leopold Senghor and Felix Houphouet-Boigny received their university education abroad. Suddenly, after the War, this situation changed as each country saw the importance of high-level academic and professional education within its own borders. Universities became one of the symbols of national identity. Whereas before 1960 full universities in Black Africa numbered only nine, in the 1960s 21 universities were added, in the 1970s another 19, and in the first six years of the 1980s

15 more.[24] Joseph Ki-Zerbo of the Voltaic Republic (UNESCO consultant on education) has underlined the importance of education as an instrument for shaping national and racial consciousness:

> For the African personality to assert itself, it is necessary to rediscover the African cultural heritage, and to this an important place must be allocated in education.[25]

Consistent with their divergent colonial philosophies, anglophone Africa witnessed a more rapid development of university education than did its francophone counterpart. Nigeria saw perhaps the most prolific establishment of universities, with Ibadan being founded in 1948, and followed by Nsukka, Lagos, Zaria and Ife. Sudan had its Khartoum University (1948), Ghana started its Legon University in Accra in 1948-9, Uganda's prestigious Makerere University commenced in 1949. But the same trend was observable in French-speaking Africa, too. Zaïre's Lovanium was founded in 1949 at Kisantu and the next year moved to Kinshasa, although the lack of secondary education in the then Congo meant that it was only four years later that it could officially function as a university. At about the same time (1950) Senegal started its *'Institut des Hautes Etudes'* at Dakar.[26]

That most of these institutions were closely modelled on and affiliated to various European parent universities and were initially staffed largely by expatriate teachers, does not alter the fact that a new intellectually, culturally, and politically aware elite began emerging from these universities from the early 1950s.

The growth of the labour movement similarly opened up new avenues of political influence, through which future leaders like Tom Mboya (Kenya) and Sekou Toure (Guinea) came to prominence. With support mounting behind them from lesser ranks of leadership and from the growing numbers of politically aware employees in the modern urban sectors of mining, trade and agriculture, as well as in university circles, pressure was increasing across many African territories for full self-government. An increasingly confident African press was meanwhile articulating the rising aspirations of the people for independence. By the late 1950s the growing African political, cultural, and educational awareness had combined to produce an almost irresistible tide-swell against the colonial experience.

It was inevitable that the rising waters would break through the retaining wall, and it was in the Gold Coast that the dam-burst eventually came. Nkrumah had been insisting that nothing short of *'self government, now'* would satisfy the people of his party, and his brief imprisonment by the British for sedition undoubtedly rallied African support to his side. In 1957 the Gold Coast became independent Ghana, with Nkrumah as its president, and other British West African countries followed. De Gaulle's France attempted to defuse the situation in her territories by offering them an attractive alternative to complete independence from France, namely autonomy as separate republics within the French 'Communauté' (with France maintaining certain military and economic responsibilities). The initiative seemed poised to succeed smoothly with almost every country opting for autonomy. However, the one exception, Guinea, had the effect of destroying the envisaged 'Communauté', and by the close of 1960, all the former colonies of both French West Africa and Equatorial Africa had become technically independent of France.

African Solidarity

Although national emancipation from colonial rule was the immediate goal (Nkrumah's statue of himself in Accra bore the inscription *'Seek ye first the political kingdom and all else will be added'*), the quest for national and racial identity or self-hood did not stop with the winning of independence. When Guinea decided against continuing in the French 'Communauté' and France in retaliation withdrew all its administrative, financial and economic support, the newly independent Ghana rallied to its side and a form of union was established between the two countries. Nkrumah envisaged not only the independence of his own country but also the solidarity of all black African nations in concerted opposition to every last vestige of colonial influence. The Pan-Africanist movement, whose early roots went back beyond the London Pan-African World Conference in 1900, found its new epicentre and fresh momentum in Nkrumah's Ghana. In 1958 Accra hosted the first ever Conference of Independent African States, and, even more important, the first All African People's Conference, attended by representatives of the nationalist movements of twenty-eight African countries, many of them not yet independent. From these meetings the organisation of Pan-Africanism was elaborated at many levels, not merely between States, but also between trade unions, political parties and other groups. Nkrumah's vision was of eventual political union between free African States along the pattern of the USSR and the USA.[27] His dream was not shared by all or even most of the new African States who were probably preoccupied with gaining their own national freedom. But whatever the short and long term views of the various leaders were, a new chapter in the history of the Continent had opened and nothing could change the course of national aspiration it had taken. Harold MacMillan, the British Prime Minister, in his famous speech to South African Parliament in 1960, admitted to having been strikingly impressed by

> the strength of African national consciousness. In different places it may take different forms, but it is happening everywhere. The wind of change is blowing through the continent.[28]

The 1960s more than any other decade saw the passing away of colonialism in Africa with 35 States achieving their independence.

If Nkrumah sought a wider solidarity than mere nationalism, he also urged a more thorough-going autonomy than merely the possession of state sovereignty. He warned against neo-colonialism,

> imperialism in its final and most dangerous form — the underlying foreign manipulation that persisted in Africa despite independence. The essence of neo-colonialism is that the state is, in theory, independent, and has all the outward trappings of international sovereignty. In reality its economic system and thus its political policy is directed from without.[29]

His book 'Neo-colonialism' discusses issues such as imperial finance, the American dollar, foreign investment, multi-national companies and combines, diamond consortia, monetary zones and foreign banks.

The United Nations Organisation provided African countries with an international forum, *'a stage on which the African personality could be produced and developed'.*[30] And whereas their individual and separate voices might not have counted for much in the balance between West and East, they found corporate strength in the emerging group of States which represented a sort of 'third way', the so-called 'non-aligned countries', committed to neither of the world's two superpowers.[31] In 1960 the General Assembly of the United Nations adopted a resolution sponsored by 43 Afro-Asian states, entitled 'Declaration on the granting of independence to colonized countries and peoples'. It condemned the *'subjection of peoples to alien subjugation, domination, and exploitation'* and declared that *'immediate steps should be taken ... to transfer all powers'* to the peoples in the colonies. The Declaration was adopted by 89 votes to none (with 9 abstentions).[32]

Within the newly independent Africa, it was recognised that some sort of more formal grouping was necessary if a united stand was to be made in relation to the outside world. Even if Pan-Africanism has never resulted in the full political union envisaged by Nkrumah, the concept of strength through solidarity and the awareness of African selfhood did lead to the founding of the Organisation of African Unity in Addis Ababa in 1963. Addressing the gathered delegates at the commencement of the Summit Conference of Independent African States which was to launch the new organisation, the Emperor Haile Selassie of the host-country Ethiopia, gave his reasons for the need for such a united approach:

> What we still lack, despite the efforts of the past years, is the mechanism which will enable us to speak with one voice when we wish to do so and take and implement decisions on African problems when we are so minded. The

commentators of 1963 speak, in discussing Africa, of the
Monrovia States, the Brazzaville Group, the Casablanca
Powers, of these and many more. Let us put an end to these
terms. What we require is a single African organisation
through which Africa's single voice may be heard, within
which Africa's problems may be studied and resolved... Let
us, at this conference, create a single institution to which we
will all belong, based on principles to which we all subscribe,
confident that in its councils our voices will carry their
proper weight, secure in the knowledge that the decisions
there will be dictated by Africans and only by Africans and
that they will take full account of all vital African considera-
tions.[33]

The Case of Zaïre: 'Authenticité'

Perhaps in no independent African country did the desire for
authentic selfhood become as strong as in the former Belgian Congo,
possibly because it was so obvious there that the mere achieving of
independence did not guarantee true emancipation. The first Premier
of the newly independent Congo, Patrice Lumumba, a radical vision-
ary, had no choice but to rely upon help from the Belgian Civil Service
and the Belgian-led army. It was this continuing commanding Belgian
presence in the form of army officers which led the army to mutiny,
and which plunged the country into anarchy, with Lumumba himself
being murdered. In the ensuing confusion the copper-rich Katanga,
vital to the economic survival of the country and itself heavily
dependent upon Belgian expertise, tried to secede from the rest of
Congo. Tshombe's attempt there failed, but later, when President
Kasavubu invited him to become his prime minister, Tshombe was
able to secure a sort of control over the whole of the country, but again,
largely due to his links with the West which assured him of resources
and mercenary troops from outside the country.

The wavering Kasavubu-Tshombe attempt to establish some sort of
parliamentary government could not command the confidence of the

majority of Africans either within Zaïre or outside and in 1965 General Mobutu at last succeeded in establishing cohesion and unity. Political independence had not really released the Zaïrians to be themselves, and the old cultural and economic atmosphere of the West still lingered on. The N'Sele Manifesto, Mobutu's political charter which launched the Second Republic, stressed the importance to Zaïrians of discovering their own personality by seeking out in the depths of the past, the rich heritage bequeathed by their ancestors. In a speech made in 1973, Mobutu declared:

> We are now embarking on our cultural liberation, the reconquest of our African Zaïria soul. We men of black skin have had imposed upon us the mentality of quite a different race. We must become once more authentic Africans, authentic blacks, authentic Zaïrians.[34]

The policy of 'authenticity' therefore, was a conscious attempt to reassert the values and traditions that the colonial period had deliberately or unintentionally suppressed. Along with the choice of a new name for the country, all place-names that evoked memories of the colonial past (eg Leopoldville, Stanleyville) were changed. Mobutu went to pains to insist that his policy was not an indiscriminate reversion to the past but rather a selective, meaningful quest:

> We use the term 'inspiration' in this connection in order to underline the fact that it is not a question of mere adoption of ancient village traditions, but rather an on-going search for certain transcendent values which belong to our people and which, in some way, constitute their genius.[35]

And further:

> Authenticity is a 'prise de conscience' by the Zaïrian nation to return to its own sources, to research the values that belonged to their ancestors, in order to be able to appreciate those which will contribute to its harmonious and natural development. It represents the refusal by the Zaïrian people blindly to adopt imported ideologies. It is the affirmation of Zaïrian man, or quite simply of man, just where he is and as

he is, with his own mental and social structures.[36]

New currency and dress, as well as personal names, all sought to affirm 'African-ness'.

The socio-cultural policies of 'authenticity' had their economic counterpart in that of 'zaïrianization' which was to follow. In 1974, all the small and medium enterprises, as well as a number of large production and distribution units that had remained in European hands were nationalized. The State, guaranteeing this mass nationalization, assigned the management and even the ownership of the enterprises to its nationals. In the financial sector, banking and insurance were also taken over by the State. Mobutu was not overly perturbed by the resulting outrage of the European states most directly affected, and he simply outlawed the issue of 'Le Monde' which headlined the policy as *'Le plus grand vol du monde'*.

The Zaïrian experience would seem to be but a particularly deliberate and radical expression of what has been taking place in all black African countries. Only in South Africa where the powerful white minority population has entrenched itself against the demands both of the black population and of the international community, have the nationalistic and racial aspirations of the Africans been thwarted. That these aspirations exist there, too, is tragically obvious.

The Religious Scene

Given the traditionally holistic view of life in Africa, it would be surprising if the Continent's drive for self-hood and identity did not have its religious dimension.

Independency

The political and cultural trends outlined so far are paralleled by the religious and the 20th Century has seen not only the rapid expansion of Christianity in Africa, but also attempts to indigenize it, to rid it of its 'foreignness', and to render it truly at home in Africa. African religious independency has been called a *'movement unique in the 20 centuries of Christian history'*[37] and its most spectacular expression is the proliferation of African Christian groups or movements, founded either by direct separation from parent, mission-linked churches, or born from African initiative outside of these historic, mainline churches. Although there had been earlier studies of individual independent religious movements, Sundkler's book 'Bantu Prophets in Southern Africa'[38] drew the Western world's attention to the importance of the trend. While Sundkler's study was limited to Southern Africa, Barrett's 'Schism and Renewal in Africa'[39] explored the continent-wide scale of the phenomenon. Barrett has continued to computerize information and was able to estimate that as of January, 1984, the independent religious movement consisted of 6,950 separate and distinct African religious denominations in 43 countries, with 71,000 churches or places of worship, with 27.5 million affiliated church members (many more millions attached less formally), and with 850,000 members being added every year.[40] Further, Barrett suggests, this situation represents just the tip of the iceberg, for

> hundreds more of such indigenous movements of renewal or protest remain in embryo inside the historical churches at varying depths without the disaffection they represent having as yet broken surface in schism.[41]

He estimates that new movements continue to break off at the rate of approximately 100 per year.

Typology

Sundkler himself distinguished between what he called 'Ethiopian' and 'Zionist' groups and while there have been attempts at reclassification, later theorists have tended to acknowledge the basic distinction. 'Ethiopian' churches are those which have seceded from white mission churches often for racial reasons, but retain to a large degree the liturgical, theological and organizational marks of the parent body from which they have split. In contrast to these, the 'Zionist' churches have neither split away from nor resemble the main-line churches, but rather have been founded by a prophet, acting under spiritual inspiration and attracting converts primarily from among traditional

42

religionists rather than from established churches. They are characterized by spontaneity, experience and authentic African liturgical
and conceptual forms. Fernandez, following Parrinder in protesting
that Sundkler's typology, while appropriate for Southern Africa, was
too restrictive for other parts of the continent, offers a more complex
classification, which elaborates, rather than contradicts Sundkler's
schema. Fernandez' 'instrumental' and 'expressive' categories coincide broadly with Sundkler's 'Ethiopian' and 'Zionist' types, but he
crosses with that continuum another, whose opposite poles 'accultur-
ated' and 'traditional' relate to the degree in which the movements
incorporate the new or perpetuate the old respectively.[42] Obviously,
the range of permutations made possible by two continua instead of
one allows a more detailed classification of religious types and indeed
the extraordinary variety of religious movements has been emphasized by many scholars. Turner, recognising the wide spectrum of new
religious movements in Africa, established four broad categories: neo-
primal (often anti-christian), syncretistic, Hebraist (identifying with
Israel and the Old Testament) and, finally, the Independent Churches.
In this last category, Turner retains, as sub-division, Sundkler's
'Zionist' and 'Ethiopian' types, although preferring for the former the
more widely appropriate term 'prophet-healing'.[43]

Causes

Even more problematic than the classification of the new religious
movements in Africa, is their relation to the political and cultural
events and trends outlined in earlier pages. Georges Balandier,
following B. Malinowski's assertion that myth should be seen as a
social charter concerning the existing form of society with its system
of distribution of power, privilege, and property goes on to state that
'le myth présente une parenté interne avec l'idéologie politique.[44]
Basing his arguments primarily on his studies of messianic groups in
the 'Bas-Congo', Balandier traces the steps by which the religious
comes to express itself as the political under the colonial situation.
First there is the coming to terms with the colonial 'fact'. Then there

is reaction to it. Thirdly is seen the growing insistence upon independence, and with it, fourthly, the emergence of political doctrine. This *'véritable phénomène de transfer'* as Balandier calls it, thus makes of religious movements a sort of proto- or embryonic nationalism: *'Ces innovations religieuses constituent, en Afrique noire, la prehistoire des nationalismes modernes.'*[45]

V. Lantenari's early work on groups in Southern Africa likewise led him to the conclusion that these religious movements were explained by colonial oppression and indeed Lantenari's general world survey of new religious movements was entitled 'The Religions of the Oppressed'.[46] However, not only is it difficult to find even one major political party that traces its origins back to a religious group, but also in many African countries nationalism and religious independency occur contemporaneously, often with very little intercourse between the two. It is significant that Lantenari has been compelled to abandon his 'colonial context' analysis in the light of his recent research into post-colonial Ghanaian movements.[47]

An opposing hypothesis, that espoused by, among others, the early Sundkler and by P. Bohannan, relates the religious and the political differently, if no less directly. There are two possible ways to react to colonial domination; the first is by nationalist revolutions and the other is by 'nativistic movements' (black independent churches). According to Bohannan the reaction chosen by the colonized will depend on the nature of the colonial power; if the colonial power is weak and somewhat paternalistic, then the dominated will choose the way of revolution. If, on the other hand, the regime is strong and tyrannical, then the reaction will rather take the form of nativistic movements.[48] J. P. Dozon insists that the proliferation of movements and sects is a response to colonial society:

> The recapture of the initiative on the part of people under colonial domination has taken place on the level of the sacred... Why? It seems that other avenues of expression and struggle were blocked because of lack of autonomous political institutions.[49]

In this light, then, nationalism and religious innovation are not to be understood as successive phases, but rather as two contemporary alternatives. Religious initiative can then be considered a pragmatic substitute for nationalism.

The weakness of both the above analyses is that the religious movements are seen too exclusively in terms of the colonial situation, committing the error (as Ranger expresses it) of

> supposing that everything that happened under colonialism
> was in some way the result of it.[50]

Buijtenhuis has attempted to steer between the two above approaches, accepting that while the so-called 'Ethiopian' Churches draw their members primarily from the elite and are a constitutive part of nationalism, the 'Zionist' groups draw theirs from the uneducated strata of society, and have an existence parallel to but unrelated to the nationalist groups. The 'Zionist' world is not that of political nationalism, but rather that of a 'counter-society', or to use Sundkler's expression, a 'church-tribe'. Buijtenhuis formulates his thesis thus:

> nationalist parties recruit their followers among those who
> perceive or experience the colonial situation mainly in terms
> of political and economic oppression, and they express a
> political protest; the Zionist churches recruit their faithful
> among those who perceive or experience the colonial situation as social destruction, cultural upheaval and they
> express a social and cultural protest, rather than a political
> one.[51]

Fernandez, as a social anthropologist, while not rejecting the political dimension of nationalism, would widen it to include much more than

> the pronouncements and programmes of the political elite... In
> the widest perspective nationalism is a response to the general
> situation of culture and social contact between societies in which
> questions of dominance and subordination arise.[52]

The role of these religious protest movements is not to achieve political emancipation per se, but rather to 'restore to their participants *autonomy and integrity in their social and cultural life.*[53]

Different disciplines use their own terminology to describe what is clearly a very complex phenomenon and some scholars have recently pleaded for interdiscplinary cooperation rather than competition. In order to do justice to what is wider than can be contained within any one branch of investigation, *'it may be that the time has come for collective research.'*[54] Says Turner:

> Such complex phenomena require a comprehensive explo-
> ration from every possible viewpoint — theological, relig-
> ious, psychological, sociological, anthropological, cultural,
> political, economic, geographical, historical, biographical,
> even physiological and medical... It is rather pathetic that
> we should still be at the stage where social anthropologists
> and historians are not quite sure that they need one another
> and where the wider possibilities of a multi-disciplinary
> approach are still largely unexplored.[55]

Similarly, Barrett decries the 'rigid departmentalization' all too often found in European studies, and in particular, the suspicion that a religious disciple has towards non-religious ones. Since religion is concerned with the ultimate and whole meaning of life, it should embrace all disciplines, and can afford less than any other discipline to ignore the others.[56]

G. C. Oosthuizen's article *'Causes of Religious Independentism in Africa'* bears out the multi-disciplinary nature of the phenomenon of the African Churches, for he lists ninety causal factors divided into categories such as political, economic, sociological, historical, de-nominational, religious, ethnic, ecclesiastical, non-religious, commu-nication, Bible, theology and sacraments. Even if some of the catego-ries overlap and many of the factors could be placed equally well into other categories, Oosthuizen is surely right when he concludes:

> the variety of causes for the existence of independent
> religious movements in Africa should guard any analysis
> from oversimplification.[57]

The complexity is further underlined by Barrett's examination of six

thousand contemporary religious movements and his discovery of a
    large number of explanatory factors held in common and...
    the many extraordinary parallels that exist in the origins,
    expansion and characteristics of independency in one area
    after another.[58]

Religious independency is bound to be complex, because tribal society
in which it has occurred is itself an intricate interplay of many features
    so closely knit together that no enforced change can take
    place in one without affecting all the others; for politics, law,
    religion, art, language, culture and society are all closely
    interlocked in a balanced and self-righting system.[59]

The traditional society that was encountered by the colonial Europeans was thus a sort of intricate spider's web of innumerable beliefs,
institutions and values and when any one element of the 'web' was
pulled away by colonial influence, it inevitably caused disequilibrium
in the whole. This in turn caused alarm and disillusionment. Society,
rather than being fulfilled by the new religion, was being demolished
and what was taking its place did not seem to fit. As a result of the
protestant missionary drive to translate the Bible into more and more
indigenous languages, Africans themselves had access to the authoritative source that the missionaries used and discovered to their
surprise that where the missionaries (and colonialists) had viewed
their African religio-cultural system almost entirely negatively, the
Bible seemed rather to affirm many of their values (eg. emphasis on
family, land, fertility).

To this surprise was added disenchantment or even resentment
when the African perceived in the missionaries a short-fall in the
biblically vital area of love. For Barratt, this *'failure of love'* in the
missionaries is the *'root cause common to the entire movement of
independency'*. It does not represent a total lack of all love, for there
is plenty of evidence of charity, sacrifice and caring. Rather it is the
failure of missions
    at one small point only — love as listening, sharing,
    sympathizing and sensitive understanding in depth

between equals... there was no close contact, so it seemed,
no dialogue, no comprehension, no sympathy extended to
traditional society or religion.'[60]

Growing disaffection eventually reaches the point of secession, often around a charismatic, prophetic figure. The resultant independent group acknowledges Christ as Saviour and Lord, but affirms in its liturgy and worship African worldview and values. It is a readjusted new community where the old equilibrium of the tribe has been rediscovered within the structures and values of the church.

Daneel paints a somewhat similar picture to Barrett, recognising the political and socio-economic dimensions of the independency phenomenon while also emphasising the distinctively religious element, too. Prophetic leaders like Shembe and Lekhanyane in South Africa, Bishop Mutendi and Johane Maranke in Zimbabwe and Kimbangu in Zaïre transformed the notion of a 'Deus remotus' into one of active involvement in tribal affairs, enabling their followers to cope with a complex and often critical political situation.[61] Even if the African churches remained aloof from violence and subversion, they were not alienated from their countries' struggle for political independence, their thriving existence apart from the Mission churches being in itself a message of hope to their nation. They aligned themselves with the cause of their people by propagating the equality between races, the dignity of black Africans and their capability of independent rule:

Their contribution towards political liberation from bondage
lay in their provision of religious justification for their
struggle, for which they found ample evidence in Scripture,
and perhaps even more importantly, in their forceful dem-
onstration of maturity and competence in handling their
own church affairs, independently of European jurisdiction.[62]

Furthermore, the independent churches provide a haven where discriminatory attitudes towards the African have no place. Educational and material advantages of the whites all too often created social distance and attitudes of superiority, paternalism, and condescension on the part of missionaries and a corresponding loss of dignity and self-esteem on the part of the Africans. Within the independent churches, however, social status and personal worth are regained.

There is an economic dimension to religious independency with some African churches. Daneel cites the 'mutual aid' systems in Zionist Churches like Mutendi's Zion Christian Church and refers to Martin West's research in Soweto to show that religious independency also helps to establish economic stability in a new and bewildering urban environment.[63] Johane Masowe received his prophetic call from God in 1932 and while many of his followers settled in eastern Zimbabwe, the inner core of his faithful band took up eventual residence with Baba Johane in Port Elizabeth in the Eastern Cape. They became known as the Apostolic Sabbath Church of God and were nick-named 'the Korsten Basketmakers' [64] — a closed and highly industrious religious community of Shona and others. Perhaps the most striking example of the economic dimension of independency is the remarkable Holy Apostles Community at Aiyetoro, coastal Nigeria. From being a marginal group of fishermen in the 1940s (though closely bound together in social and religious solidarity) they rapidly became a highly industrialized little city with a great diversification of skills, including construction and boat-building.[65]

Not all or even most of the independent African churches demonstrate the same desire for economic progress. A common feature of these churches, however, appears to be their concern for the health and welfare of their members, a care which extends beyond the emphasis on spiritual and educational progress typical of the historical churches. The combination of economic and religious activities expresses the holistic conception of life that is characteristic of African thinking.

It is clear, then, that the phenomenon of church independency in Africa is a complex one, with political, cultural and economic dimensions and involving factors other than strictly religious ones. Indeed, in a continent where life is perceived as a whole and all spheres of life are interwoven this would be expected, and it is perhaps impossible to speak of that which is 'strictly religious' where religion permeates all of life. Recent academic approaches to independency by such scholars as Fernandez, Fabian and Jules-Rosette, have warned against fitting the African phenomenon into Western conceptual categories:

> Our real enlightenment lies not in the application of image-less ideas exported from the West but in beginning with African images and by a careful method learning what they imply — what is embedded within them.[66]

Fernandez' study of the Bwiti cult of West Equatorial Africa demonstrates how their 'argument of images' maintains the integrity of their world amidst the colonial dislocation they have experienced.[67]

However, while allowing the interpenetration of spiritual and other dimensions in any attempted explanation of new religious movements in Africa, to reduce the religious dimension by explaining it away merely in terms of these other categories is to do violence to the evidence. If it is correct to call the nearly 7,000 movements 'religious' at all, it is because to a greater or lesser degree they are distinguished by that which cannot be fully explained by the political, the cultural or the economic. They all possess and express an awareness of the divine, the beyond-human and respond to this by prayer, worship and moral obedience. Recognition of the religious category 'per se' was urged by the Oxford social anthropologist Evans-Pritchard who defended his writing about Nuer religion as such, by saying in his preface:

> I have to emphasise that this is a study of religion. So strong has been the rationalist influence on anthropology that religious practices are often discussed under the general heading of ritual together with a medley of rites of quite a different kind, all having in common only that the writer regards them as irrational, while religious thought tends to be inserted into a general discussion of values. Here the view is taken that religion is a subject of study 'sui generis', just as are language and law.[68]

Turner agrees, pleading for a *'recognition of these African movements as fundamentally a religious phenomenon'*[69] and quotes Eliade in his support:

> To try to grasp the essence of such a phenomenon by means of physiology, psychology, sociology, economics, linguistics, art or any other study is false: it misses the one unique and irreducible element in it — the element of the sacred.[70]

Oosterval makes essentially the same point in speaking of the phenomenon of messianic movements around the world[71] and Zaïrian theologian Bimwenyi Kweshi similarly rejects logical positivism and affirms the validity of religious language as proper and distinct, irreducible to other language, for example that of science.[72]

Distinctives

While there is enormous variety in the thousands of independent Christian movements in Africa, certain features are present often enough to become characteristic and distinguish these churches from their 'historic' counterparts. These characteristics are of considerable significance for the theological quest in Africa.

One of these areas is worship and liturgy, that is, the manner in which people as a congregation express themselves before God. Dissatisfaction with the sort of worship patterns in the historic churches has influenced many Africans to transfer their allegiance from the mission-based churches:

> Everything is cold, lifeless, drab, boring and uninspiring. The liturgies become stereotyped, formal, monotonous, and absolutely unrelated to the African way of worship... They were not composed from the spiritual, emotional and ritual needs of the people and so have remained essentially alien to Africans.[73]

The independent churches favour a liturgy that is spontaneous rather than predictable,[74] enthusiastic rather than formal,[75] participative rather than passive,[76] and expressive bodily (clapping, marching, dancing) rather than merely verbal or intellectual. These churches have often been designated 'Spirit-Churches' because of the manifest emphasis upon the presence and power of the Holy Spirit (often through a prophetic figure) a trait largely lacking in all but the Pentecostalist historical churches.[77]

Many writers emphasise the holistic conception of life traditionally held by Africans and the pervasive and non-compartmentalized nature of religion. It is therefore not surprising that the independent churches see their faith as meeting the whole needs of their members. Healing within the believing community is thus another distinctive of the African churches, to the extent that Turner prefers to use the term 'prophet-healing' rather than 'Zionist'. It is not that the missions and their churches ignored healing altogether; indeed, medical care has from the beginning figured prominently in the agenda of missions. It is rather that

> missions treated the body and soul of man in completely
> different departments, the soul in the church and the body
> in the clinic.[78]

Hastings expresses well the all-inclusive role of the independent churches: theirs is a quest

> for a ritual, a belief, and a realised community in and
> through which immediate human needs, social, psychologi-
> cal, and physical could be met... The most characteristic
> motivation of the new Christian movements in Africa was...
> the establishing of accessible rites of healing with a Chris-
> tian reference and within a caring community by gifted and
> spiritual individuals claiming an initiative effectively denied
> them in the older churches.[79]

Healing in the independent churches stresses

> the basic unity of man, and the profound inter-relationship
> of religion and healing, in a way which has met the previ-
> ously unsatisfied needs of many Africans.[80]

Janzen and others have emphasized that since the causes of illness are understood to be social and spiritual rather than merely physiological, so must its treatment and its cure.[81]

Related to this area is that of the spirit-world, a world generally admitted verbally and conceptually rather than experientially by missionaries. Idowu[82] and Mbiti[83] distinguish divinities, spirits and ancestors (or 'living dead', Mbiti) and the importance of the spiritual beings in traditional African cosmologies and in everyday life (health, success, fertility, etc) is emphasized in innumerable African and Africanist writings. It constitutes perhaps the single most important element in traditional African world-views. Of this living, well-populated cosmos, the Zaïrian theologian-editor Boka di Mpasi states:

> the presence of ancestors and spirits constantly intervening in human activities which they preside over, inspire, prosper, protect, favour... or thwart and ruin, constitutes the basis of beliefs, practices and preoccupations of the African.[84]

In the historical churches (at least in the 19th and 20th Centuries) the typical response has been, partly through ignorance, to reject indiscriminately the reality of the spirit-world or to give the impression that such matters lie outside the realm of the church's responsibility. This, in turn, resulted in the public disavowal by church members of the influence of spirits but clandestine involvement with them in times of crisis. For Campenhoudt has truly said that *'only that which is replaced can truly be abandoned'*.[85] Within the African churches, generally speaking, the reality of spiritual forces are taken more seriously and confronted more directly. In many independent churches, the importance of ancestors continues, although as Daneel relates, with regard to the Shona Spirit-type churches the focus has shifted from

> an overriding preoccupation with and dependence upon the ancestors, to a ritually dramatized and continuously re-enacted acceptance of the reign of Christ.[86]

Within these independent churches there has taken place, according to Turner, a 'desacralization of nature', aided by the portrayal of the religion of ancient Israel as expressed in the Hebrew Scriptures readily available and used:

Formerly they believed in a range of spirits that inhabited or controlled all natural forces and objects and that had to be placated by repeated and expensive sacrifices or otherwise avoided. Now these are either believed in no longer, or amalgamated into one great evil spirit, Satan, who has been conquered by God's power; even if belief in such spirits lingers on they have lost their central position and power.[87]

The implacable hostility towards and denunciation of all forms of sorcery that characterised the preaching of William Wade Harris at the beginning of the century in the Ivory Coast continue today to such an extent that R. Bureau can say:

The majority of the'prophets' who rose up and who continue to rise up in Black Africa to save their people or their entire race, have confronted the major problem of sorcery... If large multitudes follow them, it is in the hope of finding relief from this unbearable burden. In one degree or another, all modern religious movements in Africa.... are movements aimed against sorcery.[88]

These, then, are some of the areas which feature prominently in the various independent Christian movements of Africa, despite great variation in secondary details.

Enough has been said to show that it is correct to term these movements 'religious'; they cannot be explained by merely political, social, or economic dynamics, however important these other factors might be.[89] By their acknowledgment of Jesus as Lord, the Spirit as present, and the Scriptures as Word of God, they understand themselves to be Christian. Most of the distinctives contrast sharply with the practice (if not doctrine) of the historical churches. While it is true that these latter have often been weighed in the balances and found wanting, it would be a mistake to conclude that the 'raison d'être' of the independent churches is wholly one of reaction to missions. Daneel's studies of the Shona churches led him to conclude that:

scope should be allowed for an evaluation of the genius of the independent churches in its own right. Much of what we

> observe today (in these churches) concerns a genuinely
> contextualised and originally African response to the Gos-
> pel, irrespective of and unfettered by Mission church influ-
> ence.[90]

The religious areas outlined above have their roots reaching back
into traditional pre-missionary/pre-colonial cosmologies, and this is
true of other characteristics such as the place of women, social
cohesion rather than fragmentation and the significance of dreams
and visions. There exists, therefore, a certain continuity between what
was and what is, and it is this continuity which helps to explain why
for so many Africans the independent churches are 'a place to feel at
home'.[91] There are enough points of radical departure from the
traditional socio-religious patterns, however, to question the ade-
quacy of Horton's hypothesis that 'conversion' is to be explained by the
shift from (traditional) micro-cosmology to (modern) macro-cosmology
and that in this shift Christianity (and Islam) acted merely as catalyst
for the inherent dynamics of traditional African religion.[92]

The new religious movements of Africa, therefore, express religiously
the same search for identity and self-hood in a changing world that we
have seen in other areas of social, cultural, and political experience.
Their dynamic pragmatism supports the observation that

> African religions are not closed, static systems, impervious
> to change. With their eclectic insistence on practical results,
> African religions have been flexible, open to innovation and
> thoroughly capable of assimilating new concepts.[93]

The independent churches are those movements which, while sharing
the same quest, assert Christ as Lord, and the Bible as directive of
behaviour and thought. Their faith, worship, and life-in-community
does not betray their past, but neither are they bound to their past.

> They may be described as having been founded by the
> Africans in Africa, to worship God in African ways, and to
> meet African needs as Africans themselves feel them and not
> as others feel they ought to feel them.[94]

The Report of the Second Conference of the Organisation of African Independent Churches stated:

> Authenticity is vital to our understanding of the Gospel message. I want to think like an African, worship like an African, sing like an African, live like an African. The Gospel must be presented to the African in a way he can understand and interpret in his own thought-forms and worship.[95]

It is concerns such as these that theological reflection in Africa has been addressing.

The Theological Dimension

Early Developments

By its very nature as a process it is difficult to date categorically the beginning of African Christian Theology. O. Muzorewa posits the formal inauguration of the All Africa Conference of Churches in 1963 as marking the official beginning of African theology.[96] However, his book is limited to English-speaking Protestant Africa, and any continent-wide survey must take into account the Catholic and francophone areas, too.

Without question, some degree of contextualization of the Christian message took place from the earliest times of missionary penetration into Africa. It was perhaps unconscious and intuitive and with the wisdom of hindsight the general consensus today is that it was inadequate and often unsatisfactory. Indigenous Christian leaders like Mojola Agbebi of Nigeria saw the importance of integrating Christianity with their own culture as long ago as the second half of the 19th Century.[97] Protestant Christianity, less centralized and less bound by centuries of accumulated ecclesiatical tradition, was generally speaking more open towards a sympathetic view of African culture and the need for missionary adaptation and this was formally encouraged by the 1926 Le Zoute Conference.

The process received an important academic impetus with the publication, in 1945, of Fr. Placide Tempels' 'La Philosophie Bantoue,'[98] a major challenge to Catholic (and other) assumptions that Christianity must be etched upon an African slate wiped clean of all the past. In an autobiographical account, Tempels[99] describes how in his early missionary years:

> I adopted attitudes of the white-man... the spiritual master,
> the authoritarian teacher, the religious professional, the
> chief or pastor, over against children who needed only to
> listen, to obey and to remain silent.[100]

Ten frustrating years of missionary work in the Kamina region led Tempels to rethink profoundly his whole approach. He sought increasingly to try to understand the people he was evangelizing, to get inside their skin and to see things through their eyes. His sympathetic honesty was reciprocated and in the resulting dialogue of openness, the Africans disclosed to Tempels what it was that they longed for beyond all else:

> 1) Life, intense life, full life, strong life, total life ...
> 2) Fruitfulness, fatherhood and motherhood — a fruitful-
>   ness which is not simply physical, but which is great,
>   intense, total...
> 3) Vital union with others; isolation kills us.[101]

He argued that to disapprove or reject 'in toto' this 'native philosophy' and its ensuing tribal customs, is to reject the

> characteristic feature which made the Bantu the man he
> was. It belonged to his essential nature. To abandon it
> amounts to intellectual suicide for him.[102]

Tempels perceived that if the Gospel was to be effective it should meet the Bantu in the *'wholesome desires of their own ontology'*, and that Christ was the *'triple answer, astonishingly adapted to the fundamental triple aspiration of the Bantu personality'*.[103]

His perception of 'life-force'[104] as the key to 'Bantu philosophy' with its implications for attitudes, relationships and evangelism, came to him with the power of a revelation and made some doubt his sanity. To his friend and correspondent, G.Hulstaert,[105] he wrote:

> Do not worry whether I am psychologically burnt out. Yes,
> I am. During several months I have been living in a tension,

an exaltation, a fury which surpasses human strength.[106]
Opposition from the Roman Catholic hierarchy in Zaïre, first Mgr de
Hemptinne and subsequently Mgr Dellepiane, threatened and eventually interrupted his continuing ministry in Zaïre, but his cause
propelled him forward with a crusading zeal and recklessness. Again
to Hulstaert, Tempels wrote:

> Friend, get ready... We are so strong, so terribly strong, if
> only we are allowed to speak. Sooner or later the conflict
> must erupt... Whatever might happen to me leaves me
> indifferent. I will offer this sacrifice for the salvation of Bantu
> Christianity.[107]

He was concerned to question the assumption that Christ could be
mediated to people only through the channels of Western philosophical presuppositions and concepts. In his final letter to Hulstaert,
Tempels, as if impatient with the constant arguments over fine
academic details, declared:

> What it amounts to is simply this: that Christ can be born
> and grow *within the soul* of primitive man; that these men
> can understand, experience, and express Christ just as they
> are, in the way that they think and feel and not through some
> foreign thought or mentality. This is the only issue that
> really matters. To insist that Christ can be understood,
> experienced and expressed only 'via' Greek or Aristotelian
> thought, amounts, I believe, to limiting and shrinking
> Christ, instead of allowing Him to be universal, as He is in
> reality.[108] (italics his)

Tempels is often called 'the father of Bantu philosophy'. With little
more than the statutory two years of philosophy during his ecclesiastical training, Tempels was by no means a professional philosopher.
His concerns were primarily missiological. In academic circles the
debate continues as to whether what Tempels described was truly a
'philosophy' or whether it was an unselfconscious cosmology or 'way
of seeing things' (see Ch. 2, pp. 120ff). However that may be, his
importance in the unfolding story of philosophy and theology in Africa

can hardly be overestimated. For he, perhaps more effectively and widely than any single other Africanist[109] helped to change the prevailing climate of Western academic and ecclesiatical paternalism. He also gave a rising generation of African scholars a new confidence and sense of identity to press through the door which he had opened.

The Rwandan theologian Alexis Kagame acknowledges Tempels' crucial importance by bestowing on him the honour of being 'the first to raise the problem of "Bantu philosophy"'.[110] In 1956, Kagame published his thesis in Brussels on 'La philosophie bantu-rwandaise de l'être', an 'articulate African response to Tempels and the beginning of a debate on the nature of African religion and the proper relationship of Christianity to it.'[111]

Kagame, together with a group of black priests studying in Rome in the mid-1950s, and others in Paris, produced a small book that perhaps more than any other, marked the significantly rising tide of African theological reflection. The book was called 'Des prêtres noirs s'interrogent'[112] and its list of articles reveals its central concerns: 'Nécessité d'adaptation missionnaire chez les Bantu du Congo' (V. Mulago); 'Mentalité noire et mentalité biblique' (J-C Bajeux); 'Sacerdoce et négritude' (E. Verdieu and P. Ondia); 'Catholicisme et indigénisme' (G. Bissainthe); 'Liturgie romaine et négritude' (R. Sastre); and 'Christianisme et négritude' (A. Kagame). The titles also reveal a theological dimension to Senghor's cultural quest for 'négritude', commenced as we have seen, 20 years previously and this supports the contention that the quest for an African theology is part of a wider, complex odyssey.

The Zaïrian Jesuit, K. N' soki, traces the expression 'African theology' back to the book 'Des prêtres noirs s'interrogent'[113] and in particular, the article by M. Hebga, 'Christianisme et négritude'. In it, Hebga deplored the joyless 'poor-relation co plex' in the African priesthood, the unhappy rift between wanting to live out the Gospel and being deprived of their own cultural values. He asked:

> if we admit that (we) Negroes have been called by Christ, are negritude and Christianity incompatible?[114]

African priests should rather be 'sowers of Christian enthusiasm; hence the necessity of each rethinking this problem of a "*théologie fondamentale africaine*'".[115]

The year prior to the publication of 'Des prêtres noirs s'interrogent', Ghana University's thriving Department of Theology had hosted a conference sponsored by the local Christian Council on 'Christianity and African Culture', in which Dr Busia had appealed to the Church to

> come to grips with traditional practices and with the worldviews that these beliefs and practices imply.[116]

Mbiti sees the publication of P. D. Fueter's article 'Theological Education in Africa' (1956) as being the starting point of African Christian Theology.[117]

While there are differences of opinion as to the significant moment, it is clear that by 1956, as Africa was poised to start its surge for political independence, the quest for African Christian Theology was under way, both on the Protestant and Catholic sides.

The process within Protestant Christianity received fresh stimulus with the All Africa Church Conference, held at Ibadan in 1958. It was the first major Continent-wide African Christian gathering and from it grew the All Africa Conference of Churches, officially founded in Kampala in 1963. Previously, individual churches in Africa existed in relation to their parent missionary societies in Europe and America and

> had more in common with their 'home churches' than with neighbouring African churches of other denominations.[118]

After Kampala there was, among the members of the AACC, a new point of reference and a new sense of African solidarity. Kampala spawned several consultations and sub-conferences on matters relevant to the Church in Africa. Perhaps the most significant of these was the consultation of African theologians which eventually took place at Immanuel College (Ibadan, Nigeria) in 1966 and which published its report in book form in both French and English.[119] E. B. Idowu, president of the consultation, drew attention in the preface to '*the seemingly foreign nature of Christianity'* in Africa and explained that the aim of the consultation was to seek for:

> the best way of presenting, interpreting, and implanting the Christian faith in Africa so as to permit Africans to hear God in Jesus Christ who addresses them directly in their very own situation and in their particular circumstances.[120]

Further sessions of the AACC were held in Abidjan in 1969, Lusaka in 1974 and Nairobi in 1981. Other conferences and consultations were held at Dar es Salem (1971 and 1976), Makerere (1972), Accra (1974 and 1977), Nairobi (1974), and Ibadan (1974).[121]

If the AACC was an important milestone on the Protestant side, on the Catholic side there was the publishing, as from January 1959, of the 'African Ecclesiastical Review' (AFER). It was not the first African Catholic journal; years before, the Jesuits in Mayidi (Congo), had started to produce the 'Revue du Clergé Africain'. The readership of the Revue was fairly limited and, at least in the early years, the content kept narrowly to official Roman line, by the 'magisterial manner' of Fr. Denis.[122] In some issues, there is little if anything to indicate that it was 'African' at all. In contrast to this, AFER, which rapidly became *'the chief forum for clerical discussion all across English-speaking Africa,'*[123] grappled with the relation between Christianity and African culture. It was started in response to suggestions from priests working in Uganda for a review, the purpose of which was *'to make Christ's message relevant for Africa today'*.[124] 'Inculturation' became the dominant theme of AFER. By 1971 there were 59 articles either describing attempts at inculturation, or studying its possibility. AFER in turn stimulated the publication of various 'Spearheads' by Gaba Publications, including: 'Ujamaa and Christian communities', 'Living worship in Africa today', 'Family spirituality in Africa today', 'Anointing and healing in Africa', 'Liturgy: truly Christian and truly African' and 'Life and death — a Christian/Luo dialogue'.

Vatican II

Many conservative Catholic writers and thinkers were bound by such loyalty to Rome or to official scholastic theology that even the changes brought about by independence and the 'new Africa' failed to alter their reticence to interact with non-Catholic religion (and the culture that accompanied it). Their suspicions towards the pastoral and theological concerns of AFER were to be allayed somewhat by events that took place at the highest levels of the Roman Catholic Church. In 1958 Pope John XXIII succeeded Pius XII and almost immediately ushered in the era of Vatican II. By the time the Council was over in 1965, it was clear that the official attitude of Rome had changed.

The changes that Vatican II reflected and produced were so profound that the terms 'pre-conciliar' and 'post-conciliar' far from merely expressing a chronological distinction, came to represent deep changes in attitude.[125] Hebblethwaite lists the following cluster as characterizing 'pre-conciliar' Catholicism: an excessively rationalistic approach to theology, emphasis upon individual piety, a liturgy (largely fossilized since the Council of Trent) in which the congregation remained passive spectators, a sense of superiority over and suspicion towards non-Catholic Christians and a thorough-going opposition to Communism and all other major systems of the modern world. The 'post-conciliar' cluster was the contrary of all those: revelation as a response to God's perpetually renewed summons and invitation, a willingness to relax hard scholastic categories and a move towards, among other things, a more Protestant approach to faith as 'trust', a view of liturgy that stressed its communal aspect, a more dialogical attitude towards Christians of other confessions and an openness to the world and a readiness to learn from it.[126]

With the changing self-understanding of the Church came a changing perception of the role of the theologian,[127] a change that was to be of importance in the theological scene in Africa. Whereas in pre-conciliar years the theologian had seen his role as one of 'handing on what he had received',[128] after Vatican II he became aware that his was a 'prophetic' task, that is, he could and should challenge and change the thinking of the Church. No longer were theologians merely to be the conveyor belt system for the 'magisterium'; they were to be the heralds of the new and dynamic elements in the Church. They began to argue within the church for change in the church.[129]

Not only did the role of the theologian change (at least latently) from 'scribe' to 'prophet', but theology itself, formerly considered the monopoly of a privileged 'elite', was seen to be the business of the whole church. At the 'Concilium' congress in Brussels, Jean-Pierre Jossua maintained that theology was not a specialized activity confined to those who possess some scientific competence

but simply the activity of any true Christian who reflects on his faith and is qualified by the fact that he belongs to the people of God through baptism.[130]

Even if, in more recent years, the trends expressed by Vatican II have not continued unchecked,[131] the changes within the Catholic Church have been deep. The Council came at a time when in Africa, as we have seen, increasingly articulate and forceful demands were being voiced both within the Church and outside it for new attitudes. Many within the Catholic Church in Africa gladly welcomed Vatican II and set about maximizing its effects.

In East Africa a major effort of communicating Vatican II was made, sponsored by AMECEA. From mid-1966 the joint board of bishops of five East African countries published from Kipalapala in Tanzania a fortnightly bulletin entitled 'Post Vatican II'. The effort lasted two years and worked systematically through the Conciliar documents, sending out some 5,000 copies to all the dioceses of East Africa. With Vatican II in mind, A. van Campenhoudt would write in 1970:

aggiornamento of the Church has made us discover that our Churches transmit many elements foreign to the Gospel... Vatican II has made us look beyond our own walls and be more attentive to what is going on in the world.[132]

Twenty years on from the end of Vatican II, Pottmeyer reflects that the Vatican document 'Gaudium et Spes' marked

a break with the 'a priori' suspicious attitude vis-a-vis the world, progress, democracy and science, which marked the Church in the 19th Century and at the beginning of the 20th Century.[133]

Even if his evaluation is tempered by having to speak of *'exaggerated expectations'* and subsequent disillusionment of what Vatican II has in fact produced, it is nevertheless true that the new winds blowing in the Catholic Church have encouraged rather than discouraged fresh thinking and writing by African theologians. They, together with other Catholic Church leaders, have continued to receive measured encouragement by the pronouncements of Pope John Paul II. Addressing Zaïrian bishops in Kinshasa in 1980, he said:

> The Gospel, to be sure, is not to be identified with cultures and it transcends all cultures. Nevertheless the reign which the Gospel announces is experienced by men profoundly linked to a culture... You wish to be both fully Christian and fully African.[134]

And speaking about theology as such in Africa, he declared in 1983 that doctrinal reflection on African identity was one of the main areas of concern for African theologians.

Perhaps nowhere in Catholic Africa has the challenge been taken up as eagerly as in Zaïre's 'Faculté de Théologie Catholique' in Kinshasa. Originally called Lovanium, it was intended by the colonials as a second Louvain, reflecting the cultural and academic ethos of its famous counterpart in Belgium. Inevitably, with independence and the troublesome years following 1964, the links with Brussels have become less direct. With a distinguished teaching staff, including such well-known African names as Mulago, Tshibangu and Ngindu and with a prolific literary output in three journals, it has become an important focal point in African theological reflection (see next chapter). Indeed, it is to the Faculty that N'soki traces the first use of the expression 'African theology' as such. Ironically, the first to use the term was the Faculty's Dean, Alfred Vanneste, who became the notion's chief antagonist. In an article in 'Revue du Clergé Africain' in 1958, he declared: *'We do not believe that the time has yet come for an*

African Theology to be launched.'[135] Two years later, in 1960, the Faculty organised a debate between Vanneste and Tshibangu (at that time still a student at the Faculty) on the subject of 'African theology' and the expression passed into common currency (see below, pp. 101ff).[136]

Writings and writers

Although the 1960s saw only a few serious works by African theologians, they marked a significant beginning of what was to become in the 1970's and 1980's a rising quantity of literature directly or indirectly important theologically. They included: C. G. Baëta's 'Prophetism in Ghana' (1962), E. B. Idowu's 'Oludumare: God in Yoruba Belief' (1962), H. Sawyerr's 'Creative Evangelism: Towards a new Christian Encounter with Africa' (1968), T. Tshibangu's 'Théoiogie Positive et Théologie Spéculative' (1965) which Hastings describes as (at the time): *'incomparably the most serious piece of theological scholarship yet produced by an African.'* [137] In 1969 a much earlier work by B. Danquah, 'Akan Doctrine of God'[138] was republished and in the same year J. Mbiti published his work 'African Religions and Philosophy,' the first of several books which, together with a prolific quantity of articles in dozens of learned journals, were to earn him the title of 'father of African theology'.

Since 1970 new African names have emerged that have become well-known through articles and books relating to the subject of theology in Africa. Out of these, the more important would include (alphabetically): Kofi Appiah-Kubi, Max Assimeng, Benezet Bujo (Zaïre), Bimwenyi Kweshi (Zaïre), Kwesi Dickson (Ghana), Eboussi Boulaga (Cameroun), J-M. Ela (Cameroun) E. W. Fashole-Luke (Sierra-Leone), Patrick Kalilombe (Malawi), Byang Kato (Nigeria), Charles Nyamiti (Tanzania), J. S. Pobee (Ghana), G. M. Setiloane (Botswana), Ndabaningi Sitole and Desmond Tutu (South Africa).

Sources of African Christian Theology

As would be expected, even if certain common concerns make of African Christian Theology a valid and recognisable phenomenon, there is a wide divergence of conclusions drawn by the different authors. It would be very surprising if it were otherwise. The differences can be explained to some extent by the sources or 'raw materials' used by the different theologians and especially by the relative importance granted to each of these sources for the theological task. Four of the sources are particularly important:

1. Culturo-religious heritage

Most African theologians would plead that the cultural and religious background of their world should be taken seriously. Indeed, their chief complaint is that European and American propagators of a Christianity which is understood in Western philosophical and socio-cultural categories have wanted to transfer it 'as is' to Africa. In so doing, these foreigners have related negatively to the existing African heritage; they have either ignored it as irrelevant to their purpose or sought to obliterate it as positively harmful. Examples of such attitudes (Eboussi speaks of *the language of derision* and *the language of refutation*[139]) are not difficult to find in the literature of past decades, especially the colonial phase, and are quoted in most books on African theology.

It is a common allegation by African writers that
> missionary Christianity was not from the start prepared to face a serious encounter with the traditional religions and philosophy,[140]

preferring simply to impart its message onto a clean sheet. The consequence of this 'tabula rasa' mentality is that Africa has adopted a Christianity which often does not reach down to the roots but remains superficial, overlaid. There is a lack of 'fit'. Too often, Christianity has been presented as a package of dogmas and rituals for simple credence,
> dictated understanding, evidence acquired by proxy or substitute, conformity to the system of unconditional acceptance.[141]

African theologians such as Mbiti are at pains to insist that African peoples are not religiously illiterate.[142] Kwame Bediako agrees that

this heritage is important if a meaningful Christian theology is to be
built in Africa:

>We cannot elaborate a Christian theology of religions in the
>present by assuming that a religious tradition did not exist
>in the past, nor, for that matter, that the heritage from the
>past has lost all its impact and value for the present.[143]

The same author stresses that

>theological consciousness presupposes a religious tradi-
>tion, and tradition requires memory, and memory is integral
>to identity', and quotes Mbiti 'Without memory we have no
>past and having no past, our identity itself is lost, for the
>past is also our present.[144]

Thus the familiar question of identity encountered at the beginning of
this chapter and all the way through, is discovered to be of central
importance within the theological process. As A. F. Walls puts it:

>No question is more clamant than the African Christian
>identity crisis... The Western value-setting of the Christian
>faith (is) largely rejected. Where does this leave the African
>Christian? Who is he? What is his past? The past is vital for
>all of us — without it, like the amnesiac man, we cannot
>know who we are. The prime African theological quest at
>present is this: What is the past of the African Christian?
>What is the relationship between Africa's old religion and
>her new one?[145]

Several themes offer themselves from this religious past for fruitful
theological reflection. The most obvious is the question of God. Is there
any sort of identity and continuity between the God preached by the
missionaries and the Supreme Being acknowledged apparently almost universally by African religious tradition? The question is
tackled in books and articles by many African theologians, of whom
Idowu is perhaps the most insistent on the theological importance of
the African religious past.[146] For him and for the great majority, the
answer is positive:

>There is only one God, the creator of heaven and earth and
>all that is in them; the God who has never left Himself

without witness in any nation, age, or generation; whose
creative purpose has ever been at work in this world; who,
by one stupendous act of climactic self-revelation in Christ
Jesus came to redeem a fallen world.[147]

Mbiti's book 'Concepts of God in Africa' analyses beliefs about the
'one Supreme God', taken from some 270 tribes in Africa, beliefs that
have mostly *'sprung independently out of African reflection on God'*.[148]
If the emphasis in Idowu's works is theological (in the strict sense of
the word) and falls on the vindication of the integrity of traditional
African religion, Mbiti's concern, reflected in other articles, is more
Christological and is weighted towards a Christian faith that 'fits'
because it has in the African religious past a *'praeparatio evangelica'*.

Related to the subject of God is that of the world of spirits, the
muliplicity of other-than-physical beings and this forms another
category of theological reflection. The Ibadan consultation of 1969
devoted a chapter to 'God, the spirits, and ancestors' (by S. A.
Azeanya). [149] Mbiti in a chapter in 'African Religions and Philosophy'
refers to *'spiritual beings, spirits and the living dead'*.[150] Kwesi
Dickson includes a discussion about *'God, the gods, and man'* in his
book 'Theology in Africa'.[151] In attempting to explain the plurality of
divinities and their relation to the Supreme Being, Idowu speaks of
'diffused monotheism'. Bediako finds this unconvincing:

> The fact that the African 'God', under the various vernacular
> designations made an easy transition into the Christian
> scheme of divine reality, whilst the divinities were effectively
> shut out, may even be taken as an indication that these
> spirit powers could not have been confused with or identi-
> fied with Deity in any way, nor can they now.[152]

The place, if any, of the traditional concept of the ancestors (the
'living dead') within Christian theology in Africa has provoked considerable discussion. G. Muzorewa maintains that the concept of ancestral spirits is *'a major ingredient in African traditional religion and
hence in African theology.'*[153] An example of such discussion is found
in the article by B. Bujo, where a Christian re-evaluation of

estrology as *'communion of the saints'* is advocated.[154] Masamba
Mampolo finds a vital place for *'the spiritual and symbolic effectiveness
of ancestor worship'* within the Christian churches of Africa,[155] while
Daneel sees within the Shona churches an *'adaptive remoulding'* of
ancestral practices under the influence of the Christian Gospel.[156]
A third example of theological development of traditional religious
themes is that of man and community. In contrast to the highly
individualized concept of the person that characterises the West's
view of man, the African traditional view is that

> the individual does not and cannot exist alone, except cor-
> porately. He is simply part of the whole... The individual can
> only say, 'I am because we are; and since we are, therefore
> I am'.[157]

Mulago gwa Cikala relates this sense of social cohesion to the Bantu
notion of 'la participation vitale' which he explains as

> the vital link which unites vertically and horizontally the
> living and the departed... It is the result of a fellowship, a
> sharing in one common reality... which unites together
> many beings.[158]

The concept of 'participation vitale' is of central importance in his
theological reflection. Out of it came his most representative work, 'Un
visage africain du christianisme,'[159] whose concepts also figured in
'Des prêtres noirs s'interrogent' (see above, p.52) and at the Ibadan
Conference (1969), both important early milestones in African Christian theologizing.

    The deep sense of communal solidarity bears upon the theology of
Christian conversion, engaging a debate upon the Western Protestant
insistence upon individual salvation by personal faith in Christ. It also
influences understanding of moral responsibility and what constitutes sin and guilt. Many African authors draw attention to the fact
that sin is traditionally conceived as violations against community,
order, and peace.[160] Most African authors would deny that these
moral sanctions do not relate in any way to God, for some of these
taboos and norms were instituted by God.[161] But in addition to God

there are also lesser divinities and also the spirit ancestors who,

>are believed to reward and punish because they are con-
>cerned with the effective discharge of moral obligations.[162]

These notions in turn will affect understanding as to what constitutes salvation and the soteriological place of Christ's death and resurrection. To G. Muzorewa, the African concept of 'survival' is important to any understanding of salvation.[163] Kwesi Dickson devotes a chapter of his book to 'the theology of the Cross in context', seeking to retain a significant place given by the New Testament to the death of Christ while bearing in mind traditional African ideas about death. Christ, the perfect victim, by His death

>merits, to use an African image, to be looked upon as ancestor, the greatest of the ancestors... He becomes the one with whom the African lives intimately (as well as with the other living dead) on whom he called and to whom he offers prayer,

and argues that Paul's language of the Cross would support the African belief that

>death binds up relationships in the society, revitalizing the living and underscoring their sense of community.[164]

2. African Independent Churches

As has been shown above, the all-pervasive search for identity affecting many aspects of life and thought in Africa in the 20th Century has been shared by the extraordinary proliferation of religious groups, most of which profess a Christian identity. Whether they broke away from the historical churches, or sprang up independently under prophetic leadership, they were free to be themselves and express themselves as Africans in their socio-religious life. Paradoxically, the AICs themselves have produced very little in the way of theological writings, being more preoccupied with the experience of their faith than with its theoretical formulation. Their theological contribution has been indirect, self-confessedly 'unwritten, unsystematic and undefined' and yet for all that 'implicit'.[165]

Their rituals, beliefs and historical development have, however, been the study of countless learned articles. These published descriptions and analyses have brought the Independents' religious distinctives to the attention of sympathetic, theologically equipped African thinkers within the historical churches. Muzorewa lists the independent churches as an important source of African Christian theology and says,

> African theologians turn to the independent church movement for raw materials for their work because the independent churches do indigenize the Christian message.[166]

According to S. G. A. Onibere, these churches

> par excellence constitute the institutionalization of the so much sought-for 'theologia africana,[167]

The South African A. R. Sprunger insists that

> there will be no relevant theology in South Africa and in Africa as long as the universal church and the mission churches do not start looking at, listening to and learning from our separatist brothers.[168]

Among the theologically fruitful distinctives shared by most (but not all) of the independent Churches are: attention to the ancestors, Christian healing, divination, dreams and visions, prophecy, polygamy, church discipline, the role of women, worship and liturgy.[169] Onibere adds in a shorter list the distinctive of 'communitarian character'.[170] Sprunger lists ten *'fundamentally African and genuinely Christian features'* of the so-called 'Zionist' or 'Prophet-healing' churches. Each of the features calls out for theological reflection:

1) the charismatic call of the prophet, requiring a serious examination of the doctrine of the Spirit
2) Apostolic zeal and missionary power, pointing to the need for repentance and a serious review of current theological priorities
3) Community, rediscovering the meaning of 'koinonia'
4) Universality of the Church, a new understanding of classless love

5) Tolerance, allowing for fresh thinking while remaining christo-centric

6) Worship, calling for a renewed awareness of Christ's eschatological presence

7) Healing as care and concern for illness and its causes, both physical and supernatural

8) Holistic counselling and prophetic advice, leading possibly to a renewal of pastoral theology

9) Sacramental life and symbolism, tying in with the symbolic richness evident in the Old and New Testaments

10) Generosity, pointing the way to a recovery of Christian joy.[171]

Sprunger concludes his article by saying:

> In response to the inadequacy of our church life and the ir-relevancy of our theology, the Holy Spirit Himself has lit a genuine apostolic fire in our midst... Let us listen eagerly... it may lead us to repentance and to a relevant theology.[172]

3. Nationalism

It is obvious that in the search for identity and freedom from foreign domination, African Christian Theology and nationalism have common concerns. While many of the African theologians referred to do not discuss nationalism as a theological issue, they share with the nationalist writers the mostly negative reaction to the colonial missionary period with its paternalism, domination and resulting estrangement. The colonial experience has its political reaction; it also has its theological reaction.

For some writers the lines run not only parallel but also very close. A considerable proportion of Muzorewa's book is concerned with nationalism, which he considers to be a 'major source' and 'general context' of African theology:[173]

> African theology is developing concepts that tend to rein-force political power and cultural validity. African theology's

claim to set the African at liberty to be who God created the African to be is a theological articulation endorsing what has been pointed out by African nationalists in the struggle for independence on the continent.[174]

Muzorewa argues that the close relationship between theology and nationalism have been reinforced by the creation and activities of the All Africa Conference of Churches. The fact that the 1958 All Africa Church Conference at Ibadan was held in the same place and in the same year as the All Africa People's Conference was 'not sheer coincidence'. Furthermore, it was in the one year, 1963, that both the AACC and the OAU were founded.[175]

Muzorewa insists that historical parallels are supported by conceptual affinity, for if political emancipation has been the preoccupation of nationalism,

> involvement in the political liberation struggle has also been a major theme of the AACC assemblies,[176]

and

> African nationalists are working hand in hand with African theologians, because both parties seem to share the same vision — that of a united, peaceful, dignified, self-reliant Africa.[177]

The persistence in South Africa of the white minority 'apartheid' régime has produced its own theological reaction in Black Theology, which is outside the direct scope of this study. Its emphases reflect the oppressive political and social context in that country. Shun Govender pleads for a relevant, contextualized theology and states that

> to contextualize theology in South Africa means that we have to radically redefine our theological mandate and transform theological reflection in terms of the life-death struggle of those seeking peace and justice in society.[178]

It would be totally wrong however to assume that theologians in other parts of Africa are indifferent to the issues being faced in the south of the continent.[179] The Communiqué of the Pan African Conference of Third World Theologians, sees its mandate in the context of 'the *dynamics of a conflictual history'* which includes economic, political, cultural, and sexual dimensions and states:

> We stand against oppression in any form because the Gospel of Jesus Christ demands our participation in the struggle to free people from all forms of dehumanization.[180]

Increasingly, the liberation theme is receiving attention in the writings of African theologians and church leaders. As might be expected, some discuss liberation from a Marxist politico-economic perspective, others from a Christian sin-redemption viewpoint. Whereas in past years it was possible neatly to confine socio-economic liberation theology to Latin America, ethno-political black theology to Southern Africa and the Southern USA and cultural 'African Theology' to tropical Africa, increasingly the trend is for cross-fertilization between all three.[181]

4. Bible

To say that in the modern missionary implantation of Christianity in Africa the Bible played a central role is (at least with regard to Protestant Christianity) to state the well-known. The missionary was known as 'the man of the Book' and by the high order of priority given to both the translation of the Bible into many of Africa's vernaculars and to the establishing of Bible schools at every level, the centrality of the Bible was ensured and pertains in large sections of the African Church to the present. Traditionally it was different in the Roman Catholic missionary process and Hastings can speak of

> the Catholic missionary who rarely offered his converts a Bible and had anyway set up a clearly different source of authority behind his teaching.[183]

Vatican II, however, was to bring new emphasis upon the Bible as forming, together with the Church's accumulated conciliar traditions, the basis for belief and behaviour.

The Bible features prominently in many of the independent churches. Indeed, its possession is held to be one of the causative factors in their existence for *'they found what they were looking for in the Bible, but not in the white churches'.*[184] Archbishop Ngada and his colleagues representing the independent churches declare:

> We read the Bible as a book that comes from God and we take
> every word in the Bible seriously[185]

The appeal of the Old Testament with its affinity in many respects to traditional African ethos, has been widely commented on and Dickson devotes an entire chapter of his book to 'cultural continuity with the Bible', although he does also draw attention to important points of discontinuity.[186] Turner's analysis of sermons preached in the Aladura churches of Nigeria reveal that in fact far more texts were chosen from the New Testament than from the Old, although he does allow that many independents tend to have an Old Testament interpretation of the whole Bible.[187]

The Bible and Christian Heritage' is listed first among the sources of theology in Africa by the Pan African Conference of Third World Theologians and of the Bible, the document goes as far as to say:

> the Bible is the basic source of African theology, because it
> is the primary witness of God's revelation in Jesus Christ. No
> theology can retain its Christian identity apart from the
> Scripture.[188]

Hastings, among others, has pointed out that what Africans related to in the Bible was not always what seemed to the missionaries to be most important therein.[189] In insisting that the West does not have a 'monopoly' of theology which Africa must simply receive passively as ready-made packages of dogma, African theologians are claiming the right to set their own theological agenda, asking questions and seeking answers which arise out of their authentic context.

Exactly what part the Bible will play in the theological process will vary according to the understanding of the nature of revelation. For some, like Eboussi, it is mistaken to seek a normative revelatory role in the Bible. Indeed, he speaks of the *fetishism of revelation*'[190] and insists that

> the ethical prescriptions of the Bible bear the mark of bygone
> ages. They are testimonies to history... Morality drawn from
> sacred Scripture is worth no more than politics drawn from
> the same source.[191]

The Bible, therefore, is rather

> a treasury of metaphors', a testimony of others' experience
> of God and 'survives in the fragments representing what the
> Jews perceived and felt of existence in its epochal
> novelty.[192]

What counts is rather an existential encounter with Christ 'upstream
from dogma'.[193] Dickson's evaluation of Scripture is more positive
and he urges a Biblical hermeneutic which will take seriously the
Biblical story's Ancient Near-Eastern background as well as the
particularity of the African situation. Yet he also (warily) conjectures
that the existing New Testament canon could profitably be re-exam-
ined, so that other sources of the life and work of Christ, once deemed
unworthy for canonical inclusion, might be admitted and be found

> more satisfying spiritually in the light of the African's religio-
> cultural and other circumstances.[194]

John Mbiti, as a New Testament scholar has, perhaps, done more
than other Africa theologians to interrelate the African and Biblical
worlds and has repeatedly advocated the centrality of the Bible in the
task of theology in Africa:

> Any viable theology must and should have a biblical basis
> and African theology has begun to develop on this founda-
> tion... Nothing can substitute the Bible... As long as African
> Theology keeps close to the Scriptures, it will remain rele-
> vant to the life of the Church in Africa and it will have lasting
> links with the theology of the Church universal.[195]

Mbiti's research into the African traditional religious 'possessio' is
well known.[196] One of his particular contributions has been to argue
for the 'continuum' relating the pre-Christian old and the Christian
new in terms of preparation and fulfilment. His estimate of the African
religious tradition is basically positive; its place within God's redemptive process is that of a 'praeparatio evangelica':

> African Religion reflects God's witness among African peoples
> through the ages. It has been a valuable and indispensable
> lamp on the spiritual path... It is a crucial stepping stone

towards that ultimate light (the Gospel). As Christianity develops in our continent, answering African needs and being firmly rooted in our culture, it will derive great benefits from the work already done by African Religion. The Gospel has come to fulfil and complete African religiosity.[197]

The writings of the Nigerian Byang Kato[198] stand out in contrast against most of the theological writings of his African theologian contemporaries. Whereas the majority were arguing for a positive Christian reassessment of African cultural and religious values and practices, Kato raised a dissenting, warning voice. His repeated call was for a *'Biblical Christianity'*, and his warnings were against *'syncretism, universalism and christo-paganism'*.[199] His opposition to the consensus has been interpreted as betraying a blinkered loyalty to American evangelical conservatism[200] and as repeating the mistaken perception of early missionaries who wished to wipe the African slate clean before imprinting on it an entirely new religious psychology.[201]

A more careful reading of Kato's writings, however, reveals that he, as much as anyone, was anxious that Christianity should be or become thoroughly African. He argued that Christianity could and should be considered *'an African religion'* (historically, and statistically) and he urged that *'Africans should be made to feel it so.'*[202] He insisted that *'culture is what binds a people together and gives them a sense of identity as a community'* and that therefore *'the call for cultural revival is right and necessary.'*[203] His warning was against elevating the non-Christian religio-cultural heritage (of Africa or of any country) to the status of revelation. For Kato, traditional religion in Africa as elsewhere might express an honest craving for God, a response to *'general non-redemptive revelation'*, but it is a response that bears the marks of the Fall and which must, therefore, come under the judgment of the *'special redemptive revelation'* brought in Christ and explained authoritively in the Scriptures. He thus emphasised the radical discontinuity between the Gospel and African traditional religion as a system, but not between the Gospel and the deepest needs of the African:

Christ is the fulfilment of the Old Testament and of the deep spiritual needs of human hearts, not the fulfilment of African traditional religion or any other non-Christian religion.[204]

The relation between revelation and culture remains one of the major concerns of theology in Africa, across a broad spectrum of different confessions. The Roman Catholic 'Premier Congrès des Biblistes Africains' (Kinshasa, 1979) set itself to debate the *dialogue between the Word of God and the African*[205] and listed 13 *'problèmes herméneutiques'* to resolve. For their part, evangelicals, whose *'high view of Scripture'* has sometimes in the past brought accusations of a corresponding *'low view of culture'*, have moved towards a fuller recognition that the Gospel cannot be isolated from the human culture in which it is to be proclaimed, and indeed, in which the Christian Gospel first found expression. The Willowbank Consultation on Gospel and Culture, four years after the Lausanne Congress on World Evangelization, brought together some 33 theologians, anthropologists, linguists, missionaries and pastors from all six continents. Its report reveals a new evangelical awareness of the cultural conditioning of Scripture itself which nevertheless does not put in question its *'normative quality'*[206] and a new sensitivity towards the cultural context, a replacement of a 'pre-package Gospel' approach by the incarnational model of 'identification without loss of identity'.[207]

Conclusion

In the theological task facing Africa today, the debate seems likely to centre upon the search for culturally appropriate expression of belief rather than upon cerebral speculation about abstract ideas. African theologians have established that the African context is the proper workshop within which to make meaningful theology for Africans. It is likely that for this very reason the theological process will experience an increasingly local particularization as socio-anthropological research emphasises the internal diversity of the Continent. Recently, Tienou has advocated that the only methodology which takes this diversity seriously is *'prescription theology'* which

> does not seek to develop a theology which has general validity for the entire African Continent', but which 'takes contextualization seriously in that it seeks to develop a theology capable of solving problems which are specific to a given community.[208]

It is flexible enough to determine the 'public' (ie. the constituency) and to take into account both the modern and the traditional and recognise that the two together constitute the real Africa of today.[209]

However, it is also true that many African theologians, for all their emphasis upon the socio-cultural context of Africa, are concerned that the Christianity which Africa has embraced does not lose its universality. *'African Christianity is part of a world-wide Christianity'*.[210] The question will continue to be asked *'What is it, of which we are a truly authentic African part?'* In the broad fronted advance towards reaffirmation of social, cultural, political, economic and religious identity that has caught up Africa in the past half-century, it will be remembered that the theological debate also addresses the identity of the Gospel whose common affirmation characterizes Christians of every context.

It has been seen that the quest for an African understanding of the Christian faith is the theological dimension of a very wide drive for discovering or rediscovering an identity which is authetically African rather than borrowed or imposed from outside. The process of *'faith seeking understanding'* is at work in all parts of Africa and is the monopoly of no one church, of no one 'elite' of the church, and of no one methodology. It is the purpose of the following three chapters to explore the theologizing process within the one country of Zaïre, as illustrated by contrasting approaches selected from three different confessions.

References

1. R. Oliver and J. D. Fage, 'A Short History of Africa'. Harmondsworth, *Penguin African Library*, 1972, p. 189.

2. The point is made by many writers, among them E. Mortimer:
   > A British imperialist, if he thought in terms of progress (in Africa), would think of it as an advance towards self-government; for a French imperialist, progress would imply closer integration with the mother country and political maturity would not mean the rule of Africans by the Africans (which after all had existed before the imperial powers had arrived), but the participation of Africans as Frenchmen in the government of a greater France.

   E. Mortimer, *'France and the Africans'*, Faber and Faber, London, 1969, p. 34.

3. M. J. Sampson, *'West African Leadership: Public Speeches delivered by The Honourable J. E. Casely Hayford, MBE, MLC'*. Ilfracombe. Arthur H. Stockwell Ltd., n.d. p. 79, quoted in R. Emerson and M. Kilson (eds), *'The Political Awakening of Africa'*. Prentice Hall Inc., N.J., 1965, p.10.

4. Letter from B. Diagne to Marcus Garvey in R. L. Buell: *'The Native Problem in Africa'*. New York, MacMillan Co., 1928, Vol. 2, p. 81, quoted in Emerson and Kilson, op. cit. p. 22.

5. F. Houphouet-Boigny, *'Address to Fourth Committee of United Nations General Assembly, January 7th, 1957'*, reprinted in Ambassade de France, Service de Presse et d'Information,

Speeches and Press Conferences no. 85, New York, 1957 pp. 2-8. Quoted in Emerson and Kilson, op. cit. p. 78.

6. cf. F. A. Joppa:
Les secteurs modernisant et traditionnel ne sont pas engendrés par un processus commun. Le secteur modernisant est le résultat de l'introduction d'un corps étranger — la puissance coloniale — à un moment donné de l'histoire des sociétés traditionnelles... N'ayant rien en commun, les éléments de ces secteurs se révèlent antithétiques et incompatibles.
'L'Engagement des écrivains africains noirs de la langue francaise', Editions Naaman, Quebec, 1982, p. 210.

7. M. Assimeng, 'Crisis, Identity and Integration in African Religion,' in H. Mo (ed.), *Identity and Religion*, 1978. pp.106-107.

8. E. A. Ruch, 'Philosophy of African History', in *African Studies*, Johannesburg, 1973, 32(2) pp. 113-125.

9. R. Oliver and J. D. Fage, op. cit. p. 207.

10. H. W. Turner, 'The Place of Independent Religious Movements in the Modernization of Africa', in *Journal of Religion in Africa*, Vol. 2, No. 1, 1969, p. 56.

11. J. Mbiti, *New Testament Eschatology in an African Background*, Oxford University Press, London, 1971, pp. 30-31.

12. K. Nkrumah, Address to the First International Congress of Africanists, at the University of Ghana, Legon, December 1962, quoted in Emerson and Kilson, op. cit. p. 23.

13. J. Jahn, *A History of Neo-African Literature*, trans. from German by O. Coburn and U. Lehrburger, London, Faber and Faber, 1968, p. 242.

14. L. Senghor: 'La négritude, c'est l'ensemble des valeurs culturelles du monde noir, telles qu'elles s'expriment dans la vie, les institutions, et les oeuvres des Noirs', quoted by A. Nordmann-Seiler,*La littérature néo-africaine*, Presses Universitaires Françaises, Paris, 1976, p. 17.

15. C. Achebe, quoted by G-C M. Mutiso, *Socio-Political Thought in African Literature*, Macmillan, London, 1974, p.11.

16. Quoted by C. Achebe, Johnson Reprint Corp, New York, 1967.

17. C. Achebe, quoted in G-C M. Mutiso, op. cit. p. 11.

18. Examples of works evoking the glorious past would include:
    Joseph Said, *Au Tchad sous les étoiles*, 1962
    Djibril Tamsir Niane, *Soundjata*, 1960
    Mamadou-Ouane, *Fadimata, la princesse du désert*, 1955
    examples of works evoking rural traditions include:
    J. Kenyatta, *Facing Mount Kenya*, 1938
    Camara Laye, *L'enfant noir*, 1953.

19. A. Césaire, Quoted by Oladele Taiwe, in *An Introduction to West African Literature*, Nelson, London, 1967, p. 45.

20. J. Jahn, op. cit. p. 250.

21. L. Senghor: 'il n'est pas question de ressusciter le passée, de vivre dans le Musée négro-africain; il est question d'animer ce monde hic et nunc, par les valeurs de notre passé', *Liberté I. Négritude et Humanisme*, Seuil, Paris, 1964, p. 283.

22. N. Azikiwe, *Political Blueprint of Nigeria*, African Book Co. Ltd., Lagos, 1943, Quoted by Emerson and Kilson, op. cit. pp. 60-61.

23. G. Arboussier, 'La situation actuelle du Rassemblement Démocratique Africain', in *Le Rassemblement Démocratique Africain dans la lutte anti-impérialiste*, Les Impressions Rapides, Paris, 1948, pp. 46-53, Quoted in Emerson and Kilson, op. cit. p. 80.

24. Statistics from UNESCO Yearbook, Paris, 1985.

25. Quoted in V. Ferkiss, *Africa's Search for Identity*, O. Braziller, New York, 1966, p. 165.

26. UNESCO Yearbook, op. cit.

27. K. Nkrumah, Speech, Positive Action Conference. Accra, 1960, quoted in Emerson and Kilson, op. cit. p. 147.

28. H. Macmillan, Quoted in A. Hastings, *A History of African Christianity 1950- 1975*, Cambridge University Press, Cambridge, 1979, p. 132.

29. K. Nkrumah, *Neo-Colonialism,* Heinemann, London, 1965, p. ix.

30. V. Ferkiss, op. cit. pp. 260-261.

31. In this respect, the colonial fragmentation of Africa into many states has worked to Africa's advantage, for with its 35 voices (compared with 19 Asian and 23 Latin American voices) it represents the most important bloc among the under-developed countries.

32. *Encyclopedia Britannica,* Benton, Chicago, 1974, Vol. 18, p. 903.

33. H. Selassie, 'Africa must shape its own future', from *Proceedings of the Summit Conference of Independent African States,* Vol. 1, Section 2, Addis Ababa, 1963. Quoted in Emerson and Kilson, op. cit. p. 166.

34. Mobutu S. S., Speech of 19th August, quoted in 'Church and 'authenticity' in Zaire', *Pro-Mundi Vita,* p. 2. I owe this quote to Hastings, op. cit. p. 191.

35. Mobutu S. S., conversation with P. Bernetel, quoted in Kabue Buana, *L'expérience Zaïroise,* Maury, France, 1976.

36. Mobutu S. S., *Discours à l'ONO,* 1973.

37. D. B. Barrett, From an unpublished paper presented in summary to South African Missiological Society in Jan.1984, quoted by D. Shank in 'Mission relations with independent churches in Africa', in *Missiology,* Vol.13, No.1, 1985, pp. 23-44.

38. B. G. M. Sundkler, *Bantu Prophets in Southern Africa,* Lutterworth Press, London, 1948, rev.ed. 1961.

39. D. B. Barrett, *Schism and Renewal in Africa an analysis of six thousand contemporary religious movements,* Oxford University Press, London, 1968.

40. D. B. Barrett, unpublished paper, quoted by D. Shank, op. cit. p. 28.

41. D. B. Barrett, 'Interdisciplinary theories of religion and African independency', in D. B. Barrett (ed.) *African Initiatives in Religion*, E.A.P.H., Nairobi, 1971, p. 148.

42. J. Fernandez, 'African religious movements — types and dynamics', *Journal of Modern African Studies*, Vol. 2, No. 4, 1964.

43. H. W. Turner, 'The approach to Africa's religious movements', in *African Perspective*, No. 2, 1977, p. 19.

44. G. Balandier, 'Les mythes politiques de colonisation et de décolonisation en Afrique', in *Cahiers Internationaux de Sociologie*, Paris, 33, 1962, p. 86.

45. G. Balandier, op.cit., p. 92.

46. V. Lanternari, *Religions of the Oppressed*, New York, Knopf, 1963.

47. Referred to by T. O. Ranger, 'Religious movements and politics in Sub-Saharan Africa', in *African Studies Review*, Vol. 29, No. 2, p. 2.

48. P. Bohannan, *Africa and the Africans*, The Natural History Press, New York, 1964, p. 25.

49. J-P. Dozon, 'Les mouvements politico-religieux; syncrétismes, messianismes, néo-traditionalismes', in M. Augé (ed.), *La construction du monde*, F. Maspéro, Paris, 1974, p. 88.

50. T. O. Ranger. op. cit. p. 64.

51. R. Buijtenhuijs, 'Messianisme' et nationalisme en Afrique noire; une remise en question', in *African Perspectives*, No. 2 of 1976 (issued 1977), p. 37.

52. J. Fernandez, op. cit. p. 531.

53. ibid.

54. T. O. Ranger, op. cit. p. 65.

55. H. W. Turner, 'The approach to Africa's religious movements', op. cit. p. 18.

56. D. B. Barrett, 'Interdisciplinary theories', op. cit. p. 147.

57. G. C. Oosthuizen, 'Causes of religious independentism in Africa', in *Ministry*, Vol. II, No. 4, 1971, pp. 121-133.

58. D. B. Barrett, *'Interdisciplinary theories'*, op. cit. p. 150.

59. ibid, p. 151.

60. D. B. Barrett, *Schism and Renewal*, op. cit. p.156.

61. M. L. Daneel, 'Communication and liberation in African Independent Churches', in *Missionalia*, Vol. II, No. 2, 1983, p. 60.

62. ibid, p. 65.

63. ibid, p. 72.

64. C. Dillon-Malone, *The Korsten basket-makers: a study of the Masowe apostles, an indigenous African religious movement*, Manchester University Press, 1978.

65. A. Hastings, *A history of African Christianity, 1950-1975*, op. cit. pp. 77-78. Dr. H. Fisher points out that the Holy Apostles Community began to disintegrate somewhat in the 1970's — *'a failed Utopia'* (Fisher to Molyneux, April, 1987).

66. J. Fernandez, 'African religious movements', *Annual Review of Anthropology*, quoted by T. O. Ranger, op. cit. p. 11.

67. J. Fernandez, *Bwiti, an ethnography of religious imagination in Africa*, Princeton, 1982, referred to in T. O. Ranger, op. cit. p. 12.

68. E. E. Evans-Pritchard, *Nuer Religion*, Oxford University Press, Oxford, 1962, p. viii; my attention was drawn to this by H. W. Turner's article, 'A methodology for modern African religious movements', in *Comparative Studies in Society and History* Vol. 8, No. 3, 1966, p. 287.

69. H. W. Turner, 'A methodology for modern African Religious movements', op. cit. p. 287.

70. ibid, p. 288.

71. Admitting the contribution of political liberation, social protest, nationalism, economic deprivation, culture disruption, Oosterval concludes:
    this totality of human factors worked like a mighty catalyst... but the messianic expectations 'per se' are a religious category by themselves. They are 'sui generis'; they have their own rationale and cannot be explained by non-religious factors.
    G.Oosterval, 'Modern messianic movements as a theological and missiological challenge', *Missionary Studies 2*, Elkhart, Indiana: Institute of Mennonite Studies, 1973, p. 24.

72. Bimwenyi Kweshi, *Discours théologique négro-africain; problème des fondements*, Présence Africaine, Paris, 1981, pp. 306ff.

73. A. J. Omoyajowo, 'An African expression of Christianity', in B. Moore, (ed.), *Black Theology — the South African Voice*, C. Hurst, London, 1973, p. 88. See also J. Mbiti, *African Religions and Philosophy*, Heinemann, London, 1969, p. 234.

74. A. R. Sprunger, 'The contribution of the African Independent Churches to a relevant theology for Africa', in H. J. Becken (ed.), *Relevant Theology for Africa*, Durban, 1972, p. 169.

75. ibid, p.166.

76. S. G. Onibere, 'The phenomenon of African religious independency — blessing or curse on the Church Universal?' in *African Theological Journal*, Vol. 10, No. 1, 1981, p. 15.

77. See, *Speaking for ourselves*, report by members of AICs on their pilot study of the history and theology of their churches. Publ. by I. C. T. Braamfontein, South Africa, n.d., pp. 22-23.

78. P. Beyerhaus, 'The encounter with messianic movements in Africa,' paper presented at 'Christianity and the non-Christian World Seminar', University of Aberdeen, April, 1968, p.10.

86

79. A. Hastings, op. cit. p. 72.

80. V. Hayward, 'African independent church movements', *Ecumenical Review*, Vol. 15, No. 2, 1963, p. 196.

81. J. Janzen, 'Vers une phénoménologie de la guérison en Afrique centrale', in *Etudes Congolaises*, Kinshasa, Vol. 12, No. 2, 1969, pp. 102ff.
also: Kofi Appiah-Kubi, 'Indigenous African churches; signs of authenticity', in Appiah-Kubi and Torres (eds.), *African Theology en route*, Orbis Books, New York, 1979, pp. 121ff.
J. A. Loewen, 'Mission churches, Independent churches, and felt needs in Africa', *Missiology*, Vol. 4, No. 4, 1976, pp. 410-411.
H. J. Becken, 'The experience of healing in the Church in Africa', *Contact*, (Geneva), 29, 1975, pp. 7-11.
For a fascinating account of the influence of Western medicine upon traditional concepts of illness and healing, see T. O. Ranger, 'Medical science and Pentecost; the dilemma of anglicanism in Africa', in W. J. Shiels (ed.) *The Church and healing*, Blackwell, Oxford, 1982, pp. 333-365.

82. E. B. Idowu, *African Traditional Religion*, S.C.M., London, 1973, pp. 165-178.

83. J. Mbiti, *African Religions and Philosophy*, op. cit. pp. 75-91.

84. Boka di Mpasi, 'A propos des religions populaires d'Afrique subsaharienne', in *Telema*, June, 1979, p. 32.

85. A. van Campenhoudt, 'Séparatisme et pastorale en Afrique noire', *L'Eglise vivante*, Louvain, Vol. 22, No. 5, 1970, p. 354.

86. J. Daneel, *Communication and liberation*, op. cit. p. 50.

87. H. W. Turner, 'African Independent Churches and economic development', in *World Development*, Vol. 8, 1980, p. 526.

88. R. Bureau, 'Sorcellerie et prophétisme en Afrique noire', *Etudes* Apr. 1967, p. 476.

89. See also Kofi Appiah-Kubi, 'Monography' *Bulletin de Théologie Africaine*, Vol. 1, No. 2, p. 241.

90. Daneel, 'Communication and liberation', op. cit. pp. 90-91.

91. F. B. Welbourn, *East African Rebels; a study of some independent churches*, SCM Press, London, 1961, p. 202.

92. Horton's hypothesis was originally published in *Africa*, Vol. XLI No. 2, April, 1971; it drew H. Fisher's reply in 'Conversion reconsidered; historical aspects of religious conversion' in *Africa*, in 1973; the debate continued with Horton's 'On the rationality of conversion in Africa', Vol. 45, No. 3, 1975; Fisher's response came ten years later in 'The Juggernaut's Apologia, conversion to Islam in Black Africa', in *Africa*, Vol. 55(2), 1985.

93. R. Gray, 'Christianity and religious change in Africa', *African Affairs*, No. 306:77, 1978, p. 95.

94. Letter, H. W. Turner to Molyneux, 7th Dec, 1987.

95. Report of the Second Conference of the Organisation of African Independent Churches, Nairobi, 1982.

96. G. Muzorewa, *The origins and development of African Theology*, New York, 1985, p. 57.

97. I owe this information to T. Tienou, unpublished PhD thesis, Fuller Theological Seminary, 1984, p. 8. (Permission to quote requested)

98. P. Tempels, *La philosophie bantoue*, edited by Lovanie, Elizabethville, October, 1945. A first chapter had already been published in Flemish in *Aequatoria* in 1944. Other chapters followed in *Band*, a Leopoldville (Kinshasa) periodical. Details in F. Bontinck, *Aux origines de 'La Philosophie Bantoue'* Kinshasa, 1985, p. 7.

99. Frans Tempels (his name Placide was given to him later when he joined the Fransiscan 'Ordre des Frères Mineurs') was born in 1906 in Berlaar, Belgium. He was ordained priest in 1930, sailed for Congo in 1933 for a twelve year period of service in various southern and eastern parts of the country. His ministry was one of teaching and itinerant missionary. He meantime wrote several academic studies, which were to lead up to the work for which he became most famous. The subsequent phases of Tempels story,

especially 'encounter' and the 'Jamaa', are told in, de Craemer, *Jamaa and the Church,* Oxford University Press, Oxford, 1977.

100. P. Tempels, *Notre Rencontre,* Limete, Kinshasa, 1962, quoted in Smet, 'Le Père Placide Tempels et son oeuvre publiée', in *Revue Africaine de Théologie,* Vol. 1, No. 1, 1977, p. 80.

101. P. Tempels, *Notre Rencontre,* op. cit. p. 38, quoted by Smet (see above, note 100), pp. 80-81.

102. P. Tempels, *Bantu Philosophy,* (Eng. trans. by C. King), Présence Africaine, Paris, 1969, pp. 26-27.

103. P. Tempels, 'Triple réponse étonnamment adaptée à la triple aspiration fondamentale de la personnalité bantoue', *'Notre rencontre',* op. cit. pp. 38-39, quoted by Smet, (see above, note 100) p. 81.

104. This key term in Tempels' understanding of Bantu ontology is variously translated as 'force vitale', 'force de vie', 'life-force', 'vital-force'; the word in Flemish preferred by Tempels himself was 'levenskracht'.

105. Gustaaf Hulstaert, Tempels' correspondent, was born in 1900, in Melsele, Belgium. Having been ordained priest in 1924, he sailed for Congo in 1925, where he initially had an itinerant ministry in the Boende district. For many years he edited the review *Aequatoria,* and his linguistic studies in the Mongo language are well known. His career in Zaïre has been exceptional in its length (in 1986 he was still there) and in its academic brilliance.

106. Letter from Tempels to Hulstaert, 11th May, 1946, in F. Bontinck, op. cit. p. 109.

107. Letter from Tempels to Hulstaert, 29th Nov, 1945, in F. Bontinck, op. cit. p. 95.

108. Letter from Tempels to Hulstaert, 5th Jan, 1948, in F. Bontinck, op. cit. p, 162.

109. There have been many in the history of missions in Africa who, by patient and respectful observation and research, have gained

insights just as penetrating as those of Tempels. Tempels' contribution was more far-reaching because its academic, conceptualized nature carried the debate high into academia, and far into the bastions of Roman Catholic institutionalism.

110. A. Kagame, 'L'ethno-philosophie des "Bantu"', in R. Klibansky (ed.), *La philosophie contemporaine*, Florence, 1971, p. 95.

111. A. Hastings, op. cit. p. 119.

112. *Des prêtres noirs s'interrogent*, Cerf, Paris, 1956.

113. N'Soki K., 'Génèse de l'expression théologie africaine', in *Telema*, No. 20, Dec, 1979, pp. 43ff.

114. ibid, p. 45.

1I5. ibid, p. 44.

116. quoted in Hastings, op. cit. p. 119.

117. J. Mbiti, 'Some current concerns of African theology', in *Expository Times*, Vol. 87, (referred to by Tienou, op. cit. p. 7).

118. G. Muzorewa, op. cit. p. 58.

119. K. Dickson and P. Ellingworth (eds.) *Pour une théologie africaine*, Yaounde, Editions CLE, 1969; English edition: *Biblical revelation and African beliefs*, London, Lutterworth and New York, Orbis, 1969.

120. ibid, (French editn.) p. 17.

121. See E. W. Fasole-Luke, 'Footpaths and Signposts to African Christian Theologies', *Bulletin de Théologie Africaine*, Vol. 3, No. 5, 1981.

122. A. Hastings, op. cit. p. 168.

123. ibid, p. 168.

124. J. Kearns, 'AFER's index — quite a story!', AFER, 1984, p. 14.

125. P. Hebblethwaite, *The Runaway Church*, Collins, London, 1975, p. 9.

126. ibid, p. 10.

127. ibid, p. 101.

128. ibid, p. 103.

129. ibid, p. 103.

130. Quoted by Hebblethwaite, op. cit. p. 110.

131. W. McSweeney, *Roman Catholicism; the search for relevance*, Blackwell, Oxford, 1980, pp. 245, 258.

132. A. van Campenhoudt, *L'Eglise vivante*, Louvain, Vol. 22, No. 5, 1970, pp. 352-365.

133. Pottmeyer, 'Vatican II — 20 years on', *Pro Mundi Vita* Bulletin 102 1985/3.

134. Pope John-Paul II, *AFER*, Vol. 25, No. 5, 1983.

135. A. Vanneste, 'Une Faculté de théologie en Afrique', in *Revue du Clergé Africain*, No. 13, 1958, p, 225.

136. N'Soki, K, op. cit. p. 54.

137. A. Hastings, op. cit. p. 170.

138. J. B. Danquah, *Akan Doctrine of God*, London, 1944.

139. F. Eboussi Boulaga, *Christianity without fetishes; an African critique and recapture of Christianity*, trans. from French by R. Barr, New York, Orbis Books, 1984, pp. 30-32.

140. J. Mbiti, *African Relgions and Philosophy*, op. cit. p. 232.

141. F. Eboussi Boulaga, op. cit. p. 9.

142. J. Mbiti, *African Concepts of God*, S.P.C.K., London, 1969, p. xiii.

143. K. Bediako, 'Christian tradition and the African God revisited', in D. M. Gitari and P. Benson, *The Living God*, Africa Theological Fraternity, Nairobi, 1986.

144. K. Bediako, unpublished PhD. thesis, *Identity and integrity: an enquiry into the nature and problems of theological indigenization in selected early Hellenistic and modern African Christian writers*, Aberdeen University, 1984, p. 294. (Permission to quote requested.)

145. A. F. Walls, 'Africa and Christian identity', *Mission Focus*, Vol. 6, No. 7, 1978, p. 13.

146. K. Bediako devotes a chapter to Idowu in his thesis, op. cit. pp. 332-373.

147. E. Bolaji Idowu, *Towards an Indigenous Church*, London, Oxford University Press, 1965, p. 25.

148. J. Mblti, *Concepts of God in Africa*, op. cit. p. xiii.

149. Ch. 2 in *Biblical Revelation and African Beliefs*, op. cit.

150. J. Mbiti, *African Religions and Philosophy*, op. cit. pp. 75-91.

151. K. Dickson, *Theology in Africa*, Darton, Longman and Todd, London, 1984 and Orbis Books, New York, 1984, pp. 52-62.

152. K. Bediako, 'Christian Tradition...' op. cit. p. 9-10.

153. G. Muzorewa, op. cit. p. 11.

154. B. Bujo, 'Nos ancêtres, ces saints inconnus', in *Bulletin de Théologie Africaine*, Vol. 1, No. 2, pp. 1 65-178. cf. also: E. Mosothoane, 'Ancestor cult and communion of saints', in *Missionalia*, August 1973.

155. Masamba ma Mpolo, 'Community and Cure; the therapeutics of the traditional religions and the religions of the Prophets in Africa', in *Christian and Islamic contributions towards*

establishing independent states in Africa south of the Sahara, Stuttgart, 1979, p. 125.

156. M. L. Daneel, 'Communication and liberation', op. cit. p. 84, see also his article 'The Christian gospel and the ancestor cults'. *Missionalia,* 16, Aug. 73, p. 59.

157. J. Mbiti, *African Religions and Philosophy,* op. cit. p. 108.

158. Mulago gwa Cikala:
le lien vital qui unit entre eux verticalement et horizon-talement des êtres vivants et trépassés... C'est le résultat d'une communion d'une participation à une même réalité... qui unit entre eux plusieurs êtres.
in K. Dickson and P. Ellingworth, (eds.) *Pour une théologie africaine,* op. cit. p. 192.

159. Mulago gwa Cikala, *Un visage african du Christianisme,* Paris, 1965.

160. eg. J. Mbiti, *African Religions and Philosophy,* p. 205, but see B. Kato, *Theological Pitfalls in Africa,* Kisumu, Evangel Publishing House, 1975, p. 42.

161. J. Mbiti, ibid, p. 205.

162. K. Dickson, op. cit. p. 67.

163. G. Muzorewa, op. cit. pp. 85-86.

164. K. Dickson, op. cit. p. 198.

165. *Speaking for Ourselves,* op. cit. p. 4.

166. G. Muzorewa, op. cit. p. 92.

167. S. G. A. Onibere, 'The phenomenon of African religious independency', op. cit. p. 17.

168. A. Sprunger, 'The contribution of the African independent churches to a relevant theology for Africa', op. cit. p. 163.

169. V. Hayward, 'African independent church movements', *Ecumenical Review*, Vol. 15, No. 2, 1963, pp. 193-199.

170. S. G. A. Onibere, op. cit. p. 17.

171. A. Sprunger, op. cit. pp. 165-171.

172. A. Sprunger, op. cit. p. 173.

173. G. Muzorewa, op. cit. p. 46.

174. ibid, p. 50.

175. ibid, p. 51-52.

176. ibid, p. 52.

177. ibid. p. 53.

178. S. Govender, *Christian mission and human transformation*, Report of Sixth IAMS Conference, Harare, Jan. 1985. p. 41.

179. A. Shorter, *African Christian spirituality*, London, Geoffrey Chapman, 1978, p. 7.

180. Final Communique, Pan African Conference of Third World Theologians, in K. Appiah-Kubi and S. Torres, (eds.) *African Theology en Route*, New York, Orbis Books, 1979, pp. 193-194.

181. For an exampie of 'liberation' in spiritual rather than politico-economic terms, see Bakole wa Ilunga, *Paths of Liberation*, Orbis Books, Maryknoll, New York, 1985 (Eng. tr. of *Chemins de libération*, Eds. de l'Archediocèse, Kananga, 1978).

182. cf. Kofi Appiah-Kubi, et al, *Libération ou adaptation; la théologie africaine s'interroge*, Colloque d'Accra, L'Harmattan, Paris, 1979. see espec. 3rd Section, African Theology as Liberation.

183. A. Hastings, op. cit. p. 71.

184. *Speaking for Ourselves*, op. cit. p. 71.

185. ibid, p. 21.

186. K. Dickson, *Theology in Africa,* op. cit. pp. 141-184.

187. H. W. Turner, *Profile through Preaching,* Edinburgh, 1965.

188. Final Communique, op. cit. p. 192.

189. A. Hastings, op. cit. p. 71.

190. F. Eboussi Boulaga, *Christianity without Fetishes,* op cit. pp.11ff.

191. ibid, p. 204.

192. ibid, p. 204.

193. ibid, p. 85.

194. K. Dickson, op. cit. pp. 183-184.

195. J. Mbiti, 'The Biblical basis in present trends of African Theology', in *Bulletin de Théologie Africaine,* Vol. 1, No. 1, 1979, pp. 21-22.

196. Notably his *African Religions and Philosophy,* op. cit. and *Concepts of God in Africa,* op. cit.

197. J. Mbiti, 'Christianity and African Religion', in M. Cassidy and L. Verlinden (eds.), *Facing the New Challenges -— The Message of PACLA,* Evangel Publishing House, Kisumu, p. 313.

198. Byang Kato (1936-1975), born in Nigeria, BD (London), STM and ThD (Dallas). Elected in 1973 to serve as General Secretary to the Association of Evangelicals of Africa and Madagascar (AEAM) and in 1974 as Vice-President of the World Evangelical Fellowship (WEF). He wrote only one book, *Theological Pitfalls in Africa,* Evangel Publishing House, Kisumu, 1975. He was, however, a prolific writer of articles, many of them transcriptions from public addresses at popular congresses, which accounts in some measure for their frequently polemic style. Some of these addresses have been edited as other books and booklets (see below). He died in a swimming accident on the Kenya coast.

199. B. Kato, in *Biblical Christianity in Africa,* African Christian Press, Achimota, Ghana, 1985, p. 11.

200. for instance by T. M. Njoya, 'Dynamics of change in African Christianity; African theology through historical and political change', PhD. Thesis, Princeton Theological Seminary, 1976, p. 60. I owe this information to Kwame Bediako, thesis, op. cit. p. 470.

201. Kwame Bediako, PhD. thesis, op. cit. p. 476.

202. B. Kato, 'Christianity as an African Religion', ch. 4 in *Biblical Christianity in Africa,* op. cit. pp. 32ff.

203. B. Kato, *African Cultural Revolution and the Christian Faith,* Challenge Publications, Jos, Nigeria, 1976, p. 6.

204. B. Kato, *Theological Pitfalls in Africa,* op. cit. p. 155.

205. D. Atal et al, (eds) *Christianisme et identité africaine,* Actes du Premier Congrès des Biblistes Africains, p. 17.

206. *The Willowbank Report of a consultation on Gospel and Culture,* LCWE, Wheaton, 1978, p. 9.

207. ibid, pp. 14, 18.

208. T. Tienou, unpublished PhD. thesis, Fuller, 1984, op. cit. p. 191ff.

209. ibid, p. 185.

210. *Final Communique,* op. cit. p. 193.

Chapter Two
Faith seeking (published) understanding; the contribution of Kinshasa's 'Faculté de Théologie Catholique'

It is not only in virtue of its geographical position ('set in the heart of the Continent'[1]) that the'Faculté de Théologie Catholique de Kinshasa' FTCK) can claim to play a central role in the emergence of so-called 'African theology'. Of greater importance is its position in the capital of the country that has been called, on account of the sheer numbers of priests and members,'the giant of Catholic Africa'.[2] More important still is the academic stature of the Faculty itself, expressed not only internally through the rigorous standards of teaching up to doctorate level, but also externally through the Faculty's numerous publications. (see Appendix I)

Early history of the 'Faculté'

The birth of the Faculty was inextricably bound up with the University of Louvain (Belgium). Indeed, so consciously was it modelled on its famous Belgian counterpart that the African daughter-university was even called Lovanium. The connections that bound the two together extended far beyond the mere name: R. Yakemtchouk can write:'The University of Lovanium and its Faculty of Theology were a creation of the Catholic University of Louvain; they belong to her spiritual heritage and are part of her history.'[3] Set just above foundation level in the wall of the present Faculté des Sciences building on the 'Campus Universitaire' in Kinshasa (and almost totally hidden by long grass) is a white stone originating from Louvain in Belgium; it bears two dates, 1425 and 1954, the former the year of Louvain's founding, the latter that of its Zaïrian counterpart. Yakemtchouk traces the earliest notions of university-level institutions in Africa back to Father Charles (SJ), the first occupant of the newly endowed Chair of Missiology in Louvain in the early 1920's. His enthusiasm for missions in Africa received impetus from the then Pope, Pius XI, whose missionary vision earned him the name 'pape des missions'. The following years were to see the creation of relatively advanced medical and agricultural institutions in the Belgian Congo.[4] Bishop Dellepiane, the Holy See's representative in the Congo, brought the project of a Catholic University a step nearer fulfilment by persuasively stressing the inevitability and imminence of university-level education and warning that if the challenge were not met by the Catholic Church, then the initiative would fall to lay or even Protestant elements. He argued for the establishing of a Catholic University having the same character and legal standing as the Catholic University of Louvain. Realization of the project was hindered by indecision and even rivalry between Louvain, the Jesuits and the representatives of the Holy See as to who should be responsible and in what way.[5]

It was in 1954, in the colonial capital Leopoldville, that the University of Lovanium eventually opened officially, under the jurisdiction of Louvain. It was the ambition of the founder of the new University that it would have an academic level comparable to that of European universities and it was their conviction that it was

> destined to become a beacon of Christian culture shining out over the whole of Africa.[6]

Three years later the Sacred Congregation of Seminaries and Universities in Rome conferred upon the new institution the status of Catholic University and in the same year ordered that a Faculty of Theology be set up in the University. Its admission requirements would, like those of Louvain, be very strict. So, just three years before the Belgian Congo entered independence, the country had a Faculty of Theology, which although small in numbers (there were only seven students in that first year), was of a very high academic level, not only modelled on, but also governed from its mother-university in Belgium. At the opening ceremony, the Rector, Mgr. Gillon, spoke with pride of the links with Louvain, but insisted also that the research which the Faculty would promote would 'include specifically African aspects.'[7] The first seven teachers were all Belgian, some seconded by Louvain University, others already teaching in different institutions in Congo.[8]

The anomaly of a Faculty of Theology in Africa governed by a board in Belgium, became increasingly glaring as the country moved rapidly towards independence. The need to adapt the programme more to the African situation was becoming more pressing and African students, exasperated by the conservatism and rigidity of colonial structures, delighted in calling into question the presuppositions of some of their European teachers.[9] They found some of their support in unlikely places: some 15 years earlier, in the mid-1940s, the Belgian priest Placide Tempels had similarly argued (see Ch. 1) that the African way of understanding needed to be given serious consideration. His book, 'La philosophie bantoue' [10] was to have widespread repercussions in Africa and beyond.[11] The publication of the hard-hitting 'Des prêtres noirs s'interrogent'[12] in Paris in 1956[13] was becoming influencial and was further unsettling Western complacency.[14] One of the leading contributors to the book, Mulago gwa Cikala, joined the Faculty of Theology after completing his studies in Rome as the Faculty's first African teacher.[15] The students' sentiments also received backing from closer at hand from the then Abbé J. Malula of Leopoldville, who spoke out against an 'imported Christianity' which fails to distinguish between that which is divine and that which is 'simply Western'. According to the future Cardinal, missionaries, while making real efforts at adaptation, remain strangers and 'the African soul remains untouched'. He urged the start without delay of an in-depth task of adapting the Gospel message to the Bantu soul, arguing that

it is to the substratum of this soul, by means of an indigenous hierarchy, that Christianity must be joined.[16]

Most of all, however, it was political events which were to precipitate action which otherwise might have taken many years. The date for

Congo's independence from Belgium was set for June 30, 1960. It was barely over a month before that, on May 21st, that Mgr. van Waeyen-bergh, the Rector of Louvain and President of the Board of Governors of Lovanium, called a meeting of the Board to discuss what was now seen as the inevitable transfer of the Board from Belgium to Congo. On June 10th (barely three weeks before independence) the new Statutes were unanimously accepted, with Louvain Board members being replaced by Bishops and lay people in Congo, selected in such a manner as to emphasize the national character of the new Board.[17] The first meeting of the new Board on African soil took place, almost literally at the 11th hour, on June 29th, the day before independence.

If the transfer of the Board to Congo was symbolically important as it undoubtedly was, perhaps so, too, were the tardiness and hesitation (one might almost say reluctance) of that transfer, which seemed to express the uncertainty on the part of many Europeans as to the possibility and place of a specifically African ecclesiastical and theo-logical contribution. Already, the year before, Tharcisse Tshibangu (at the time a student in the Faculty) had written in a university publication of the need in Africa

> to pass from a Christianity which is merely received to a
> Christianity come of age, which is understood in all its
> dimensions and is embraced consciously and freely...[18]

For his part, the Dean of the Faculty, A. Vanneste, while acknowledg-ing the European coloration of theology after almost two thousand years of history and admitting the need for pastoral adaptation in the Church, warned:

> But let us be careful to avoid all misunderstanding. The
> Christian religion bears within itself a truth which is divine
> and therefore universal and eternal in a way which is wholly
> unique. In some ways, therefore, it can never adapt to local
> and temporal circumstances, but must rather seek to be
> constantly itself, as completely and as radically as pos-
> sible... We wish to declare frankly, we do not think that the
> moment has come yet to launch an 'African Theology'. We

prefer rather that theology in Africa should seek to be a real theology; as with Christianity, theology must first of all be itself.[19]

His article did not rule out an eventual African theology but underlining the relative and contingent nature of any culture, African included, he saw it as being no more than *'a particular expression of the eternal truth'*.[20]

The debate

The Faculty, therefore, was born into a world of political and cultural ferment and turmoil and the debate on 'African Theology' which was organized by the 'Cercle Théologique' of the Faculty in 1960 (the very year of independence) between Tshibangu and Vanneste, must have taken place in an atmosphere which was much more than merely academic. The debate was published in the widely-read and influential 'Revue de Clergé Africain'[21] and thereby received national and international diffusion. Tshibangu continued to insist on the existence in Africa of a thought-pattern different from the Aristotelian-Thomist systems of the Western Church, a world-view which was global, synthetic, existential, holistic, which, while finding echoes in some Western philosophers and writers, nevertheless was recognizably African. He went on to argue that if this were so, then a theology of 'African colour' should be possible.[22] Vanneste, for his part, questioned gravely the value of insisting upon African specifics. Coming close to contradicting what he himself had said in 1958 about the relative nature of each and every culture, he envisaged a world where universal values were accepted, values which had grown up in Europe through successive centuries turning again and again to Graeco-Roman models for inspiration and which had provided European culture with that *'high degree of perfection which the entire world recognizes'*. The future of theology in Africa, if Africans did not want to be merely turned in upon themselves searching for their own distinctives, was to seek to contribute towards the emergence of *'universal catholic theology'*.[23] Tshibangu, at the conclusion of his

article, agreed that the movement was indeed towards a universalization of thought, but maintained that this universalization would not
mean the obliteration of cultural differences but rather their
integration.

The debate was to continue for years to come during which the voices
taking the side of Tshibangu became ever more numerous, while those
siding with Vanneste became fewer. In 1964, the FTCK organized its
first 'Semaine Théologique de Kinshasa', a week-long open-forum
debate on a subject deemed important for the Church in Africa.[24] The
influence of these 'Semaines' extends beyond the many who attend its
public sessions as the official reports are published by the Publication
Department of the Faculty and find their way to libraries in many
different parts of the world. The fourth 'Semaine Théologique de
Kinshasa' in 1968 was devoted to the subject of African Theology and
is often referred to in subsequent literature as being of particular
importance. Vanneste once more appealed for the essential unity of
Catholic theology towards which all theologians should direct their
efforts. Perhaps moving away from his earlier European-centred
remarks of 1960, Vanneste acknowledged the existence of theological
plurality (which, indeed, could even be considered in a positive light
as a *pluralisme par richesse*'), but his remarks seemed, at least to his
African colleagues, to be a rather reluctant concession to expediency,
a temporary if inevitable stage in the progress toward a universal
world theology'. Anything short of that goal was suspect: *We must
struggle against Western theology, Eastern theology, African theology*'.[25] His remarks provoked accusations of exaggerated Hegelianism
from a Congolese fellow-speaker, Tshiamalenga, as indeed they did
from another staff-member, Ngindu, who registered his obvious
disagreement with Vanneste in his report of the Conference:

> It must be said right away that, for Canon Vanneste,
> diversity, plurality, multiplicity must all be superseded, in
> the hegelian sense of the term, that is, they must be
> assumed, integrated into a superior synthesis and that it is
> towards this synthesis that every effort of understanding

and of theological investigation should tend.[26]

While Ngindu in his detailed report on the fourth 'Semaine' lists only Vanneste as the protagonist of the *'unity-not-plurality'* position, he chooses three of many protagonists of the *'plurality-therefore-African'* position. Two of the named, Mulago gwa Cikala and Mgr. Tshibangu, as Zaïrians, would have been expected to endorse the pro-African position. Their cause received important support from the non-African, internationally recognized figure of theologian-author J. Danielou, Dean of the Faculty of Theology of the Catholic Institute of Paris.[27] Danielou understood African Theology to mean the seeking of understanding of the Christian revelation by the African. The one Christian truth needed to be assumed by each type of humanity according to his own particular manner. Hence there was incontestably a proper place for African Theology. It implied, according to the French theologian, two things: on the one hand it had its starting point in Holy Scripture and Church Tradition (the twin sources of traditional Catholic authority) and on the other hand a taking seriously *(une prise de conscience)* by the African of his own values; in other words, not only an experience of these values but a reflection upon them.[28] The lecture given by Tshibangu was a detailed spelling out of the implications and methods of the sort of African Theology that Danielou envisaged — a theology that would need to be scientifically rigorous, not only to search and ponder carefully the sources of Christian belief, but also to seek to understand with the help of human and social sciences, the African human reality in which the Christian message is received.[29]

The 1968 'Semaine Théologique' was something of a landmark in the mounting acceptance of the possibility of African Theology. In its struggle for wider recognition of the legitimacy of religious pluralism in which the quest for African Theology could be made, the Faculty found a powerful ally in Pope Paul VI and in the Second Vatican Council summoned by Pope John in 1962-65.[30] The Council assembled for the first time in Rome representatives from every continent, and it marked

a turning point in the history of the Church in the sense that
it expressed a much greater openness towards non-Western
cultures and non-Christian religions.[31]

Vatican II's 'Ad Gentes' on missionary activity taught clearly that orthodoxy and pluralism were not necessarily mutually exclusive. Paul VI, for his part, did not delay in applying what Vatican II had postulated in his 'Africae Terrarum' (1967) and in his address to Ugandan bishops in 1969. Only 10 years separates Paul VI's 'Africae Terrarum' from Pope Pius XII's encyclic 'Fidei Donum' (1957) yet the two discourses represent two different eras in Catholic history. The earlier homily was essentially an appeal for the implantation[32] of the Catholic faith in Africa by means of European Bishops releasing at least temporarily some of their priests for this task. Paul VI, on the other hand, addressing African peoples, listed moral and religious values contained within traditional African cultures, values which were worthy of *'attentive consideration'*. He went on:

The teaching and redemption of Jesus Christ constitute, in
fact, the fulfilment, the renewal of all the good which exists
in human tradition. That is why the African, in becoming a
Christian, does not have to deny himself, but rather he
affirms the old values in spirit and in truth.[33]

Here, then, was official recognition, at the highest level, of a true African identity. Two years later, at the Symposium of African Bishops in Kampala, in July, 1969, Paul VI was no less outspoken in approving that pluralism which, while remaining faithful to official Catholic teaching, is also faithful to the *'style, temperament, genius and culture'* of those who profess that faith. And he concluded: *'In this sense, you can and should have an African Christianity.'*[34]

Remarks such as these were widely reported in Africa, not least in the publications of the Faculty and theologians like Mulago and Tshibangu did not hesitate to quote them in defense of their advocacy of an African Theology.[35] The decade of the 1960s, therefore, (the early years of the Faculty) saw the issue of African Theology push beyond the tentative questionings as to the legitimacy or otherwise of such a theology, to a position where the question was no longer 'if' but 'how'? By 1970, Tshibangu felt able to write:

We have reached a place where the problem of African Theology is no longer one of principle, for that is now settled.

The problem now is the elaboration of that theology.[36]

Even Vanneste, who had long expressed scepticism about such a theology, was coming to admit that 'theological pluralism has become a "doctrina communis"', but insisted (perhaps wistfully?) that the very resistance that had been expressed, by himself and others, had contributed in its own way, for it had compelled African theologians to justify the legitimacy of their claims and to constantly deepen the theological and epistemological bases of their assertions.[37]

Perhaps it can even be said that the period of theological controversy in the 1960s were the Faculty's most important years. The FTCK was an arena in which the struggle was actually taking place, its lecturers and writers not mere spectators but contestants.[38] In the important debate, the FTCK played an active role, not only by the international conferences and discussions which it organized, but also, and perhaps especially, by the wider diffusion of the debate by means of its publications. Had it not been for these latter, the influence of the Faculty would have remained local and circumscribed.

Vanneste admits that with time his position has modified, but he also insists that he still prefers to lean towards the universal nature of Christian theology, rather than towards any specific, particularist expression of it.[39] His evolving position on the question of 'African Theology' is evident in a series of three articles in the journal 'Cultures et Développement'. The first was written 14 years after the Kinshasa debate and the other two followed at intervals of three years, so that, in all, 20 years are represented. The first article acknowledges that, looking back 14 years to the debate, it is obvious that the two 'theses' (his and Tshibangu's) were not so much contradictory as representing different but complementary emphases. Having admitted this much, Vanneste nevertheless maintains that while a certain pluralism is permissible, it cannot be an end in itself, but should serve as a means to enrich the universal.[40] The second article acknowledges the increasingly wide support for the idea of African theology. Vanneste underlines the different 'raisons d'être' of Western theology and African theology; while the former tends to be speculative, the latter is more pastoral, concerned not so much with the risk of asking radical questions about the Christian faith as with ridding Christianity of its 'foreignness'. While noting the contrast between the two theological paths, Vanneste again emphasizes their possible fruitful complementarity.[41] In the third article, Vanneste shows how African theology is burgeoning (conferences, bibliographies, etc.) and devotes considerable space to discussing admiringly the doctoral thesis of the young Zairian theologian Bimwenyi Kweshi: *'Discours théologique négro-africain; Problème des fondements'* which, in Vanneste's opinion, *'far surpasses anything yet written on the meaning, the possibility and the necessity of a truly African theology'*. It marks perhaps the largest step in the move on Vanneste's part from a reluctant scepticism to a cautious affirmation of the possibility and desirability of theology in Africa which is worthy of the name 'African Theology'.[42]

Although the important differences of opinion within the Faculty over the question of 'African theology' were most conspicuous during the 1960s, they have not been entirely resolved in the years since. Three different Faculty staff members, representing either side of the 'divide', volunteered separately to the author that the names of the Kinshasa periodicals are significant, reflecting the opposing viewpoints of scholars.[43] It was decided[44] in 1977 that the name of the periodical published by the Faculty would be called 'Revue Africaine de Théologie' — it represented a publication produced on African soil reflecting on theology (whose universality was thereby implied). The 'Bulletin de Théologie Africaine', on the other hand, which was created a year or two later by the Ecumenical Association of African Theologians (in which several Faculty professors figure prominently) was, by clear inference, a publication which expressed theological reflection of a specifically African dimension. This was spelt out in its first editorial by the Coordinator of the Provisional Committee of the EAAT,

Englebert Mveng:

> Our Bulletin is a BULLETIN of AFRICAN THEOLOGY... We
> no longer need to wonder whether an African theology is
> possible. From now on we are in the workshop (chantier) of
> African theology... To insist on the birth of African theology
> is, for us, to liberate the Holy Spirit, who until now has been
> enchained within categories which are foreign to us, and
> which prevent us from fully grasping the message which he
> addresses to us today.[45] (capitals his)

Conversations in Kinshasa revealed a certain impatience felt by
more than one Zaïrian Faculty member about the non-specific nature
of the 'Revue' and a hope that before much longer it will become more
wholeheartedly African in its stance.[46]

African Theology and 'authenticité'

The controversy of the 1960s was just over when a storm of a different
nature gathered. Not for the first time in its history, national political
events were to affect the Faculty profoundly. On October 4, 1971,
Zaïre's President Mobutu launched his drive for 'authenticité'.[47] It is
at first view surprising that the President's veritable crusade for a
reassertion of traditional Zaïrian culture does not find in the publications of the Faculty a more sympathetic echo. The RAT does not
contain a single article on the subject from its launching in 1977 until
1984. A thesis on 'Christianisme et discours politique au Zaïre'
summarized in CRA (1979) by its author Nyunda turns out to concern
only the pre-Mobutu years, while an article in the same periodical in
1980 entitled 'Evangélisation et authenticité' (1980) concentrates
wholly on steps towards inculturation advocated by the post-Vatican
Catholic Church.

If the response by the Faculty was less than enthusiastic, the reason
becomes apparent in the only article that directly addresses the
'ideology of recourse to authenticity'.[48] The article prints the address
given by Faculty Professor Ngindu Mushete at an international
conference on traditional religions held at Abidjan, Ivory Coast, in July

1974. In it, Ngindu gives a blow by blow factual account of the astonishing measures taken by the Mobutu Government in its authenticity drive. It is clear that Western Christianity in general and Catholicism in particular, were singled out as one great obstacle in Zaïre's quest to *'rediscover its soul'*.[49] In 1972 Catholic (ie 'foreign') first names were outlawed, only genuine African names were permitted. Soon after, Cardinal Malula was banished from his residence, accused of authoring a subversive document. In 1973, 31 journals, most of them Catholic, were suppressed. The day following the suppressions, the political party 'dissolved' the Episcopal Assembly which it accused of subversion. In 1974, Zaïre as a *'secular state beyond religion'*, abolished December 25th as a public holiday. Later in the same year the State Commissioner for political affairs ordered the removal of crucifixes, pictures, or photos other than those of the President from all public buildings (private dwellings and places of worship were exempt). That it was the Catholic Church in particular that Mobutu saw as a threat is clearly spelled out in a newspaper article ('Le Soir', April 6th, 1973):

> The human institution, I say human, which is called the Church, which exists at the Vatican, has nothing to do with Zaïre, with Mobutu... We will no longer accept political, economic, religious, or spiritual domination imposed from the outside. Before independence, three authorities were acknowledged: Administration, Business firms, and the Church. The first two have given way; there is no reason why the Church should not do the same. I have never had any trouble from the Protestants, nor from the Kimbanguists, because they do not receive their orders from overseas. But the Zaïrian Bishops do... They are nothing more than agents working for foreign powers.[50]

The Catholics, for their part, rightly diagnosed the clash as essentially *'un affrontement des pouvoirs'*. A special note on Church-State relations in Zaïre in 'Pro Mundi Vita' (1975), pointed out that it was not essentially an ideological or religious conflict; it was rather that the Catholic Church (and to a lesser extent other Christian bodies,) is the only solidly implanted institution in Zaïre which still dares to pass judgement or give directives independently from the political party... The regime feels it is being observed, scrutinized, and even condemned by the international character of the Catholic Church.[51]

In time the tension between the Catholics and the State relaxed somewhat with hostility giving way to a mutual if wary respect. But in view of all that happened and was said, it is not difficult to appreciate why the Faculty has viewed the potential ally of 'authenticité' with such coldness and has given the notion such scant room in its publications.[52]

If the cause of African theology in the Faculty owes little or nothing (at least openly) to nationalistic trends embodied in Mobutu's authenticity drive, it continues to find inspiration in post-Vatican II events and innumerable articles in their publications refer to the travels and pronouncements of the present Pope, John-Paul II, who is seen as a continuum rather than a rupture with his predecessor, Paul VI. Most notable among these events chronicled in FTCK publications are the visits of the Pope to Africa in 1980 and the visit to Rome of Zaïrian Bishops in 1983. The Pope acknowledges building on the foundation laid by his predecessor Paul VI but goes further, exploring the implications of 'africanization' into the recesses of liturgy, catechism, art and community life and seeking to find the balance between what is constant and what is cultural:

> Of course, the Gospel is not to be identified with cultures; it transcends them. But the reign which the Gospel announces is lived out by people profoundly tied to a culture; the construction of the Kingdom cannot do without borrowing elements of human cultures. And from these elements evangelization should cause original expressions of Christian life, celebration and thought to surge forth from traditional culture. You wish to be at one and the same time fully Christian and fully African. The Holy Spirit is asking us to

believe, in fact, that the leaven of the Gospel, in its authenticity, has the power to raise up Christians within diverse cultures, with all the richness of their heritage purified and transfigured.[53]

To the Bishops of Kenya the Pope clarified further what 'Africanization' meant:

It is not a question of falsifying the Word of God or of emptying the Cross of its power (cf I Cor. 1:17), but rather of bearing Christ into the very heart of African life and to raise the whole of African life up to Christ. Thus, not only is Christianity important for Africa, but Christ himself, in the members of His body, is African.[54]

These remarks, designed to affirm the special contribution that Africa can make, are balanced by the Pope's frequent reminders of Papal and episcopal authority:

Theologians are the formal 'co-adjudicators' of the Magisterium, especially in approaching new questions... But it is no less true that only the Pope and the episcopal college are the organs of the Magisterium and the Magisterium is not delegated out to others. Do not forget that it is up to you, the Bishops, in union with the Successor of Peter, to judge in the final resort the Christian authenticity of ideas and experiences.[55]

In this way the Pope has sought at one and the same time to stress both the extent and the limits of the post-Conciliar flexibility of the Catholic Church.

The years since 1970 have thus seen the expanding Faculty working at elaborating the infrastructure of the African theology whose legitimacy it had fought hard to establish back in the 1960s. Its four 'Départments' have a current total of 370 students of whom 173 are 'séminaristes', destined to have a career of some sort in the Catholic Church.[56] A recent inventory established that the Faculty library has over 21,000 books, a total which is brought up to nearly 28,000 if current periodicals and their back-numbers are included.[57] From the

Faculty and its Departments flows a constant stream of published material which does more than anything else to emphasize the research leadership, within its field, of the Faculty within the continent of Africa. The Louvain principle 'On ne croira pas à une recherche qui n'aboutit pas à une publication' (no-one will take seriously a piece of research which is not published) was, from the early years of the Faculty, put into practice in Kinshasa.[58] One of the Faculty's requirements for the doctoral qualification is that part of the thesis should be published. The two major periodicals relating to African Theology[59] contain, therefore, much material emanating from the Faculty itself.

The 'Centre d'Etudes des Religions Africaines' and its 'Cahiers'

One major contribution to the emergent African theological task has been the scientific investigation of that cultural, religious and philosophical world which form its context. In this investigation the 'Centre de Recherches Africaines' (CERA) has played an important part. Back in 1967, Vincent Mulago questioned:

> Can we really hope for the blooming of an African theology
> as long as we lack an explicit and scientifically organized
> system of noting and interpreting the (African) reality?[60]

The year before, Mulago had been appointed director of the newly created centre, which, as its name implies, is a department for research rather than for teaching. He set about his task with energy and enthusiasm. Sensing the full support of Vatican II (the 10th Anniversary report of the CERA quotes extensively from 'Ad gentes' and refers the reader to 'Lumen gentium'),[61] the new Centre had as its task the

> scientific understanding of African religions, beliefs and
> customs, both traditional and modern, in order to resolve
> the problem of the integration of Christianity to the way of
> life of Africans.[62]

A library centre was set up to facilitate research; it currently houses some 2,500 volumes, of which the large majority relate to the African religious, ethnographic and linguistic context.

According to Mulago, the rigorous scientific research that 'CERA' was committed to was actively encouraged by the then rector of the University, M. Gillon.[63] And characteristically, not content merely to discuss and research, the Faculty decided from the outset that there should be a published review, 'Cahiers des Religions Africaines' through which the discussion could be widened both as to input and as to readership. Its editorial committee was made up of staff of the FTCK and of University specialists (particularly of the Literature and Social Science Faculties) both in Kinshasa and from other African and even European countries.[64] The first edition appeared in 1967, a modest, double number in type-style offset form. Publication has continued since then bi-annually and the quality of printing was established at its present high standard as from No. 3 (1968). According to the subscription and despatch files in the Faculty Library, the 'Cahiers' is exchanged with some 66 other journals from around the world (see Appendix II) quite apart from direct subscriptions, which indicates both the wide circulation of the journal and also the wealth of the Centre as a focal point of documentation.[65] In addition to the 'Cahiers', the Centre also has a published series 'Bibliothèque du CERA', which by 1985 had published eight significant works, ranging in subject matter from African world view to Islam and from African philosophy to the Kitawala sect.[66]

An analysis of all items (ie., essays, monographs, reviews, reports, bibliographies, etc.) appearing in the 'Cahiers' between 1967 and 1985 is given in Table 1. It reveals a penchant for studies in the realm of traditional Black Africa. Of the 337 items, no less than 211 (over 60%) are of this nature and the fact that almost half of the items in this category are longer articles and monographs representing some sort of original research (rather than commentaries on what others have said) is further evidence that the journal seeks to provide a serious channel of research. Most of the 108 items which concern specific African tribes (traditions, institutions, language, etc.) are to be found in this category; some of these are ethnographic bibliographies serving the researcher with valuable resource tools. The tribes most frequently represented are: BaKongo (11 items), BaLuba (11), Mongo (7), Bashi (7), Igbo (6), Batetela (4) and Chokwe (3).

Several *CRA* articles explore the African traditional understanding of sin and forgiveness or reconciliation.[67] Mbonyikebe debates the African understanding of 'moral fault' and culpability.[68] The reprehensible act, firstly, has a primarily social dimension, its gravity measured by the degree of harm it inflicts upon human relationships. Secondly, it has less to do with inner intention and more to do with tangible consequences. In support, the author quotes as broadly representative of African societies the statement of K. Nange, who wrote concerning the Chokwe tribe: *'The seriousness or otherwise of an act depends on its object more than on the will of the offender.'*[69] He gives a widely accepted catalogue of serious moral misdeeds: sorcery (attacking the very life-force of others), theft (possessions constitute a sort of extension of the person and thus have a value far greater than their intrinsic, material worth), adultery (a particular form of robbery), disrespect of elders and exploitation of the weak, innocent and of strangers. The source of evil is located either in the person of the sorcerer, or in Fate. As regards remission of evil, it is never automatic, but is usually the outcome of much deliberation by the wider group. It often entails public examination of the facts, avowal of the misdeed by the culprit, and restitution toward the one offended against. Sometimes God and/or the ancestral spirits are called upon to witness (and, indeed, participate in) the reconciliation and a libation or prayers are accordingly offered. Forgiveness, according to the author, is consequently total. The author concludes that the African conception of wrong is based on the essential idea of a 'sacred order' involving societal harmony and in which the ancestors have a determinant role. The ancestors, in turn, are a link in the overall and original life-force who is the Supreme Being, although the author admits that moral motivation in African traditional thinking has more to do with human-community ethics rather than religion as such.[70]

A large number of the remaining items concern the interrelation of traditional views with Christianity (see, for example, the categories

Table 1: Cahiers des Religions Africaines
Subject categories 1967-1985

Subject	No. of items	Tot	Articles
African Traditional, mainly religion:			
Religion (general)	22		
God	16		
Death and hereafter	12		
Sorcery, magic, divination	12		
Man	11		
Marriage and lineage	11		
African philosophy	10		
Rites	9		
Spirituality	8		
Cosmology	7		
Prayer	6		
Myths	6		
Spirits and ancestors	6		
Art, cinema, drama, dance	23		
Bibliographies (ethnogr.)	20		
Other (healing, initiation, proverbs, sin/evil, etc.)	32		
		211	92
Africa and Christianity:			
Independent Churches	34		
African Christian Theology	31		
African Church	20		
African history, biography	15		
RC Church and doctrine	11		
		111	37
Other:			
Islam	8		
Politics	4		
Literature	6		
Others (media, theory, development, education, etc.)	18		
		36	7

NB. Several items have more than one valid categorization. 'Articles' are longer items which seek to make a significant, original contribution.

'Independent Churches' and 'African Christian Theology' under 'Africa and Christianity' in Table 1). The last category, 'Other', includes a very wide spectrum of subjects, many of which relate to contemporary (rather than traditional) African concerns and various international questions. Taken as a whole, the 'Cahiers' constitute an important contribution to African studies, concerned primarily to examine the traditional thinking and society of Black Africa, yet aware that the Continent unavoidably is influenced by and open to the rest of the world.

Two entire volumes (Nos. 21-24) were devoted to full reporting on a conference organized by 'CERA' in Kinshasa in 1978 on African Religions and Christianity. The Conference was international, ecumenical and multi-disciplinary with some 38 participants from nine countries. Almost half of these were theologians, but there were also five philosophers, 12 social science specialists, two historians and a psychologist. The first part was devoted largely to African traditional religion, including for example Malula's 'Elements fondamentaux de la religion africaine', but including also more modern elements of African experience (messianic movements and Tempels' Jamaa movement). The second part concentrated on the relations between the African world and Christianity. Mulago, summing up the Conference, could speak of the wisdom and originality of traditional African thought and its persistent importance in individual and communal life of Africans. He stressed the need for open and sensitive dialogue between that thought and the Gospel for there to come into being an African theology which would be more than

> a simple echo of theologies elaborated in the home-countries
> of the first heralds of the Gospel,

Such a theology, Mulago insisted, would be one

> resolutely informed by and open to life in all its dimensions,
> capable of establishing an ethic, a social practice, a specific
> spirituality and one which would be able to integrate within
> itself that religious sensibility which is proper to Africans.[71]

Two entire numbers of the 'Cahiers' in 1982 were devoted to African music, art, theatre and literature, serving to illustrate again the

African preference to understand 'religion' in its many-faceted dimensions.

The Faculty's 'Revue Africaine de Théologie'

While both the name and the objectives of the 'Cahiers des Religions Africaines' indicate a well-defined aim, the 'Revue Africaine de Théologie' displays a much broader range of interests. It too, enjoys a wide international circulation (see Appendix III). In any given issue of the 'Revue' might be found articles on New Testament exegesis, essays on European philosophers, reports of international conferences and debates on African Church problems (see Table 2 below). This is in keeping with the stated aims of the journal:

> It seeks to contribute to a new synthesis of Christian life and
> thought, in conformity with the genius and aspirations of
> African peoples.[72]

The majority of articles have some direct or indirect bearing upon Africa, but by no means all. Among the more important fields addressed by *RAT* are: Biblical studies, philosophy, ethics and sacraments.

Biblical studies

This category is discussed first because of its evident importance in the overall analysis of the 'Revue'. Admittedly, there are only some 27 items in this category as opposed to 138 in that of 'Africa and Christianity'. However, if full-length articles are considered (which probably, more than the other types of items, represent original research) then the largest number of contributions, almost one third, are to be found in the field of Biblical studies (exegesis and hermeneutics). Almost 90% of all items in the 'Bible' category are full-length articles.

Despite a much talked of African predilection for the Old Testament, the overwhelming majority of these studies are in the New Testament (23 NT : 1 OT). The 'Secrétaire du Département de Théologie' and Professor of New Testament at the Faculty, Atal sa Angang Andziegu, explained this inbalance as due in part to the specialization of the teachers.[73] But he also insisted that it would be hermeneutically and methodologically incorrect to

> indulge in merely establishing parallels between the Old
> Testament and African thinking

and quoted Luke 24:27 as establishing that it is through Christ that the Old Testament is truly understood. Accordingly, any hermeneutic which has as its goal a simple correlation of Old Testament and pre-Christian African thought and values is falling short of its true purpose. Most of the studies are detailed textual criticism or exegetical essays which would be just as at home in any European journal and apparently not designed to integrate in any direct way with the African scene. Examples of these might include Kuzenzama's article: 'La préhistoire de l'expression "pain de vie" (Jn. 6: 35b, 48), 'Continuité ou émergence?' (RAT, Vol. 4, No. 7, 1980, pp. 65ff), or Seynaeve's 'Le thème de "l'heure" dans le Quatrième Evangile', (RAT. Vol. 7, No. 13, 1983, pp. 29ff.). Atal would make no apology for the 'non-African' nature of these articles:

> We oppose the idea of an 'African selection' of Scripture. Of
> course, there must be application (to the African context),
> but this follows and indeed it presupposes a prior strict
> exegesis.[74]

Other studies, however, seek to address issues of importance in the Church in Africa. Buetubela's detailed exegetical analysis of Mark 14:25 concerning Jesus' saying on the 'new wine'[75] is of topical interest (see also below, p.123 for further discussion on the sacraments).   Ukachukwu's article on 'The subordination of the women in the Church, I Cor. 14: 33b-36', likewise seeks to combine detailed exegesis of Scripture with a concern for major issues in the African (and worldwide) Church. Ukachukwu opposes the usual (according to him, mistaken) interpretation of the text which not only condemns women for ever to silence in the Church, but also seems to be at variance with Paul's teaching elsewhere excluding any complexes of superiority/inferiority between the sexes. His exegesis

Table 2: Revue Africaine de Théologie
Subject categories 1967-1985

Subject	No. of items	Tot.	Articles
African Traditional:			
Philosophy	20		
Religion, religions	4		
History	3		
Ethnographic studies	2		
Spirituality	2		
Other	9	40	12
Africa and Christianity:			
African Christian Theology	55		
African Church	28		
African Church History	21		
Conferences	10		
Independent Churches	7		
Pope in Africa	6		
Other	11	138	22
International Christianity:			
Vatican, RC (eucharist, etc.)	15		
Theology	7		
Conferences	6		
Missions	3		
Other	10	41	9
Bible:			
Old Testament	1		
New Testament	23		
Hermeneutics	3	27	24
Faculty:	10	10	0
Other:			
Islam	7		
Philosophy	6		
Biography	3		
Other	17	31	7

NB. Several articles have more than one valid categorization. 'Articles' are longer items which seek to make a significant, original contribution.

appeals for the Greek particle 'η' at the beginning of v. 36 to be given disjunctive rather than conjunctive value. The injunction for women to keep silence accordingly represents not Paul's opinion, but a report which he had heard and which he emphatically challenges. Ukachukwu concludes his article by rejecting 'the male dominated hermeneutics' of many commentators and by calling for a review of attitudes towards women and a reconsideration of their role in the Church.[76]

Two further items in RAT seek to point the way beyond textual exegesis for its own sake. The report of the 'Premier Congrès des Biblistes Africains', held in Kinshasa in December 1978, is chronicled in RAT, 1979. While covering such subjects as continuity and discontinuity between the Testaments and that between the Old Testament and African traditional religions, the report concludes with Mgr Mukeng'a Kalond's insistence that

> the task of biblical exegesis is not so much to make lots of analyses, but rather to reveal a living Christ who meets a given people in order to bring them God's salvation.[77]

Mgr Monsengwo's address in 1982 to the Pontifical Bible Institute in Rome is published in RAT 1982. In it, the Auxiliary Bishop of Kisangani pleads for the *'eminently ecclesiastical and pastoral function of Scripture, too often befogged by a show of erudite wisdom,'* and urges a constant dialogue between the *'professionals of the Word of God'* and its *'users'* (preachers and hearers).[78]

Philosophy and Ethics

Philosophy, asking as it does questions of the ultimate meaning of human existence, finds coverage in both of the Faculty's major journals. The RAT has a total of 26 philosophy items, half of them articles, the rest mainly reviews on books published either at the Faculty or elsewhere. The CRA has 11 (four articles) directly concerned with philosophy, although statistics become less meaningful where the different categories religion/philosophy/cosmology, etc., are so interrelated.

Several articles point to the difference between traditional Western analytical and scholastic philosophy, with its roots in ancient Greece and Rome, on the one hand, and the practical, synthetic, global categories more familiar to African thought, on the other. Certain European authors (theologians and philosophers) are appealed to, however, as making important breaks with the mainstream of Western speculative philosophical thinking and opening new tracks which run closer to African insights. Among these would be Karl Rahner with his notion of 'transcendental anthropology' — a theology which has man at its centre, not in a God-less but in a God-affirming manner and which Ngimbi-Nseka (RAT, 1979) sees as fitting well with African cosmology. He concludes that metaphysical anthropology (philosophical discourse on man) is essentially theological and theology, (human discourse about God) is necessarily anthropological.[79] Gabriel Marcel's emphasis upon 'inter-subjectivity' ('Nous sommes' rather than 'Je suis') finds a ready response in the African notion of corporate solidarity, according to the same author Ngimbi-Nseka in another article (RAT, 1979).[80] Nkeramihigo favours Paul Ricoeur's rejection of that form of existentialism which falsely opposes creation and liberty and he approves of insistence that justification is the secret of liberty (RAT, 1981)[81] Perhaps most of all, the French philosopher Bergson is considered (notably by Tshibangu[82]) to have called radically into question the 'aristotelianism' which is at the base of Western philosophy. It is perhaps for this reason that a large number of the theses and dissertations produced by the students at the Faculty concern 'bergsonisme' (see below, pp.126ff).

Turning from Europe to Africa, the publications of the Faculty reflect the differences of opinion as to whether there exists such a thing as 'African Philosophy'.[83] On the one hand Professor Smet has produced a large bibliography of philosophy in Africa. There is a flourishing department of Philosophy and African Religions. Louvain's Professor Ladrière is quite categoric:

> African philosophy is today a well-established reality, as is attested by a constantly growing list of works.[84]

Others, on the other hand, are sceptical. P. J. Hountondji, whose book 'Sur la "philosophie africaine"' is reviewed by Basinsa in RAT 1979,[85] insists that philosophy as a theoretical discipline cannot, by definition, be unconscious. So Tempels was wrong to speak of a 'Bantu philosophy' which existed collectively though inexplicitly. Moreover, true philosophy must be written, for only then is the memory freed to be critical. Oral tradition, therefore, cannot count as philosophy.[86] The Zaïrian reviewer, Basinsa, disagrees with such a narrow definition, claiming that philosophy can be widened to include all 'explication of human experience'.[87] Faculty member Tshiamalenga directly addresses the question in his article 'La vision Ntu de l'homme'[88] listing those who affirm an African philosophy (Tempels, Kagame, Rubbens, Mujynya) and those who reject it, at least in traditional Africa (Crahay, Hountondji and Kagame, latterly). Tshiamalenga seeks a position between the two groups; he sides with this second group in proposing that the rising generation of African philosophers be done with the tempelsian notion of a *it goes without saying* African philosophy, which confuses the African 'vécu' with the 'réflexif' which is the proper area of philosophy in the strict sense.[89] But he claims that the rigid definitions prescribed by this group are arbitrary and too narrow (Laleye would speak of 'impérialisme par les textes'). He concludes:

> We hold, therefore, that certain stories, accounts and proverbs, etc., are the means deliberately chosen by traditional Bantu to transmit the fruit of their reflection about the world, man and the Absolute. It is, of course, a philosophy which is incomplete and fragmentary. But then, all philosophy, even the best, is incomplete insofar as it is a human undertaking. There are merely degrees of incompleteness.[90]

Apart from the obvious, but important, distinction that the debate clarifies between traditional implicit 'philosophy' and modern explicit philosophy, there remains great diversity of philosophical reflection in black Africa. In August 1978 in Dusseldorf, during the 16th World Congress on Philosophy, there took place a symposium on philosophy in Africa, at which nine Africans (five of them authors) contributed. The results were edited by A. Diemer into a book entitled 'Philosophy in the present situation of Africa'. The book is reviewed by FTCK's Laleye, who concludes:

The African philosophers present have illustrated eloquently the great diversity — and therefore the richness — of current African philosophical activity... They will have given the other participants the impression that they are free thinkers, freely going different ways. [91]

Despite the diversity, it seems clear that increasingly the existence of African philosophy is an accepted fact. Without doubt, the increasing volume of published material helps to establish its validity and assists its development and the Faculty is in the forefront of publication (see Appendix I). In 1983 the bi-annual 'Revue Philosophique de Kinshasa' was launched by the Département de Philosophie et Religions Africaines' of the Faculty. Its inaugural issue included 18 articles covering African philosophy, philosophy of language, moral philosophy, esthetic philosophy and the philosophy of development. Evidence of the original reflection contained in the *RPK* is an article by the Present 'Chef de Département', Mudiji, 'La forme et la transforme du masque traditionnel africain', based on his doctoral thesis at Louvain on Pende masks.[92] Besides full-length articles, the *RPK* contains book reviews, reports of conferences and occasional interviews on philosophical subjects.

The step from philosophy to ethics is not a large one given what many report to be the holistic, integrated nature of African thinking. Most African thinkers seem to agree that the notion of 'life force' or, better (since it excludes individualism), 'life participation' is of prime importance to the African and that this being so, communal harmony and equilibrium are central to ethics. Ngimbi Nseke explores the ethical implications of an ontology of 'inter-subjectivity' where *'esse est coesse, être est coêtre'*, where the emphasis is not so much on 'Je pense' as on 'Nous sommes' and where 'Etre' is more important than 'Avoir'. Such an ontology provides a powerful base for the ethic of faithfulness and love and this love, far from degenerating into individualism, permits true personhood.[93]

Sacraments

The two Roman Catholic sacraments of the Eucharist and Ordination receive considerable coverage in the *RAT*. Some eight entries relate to the first, and two or three to the second. The debate is to ascertain to what degree decisions made by the Church (in Rome) in past centuries are binding upon the very different world of modern-day Africa.

Must the Eucharist be celebrated only with grape wine and wheat-flour? The question was debated at the Faith and Constitution Congress in Lima in 1982: 'Which aspects of the Eucharist are unchangeable because of their institution by Jesus and which aspects should depend on the competence and decision of the Church?'[94] Vanneste takes up the debate.[95] After distinguishing between 'specific' (Christ-ordained) and 'generic' (Apostles and Church-ordained) sacraments, Vanneste asks if the Eucharist can really be considered a generic sacrament, whose meaning is sacramental but whose elements can be modified. He concludes that it cannot and that wine and bread should be maintained, arguing that those who wish to substitute (say) bananas and palm wine want at one and the same time to maintain a resemblance to Jesus' rite and to Africanize it. He is supported by Nothomb. In opposition to this position, Mampila[96] urges a more flexible notion of the Eucharist. Using R. Didier's distinction between 'index' and 'symbol', Mampila retains that the index (the 'real-thing-to-be-remembered') is Jesus-Christ and his Paschal mystery; the bread and wine are symbolic, necessary but secondary and therefore susceptible to alternatives (although he does insist on the efficacy of the words of institution). His conclusion follows:

> It isn't the use of the elements of wheat-bread and grape-wine that guarantees the conformity of our Eucharists with the Last Supper of Jesus, but rather their symbolic character... The word of institution which is not inextricably connected to the symbolism of bread and wine can be said

over new elements, as long as they are selected by the Magisterium of the Church to serve as sacramental matter.[97]

Substantially the same conclusion is reached by Buetubela in his exegetical article on Mark 14:25 concerning the new wine: the eucharist symbolizes the divine meal ('the vital exchange of which God is the Author'). Any element capable of expressing the festive character of wine can successfully represent the 'new wine', and so bread and grape-wine are not the only elements possible for a meaningful celebration of the eucharist.[98]

No less topical is the issue of whether only ordained priests may consecrate the Eucharist or whether provision can be made for Church-recognized married personnel to do so. The question is not merely academic but urgently practical. R. Luneau advances the pragmatic argument that ordained priests are pitifully few in number, and illustrates the problem by referring to his two parishes in Chad (comprising between them of 80 scattered villages) for which he alone had to be responsible. Luneau states:

To maintain rigidly and to the letter (the law linking priest-hood and celibacy) when times have changed, is to sin against the Spirit.[99]

He is supported in his opinion by M. Ela (Cameroun):

To impose celibacy upon elders of the Church so that they might be eligible to administer the Eucharist is contrary to the Gospel.[100]

In his article in *RAT* (1983), Nothomb is admirably impartial in presenting Biblical, theological and other arguments for and against the ordaining of married elders for the celebration of the Eucharist. In the end, however, he believes that Vatican II's decision (and its subsequent restatement) not to permit the ordination of married men, is the right one. Short-term pragmatic solutions to the Church's need must not override the all-important theological understanding of the Priest as 'Christ's man'.

The priest must model his whole life upon his Master. If he is to participate in His mission, it is only normal that he shares His 'options de vie'. Celibacy, or absolute sexual abstinence, was one of the options chosen by Christ to fulfil His mission. There is thus a deep and perfect coherence, an internal logic, between priestly ministry and celibacy (or abstinence).[101]

The question of married priests returns in *RAT* (1984) with the official Rome statement in a 'Letter of the Congregation for the doctrine of the faith', signed by Cardinal Ratzinger, who adds his own commentary at the end. The letter exposes what it sees to be erroneous teaching advocating married priesthood, warns the Church to be vigilant and restates in very definite terms the traditional position of celibate priesthood. The articles are followed by an explanation of the theological and pastoral context of the letter by Vanneste, who makes clear his own approval of the position taken by Rome.[102]

It has been shown that the journals of the FTCK cover a wide range of subjects and overall it is difficult to discern an official FTCK 'line'. Authors are free to express themselves and frequently they reveal differing, even opposing positions. While there are articles which have little or nothing to do with Africa directly, they are in the minority and the journals incontestably are orientated towards Africa.

The frequency with which articles refer to documents of Vatican II or to papal pronouncements give the journal (and especially the *RAT*) an unmistakably Catholic stance, though occasional Protestant contributions are made too.

The frequent chronicling of international events and conferences is designed to broaden the horizons of the readers to encompass trends beyond the boundaries of Africa and the book reviews (four or five per *CRA* issue, twice that number in *RAT*) inform readers of what others, elsewhere, are thinking. The *RAT* has for many years published a classified 'bibliographie sélective' of African Theology, which now comprises well over 6,000 items.[103]

Theses

As with all higher-level institutions of learning, the FTCK stipulates that students submit a thesis as part of their graduation requirement. The theses initiate the students not only into personal research but also into expressing that research by writing.

Since the beginning of its history, there have been well over one thousand theses presented at the Faculty.[104] The largest number of theses (about 58%) is accounted for at Graduat level, where the dissertation is usually of about 50 pp. long. First degree level (Licence) accounts for another 38%; theses in this category are anything from 60 pp. to 180 pp. long. The remainder of the theses have been done either at doctorate level (200 pp. to 400 pp.) or at the pre-doctorate 'Diplôme d'Etudes Spéciales' (D.E.S.) level[105] (30 pp. to 40 pp.)

An analysis of the theses (see 'Table 3' below) reveals that by far the majority of the theses are in the field of non-African philosophy.[106] The student choices are influenced both by the *recognized universal influence* of the philosophers in question or by the preference and competence of the thesis supervisor.[107] Most of the theses related to African philosophy explore the writings of Placide Tempels or of the Zaïrian theologian/philosopher Bimwenyi Kweshi.[108] Several attempt to develop philosophical terminology in African languages.[109] The high number of theses in the category 'African Traditional Religion' are, with only three exceptions, specific tribal studies rather than general and theoretical works. Church History, either Western or African, is notable for its absence, although there are several theses (including four doctorates) which research historical theology.[110] The highest number of doctoral theses relate to Biblical studies, although it must be said that they and indeed the large majority of all doctoral theses were written early on in the history of the faculty, perhaps indicating that despite the enviable academic level of the FTCK, the preference is still to do research degrees in the West.[111]

Table 3
FTCK Student theses 1961-1985

Subject	Academic Level				
	Doc	D.E.S.	Lic	Grad	Tot
Philosophy	2	5	136	300	443
Afr. Trad. Relig.	0	2	50	129	181
Bible	9	0	23	27	59
(OT : NT)	(3:6)		(8:15)	(11:16)	
Theology	1	1	14	39	55
Development	0	3	19	25	47
Ethics	0	2	23	20	45
Afr.Phil.	2	2	20	18	42
Vatican	2	0	12	21	35
Church	0	1	13	19	33
Afr.Theol.	0	0	16	13	29
Politics	0	1	13	10	24
Patristics	4	0	13	0	17
R. C. Doctrine	0	0	2	8	10
Education	0	0	9	0	9
Afr. Indep. Ches	0	0	3	1	4
Other	0	0	0	6	6
	20	17	363	636	1,039
	(20)	(17)	(344)	(634)	(1,015)

The totals in brackets represent the actual number of theses to date per academic level; the larger totals above these reflect the fact that certain theses can have more than one valid category.

Conferences

The influence of the Faculty is further extended by conferences organized by its different Departments. They permit the visit to Kinshasa and to the Faculty of internationally known participants and allow the cross-fertilization of ideas. The conference lectures and debates are attended by a public of several hundred and the proceedings, since they are reported in detail in the Faculty's periodicals or in other Kinshasa-based reviews, enjoy a wide readership both within the country and internationally.

The 'Semaines Théologiques de Kinshasa' were started in 1964 and have taken place almost every year since then.[112] The full reports were originally published by the Jesuit 'Revue du Clergé Africain' until it was suppressed in 1972, since when the Faculty itself has continued with the series. Formerly, each diocese in Zaïre used to be encouraged to send one or two delegates, but financial and transport difficulties within the country have made this increasingly impractical. Between 200 and 300 attend the 'Semaines', which are usually held in the big Catholic conference and retreat centre at Nganda in Kinshasa, although one year it was held at the Faculty itself.

The 'Centre d'Etudes des Religions Africaines' organized its first 'Colloque International' to mark the tenth anniversary of its existence, in 1978. Its themes have sought to move from the general to the increasingly specific[113] and its 'Actes' (proceedings) are fully reported in CERA's own 'Cahier des Religions Africaines'.[114] The large cost of organizing such a 'Colloque' (approximately $40,000 each) is met in large part by interested donors (individuals and groups).

Since 1976 the 'Départment de Philosophie et des Religions Africaines' have similarly organized their 'Semaines Philosophiques'. The 'Semaines' have taken place almost yearly and the proceedings have been published by the Faculty as a series entitled 'Recherches Philosophiques Africaines'.[115]

Conclusion

Exactly how influential the Faculty is in helping to bring about an African theology is probably impossible to determine. While the periodicals with their nation-wide and international readership have done much to establish Kinshasa in the very forefront of theological debate and research in Africa, it is more difficult to ascertain to what extent the views expressed therein have practical repercussion at the various levels of church life. Even amongst the Faculty members and editorial staff themselves there is disagreement as to the influence or otherwise of the published material. The compiler of the 'Bibliographie Sélective de Théologie Africaine' expressed doubt as to whether the academic discussions of the periodicals had much importance for people at grass-roots level and felt that the theologians task was merely in the scholarly domain.[116]

In contrast, the 'CERA' Director, Mulago, is of the opinion that the impact of thinking at the Faculty is, indeed, felt at other, non-academic levels. He cited the example of the 'Huitième Semaine Théologique de Kinshasa'[117] (1973) as having had a profound influence upon Cardinal Malula, who was compelled to rethink the role of the local church and its leaders (Lingala: 'bakambi') and has sought, consequently, to increase the responsibility of the 'communautés de base' within the traditionally strongly hierarchical Catholic Church in Zaïre.[118] He also explained that in an effort to avoid theological elitism, the 'Colloques Internationaux' have sought to include in their programme an evening assembly of a less specialised nature, open to the public and held in a church building in the city, thereby encouraging public participation.[119] As yet another example of the 'filter-down' effect of academic thinking, Mulago cited the 15th Semaine Théologique de Kinshasa (1985), entitled 'Charisme de la vie consacrée', the subject of which was taken up by the episcopal conference (whose concern is pastoral rather than academic) the following year.

Bishop Tshibangu who, from the beginning of the Faculty's history, has been a key figure in the on-going debate on African theology, is also insistent that there is and must be a close relationship between the academic and the practical. He explained this conviction as a 'personal intuition', that African theology cannot be truly scientific unless it reflects upon the *'réalités de base'*. When he was a teacher at the Faculty he used to send his students out into the streets of Kinshasa to seek by means of questionnaires to understand the different concepts of divination and death and the here-after held by ordinary non-academic people; then his students would come back to the classroom to report. The creation of 'CERA' was partly a result of this concern and methodology. However, Tshibangu admitted that often a great distance separates much of academia from everyday life; when he sought in his preaching in local churches to 'translate' into simpler form the learned homilies that he had had to prepare for academic circles, he found that he simply was not communicating. While the academic debates have their place, Tshibangu observes that it is spiritual renewal which does most to purify and enrich Christian living. Through the working of the Holy Spirit

> the simple come to an understanding which is more pro-
> found than that of the learned; a discernment come from the
> Holy Spirit.

For Tshibangu, therefore, the local church is a most important 'lieu théologique' and spiritual (charismatic) renewal succeeds in exposing the whole of life to the Gospel.[120]

The view is also expressed by yet other that the influence is not only (or even primarily) downward from the Faculty to the Church grass-roots, but rather the reverse:

> things are happening at the grassroots level, people are
> thinking in certain ways, seeing things differently. The
> theologians in turn are seeking to conceptualize these
> behavioural trends and tendencies[121].

If it is true, as M. E. Andrews claims, that no people can ever produce a theology who are not first

> prepared to take themselves seriously and this means in
> part seeing the importance of the details that are near and
> not far,[122]

then the Faculty is helping to provide the essential infrastructure of an African theology. The colonial years, by and large, caused Africans to lose pride in their world and in their past and present values. The last thirty or forty years have seen a gradual and multidimensional recovery of that lost pride. The FTCK has sought to contribute to that recovery in a theological dimension. The emphasis upon publishing that has characterized the Faculty from the outset, is one clear indication of Africa taking itself seriously.

References

Note: CRA = **Cahiers des Religions Africaines**
RAT = **Revue Africaine de Théologie**

1. Ntedika Konde, 'Adresse d'ouverture', *CRA* Vol. XI, No. 21, 1977, p. 10.

2. Hastings A. *A History of African Christianity 1950-1975*, Cambridge, 1979, p. 62.

3. Yakemtchouk R. *L'Université Lovanium et sa Faculté de Théologie* Chastre, 1983, p. 7.

4. The medical institution was known as 'Fomulac' ('Fondation Médical de l'Université de Louvain au Congo'), dating from 1925; the agricultural initiative was called 'Cadulac' (Centre Agronomique de l'Université de Louvain au Congo'), founded in 1932. Yakemtchouk, op. cit. pp. 12-13.

5. ibid, pp.18-37.

6. Vanneste A. 'La Faculté de Théologie Catholique de Kinshasa. Vingt-cing ans d'existence', *RAT*, Vol. 6, No. 12, 1982, p. 219.
7. Yakemtchouk, op. cit. p. 67.

8. The seven teachers were: A. Vanneste, professor of theology at Brugges, (Belgium) - Dean; P. de Locht, Louvain; F. Bontinck, Lisala (Zaïre); J. Seynaeve, Nyakibanda (Zaïre); Vander Perre, Malines (Belgium); J. van Torre, Louvain; A. Crève, Niangara (Zaïre). Yakemtchouk, op. cit. pp. 59-60.

9. ibid, p. 83.

10. P. Tempels, 'La philosophie bantoue' *Présence Africaine*, Paris, 1949. For discussion on Tempels and his writings, see ch. 1.

11. The repercussions of Tempels writings (favorable and hostile) both within Congo and in Europe are indicated in the fascinating exchange of letters between Tempels and Hulstaert in F. Bontinck, 'Aux origines de la Philosophie Bantoue; la correspondence Tempels-Hulstaert' FTCK (Kinshasa, 1985).

12. The book is discussed more fully in ch. 1.

13. ' Des prêtres noirs s'interrogent' *Rencontres 47*, (Paris, 1956).

14. Although the book caused a stir in some circles immediately, it was only later that the full importance of the book was realized. 1956 is often spoken of in the francophone world as something of a watershed date on account of the book.

15. In conversation (Kinshasa, 1st Feb, 1987), Mulago explained that at the time, African Catholic students in Rome had formed an 'Association' with its own stencilled review of theological reflection. Alioune Diop, the General Secretary of 'Présence Africaine' (an African cultural and publishing society in Paris) took the initiative to publish certain of the review's articles (among which were Mulago's outlines of his doctoral thesis which was eventually published with the title *Un visage africain du christianisme*). Mulago was at pains to insist that it was not they (the students) who pushed to publish their articles, and it was Alioune Diop who chose the title 'Des prétres noirs s'interrogent'.

16. Malula J. 'L'âme bantoue face à l'Evangile', in *Vivante Afrique*. 1958, p. 13.

17. The new Administrative Council included six bishops (some of them national) of different regions of Congo and several lay figures of national repute, such as the Congolese Governor of the 'Banque Nationale'. Yakemtchouk, op. cit. p. 99.

18. Tshibangu, T. *Présence Universitaire*, (Kinshasa, 1959), p. 16.

19. Vanneste, A. *Revue du Clerge Africain*, May, 1958, pp. 225-236.

20. ibid.

21. The Jesuit *Revue du Clergé Africain* produced at Mayidi, Congo, continued publication until it was suppressed in 1972. Especially in its earlier years it bore the mark of the magisterial character of Father Denis (SJ). *Telema* started publication in 1975 under its Zairian editor Boka di Mpasi (SJ) and represents the continuation of the previous *Revue,* although its first editorial avoids any reference to it.

22. Tshibangu T., 'Débat sur la théologie africaine' in *Revue du Clergé Africain* Vol. 11: No. 4, July 1960, p. 346.

23. Vanneste, ibid, p. 351.

24. On the 'Semaines', see also below, p. 143.

25. Vanneste, A., quoted by Ngindu, 'La Quatrième Semaine Théologique de Kinshasa et la problématique d'une théologie africaine', in *CRA*, Vol. 2, No. 4, 1968, p. 359.

26. Ngindu M., ibid, p. 359.

27. The Faculty makes it a practice to invite prominent theologians to heighten the value and influence of the 'Semaines'. Other well-known participants have included: Prof Von Allmen (Neuchatel), Rector Garofano (Universite Urbanium de la Propagande, Rome), Mgr Delhaye, General Secretary of the International Theological Commission. (conversation with Mulago, Kinshasa, 1st Feb, 1987).

28. Reported by Ngindu, op. cit. (note 25), p. 361.

29. Tshibangu, T., ibid, pp. 363-372.

30. Discussed more fully in ch. 1.

31. Quoted by Yakemtchouk, op. cit. pp. 178-179.

32. The notion of 'implantation' seemed, at least to many Africans, to represent the mere transplantation of European ecclesiastical

teaching and institutions into Africa and was roundly rejected by the Declaration of Bishops of Africa and Madagascar (1974) who favoured rather the expression 'incarnation' of the Christian message in Africa.

33. Quoted by Vanneste, 'Bilan théologique d'un voyage apostolique' in *RAT*, Vol. 4, No. 8, 1980, p. 228.

34. ibid, p. 229.

35. eg. Mulago V. 'Le problème de la théologie africaine à la lumière de Vatican II', in *Renouveau de l'Eglise et Nouvelles Eglises*, Colloque sur la théologie africaine, Kinshasa, 1967, p. 115-152.

36. Tshibangu T., quoted by Vanneste, 'La théologie africaine... Note historique', in *RAT*, Vol. 7, No. 14, 1983, p. 273.

37. ibid, p. 274.

38. The debate on 'African Theology' continued at the 7th International African Seminar, held at the University of Ghana, April, 1965, the report of which was published for the International Africa Institute, C. G. Baëta (ed.) *Christianity in Tropical Africa*, O.U.P., 1968. The discussion reported on p.148 of that document, concerning Mbiti's paper and involving R. Bureau and V. Mulago, was, according to Prof Richard Gray (one of the participants) very serious and even heated, reflecting that the debate was much more than academic. (Conversation with R. Gray, July, 1987).

39. Conversation with A. Vanneste, 28th Jan,1987, Kinshasa.

40. A. Vanneste, 'Où en est le problème de la théologie africaine?', in *Cultures et Développement*, Vol. 6, 1974, pp. 149-167:
    Personne ne prône le culte de particularité pour elle-même; la particularité ne se justifie que dans la mesure où elle renvoie à des valeurs universelles... La théologie africaine n'echappera guère à cette loi: elle sera riche de sa propre spécificité et de son originalité dans la mesure où elle s'efforcera sans cesse de les dépasser et de les supprimer. (pp. 164-165.)

41. A. Vanneste, 'L'actualité théologique en Afrique', in *Cultures et Développement*, Vol. 9, 1977, pp. 631-650. On the differences between Western and African theologies: the former

    doit son origine avant tout au désir de connaître, elle est
    de par sa nature une interrogation spéculative,

while African theologians

    se veulent plus directement 'au service de leurs églises'...
    ils s'efforcent de contribuer à l'incarnation toujours plus
    profonde de l'Eglise dans le milieu africain. (pp. 649-650).

42. A. Vanneste, 'La théologie africaine en route', in *Cultures et Développement*, Vol. 12, 1980, pp. 325-346. On Bimwenyi Kweshi's thesis: *Discours théologique négro-africain. Problème des fondements* (Louvain, 1977): a work which

    dépasse de loin tout ce qui a été écrit jusqu'à présent, sur
    le sens, la possibilité et la nécessité d'une théologie
    vraiment africaine (p. 337).

43. The fact that all three expressly wished to remain anonymous on the point indicated that the issue still remains a sensitive one within the Faculty.

44. It has been difficult to ascertain how the decision in 1977 was made, but it may be supposed that Vanneste as Dean at the time had a prominent part in it.

45. E. Mveng, 'Editorial', *Bulletin de Théologie Africaine*, Vol. 1, No. 1, p. 6.

46. For instance, Mulago stated: 'Les abonnés cherchent de nous quelque chose de spécifique. La *Revue Africaine de Théologie* est édifiante, mais l'on peut lire de tels articles ailleurs. Les numéros du *Bulletin de Théologie Africaine* sont vite vendus, tandis que les numéros de la *Revue* traînent.' (Conversation with Mulago, Kinshasa, 1st Feb, 1987).

47. See ch. 1.

48. Ngindu M., 'Le propos du recours à l'authenticité et le christianisme au Zaire', *CRA* Vol. 8, No. 16, 1974, pp. 209-230. The same article, a slightly abridged translation of the French, appears as 'Authenticity and Christianity in Zaïre', in Fashole-Luke, J. R.

Gray, A. Hastings, G. Tasie (eds), *Christianity in Independent Africa*, Rex Collings, London, 1978, pp. 228-241.

49. Ngindu M., 'Le propos du recours...' op. cit. p. 210.

50. Quoted by Ngindu M., ibid, p. 217.

51. ibid, p. 221.

52. Vanneste commented in conversation:
    Il est vrai qu'à première vue les soucis d'authenticité et ceux de la 'théologie africaine' se ressemblent. Mais la première manque la dimension chrétienne que la deuxième affirme. Si la Faculté avait pleinement appuyé la doctrine de l'"authenticité', les gens auraient compris cela à travers. (Kinshasa, 28th Feb, 1987).

53. 'Le Pape chez nous, Discours de S.S. le Pape Jean-Paul II, prononcé à loccasion de son voyage au Zaïre, 2-6 mai, 1980', in *RAT*, Vol. 4, No. 4, 1980, p. 232.

54. Pope John-Paul II:
    Il n'est pas question de falsifier la parole de Dieu ou de vider la croix de sa puissance (cf. 1 Cor.1,17), mais plutôt de porter le Christ au coeur même de la vie africaine et d'élever la vie africaine toute entière jusqu'au Christ. Ainsi, non seulement le christianisme est important pour l'Afrique, mais le Christ lui-même, dans les membres de son corps, est africain.'
    Quoted by Vanneste, 'Bilan théologique... in *RAT*, Vol. 4, No. 8, 1980, p. 233.

55. 'Discours du Pape aux Evêques du Zaïre', Kinshasa, May 3, 1980, in *RAT*, Vol. 4, No. 8, 1980.

56. *Faculty statistics for 1986-87*, compiled and supplied by Léon de Saint-Moulin (Academic Secretary):

Department	G1	G2	G3	L1	L2	tot.
Theology	35	33	27	11	30	136
Theology & Human Sciences	12	6	13	4	13	48
Philosophy & Afr. Religs.	31	28	30	42	29	160
others, (eg. doctoral and pre-doctoral students):						26
Total:						370

For the year in question, the places of origin of the students were: Zaïre - 296 (51 from Kinshasa); Brazzaville - 9; Nigeria - 3; Rwanda - 2; Angola - 2; Ghana - 2; Cameroon, Colombia, Burundi, Germany, Central African Republic - 1 each.

Since 1957, graduates total:	Zaïrians	3,428
	other Africans	189
	non-Africans	66
	Total:	3,683

57. Figures are from the FTCK *Programme des Cours*, 1986-87.

58. The Louvain 'saying' was quoted to me by F. Bontinck to explain the prominence given to publishing by the Faculty in Kinshasa. (Kinshasa, 1st Feb,1987).

59. The third Faculty periodical *Revue Philosophique de Kinshasa*, has not been included for consideration in this thesis. While it is true that theology and philosophy share certain common concerns and while several articles in *CRA* and *RAT* explore the contribution of the one to the other (see pp.), the *RPK* sees itself as a 'specialist organ of current research for Zaïrian and non-Zaïrian philosophers' (editorial Vol. 1, No. 1, 1983). Many of its articles relate to specialist and technical aspects of philosophy in Europe and Africa; eg., 'Pensée-langage: le problème de la "rélativité linguistique", and: 'La forme et la trans-forme du masque traditionnel africain', both in Vol.1, No.1. Its thrust is thus tangential to that of the thesis.

60. Discussion at the fourth 'Semaine Théologique', Kinshasa, 1968, in *CRA*. Vol. 2, No. 4, 1968, p. 367.

138

61. *CRA*, Vol. 9, No. 17, 1975, p. 9.

62. ibid, p. 10.

63. Conversation with Mulago, Kinshasa, 1st Feb, 1987.

64. The list of these editorial members and also that of 'associated researchers' are given in *CRA*, Vol. 12, Nos. 23-24, pp. 270-271.

65. This figure does not compare exactly with the '140' exchange subscriptions referred to in *CRA*, Vol. 9, Nos. 17-18, 1975, p. 11, although perhaps the expression
    140 périodiques avec lesquels nous entretenons des
    rapports des échanges
indicates enquiries rather than firm subscriptions.

66. The series 'Bibliothèque du CERA' includes: Mulago g.C., *La religion traditionnelle des Bantu et leur vision du monde*, P.U.Z., (Kinshasa, 1980); A. J. Smet, *Philosophie Africaine* — textes choisis I & II P.U.Z., (Kinshasa, 1975); Buakasa T., *L'impensé du discours. 'Kindoki' et 'Nkisi' en pays Kongo du Zaïre*, Kinshasa, ?); Ngindu M. et al, *Combats pour un christianisme africain. Mélanges en l'honneur du Prof V. Mulago*, (Kinshasa, 1981); J. Jomier, *L'Islam. aux multiples aspects*, (Kinshasa, 1982); Mwene-Batende, *Mouvements messianiques et protestation social. Le cas du Kitawala chez les Kumu du Zaïre.* (Kinshasa, 1982); Nkiere B., *La parenté comme système idéologique. Essai d'interprétation de l'ordre lignagère chez les Basakata*, (Kinshasa, 1984); F Bontinck, *Aux origines de la 'philosophie bantoue'. La correspondence Tempels-Hulstaert*, (Kinshasa, 1985). Two other books in the series are out of print.

67. Included in these *CRA* articles on sin and forgiveness are: Mbonyikebe S., 'Brèves réflexions sur la conception traditionnelle du péché en Afrique Centrale', Vol. 8, No. 16, pp. 155-166; Tshiamalenga T., 'La philosophie de la faute dans la tradition luba', Vol. 8, No. 16, pp. 167-186; Buakasa T., 'Le projet des rites de réconcilliation', Vol 8, No.16, pp. 187-208; Mbonyikebe S., 'Faute, péché, pénitence, et réconciliation dans les traditions de quelques sociétés en Afrique Centrale', Vol. 14, Nos. 27-28, 1980, pp. 265-282.

68. Mbonyikebe S., 'Brèves réflexions' op. cit.

69. ibid, p. 159.

70. The conclusion of Mbonyikebe's article reads in French:
En conclusion, notre réserve terminologique peut faire place, pensons-nous à l'affirmation d'une conception authentiquement africaine du péché. Nous reconnaîtrons toutefois que les motivations morales propres à nos cultures relèvent plus d'une Ethique de l'Homme communautaire que de la religion proprement dite et que par là elles ont, non pas tant au niveau de la logique du système que du vécu des personnes, une résonnance laïque.' (p. 165).

71. Mulago gwa C. 'Discours de clôture', in CRA, Vol. II, No. 21-22, p. 284.

72. Vanneste, 'La Faculté... Vingt-cinq ans' RAT, Vol. 6, No. 12, p. 223.

73. Conversation with Atal sa Angang, FTCK, 4th Feb, 1987.

74. The purpose of exegesis, according to Atal, is first to understand the biblical text. The message was expressed in human language, to real men and women at a specific time and place. This means that there has to be due consideration to the historical background and to the grammatical and linguistic expression of the text. Having done everything possible to understand the author's intention, the exegete's task is then to convey faithfully the same message to people of a different time and place. There is danger in seeking a 'pre-existent Christianity' (in African traditional religion) and 'concordisme' must be avoided. For Christianity is new ('un nouveauté'). Some Africans, in their antipathy to colonialism, have ended up reacting against Christianity. (Conversation with Atal sa Angang, FTCK, 4th Feb, 1987).

75. Buetubela B., 'Le produit de la vigne et le vin nouveau', in RAT, Vol. 8, No. 15, 1984, p. 5-16.

76. Ukachukwu M., 'The subordination of women in the Church', in RAT, Vol. 8, No. 16, 1984, pp. 183-196.

77. Mukeng'a Kalond, quoted in 'Le premier congrès des biblistes africains', in *RAT* , Vol. 3, No. 6, 1979, p. 84.

78. Monsengwo P., 'Exégèse biblique et questions africaines', in *RAT*, Vol. 6, No.12, 1982, p. 165.

79. Ngimbi-Nseka, 'Théologie et anthropologie transcendentale', *RAT*, Vol. 3, No. 5, 1979, pp. 5-29.

80. Ngimbi-Nseka, 'Esquisse d'une éthique d'intersubjectivité', *RAT*, Vol. 3, No. 6, 1979, pp. 185-203.

81. Nkeramihigo T., 'La problématique de la transcendance chez Ricoeur', *RAT*, Vol. 5, No. 9, 1981, pp. 7-18.

82. Tshibangu T. in 'Intelligence de la foi et voies non-occidentales de la théologie'; lecture given at the 'Quatrième Semaine Théologique de Kinshasa, July, 1968, and discussed by Ngindu Mushete in *CRA*, Vol. 2, No. 2, 1968, pp. 353-372. cf. also Tshibangu's doctoral thesis: 'Théologie positive et théologie spéculative. Position traditionnelle et nouvelle problématique' Louvain, 1965, pp. 384-385. According to Mudiji (Head of Philosophy Department), Bergson argues that conceptual analysis is not the totality of philosophical thought; intuition has a role alongside rationality. (Conversation with Mudiji, FTCK, 4th Feb, 1987).

83. cf. Article by H. Lodewyckx, 'Philosophie Africaine, Origines et Perspectives' in *Bijdragen, tijschrift voor filosofie en theologie* 47 (1986) 141-169. The article helpfully sets out different stages in the 'evolution' of African Philosophy, and is well regarded by Faculty teachers of philosophy.

84. J. Ladrière, 'Perspectives sur la philosophie africaine', in *RAT*, Vol. 5, No. 9, 1981, p. 57.

85. Basinsa, *RAT*, Vol. 3, No. 5, 1979, pp. 133-138.

86. Hountondji states clearly in his book what he understands to constitute 'African Philosophy':
J'appelle 'philosophie africaine' un ensemble de textes; l'ensemble, précisément, des textes écrits par des Africains et qualifiés par leurs auteurs eux-mêmes de

'philosophiques',
P. J. Hountondji, *Sur la 'philosophie africaine'. Critique de l'éthnophilosophie*, Maspéro, (Paris, 1977), p. 11.

87. Basinsa, op. cit, p. 137.

88. Tshiamalenga N., 'La vision Ntu de l'homme', in *CRA*, Vol. 7, No. 14, 1973, pp. 175-198.

89. ibid, p. 176.

90. ibid, p. 179.

91. Laleye I-P., in *RAT*, Vol. 6, No. 12, 1982, p. 266.

92. Mudiji M., *'Formes et fonctions symboliques des masques "mbuya" des Phende. Essai d'iconologie et d'herméneutique'*, Louvain, 1981. Mudiji stated that he did his 'Licence' thesis on the philosopher Blondel, but that he derived little benefit from it. For his doctoral thesis he *'preferred to be open towards the African milieu'*. (Conversation with Mudiji, FTCK, 4th Feb, 1987) .

93. Ngimbi-Nseka, 'Esquisse d'une éthique d'intersubjectivité', in *RAT*, Vol. 3, No. 5, 1979, p. 185-202.

94. Faith and Constitution Congress, Lima, 1982. 'Baptême, Eucharistie, Ministère', discussed by Mampila, 'Une eucharistie sans pain ni vin?' in *RAT*, Vol. 8, No.16, p. 19.

95. Vanneste A,, 'Une eucharistie sans pain ni vin?', in *RAT*, Vol. 6, No. 12, 1982, pp. 205-218.

96. Mampila A. *RAT*, Vol. 8, No. 16, 1984, p. 17-32.

97. ibid, p. 32.

98. Buetubela B., 'Le produit de la vigne et le vin nouveau', *RAT*, Vol. 8, No. 15, 1984, pp. 5-16. Buetubela concludes his article:
Il n'est nullement dit que le pain *de froment* et le vin *de raisin* soient la seule manière de signifier le rapport nouveau qui unit l'homme à Dieu. La fidélité à la réalité de l'Incarnation du Christ n'est pas l'absolutisation de la

matérialité des éléments culturels utilisés par Jésus.' (p. 16) (italics his).

99. R. Luneau: *'Maintenir (la loi qui lie sacerdoce ministériel et célibat) dans sa rigueur et sa lettre, alors que le temps a changé, c'est pécher contre l'Esprit'*, quoted by Nothomb, *RAT*, Vol. 7, No. 14, 1983, p. 184.

100. Nothomb, op. cit. (note 99), p. 184.

101. ibid, p. 202.

102. A. Vanneste, 'Le contexte théologique et pastoral de la Lettre', in *RAT*, Vol. 8, No.16, 1984, pp. 87-99.

103. The 'bibliographies sélectives' were started by Prof. Ntedika Konde, *RAT*, Vol. 1, No. 2 and have continued ever since, with Mbiye Lumbala taking over from Ntedika. To date the bibliographies list publications up until 1980, but the series is to continue in future issues.

104. Each year's theses are listed in *RAT* the following year. The last records (1984-85) appear in *RAT*, Vol. 9, No.18 and the total to that date was 1,015 theses. The two most recent years' thesis lists have not yet been published.

105. The 'Diplôme des Etudes Spéciales' is a pre-doctoral programme open to those who have gained a distinction in their first degree results. It lasts one year.

106. In order of preference, the 10 most popular philosophers represented by the theses are: J-P. Sartre (30 theses); Karl Marx (23); G. Marcel (20); H. Bergson (17); M. Heidegger (15); E. Mounier (15); E. Kant (15); M. Merleau-Ponty (13); F. Nietzsche (11) and S. Kierkegaard (10).

107. Conversation with Mudiji M., director of the 'Département de Philosophie et des Religions Africaines', FTCK, 4th Feb, 1987).

108. Bimwenyi Kweshi's most important work is his doctoral thesis: *Discours théologique négro-africain. Problème des fondements*, Louvain, 1977 (796 pp.) (Published by Présence Africaine, Paris,

1981.) It received Louvain's 'la plus grande distinction'. Ngindu Mushete, reviewing the thesis, concludes:

(Bimwenyi) vise à faire une théologie africaine compréhensive et explicative, une théologie où la culture africaine n'est pas seulement décrite, mais intégrée à un ensemble conceptuel plus vaste, permettant une reprise critique des données fondamentales de la révélation chrétienne.

in *Bulletin de Théologie Africaine,* Vol. 1, No. 1, (Kinshasa, 1979) p.135.

109. e.g. Monzelo L., 'Vers une terminologie philosophique en langues bantu. Essai de traduction en lingala d'*Amour et responsabilité* de Karol Wojtyla', Mémoire de Licence en Philosophie et Religions Africaines, 1980.

110. e.g. patristic, medieval, or reformation studies.

111. However, a recent FTCK 'Bulletin d'information' (No. 23, December 1986) says:

Dans le but de promouvoir des recherches approfondies, en théologie, en philosophie, dans les religions africaines et les sciences humaines, la Faculté a enrégistré toute une série d'inscriptions au D.E.S. et au Doctorat, p. 92.

112. *Semaines Théologiques de Kinshasa:*

1.	1964	La théologie à l'heure du Concile
2.	1965	L'Eglise et le monde
3.	1966	Le Dieu de nos pères
4.	1968	Renouveau de l'Eglise et nouvelles églises (Colloque sur la théologie africaine)
5.	1970	Le mariage chrétien en Afrique
6.	1971	La pertinence du christianisme en Afrique
7.	1972	Foi chrétienne et langage humain
8.	1973	Ministères et services dans l'Eglise
9.	1974	Péché, pénitence, et réconciliation. Tradition chrétienne et culture africaine
10.	1975	L'évangélisation dans l'Afrique d'aujourd'hui
11.	1976	Pastorale et épanouissement des vocations dans l'Afrique d'aujourd'hui
12.	1977	Libération en Jésus-Christ
13.	1979	Justice chrétienne et promotion humaine

144

      14. 1981   Les intellectuels africains et l'Eglise
      15. 1985   Charisme et la vie consacrée

113. According to Mulago g. C, in conversation, Kinshasa, 4th Feb, 1987.

114. The three 'Colloques Internationaux' to date are:
      1. 1978   Religions africaines et christianisme
      2. 1983   Afrique et ses formes de vie spirituelles
      3. 1986   Médiations du sacré, célébrations créatrices.

115. The nine 'Actes des Semaines Philosophiques de Kinshasa' (and two other works) are listed in the duplicated document of the Faculty's theological and philosophical publications.

116. Conversation with Mbiye L., FTCK, 30th Jan, 1987.

117. see note 112 (8), above.

118. Conversation with Mulago g. C, Kinshasa, 1st Feb, 1987.

119. Thus, for example, while all the more technical meetings of the most recent 'Colloque' (February, 1986) were held at the Conference Centre at Nganda, evening meetings were open to the public and were held at the Salle Paroissiale de Matonge, St. Joseph. The evening lectures included a talk on African liturgy and religious architecture and another on 'la drummologie africaine'.

120. Conversation with Tshibangu, 2nd Feb, 1987. Tshibangu was anxious to insist that lest it should become nothing more than individualistic piety, charismatic renewal should express itself within a local church where it can be guided aright.

121. In a conversation with two Bishops and three priests, at the Scheutist 'Centre d'Accueil', on 31st Jan, 1987.

122. Andrews M. E., The O.T. as Israelite Theology and its implications for a New Zealand Theology', *South East Asia Journal of Theology*, 17 (Issue 2), 1976, pp. 32-40. I am grateful to Dr. H. W. Turner for drawing my attention to this article.

Appendix I

Publications of the
'Faculté de Théologie Catholique de Kinshasa' (FTCK)

1. Theological
Revue Africaine de Théologie (1977-) twice yearly. Journal devoted to scientific study of Christian sources and the confrontation between Christian religious heritage on the one hand and African realities on the other. Seeks to contribute to the elaboration of a new synthesis of Christian life and thought which will be in conformity with the genius and aspirations of African peoples.

Series: *Recherches Africaines de Théologie* (1971-) 8 works. Devoted to scientific work in biblical, historical and systematic theology.

Series: *Eglise Africaine en dialogue* (1975-) 5 works. To promote dialogue between theological and religious science specialists on the one hand and the non-specialist Christian and non-Christian public on the other.

Series: *Semaines Théologiques de Kinshasa* (1964-) almost yearly. Full report of lectures and discussion of the nearly-annual public conferences organised by the FTCK on matters of theological importance.

2. Philosophical
Series: *Recherches Philosophiques Africaines* (1977-) 11 works. Concerned to organise Africa's thinking of yesterday and today, in response to its historic existence, liberation and integrated development.

Series: *Cours et Documents* (1979-) 6 works by Faculty professors, designed for use as teaching and research texts.

Series: *FILOZOFI* (1979-) 4 works. Philosophical reflection in African languages in order to promote the scientific use of African languages, translate important Western texts and encourage the formation of a philosophy in African languages, so as to revitalize the African genius and its creative capacity.

Revue Philosophique de Kinshasa (1983-) twice yearly. Will publish any research likely to promote philosophical reflection in Africa.

Afrique et Philosophie (1977-) Student journal, designed for student philosophical 'target practice'.

3. Centre d'Etudes des Religions Africaines
Cahiers des Religions Africaines (1967-) Twice yearly.

Series: *Bibliothèque de CERA* (1973-). Designed to permit a systematic and scientific study of African traditional and modern religions and customs. 8 works.

Appendix II
Revue Africaine de Théologie
Subscriptions analysis, as of January 1987
(Source: FTCK files)

Continent	Country	Type of subscription			Tot.
		University	Individual	Exchange	
Africa	Zaïre	42	122	5	169
	Rwanda	1	7	1	9
	Angola	2	1	1	4
	Congo	1	3		4
	Gambia	4			4
	Mozambique	1	2	1	4
	Togo		3		3
	Burundi	1	1		2
	Cameroon	2			2
	Egypt	1		1	2
	Ghana		2		2
	Benin	1			1
	Burkina Faso			1	1
	Chad	1			1
	Ivory Coast			1	1
	Liberia		1		1
	Mauritius	1			1
	Nigeria			1	1
	Tanzania	1			1
		59	142	12	213

Europe	Italy	11	9	31	51
	Belgium	5	19	15	39
	France	3	4	19	26
	Spain	3		11	14
	F.G.R.	3		9	12
	U.K.	2	1	5	8
	Switzerland		1	7	8
	Poland	1		6	7
	Portugal	2		3	5
	Holland	4			4
	Austria		1	2	3
	Sweden			1	1
		34	35	109	178
N. America	Canada	3		5	8
	U.S.A.	14		7	21
		17	0	12	29
Other	Brazil	4		2	6
	Colombia			3	3
	Chile			2	2
	Israel			2	2
	Peru			2	2
	Philippines			2	2
	Argentina			1	1
	Equador			1	1
	India			1	1
	Japan			1	1
	Taiwan			1	1
		4	0	18	22
	Totals	114	177	151	442

Appendix III
Cahiers des Religions Africaines Subscriptions analysis, as of January 1987, (Source: FTCK files)

Continent	Country	Type of subscription			
		University	Individual	Exchange	Tot.
Africa	Zaïre	28	55	8	91
	S. Africa	2		2	4
	Algeria			3	3
	Burundi	2		1	3
	Kenya	1	2		3
	Cameroon	1	1		2
	Congo	1	1		2
	Gabon	2			2
	Guinea		2		2
	Ivory Coast			2	2
	Malawi	1	1		2
	Mozambique	1	1		2
	Tunisia			2	2
	Angola		1		1
	Mali		1		1
	Morocco	1			1
	Nigeria			1	1
	Rwanda			1	1
	Senegal			1	1
	U.Volta		1		1
		40	66	21	127

Continent	Country	Type of subscription			
		University	Individual	Exchange	Tot.
Europe	France	11	4	14	29
	Holland	14	4	2	20
	Italy	11	3	4	18
	Belgium	7	1	6	14
	U.K.	5	1	4	10
	Switzerland	3	3	3	9
	F.R.G.	6	1		7
	Spain	3			3
	Sweden	1	1		2
	Austria	1			1
	Greece	1			1
	Portugal	1			1
		64	18	33	115
N. America	Canada	9	1	4	14
	U.S.A.	37	3	2	42
		46	4	6	56
Other	Brazil	3	3		6
	Colombia		1		1
	India			1	1
	Japan			2	2
	Pakistan			2	2
	Saudi Arabia			1	1
		3	4	6	13
Totals		153	92	66	311

Chapter Three
The Oral Dimension of Theological Expression
The place and function of hymns in the EJCSK (Eglise de Jésus-Christ sur terre par le Prophète Simon Kimbangu)

Introduction

The role of written expression in the literate Western academic world is so prominent that it might be assumed to be the only medium of communicated thought worthy of serious attention. W. A. Graham observes:

> We are a typographic culture in which it is unconsciously assumed that the really fundamental form of language is the written or the printed word. We have lost to a large degree the oral-aural dimensions of literate culture that characterized our own civilization well beyond the Gutenberg revolution up to perhaps the Enlightenment and that still characterize most other literate cultures of the world today.[1]

In reality, oral expression and communication are still the major means of sharing and spreading ideas and experiences in the world.[2] This is especially true (even within the 'literate world') in those areas of cognition where purely speculative, cerebral processes are joined by strong volitional and emotive ones. One such cognitive area would be that of religion. And where religion is expressed and communicated within societies where non-literacy represents the familiar, traditional norm, the processes of speak/hear/do will be more significant, more representative of local understanding than those of read/write/speculate.[3] To restrict the theological process to what is written and thereby to exclude from it the oral dimension is arbitrary and incorrect. While it is true that analytical and speculative theology finds its ideal medium in the written word, it is wrong to suppose that that sort of theology is the only one in which faith seeks understanding and expression.

There exist, in fact, several different sorts or levels of theology, as J. Mbiti insists, in discussing the African theological scene. There is, obviously, written theology, the privilege of an educated minority and produced mainly in European languages. But in addition there is oral theology:

> Oral theology is produced in the fields, by the masses,
> through song, sermon teaching, prayer, conversation, etc. It
> is theology in the open air, often unrecorded, often heard
> only by small groups of audience and generally lost as far as
> libraries and seminaries are concerned.

Mbiti goes on to speak of a third theology, the symbolic, expressed through art, sculpture, drama, symbols, rituals, dance, colours, numbers, etc.

It is appropriate, in considering the expression of beliefs of the Kimbanguist Church, to pay attention to the second of Mbiti's categories, that of the oral dimension. The Kimbanguist Church is probably the largest of the so-called Independent African Churches; membership estimates vary widely from a cautious 227,000,[5] to an official Kimbanguist figure of 5 million quoted by His Eminence Diangienda Kuntima, third son of Simon Kimbangu and spiritual head of the Kimbanguist Church.[6] While the Kimbanguist Church might include France and Belgium in its 'champ d'action',[7] its membership and influence is almost entirely within Central Africa and, in particular, Zaïre. Asch's 1976 research of the Kinshasa Kimbanguist churches[8] revealed that 33.6% of the membership were illiterate; another 49.3% were literate, but only with primary school education.[9] These two categories together comprise those whose world is overwhelmingly oral and together they account for 82.9% of the membership. If these proportions are accurate for the capital where presumably exposure to literacy is greater, the orality of the overall Kimbanguist situation is even more marked. This is not to deny that the Kimbanguist Church has its literate theological dimension; indeed, recent years have seen an increasing quantity of documents, articles and books written by Kimbanguist church leaders,[10] not to mention the theses and dissertations produced each year by the students at the Kimbanguist Faculty of Theology in Kinshasa. Nor is it to suggest that the EJCSK is without its intellectual élite.[11] It is rather to suggest that the written theological product is not the only or even the most important expression of belief and practice within the Kimbanguist Church.

The Prophet and his Church

Since Kimbanguism relates importantly to the historical figure of Simon Kimbangu and has been influenced by the course of historical and political events, any discussion of its oral theology must take into account the development of the movement from its beginnings in the early 1920's. Born at Nkamba (south west of Kinshasa in Bas-Zaïre) in the late 1880's,[12] Simon Kimbangu was orphaned at an early age and fostered by his aunt Kinzembo who introduced him as a youth to the Baptist Missionary Society. At the BMS mission school at Ngombi-Lutete Kimbangu learned to read and write and it was there, too, that he became familiar with and versed in the Bible. He and his wife were baptised by immersion in 1915 and were religiously married at Ngombe-Lutete the same year. According to official EJCSK documents, Kimbangu was appointed as catechist for the area of Kamba and its surrounding villages, although some authors would question the place and even the fact of this appointment.[13] Some of his studies at least were with a travelling pastor named Kimbangudi who said of Kimbangu that he did not have the spirit to read but that he had much understanding of religion.[14]

These were the years of the First World War and, in addition to being shaken by the international political turmoil, the lower Belgian Congo was being ravaged by epidemics of sleeping sickness and, immediately after the War, Spanish influenza, typhoid fever, smallpox and drought.[15] Asch considers it to be significant that Kimbangu's vision and call came at this time of apparent powerlessness of European medicine on the one hand and the weakening of the Belgian administration as a result of the War on the other.[16] According to Diangienda, it was Christ Himself who addressed the call to Kimbangu while he was in prayerful meditation:

> Simon Kimbangu, my people are unfaithful. I have chosen
> you to be my witness and to lead them on the path of truth
> and salvation. Your mission will be difficult, but do not fear,
> for I will always be at your side.[17]

Kimbangu, like many prophets before him, shrank from the call and, possibly to escape it, went alone to Kinshasa, where he worked in the 'Huileries du Congo-Belge', a palm-oil factory, though he appears never to have received his pay. Asch conjectures that Kimbangu would have almost certainly have come in contact in Kinshasa with the revolutionary panafrican teachings of Emmanuel John and the American, Wilson,[18] but of this there is no direct evidence. After several months Kimbangu returned to his native Nkamba and it was as he was on his way to market on April 6th, 1921, that he healed the woman Nkiantondo.[19] This is the event and the date quoted in official Kimbanguist literature as signalling the start of what was later to become known as Kimbanguism.[20]

For some two months after that April date, thousands of people from all over the province and even from the capital made their way to Nkamba to see first-hand what was being rumoured. Jobs were abandoned, contracts broken, as workers deserted their posts to make their way to Nkamba (often by night to avoid detection).[21] Many sick and suffering were among the crowds and the convergence of so many ill people to one area aroused fears that an already serious health problem would be made worse.[22]

Inevitably, perhaps, the reaction came. Kimbangu was accused of causing his fellow-BaKongo to desert their work, to be xenophobic, to refuse to pay taxes and he himself of being insane or of provoking unrest. Accusations such as these were advanced by persons in the Belgian administration, the Roman Catholic Church (often expressed by Father Van Wing whom Diangienda calls an 'antikimbanguiste notoire'[23]) and by the majority of the press.[24] Although most sources have less to say about Protestant opposition, Diangienda describes in detail the hostility of certain Baptist missionaries, jealous of Kimbangu's success and popularity.[25] Kimbangu managed to elude the military detachment that was sent to Nkamba to arrest him on June 6th, 1921, but the administration took the situation seriously enough to place the region under semi-military regime. Many were arrested and led in chains to the tribunal at Thysville, later to be deported in internal exile to camps in Haut-Congo beyond Kisangani, which in turn became centres of Kimbanguist influence. On 12th September, however, Kimbangu gave himself up to the authorities, together with certain of his closest co-workers.

The judiciary process of Kimbangu's trial (he and his followers were allowed no defense) is described in detail in Jules Chome's book[26] and in that of Diangienda.[27] He was judged by a military tribunal. On October 3rd, 1921, the court sentenced Kimbangu to death and most of his collaborators to penal servitude for life. The Belgian procurator, Dupuis, together with support from Protestant missionaries, obtained from King Albert the commutation of the death sentence to life imprisonment. Kimbangu was deported up the Congo river by boat and train to a prison in Elizabethville (Lubumbashi) where he remained until his death on October 12th, 1951. Thirty years of imprisonment for six months of prophetic activity.

The years from 1921 to 1959 (when Kimbanguism was at last legalized) were ones of persecution for the Kimbanguists. Loyalty to Kimbangu was sufficient cause for deportation to the 'Colonies Agricoles pour Relégués Dangereux' (detention-labour centres) in the provinces of Coquilhatville (Equateur), Léopoldville (Bandundu), Elisabethville (Shaba) and Stanleyville (Haut-Zaïre). Although

Kimbangu himself was more or less cut off from all contact with the outside world, his wife Marie Mwilu and a group of faithful Kimbanguists maintained a network of contacts, even with those in the detention centres. A secret, coded alphabet permitted messages to pass undetected between members and so liberally were Biblical references used in correspondence that the coded symbols eluded the scrutiny of the uninitiated authorities.[28]

The years of 'clandestinité' not surprisingly saw a diversifying complexity of the scene surrounding the embryonic Kimbanguism. The Salvation Army attracted some Kimbanguists who saw in its khaki uniforms, brass bands and especially its red flag bearing the letter 'S' evidence of a prophesied return of Simon Kimbangu. In 1939 a Salvationist Simon-Pierre Mpadi founded his 'Mission des Noirs', ostensibly of Kimbanguist inspiration, but overtly political and asserting several of the cultural traits or practices that Kimbanguism rejected (polygamy, smoking, etc).[29] The Mpadists, too, suffered deportation to the labour camps where, however, the Kimbanguists would have nothing to do with them. Then there were various prophetic individuals and their followers ('ngounzists' from 'ngunza', prophet), some of whom acknowledged Kimbangu, others not. Any simplistic generalization as to the cause of the emergence of these groups ('political', 'religious', 'oppression', 'healing', etc.) fails to take into account the diversity of the groups concerned.

Shortly before his death, Kimbangu stated that his three sons should continue the work that he had begun.[30] As the 1950s progressed, the third son of Simon Kimbangu, Diangienda Kuntima, was transferred from Kasaï to Kinshasa where he served as clerk in the administration of the Governor General Pétillon. He began working towards the regrouping of Kimbanguist members, urged them to come out of hiding and out from missionary churches, even if it meant incurring the opposition of the authorities. Active too, was the young Lucien Luntadila (later to become the General Secretary of the Kimbanguist Church). He chanced, one day, upon a copy of the Declaration of Human Rights. Belgium was signatory to the Declaration but was openly flouting it by continuing to repress and deport the Kimbanguists. In July 1957, during a period of further recriminations against Kimbanguists, Luntadila and a colleague Albert Yowani decided to force the Government's hand. They handed in to Governor Pétillon a 600-signature petition demanding either that the authorities massacre the crowd of Kimbanguists who, in full knowledge of possible consequences, were at that moment and for the purpose gathered in the Baudouin Stadium,[31] or that they once and for all cease the persecution against the Kimbanguists. Restrictions were eased, but not lifted altogether. In September of the same year the emerging leadership published a *'Mise au point sur le Kimbanguisme'*, affirming the character of Kimbanguism to be 'purely religious' (i.e., non-political). The legal status which the Kimbanguists worked so hard to obtain was eventually granted on December 24th, 1959, just months after the decease of Kimbangu's widow, Marie Mwilu. It is the date quoted by the Kimbanguists themselves as marking the creation of the Kimbanguist Church. After nearly 40 years of persecution, it was a triumphant moment for the Kimbanguists. But, according to Asch, there was a price to pay; the quest for legal recognition cost an important shift in the spirit and direction of Kimbanguism, away from the 'engagement' which historically characterized the 'underground' years:

> From the time when the EJCSK, under Joseph Diangienda's leadership, started negotiations with the colonial admini-stration with a view to obtaining legal recognition that would put an end to persecution 'for the cause of Kimbanguism', the ideological content of official Kimbanguism changed sig-nificantly.[32]

Nor was it the only such shift. Asch argues that with the desire (and eventual success) first, of being accepted by the World Council of Churches (1969) and then, secondly, of gaining the graces of the Mobutu régime as it severely restricted legal recognition of religious groups (1971), the Kimbanguist leadership has had repeatedly to sacrifice something of its essential self; that it has been compelled to embrace internal contradictions, a 'double discourse' in which an unofficial kimbangucentrism is tolerated in the majority of members, while an official christocentric 'front' is projected to the Western, outside world. Asch expresses the three-fold 'adjustment' thus:

> To the colonial administration, the EJCSK declared itself to be apolitical, which enabled it to obtain official recognition. Thereafter, the EJCSK obtained its admission to the WCC at the cost of a 'restatement' acceptable to international Protestantism. Finally, its political conservatism towards Mobutu's State has enabled it to procure the status of third religious power among the official national institutions.[33]

Kimbanguist leaders protest bitterly that Asch has not only erred on many factual, historical details but has also judged events and beliefs with the easy prejudices of an outsider.[34] The complexity of the situation is a further reminder that written theological statements (the catechism, the 'Essence de la théologie Kimbanguiste', the liturgy)[35] are not necessarily the only ones and that oral expressions of belief are also important. As Professor Hollenweger has put it:

> The Kimbanguist Church communicates its witness through African forms of communication: songs, ballads, proverbs. Asked by the WCC to write a confession of faith they produced a document which could classify them amongst evangelical Christians. But this document, copied from Western sources, gives only a very inaccurate insight into the life of the church. More important are their hymns, their prayers, the symbols of their liturgy, their festivals and processions.[36]

André Droogers makes the same point, directing criticism against M-L Martin's book on Kimbanguism which presents essentially the 'official face' of Kimbanguism (indeed, Martin's close involvement, even identification with, the Kimbanguist Church is often claimed to have been instrumental in gaining for the EJCSK membership of the WCC). His article seeks, by participant observation, to look at 'Kimbanguism at the grass roots' and to do so by content analysis of prayers, speeches, sermons and songs as recorded in eight church services.[37]

Hymns in the EJCSK

Hymns are not the only element of oral credal expression, but within the Kimbanguist Church they are of special importance, as many articles point out.[38] Kimbanguists themselves believe that their hymns are not ordinary religious songs composed by those with a musical gift. Rather, they are 'captés', received by revelation and under inspiration. This belief goes back to the very first year of the Kimbanguist 'event', 1921. The story is frequently told[39] how Kimbangu sent some of his helpers to the BMS station at Ngombe-Lutete to purchase hymnbooks. They were rebuffed by the sarcastic reply:

Has your prophet Simon Kimbangu only received the gift of healing the sick and raising the dead? Has he not also received the gift of inspired hymns?

When some time later the missionary Jennings went to Nkamba to get back some books that Kimbangu had in his possession, Kimbangu was told by God that from then on he should never look to the missionaries for anything; he would be granted all he needed for his mission of evangelization. There and then, in the presence of the missionary, a close colleague of Kimbangu, Mukoko Jean, 'received' the first hymn: *'Soldiers of righteousness, put on your armour.'* (see Appendix I)

While the years immediately following Kimbangu's arrest and deportation saw a few inspired hymns, in general the years of 'clandestinité' were relatively barren of hymns, with apparently only one between the years 1926 and 1955.[40]

Nsambu and Fwasi

The current status of inspired hymns in the EJCSK must be linked with two figures. The first is Pastor Nsambu Twasilwa,[41] the Director of the 'Bureau des Chants Kimbanguistes' in Kinshasa. Born and brought up in BMS circles, Nsambu secretly became a Kimbanguist in 1950, but continued actively in the BMS church in Kitega, organizing choral activities. In 1956 the Baptists expelled Nsambu for his Kimbanguist tendencies and soon after other Kimbanguist sympathizers were similarly excluded. 1956 was the year of 'Bolingo na 56', ('bolingo' = love, Lingala) when Kimbanguists, thrown out and thrown together, experienced an intensification of solidarity and a spirit of abandon, heedless of possible consequences. In March of that year Nsambu decided to return to his village in Bas-Zaïre and made visits to Nkamba, the birth-place of Kimbangu. On his second visit, as he crested a hill near to Nkamba and caught sight of the 'Holy City', he heard celestial music and 'received' his first hymn: *Mbanza mpa ya kubamene* (The New Jerusalem is ready...). Nsambu returned to Kinshasa and reported back to Diangienda who authorized him to teach his new hymn to the Kimbanguists. *'From that moment, the way was open'*, states Nsambu.[42] Not only did the first organized choir take place in the then Kimbanguist office in the urban zone of Kasa-Vubu, but others besides Nsambu began receiving inspired hymns. From December 1959, on the instructions of Diangienda, Kimbanguists met openly in other places and wherever they met, choirs were formed and began to assume their present important role. In 1963, during a major reorganization of the Kimbanguist Church, Nsambu was designated by S. E. Diangienda as 'Directeur des Chants Kimbanguistes', responsible for developing and supervising the choirs which in 1987 numbered between 50 and 60 in the city of Kinshasa alone, with an official total membership of some 6,424.[43] The 'Bureau des Chants' is on the third floor of the large Kimbanguist administrative headquarters (urban zone of Bongolo) whose foundation stone was laid by President Mobutu on March 20th, 1966. It comprises several offices, including the 'Bureau Téchnique' where hymns are processed (see below, pp. 163ff).

Of no less influence in the story of Kimbanguist hymns was Fwasi Lucien ('Mista Fwasi'). If Nsambu's gifts are organisational, Fwasi's were musical and spiritual. Already at the age of 14 or 15 Fwasi composed hymns at the BMS station at Ngombe-Lutete. Although more or less blind from birth, (and therefore with very little formal education) Fwasi had a thorough knowledge of the Bible and memorized large portions of it. He was put out of the BMS Church at Ngombe-Lutete on account of one of his hymns which was deemed to be schismatic. The offending final verse of Fwasi's hymn reads:

> Yabanza vo, lolo inti'angiekama
> (I thought the fire-charred branch a good support to lean on)
> Kinga nkulukulu a mwilu kwandi
> (in fact it only soiled me further)
> Owau nki ndenda vanga?
> (what shall I do now?)
> Mono se ilembi vuluzwa
> (I have missed being saved)

The 'lolo' (charred branch) was understood by the missionaries to be a camouflaged accusation against themselves and against their Church, which, far from providing salvation, had in fact only worsened the plight of those who had sought refuge therein. Interestingly, if the indigenous hymns were deemed by the one side to hide dangerous truths, missionary hymns were occasionally considered to do the same by the other side.[44]

Fwasi was imprisoned briefly in Mbanza Ngungu in 1955 over a minor village dispute, but before the two months of his sentence were ended he had organised a prison choir. In 1956 he was readmitted to the BMS Church and eventually some 13 of his hymns were included in the hymnbook *Nkunga Mia Kintwadi*, used by several of the missionary societies working in Bas-Zaïre.[45] It was in September 1958 that Fwasi met up with Nsambu Twasilwa who was in the region for a wedding. Nsambu persuaded Fwasi to return with him to Kinshasa where Fwasi spent many hours singing his hymns from memory (all four parts) into a tape-recorder.[46] S. E. Diangienda had Fwasi visit all the 'paroisses' in Kinshasa where he preached and sang his hymns. His extraordinary abilities and zeal, combined with the official approbation of the Chef Spirituel, all constituted a powerful impetus to the new wave of inspired hymnology. Fwasi returned before long to Nkamba, where he continued to receive many hymns, despite a serious rheumatic illness to which he eventually succumbed in 1973, aged 53.[47]

From 'revelation' to 'canonization'

Not everyone in the EJCSK is an 'inspiré' (capable of receiving hymns by inspiration). There are 46 people who are currently (1987) registered as exercising the gift. It is regarded as any other spiritual gift, granted by God at His discretion to those of His choice, both male and female. No pride is evident in those who have the gift, no resentment in those who lack it. The gift is by no means rare. While some choirs might have none with the gift, others of, say, sixty members might have two or three 'capteurs'. Conversations with several 'inspirés' of various ages revealed that there are broad similarities of experiences. Nsambu states that hymns can be received in at least three ways. First, while the 'capteur' is asleep, he will have a dream or a vision, in which he first hears and then sees an angelic choir. He draws near and finds himself joining in, adding his voice to those of the celestial singers, learning by participation. Upon waking he remembers the tune he was singing and the words. Sometimes it is only the air that he will recall, sometimes all four parts. Secondly, the same thing can happen during the waking hours, while walking along the street, or in the fields. A distant but gradually more distinct sound of singing will cause him to stop and take note (this would not normally be accompanied by a visual experience). This was how Nsambu received his first hymn. Thirdly, the words and music can simply 'well up' ('les choses arrivent au coeur') and the individual will sense that it is a hymn communicated by God. Nsambu stated that for him this was the most usual means of receiving hymns. The intensified spiritual atmosphere of the weekly retreats held at a location not far from Kinshasa is particularly conducive to inspired hymnology.[48]

The present Secretary of the 'Département des Chants', Mabika Masala, recalls that he was only 14 years old when Mista Fwasi came to Kinshasa and visited the different Kimbanguist parishes, among them his own of Njili. After listening to Fwasi, Mabika returned home exhilarated with what he had heard. That night, in a dream, he heard the angelic choir and so received his first hymn. After much hesitation he went to the 'Chef Spirituel' who encouraged him and sent him to

Nsambu so that the hymn might be noted and taught. He received his second hymn two days later, but then there was a period of several years before he was granted a third. Explaining this to Fwasi one day in Nkamba, Fwasi reassured him and told him to expect 'seasons of drought'.[49] It is held to be especially important in such periods when God chooses to withhold his revelation, that the individual refrain from 'forcing' a hymn. Those who do so in an attempt to attract admiration are apparently easily exposed as mere 'composers' and fall under the censure of the 'Chef Spirituel'.

A third 'capteur' relates that he received three hymns when he was 16 years of age, but kept them to himself. The 'Chef Spirituel' insisted that if they had been given, they should be put to use and sung in the Church. His first hymn turned out to be very successful (ie. widely sung). It had five verses to it and the music was revealed in all its four parts. He claims he had no trouble remembering it; it was as if he had known it for a long time. However, since 1970 he has received hymns only rarely.[50] Sometimes, like any gift, that of 'captage' can atrophy through disuse. The present 'Chef de Protocole' confided that although he used to receive hymns by revelation, he is now so busy with his duties that he no longer exercises the gift. He does not feel guilty about this necessary adjustment, seeing it as within God's will.[51]

Like any spiritual gift, inspired hymnology is open to abuse and counterfeit, for the Kimbanguists believe that its source may be not only angelic, but also satanic.[52] If part of the function of the 'Bureau des Chants Kimbanguistes' is to collect inspired hymns and to make them available for the whole Church, the other part of its duties is to sift the true from the false. The current process involves a number of steps. First, the 'capteur' will report to Nsambu as Director of the Bureau who will give the hymn its first critical hearing. He (or she) will then be sent along to the 'Bureau Téchnique', a room on the same floor of the Bongolo Headquarters. Here, the two or three persons concerned with the 'enrégistrement' will pray with the 'capteur', then request him to sing his hymn, several times over. This will enable them to transcribe the tune in tonic sol-fa, but will also serve to reveal whether the singer has genuinely 'received' the hymn. As he sings, the recorders will be noting the quality of the music (as to whether it is distinctive and 'excites the heart')[53] and that of the text (as to whether it is edifying and 'conforms to the will of God').[54] They will also pay heed to the manner of the singer. For if one indication of true inspiration is the look of calm and joyful assurance on the face of the singer, then hesitation, anxiety and undue sweating will all betray the fake.

In rather the same way that the gift of glossolalia in charismatic circles imparts a sense of divine immediacy to both the speaker and (if he is exercising his gift in public) hearers, so the gift of inspired (revealed) hymns is an important indication to the Kimbanguists that their experience of God is not second-hand but direct. The fact that many of the 'capteurs' apparently have no human qualifications such as a fine voice, musical ability, advanced education, etc., to explain their ability only emphasizes to the Kimbanguists that these hymns are evidence that God is at work among them:

> It must not be forgotten that these hymns are 'received' by
> Christians without any special training, often cultivators,
> sometimes children, who would not normally be expected to
> know the essentials of evangelical theology... And above all,
> these hymns, given to us Blacks by inspiration from the Holy
> Spirit, are the striking manifestation that for us Africans
> Jesus Christ is really our only Lord and Saviour by the
> intermediary of the ministry of our 'Papa', Simon Kimbangu,
> openly and with power... [55]

So as not to discourage or shame the 'capteur', it is very rare that either Nsambu or the 'Bureau Téchnique' will reject an inspired hymn while it is being sung. Usually, the hymn will be transcribed and the singer dismissed with thanks; only then will the singer and song be assessed. A minority of the hymns will be rejected on the basis of the above criteria and be filed away accordingly.[56] The majority will move on to the next stage of the process: composition. The four-member Composition Committee, supplied with the soprano air, will work out on a blackboard the other three parts: alto, baritone and base and will write it in tonic sol-fa (see Appendix II). Thereafter, the hymn will pass to the Transposition Committee (also officially 4 members), who will transcribe the tonic sol-fa into staff notation. A select minority of hymns will go to the Translation Committee, headed by the senior figure of the 'Chef de Cabinet', Bena-Silu, for transposition from Kikongo to Lingala or French. Characteristically of Zaïrian bureaucracy in general and Kimbanguist in particular, the 'Bureau Technique' (itself just one of the several departments in the 'Bureau des Chants') is highly structured with three administrative and five technical 'services'. Only a fraction of the total personnel in the 'Bureau des Chants' is full-time; the others have salaried employment in various parts of the city and converge on Bongolo after work hours to put in time voluntarily. The 'Service Statistique' of the 'Bureau Téchnique' is responsible for keeping a monthly and annual count of the various categories of hymns processed at the Bureau. For the year 1986, a total of 277 hymns were processed, (see Appendix IV) although it is admitted that many hymns that are sung both in Kinshasa and elsewhere never pass through the official channels.

Into the life of the Church

Once the process of 'canonization'[57] of a hymn has been completed, there remains the task of introducing it into Church usage. Apart from the dozens of parish and organisation choirs that exist in Kinshasa, there is a central choir composed of the leaders of all the other choirs. This 'Chorale des Dirigeants' meets for rehearsals three times a week at the 'Bureau des Chants' and it is here that the new hymns are taught to the leaders, who in turn teach the choirs for which they are responsible. These choirs meet on designated evenings of the week, either in their parishes, or (if the choir is of a particular organization rather than of a parish) in the grounds of the 'Centre d'Accueil' (the guest and conference centre in Kinshasa's Kasa Vubu Zone). Members will often have to walk long distances after a full day's work to arrive at the rehearsal by early evening and the spirit of serious and solemn dedication is apparent throughout the long rehearsal. Typically, before joining in the rehearsal, the newly arrived member will remove his/her shoes[58] and kneel to pray. The leader will have the duplicated sheet of the hymn in tonic sol-fa and will proceed with the teaching of each part in turn. Members will note down the words as they are given. The hymn will be sung repeatedly until it is well mastered. Not infrequently the rehearsal will include an offering for the current building project. The total absence of frivolity and idle chat is especially striking in the choirs comprising young people; the choir rehearsals are not entertainment, but intense spiritual exercise. Many choirs designate one or more counsellors to watch over the spiritual health of their members.[59]

The hymn thus memorized will be sung by the choir at the Sunday service either in the local parishes, or at the twice-monthly central rally which normally lasts nine hours (9am-6pm) and which takes place at an open-air venue large enough to accommodate the enormous numbers (roughly estimated at 15,000[60]) that congregate around a large square space. In the centre of one side of the square is the long podium where visitors and dignitaries (notably the 'Chef Spirituel' Diangienda and his college of elders) normally sit, under shelter from the sun or rain. The programme traditionally falls into two quite distinct sections: the service proper (Fr.'culte') and the 'nsinsani'offering, (Fr. 'partie sociale'). The 'culte' (again characterized by its order and solemnity) follows a standardized liturgy[61] and includes a communal hymn, the reading of a psalm and the Ten Commandments, prayers, dedication of infants and a formal collection. It is during this service part of the day that choirs stand in turn to sing their hymns. There is also a sermon preached by a designated man or woman,[62] or even by the 'Chef Spirituel', but the time devoted to preaching is considerably less than for the hymns. As one choir leader explained: *The hymns preach a lot; the Bible preaches a little'.*[63]

The service is marked by a solemnity and order which seem unaffected by the oppressive heat of the sun or the sudden onset of rain (only a tiny minority are under shelter of any sort). The uniformed 'sentinelles' who stand motionless for hours on end in front of the podium and at given points around the square, are there not to establish order but to express it. The service proper ends with a military-style march-past of nearly three thousand Kimbanguists (ranging from the very young to the very old, all still shoe-less and dressed mostly in green and white uniforms), representing all the different EJCSK choirs and organizations. As they pass the podium they wave fronds or salute, while all the time an official keeps up a non-stop commentary over the loud-speaker system on the identity and history of each group and the brass band plays at full volume. At a designated place towards the end of the march-past the marchers (the women more frequently than the men) deposit gifts of soap, rice, tea, or bananas. These rapidly growing heaps of non-monetary gifts are periodically evacuated whenever they threaten to obstruct the march-ers; they are sorted by stewards and later used for the many visitors at the 'Centre d'Accueil' or at the residence of the 'Chef Spirituel'.

The second part of the day-long programme is essentially the 'nsinsani' offering, the principal fund-raising means for the EJCSK which traditionally has looked to its own members rather than to the West for its finance. After opportunity has been given for anyone so inclined to make a really substantial gift in public, the 'nsinsani' is thrown open to all. Groups representing choirs or other Kimbanguist organizations form into columns and, keeping step to a lively rhythm from the brass band, weave in and out of each other, until the large central space is quite full. Gradually each column approaches its designated green plastic bowl into which each marcher drops his gift. The column then weaves off and away, only to come back again after more circuitous marching to deposit a second offering, and a third and so on, even to a sixth or eighth.[64] Each time the bowl is emptied and its contents counted, the totals are totted up so as to enable groups to compete good-humouredly against one another ('nsinsani' = com-petition, kikongo). Usually, so as to encourage generous giving (as well as to be available for counselling) the 'nsinsani' is conducted under the watchful eye of either Diangienda or one of his family, or of one of the early contemporaries of Simon Kimbangu, like Mama Mikala. If the 'Mvwalas' (the three sons of Kimbangu) cannot be there physically, it is believed that they are really there in spirit and their chairs are placed somewhere near the offertory bowls. These big 'nsinsani' offerings at the central meeting can last three or four hours, but they are only the most spectacular of the 'nsinsanis', for almost any gathering of Kimbanguists will provide an excuse for another 'nsinsani', the proceeds of which will contribute to whichever construction project the 'Chef Spirituel' is promoting. The constant money collecting is criticized, but by those outside rather than inside the EJCSK. The majority of the Kimbanguists belong to the poorer classes, but in marked contrast to many of the established, mission-related churches who lean on overseas or missionary sources of income, the Kimbanguists do not appear to resent the calls on their money and the 'nsinsani' is conducted in a spirit of carnival.[65]

Director Nsambu estimates that the collection of hymns in the 'Bureau' must number 6,000. Plans for systematic classification are as yet unrealized, although there does exist a categorized assortment of almost 500 Kikongo hymns designed to constitute an official hymnal (see Appendix III).

Three attempts to have the hymns printed in Belgium, Greece and finally by the Protestant publishing centre in Kinshasa (CEDI) respectively, all foundered for financial reasons. To date, the EJCSK is without an official hymnbook. By far the majority of the hymns in the 'Bureau' are in Kikongo; some in Lingala and French and occasional hymns in English are also encountered.

Selection and interpretation

Rather than use the collection once proposed as the official printed hymnbook (and whose selection might have been affected accordingly) the hymns used for this study are from five different sources:

First and most important, was an 'ad hoc' assortment in a card folder in the 'Bureau', consisting of 385 hymns from all periods and by many different 'capteurs'. It was an arbitrary rather than an official collection and therefore deemed likely to present a truer hymnological picture, and, from the practical point of view given the limited time available, it was of manageable proportions. With the tireless assistance of a MuKongo Kimbanguist, Cit. Nziama, who also had a good command of French, a quick running translation of all the hymns was made. Those hymns considered to be of special interest were asterisked for subsequent scrutiny. Hymns which, when translated, were found to be 'ecumenical', that is which expressed standard Christian beliefs in such a way as to be indistinguishable from Christian hymns of any other continent, were deliberately left, although it has to be emphasized that these 'ecumenical' hymns constitute part of the total picture of Kimbanguist hymnology. However, the hymns selected for more careful translation and analysis were distinctively Kimbanguist, that is, they recognizably reflected historical or doctrinal distinctives of the Kimbanguist phenomenon. Among these distinctives would be: the African and Kimbanguist perception of the colonial situation with its accompanying persecution, deportations, suffering and racial injustice; the Kimbanguist sense of vindication in the period following the gaining of national independence and the official recognition of the EJCSK; the Holy City of Nkamba-Jerusalem; and perhaps most of all, the historical and current role of the Prophet Simon Kimbangu and the role of his three sons who lead the present church. Again, the vast majority (over 80%) of the hymns in this collection were in Kikongo, others were in Lingala and a few were in French.

The second source of hymns was a folder of 1921 songs filed in the Secretary's office at Bongolo. All of these 24 early hymns are in Kikongo.

Third, use has been made of Boka and Raymaekers' 1960 collection of 85 hymns by Nsambu Andre.[66] The hymns are all translated into French from Kikongo and Lingala originals and appear in full, with no added commentary. They were intended to be part of a larger collection which never materialized.

Fourth, the document produced by the Swiss pastor Heintze-Flad, *L'Eglise kimbanguiste, une église qui chante et qui prie*[67] furnished at least extracts from 53 hymns.

Finally, there are about a dozen other hymns recorded personally at services and choir rehearsals in Kinshasa during the month of February, 1987.[68]

Putting all the sources together gave a total of some 560 hymns on which the present analysis was based.

It is true that the large majority of the hymns in question have been consigned to writing, but this does not, in and of itself, transfer them from the oral to the written realm. It is also true, as Finnegan has pointed out, that where hymns and lyrics have arisen following the impact of Christianity, it is common for a written tradition of religious literature to coexist and to some extent overlap with an oral tradition. But it is a mistake to assume that the advent of Christianity and its associated literate traditions has diminished the importance of oral religious utterances. Indeed, as Finnegan insists, taking African churches as an example, the opposite would appear to be the case:

> It is precisely in the religious sphere that there has been a marked development of oral forms in lyrics, prayers and testimonies... Sometimes these utterances are subsequently reduced to writing or even make an appearance in written form, but even in these cases, their spread and significance among their largely non-literate patrons is primarily oral.[69]

As to the task of theological analysis from oral sources, a cautionary note has rightly been sounded by Bengt Sundkler, in his critique of G. C. Oosthuizen's *The Theology of a South African Messiah* (an analysis of the hymnal of the 'Church of the Nazarites').[70] Sundkler is uncharacteristically scathing[71] in his comments of Oosthuizen's approach and conclusions:

> We suggest that Shembe's hymnbook should be understood not from the outside, from a Western point of view, measuring its contents according to the standards and ideas of a European catechism, but rather from its own presuppositions...[72] We suggest that one should discard such heavy and learned Western panoply and let Shembe walk along as he used to and loved to: moving light, barefoot.[73]

Sundkler was making the obvious point that the difference between orality and literacy must be respected and was, in effect, accusing Oosthuizen of unfairly judging the former on the stringent analytic grounds of the latter. W. J. Ong listed no fewer than nine character-istics of orally-based thought and expression.[74] Some of these distinctives are important enough to merit brief discussion here.

First, orally based expression is redundant or copious. Whereas writing can be word-economical since the reader's eye can 'back-scan' if necessary to pick up forgotten or missed information, orality depends on repetition of the 'just-said', which keeps both speaker and hearer surely on the track.

> Sparsely linear or analytical thought and speech is an arti-
> ficial creation, structured by the technology of writing.[75]

Then, because it relies upon repeating what has been said in the past, it tends to establish a conservative or traditionalist set of mind that with good reason inhibits intellectual experimentation.[76] Fur-ther, it is close to the human life-world:

> In the absence of elaborate analytic categories that depend
> upon writing to structure knowledge at a distance from lived
> experience, oral culture must conceptualize and rationalize
> all their knowledge with more or less close reference to the
> human lifeworld.[17]

Thus, it is situational rather than abstract. Whereas writing separates the knower from the known and thus sets up conditions for 'objectiv-ity' in the sense of personal disengagement or distancing, learning or knowing in an oral culture means achieving close, empathetic, communal identification with the known.[78]

All these special properties of oral (as opposed to written) expression will dictate that different criteria be brought to bear upon oral utterances in general and hymns in particular. Hymns constitute a sub-category of oral utterance and have their own, additional, char-acteristics. They share, with other verse and poetry, a language which is allusive rather than direct, affirmational rather than rationalistic (from the mind to the mind).[79]

These distinct features of oral expression generally and hymn expression in particular impose limitations on the sorts of analytical questions that can be asked. The medium does not lend itself readily to rigorous cartesian dissection; it would break under the strain.

One important obvious observation can be made. The Kimbanguist hymns (like most hymns) are for communal use and derive part of their significance from this very fact. They are for corporate rather than solitary use. All the literature about the Kimbanguist Church emphasises the central place that singing plays in their worship and hymns are perhaps the major means by which members affirm together their sense of community, so important in African society. Whereas theology books are written by individuals in their solitary silence and are designed to be perused by other scholars in theirs, the Kimbanguist member affirms his identity by joining his voice with that of the rest of the singing community. The vast majority of the hymns are other than in the first person singular and are expressions, not of individual piety but of corporate identity and common aspiration. Ritual finds part of its meaning in its communal participation. By their singing, Kimbanguists declare: 'We participate, therefore we are'.

The compilation intended for publication ('Ndandani za mi Nkunga') followed a standard 'Table of Contents' grouping of hymns (see Appendix III). However, a totally different classification can be attempted, on the basis not of themes, but of referent (see Fig. 1).

The first category can be termed 'Godward', that is, hymns addressed to God. The type can be subdivided into four categories: hymns of praise and worship, those of confession, those of petition and those of response. The second category can be termed 'mutual', where the hymns are addressed from member to member and the type subdivided into three: exhortation, instruction and affirmation (testimony). Hymns of the third category are oriented towards those outside the Kimbanguist fold and may be termed 'outward'. These are evangelistic hymns of entreaty or warning. There is a fourth group,'others', comprising hymns for special occasions: Christmas, marriage, bereavement, greeting of visitors, child dedication, etc. (see Appendix V for category examples).

Patterns of concern

Reading and rereading of the Kimbanguist hymns reveals certain themes, tendencies, or patterns of concern and, given the 'genre' in question, it is probably more instructive to consider these broader patterns than to attempt close verbal analysis which would not only require an intimate knowledge of kikongo, but also strain the limitations of oral expression.

1. Jesus, the Holy Spirit and Kimbangu

Of the 560 hymns under analysis, the great majority (over 400) mention Jesus Christ under the various Kikongo terms of 'Yisu', 'Mfumu Yisu' (Lord Jesus), 'Mvuluzi' (Saviour), 'Mwana Nzambi' (Son of God). It is difficult not to conclude that Jesus Christ is central to the beliefs of Kimbanguists as he is for other Christians.

As might be expected, the inspired 'reception' of Christmas carols occurs in the weeks leading up to Christmas (see Appendix IV). However, they are sung not only around December 25th, but also to mark any joyous occasion, such as the birthday of one of the 'Mvwalas', or the welcoming of a visitor of note.[80] The carols celebrate in standard 'nativity' language and with joyful tunes, the birth in Bethlehem of the baby Jesus. Many of the hymns which speak about the death of Christ could as well be found in hymnbooks used by Protestant denominations in Zaire or elsewhere: '*We thank the Saviour Jesus for the death He died for us* .'[81] An early hymn of 1921 declares: '*Jesus gave Himself up / He was nailed to the tree / His blood dropped down / that we might be cleansed.*' [82] His resurrection is affirmed: '*To save men upon the earth, He (Jesus) rose victorious from the dead.*' [83]

The acknowlegement of Jesus is not merely with reference to the remote historic past; it bears equally on the present belief structure of the Kimbanguists. In the hymns, it is to Jesus that the faithful abandon themselves; it is in Him that they find their peace, tranquillity, riches, rest (on condition that they believe); He forgives their wrong words and actions; He procures victory for them; He is their pastor (shepherd), brother, liberator, healer, miracle worker,

Fig.1. A typology of Kimbanguist Hymns

Category A: Godward

1. Praise	46
2. Confession	21
3. Supplication	101
4. Response	19
	187

Category B: Mutual

1. Exhortation	150
2. Instruction	36
3. Affirmation	19
	205

Category C: Outward

1. Evangelism	74

Category D: Other   99

Total   565

NB: The total reflects the fact that several of the 560 hymns exactly fit more than one category.

Graph representation of
the above categories:

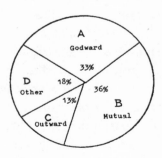

redeemer, saviour, He is the 'ntu' (head) of the Community. All these epithets could be found in Western Christian hymns and in those of African mission-related churches and re-emphasize the historical links that Kimbanguism has with Protestant missionary Christianity.[84]

What is more controversial is the place that the Prophet is accorded in Kimbanguist understanding, Asch quotes many witnesses from different parts of Zaïre to support her claim that the unofficial Kimbanguism of the majority believes that Simon Kimbangu was/is the manifestation of the Holy Spirit, the Third Person of the Trinity.[85] Droogers, in his study of grassroots Kimbanguism in the 1970s, comes to the same conclusion:

> Whereas the Holy Spirit was given to the Whites in an invisible way and did not succeed in His work, Kimbangu is the visible Holy Spirit given to Africa — but for the benefit of all mankind.[86]

Of the 569 hymns, some 135 (almost a quarter) speak of the Prophet, using a variety of different names: Tata Simon, Kimbangu, 'Ngunza' (Prophet), 'Ngunza Nzambi' (Prophet of God), 'Ngunza Yisu' (Prophet of Jesus), 'Ngunza Mvuluzi' (Prophet of the Saviour), 'Ntumwa' (Sent One, Apostle), 'Ntumwa a Se' (Apostle of the Father). According to the hymns, Kimbangu is

> the visible sign, given by Jesus for men on earth, in whom the glory of God has appeared to us;[87]
> the Apostle whom God sent in order to fulfil the promises made by Jesus to the Blacks and to make clear the mystery of Jesus, to save men upon the earth.[88]

He is

> the prophet who announced the news of Jesus; Jesus will curse those who refuse to believe Kimbangu's testimony.[89]
> It is by this Prophet that we receive (in the successive verses of one hymn) 'Jesus the love of God, the mercy of God, the voice of Jesus'.[90]

He is

> the Messenger, the Apostle of Jesus, who is truly our strength.[91]

It is

> the Prophet of the Lord whom we praise, let us tell the good deeds of his life.[92]

Indeed, so closely do Kimbangu and Jesus come in some of the hymns that it becomes difficult to separate them:

> Thanks be to Jesus, I will tell out the name of the Prophet;[93]
> the Lord loves us, he sent us the Prophet... if we believe in him (the prophet? Jesus?) we will be saved;[94]
> Did you see, when he raised the dead? Believe in the Prophet so that you may be saved[95]
> Do you know the day of Jesus' return? / the dead will be judged; Do you know the day of Tata Simon's return? / The dead will be raised.[96]

In the texts of the hymns, it is not to the Holy Spirit that Kimbangu is assimilated, so much as to Jesus Christ.

The association with Jesus is made even closer by numerous parallels in the lives and ministries of the two. Like Jesus, Kimbangu healed the sick and raised the dead. The solo part of one hymn seeks to report testimonies given by those who were healed:

> I was dead for three days, he raised me / I was blind, he gave me back my sight / I was paralysed, he made me walk / I was leprous, he made me clean.

Between each testimony the choir sings: 'Let us get ready to receive the Saviour.'[97] The testimonies are of those who found healing in the Bas-Congo in the 1920's. But they could equally be testimonies of the sick and needy of first century Galilee and Judaea. Kimbangu, like his Lord, suffered from the accusations and cunning of powerful religious and political enemies and he too was condemned to death after being falsely accused. Kimbangu, of course, had his sentence commuted to life imprisonment, but he too died as a result of his sentence. Many hymns relate to the unjust sufferings of the Prophet:

The Apostle of the Lord died here below, in a damp prison,

    He was persecuted here below, like a wrong doer.

Refr: O woe on the earth! The Prophet was killed on earth,

the world afflicted him because it did not know him.[98]

This area of assimilation in the Kimbanguist body of beliefs found strong encouragement from a surprising source. Jules Chomé, a left-wing Belgian, wrote his book: *'La passion de Simon Kimbangu'*[99] in which he drew comparisons between the arrest, trial, sufferings and eventual death of Kimbangu and those of Christ. Chomé had no religious inclinations and the intentions behind his book were not so much to plead the cause of the Kimbanguist religion as to discredit the practices of the colonial administration,[100] but the book is admired in Kimbanguist circles.[101]

With the Prophet's ministry perceived to re-enact that of Christ, it is hardly surprising that the hymns also express parallels extending beyond Kimbangu's death:

Risen, he is risen! Risen, he is risen!

  Let us praise Almighty God for having raised him from the dead.

Killed by a horrible death, killed by a horrible death,

  Let us praise the Lord Jesus for having raised him from the dead.

Our Prophet has risen! Our prophet has risen!

  Let us praise the Lord Jesus for having raised him from the dead.[102]

The existence of the mausoleum at Nkamba, sacred resting place of Kimbangu's earthly remains, far from diminishing the Kimbanguist's conviction that Kimbangu is not dead but alive, rather increases it. For in Kongo cosmology, as MacGaffey emphasises,[103] the noble dead are more alive than the living and consequently, the grave is not a cul-de-sac, but a gateway to the world of spirit:

The Prophet of God is risen! He returns from the land of the dead,

  The angels of God have brought him out from the land of the dead.

Refr. He returns from the dead, he is transformed into spirit,
He has come out of the tomb, he has met his Lord.[104]

The parallel continues beyond the resurrection to the present intercessory role of Kimbangu for his followers. Prayers are sometimes made in his name, not least through the supplicatory hymns of Category A, beseeching him for protection, for help or for peace.[105] And indeed, in the many apocalyptic hymns of the EJCSK, Kimbangu shares with Christ the role of returning king and judge (see section on Eschatology, pp.197ff). The parallel with Christ, projected forward into eternity, is also extended backward into eternity, too (for example by the three-language chatechism of 1970).[106]

In view of this comprehensive Christic assimilation, then, could Oosthuizen say of Kimbanguism what he concluded in his chapter entitled 'The Messiah' in his study of the hymnal of Shembe's 'Church of the Nazarites'?

> Messianism in the Bible is inseparably linked up with Jesus Christ while it is in the *'iBandla lama Nazaretha'* insepara-bly linked up with Isaiah Shembe. He is more than the promised prophet of Deut. 18:15... he is truly a Messiah to his followers, a god in whom the divine and human are inseparably associated; he is to them truly Christ, the holy one who has risen and continues to live at Ekuphakameni. The cornerstone of this movement is thus not Jesus Christ but Isaiah Shembe. He wished to be the political, social and religious Saviour of the Zulu nation in the first instance but also of all other nations.[107] (Italics his.)

It is difficult to imagine that he could say the same of Kimbangu and his Church — at least, not for the same reasons. Firstly, Kimbangu himself, by all accounts, made no messianic claims about himself. Early accounts of his ministry agree that he preached and healed not in his own name, but in the name of Jesus Christ. At his trial before the military tribunal in 1921, Kimbangu claimed his ministry was concerned only with preaching the Gospel of Jesus Christ. The questioning at the trial is reproduced in Diangienda's book:

De Rossi: Are you the 'mvuluzi' (saviour)?

Kimbangu: No, Jesus Christ is the Saviour. I received from
             Him the mission of proclaiming the good news
             of eternal salvation to my people.

De Rossi: Have you raised the dead?

Kimbangu: Yes.

De Rossi: How did you do it?

Kimbangu: By the divine power that Jesus gave me.[108]

Back in 1924, when it could be expected that the colonial powers would be quick to emphasize discrediting elements among the Kimbanguists, the 'Administrateur Territorial' of Thysville (Mbanza Ngungu) concluded his report on their beliefs by saying:

> They do not pray to Simon Kimbangu; they pray to God,
> Kimbangu is an emissary of God.[109]

Martin was able to say in 1968, while still professor at the University of Botswana and having completed comparative research into African Independent religious movements in Southern Africa:

> Simon Kimbangu is not in Christ's place... Simon Kimbangu
> is thus not a black messiah who opens the door of heaven
> (like I. Shembe in Zululand, for instance) but rather the
> finger of John the Baptist, pointing towards the Lamb of God
> who takes away the sin of the world.[110]

Secondly, besides Kimbangu's own disclaimer of messianic pretensions, the hymns give to Jesus Christ a place of striking prominence. Whereas the mention of Jesus in the Shembe hymnal is conspicuous by its rarity (only two of 243 hymns specifically refer to Jesus; one other, No. 87 is clearly allusive to Him[111]) the Kimbanguist hymns that omit mention of Jesus Christ are the exception rather than the rule. The Kimbanguist hymns, therefore, can be said to be not 'Jesus-excluding' but rather 'Kimbangu-including'. This conclusion is borne out in prayers, sermons, Kimbanguist writings and in personal conversations at every level. There appears to be no conscious minimizing of Christ, no sense of rivalry in Kimbanguist belief between Christ and Kimbangu. It is not that Jesus is the white man's messiah while Kimbangu is the black man's. Nor is it to deny that Christ performed miracles, suffered, died, rose again and will one day return in judgment. It is rather that all that Christ did, Kimbangu did, too.

If it is simplistic to perceive Kimbangu as a divine Christ-substitute, a second, more subtle interpretation draws on the ikonic model. Sundkler proposes this solution in opposition to Oosthuizen's overly theological analysis of Shembe's hymns.[112] It seems to fit the Kimbanguist hymns even better than those of the Church of the Nazarites. Kimbangu is the ikon (mask) of Christ. Of the Eastern Orthodox ikon, Timothy Ware says:

> The ikon is not an idol but a symbol; the veneration shown to images is directed, not towards stone, wood and paint, but towards the person depicted... (The ikon) is one of the ways whereby God is revealed to man. Through ikons the Orthodox Christian receives a vision of the spiritual world.[113]

To the Kimbanguist, the Prophet is the visible, local representation of Jesus in the African world. By looking believingly on the miracles the Prophet performed and the example of his humility and courage in the face of adversity and suffering, the eye focuses clearly on Christ. For in the person and deeds of Simon Kimbangu, God has in the clearest possible way affirmed His love and purposes for the BaKongo (and for other Africans, and indeed, for the whole world). Whereas, before, the Blacks had to take the Whites' word that God loved them and sent His Son to redeem them, now they see for themselves. Like the Samaritans in Jesus' day, Kimbanguists can say (to the Whites), 'We no longer believe just because of what you said; now we have heard for ourselves, and we know that this man (Jesus) really is the Saviour of the world.' (John 4:42) Thus it becomes right, within the ikonic model framework, to make much of Simon Kimbangu. He is the *visible sign, given on earth to give us life*';[114] he is *'the reflection of the love of Jesus, the glory of God appeared to us'*[115] and it is *'by (receiving) the Prophet that we receive Jesus... the love of God... the mercy of God... and the voice of Jesus.'*[116] If another hymn can exult: *'Jesus is the magnificent miracle-worker, He heals our sicknesses and forgives our sins'.*[117] is it not because His power has been clearly manifested in the deeds of Simon Kimbangu? So closely does the ikon of Kimbangu represent the Christ, that to reject the one means rejecting the other: *'You who despise the Prophet of God, Jesus will curse you';*[118] *'You who do not believe in the Prophet, your soul will perish'.*[119] In just the same way, Jesus could blame the religious leaders of His day for not believing the testimony of John the Baptist; it was not possible at the one and the same time to believe in Christ and disbelieve John who testified of Him. From the ikonic perspective, it is in this sense that Kimbangu must be 'believed' and that his 'good news' must be proclaimed everywhere.

The pluralism of perception that exists within the Kimbanguist Church might be due to the susceptibility of any ikon to drift away from that which it represents to become an object of veneration in and of itself.[120] The language of the hymns is ambiguous enough to permit this plurality of perception about the person and role of Simon Kimbangu. Different people can sing the same hymn and understand different things, yet remain part of the same church. McKay's statement with regard to earlier missionary/Kongo ambiguities has its modern counterpart:

> The fact that missionaries and converts shared a common religious vocabulary masked the difference in their cosmologies.[121]

The ikonic paradigm thus permits that theological sliding-scale flexibility that is a feature of Kimbanguist language about Kimbangu and Christ. However, in itself it does not explain sufficiently the controversial belief about Kimbangu as the Holy Spirit. This belief is publically denied by the leadership in Kinshasa. Although opportunity was repeatedly sought to speak with the 'Chef Spirituel' on the subject, his busy schedule and poor health did not make this possible. In an address at one central 'nsinsani' service,[122] Diangienda criticised the foreigners who betray the trust and kindness shown to them by crudely misrepresenting what Kimbanguists believe about the Prophet and he insisted that 'Kimbangu is not God'. The official

'Catéchisme kimbanguiste' reproduced in Diangienda's book states that the Holy Spirit has come, as Jesus promised; that the Apostles, by the power of the Holy Spirit, accomplished the same miracles as Jesus did and that in Simon Kimbangu 'the Holy Spirit has manifested Himself... Simon Kimbangu is the witness of Jesus-Christ, before Whom he is our advocate (French'appui').[123] Bena-Silu, in his detailed refutation of historical and doctrinal 'errors' in Asch's book, insists that 'there exists no document written by EJCSK leadership stating that Simon Kimbangu is the incarnation of the Holy Spirit' and denies emphatically and repeatedly any such identification.[124] The position of the 'Faculté de Théologie Kimbanguiste' would follow this official understanding: one Diploma dissertation devotes an entire chapter to the question 'Is Simon Kimbangu the Holy Spirit?' and concludes that he should rather be understood as 'a man filled with the Holy Spirit... invested with a prophetic authority'.[125]

Nevertheless, despite these official pronouncements, almost without exception[126] personal conversations with Kimbanguists in Kinshasa gave the impression (at least to an outsider) that Kimbangu is believed not merely to have been powerfully anointed by the Holy Spirit, but that he actually was/is the Holy Spirit. Whether speaking in French, Lingala, or Swahili, the Kimbanguists, in talking about the identity of the Prophet, will appeal in an almost stereotyped way to a cluster of biblical texts, which concern Christ's promise of the Spirit to His disciples. The texts are, with slight variations, quoted correctly or incorrectly as follows: John 14:16 'I will ask the Father and He will give you another Counsellor, to be with you forever' (proving the continuity between Jesus and Kimbangu). John 14:12, 'He will do even greater works than I have done, because I am going to my Father' (hence Kimbangu's miracles). John 15:26, 'When the Counsellor comes, whom I will send to you from the Father, the Spirit, he will bear witness about me' (hence Kimbangu's constant pointing away from himself to Christ). John 10:16 is sometimes quoted as Jesus saying to the Jews: 'I have other sheep which are not of this sheep pen; he (sic) must bring them into the pen also' (to support the claim that Jesus had the

Africans in mind when He sent Kimbangu). And sometimes Deut 18:15 (quoted by Peter in Acts 3:22) is used to identify Kimbangu as the one Jesus would choose to bring those sheep into the fold: 'The Lord your God will raise up for you a prophet like me *from among your own people*' (italics theirs).[127]

The conclusion, sometimes emphatically stated, is that these promises made by Jesus to His disciples found their fulfilment on April 6th, 1921, in the Bas-Zaire village of Nkamba, when Simon Kimbangu started his ministry of healing the sick and raising the dead. When it is asked if these promises were not fulfilled on the Day of Pentecost in the First Century, the answer is usually given that that was something else — an effusion of God's power, whereas in Kimbangu we have the person or man that Christ promised. For the Kimbanguist will sometimes insist openly that the Spirit promised is a man (Lingala 'moto', Swahili 'Mutu', French 'homme') and not just an impersonal power. This belief, in turn finds support from the unexpected source of a biblical reference book once widely used in the West in Protestant Circles: R. A. Torrey's *Topical Text Book* and published in Kikongo in 1946 by Flemming H. Revell Co. under the title *Nkanda Wa Ngionzokolo A Minsamu*. The book was obviously intended by the translator and publisher for use by Kongo pastors and Bible students. Under the section entitled 'The Holy Spirit' (Kikongo:'Mpeve yaNlongo') it is clearly stated, with many Bible verses to support the claim 'Mpeve yaNlongo I Muntu'. Torrey's aim was to show from Scripture the personhood of the Spirit (eg. one who guides, corrects, may be grieved etc.); the translator sought to get the idea across by using the attribute 'muntu' (man/person/human being), thereby unwittingly fuelling the belief that the promised Holy Spirit is in fact a man.[128]

The hymns under analysis do contain a few where a distinction is made between Kimbangu and the Holy Spirit:

Living God, we implore you; we your children implore you. Draw near.
Father God, we implore you; grant us the Holy Spirit.
Refr; Grant us the Holy Spirit! (x 4)

Lord Jesus, we implore you; we your sheep implore you.
Draw near.
Lord Jesus, we beseech you; grant us the Holy Spirit.

Tata Simon, we implore you; we your sheep wander
about,
Bring us back into the fold of the Father; grant us the
Holy Spirit.[129] (see also Appendix V. A3)

Far more common are the hymns that establish a trinitarian
structure where the Prophet takes the place that an outsider would
expect to be occupied by the Holy Spirit. Among the many examples:

Father God has done His work... with all power, with all
power,
The Lord Jesus has done His work... with all power, with
all power,
Tata Simon has done his work... with all power, with all
power.[130]

Jehovah God has called me, has shown me his glory;
He has told me to convert, that he might give me a crown.

Refr: A crown a crown a crown... which he has prepared,
Solo: Jehovah God... Lord Jesus... Tata Simon...

The Lord Jesus has called me, has shown me his glory;
He has told me to convert, that he might give me a crown.

Tata Simon has called me, has shown me his glory;
He has told me to convert, that he might give me a
crown.[131]

O our God, give us all we need,
 see how we are consumed, our eyes are on you, our Father.

Lord Jesus, look upon us,
see how we are consumed, our eyes are on you, our Lord.

Tata Simon, look upon us,
see how we are consumed, our eyes are on you, our Father.[132]

In several hymns, the 'trinitarian structure' is further expanded to accommodate a fourth person — that of the 'Chef Spirituel', the Prophet's son, Diangienda, or indeed all three sons, the 'zimvwala' (sceptres, staffs).

We thank our God/who gave us a Saviour,
We thank him/infinitely.

We thank the Saviour/who requested a Helper for us,
We thank him/infinitely.

We thank our Prophet/who left us the 'zimvwala',
We thank him/infinitely.

We thank the 'zimvwala'/who show us the way to the
Father,
We thank them/infinitely.[133]

The picture becomes one of a descending stairway, stretching down from God the Father through Christ and then Kimbangu to the 'zimvwala' and indeed through them to the faithful themselves. The hierarchical structure portrayed in these hymns fits comfortably the Kongo (and Bantu) cosmology, which, along with the Bible and missionary Protestantism, forms the third major element in Kimbanguist beliefs. The supreme and most remote Being is 'Nzambi a Mpungu'. Between Him and the living on earth are ranged a whole descending hierarchy of spiritual beings known as 'bisimbi' (spirits) or occasionally as 'nzambi' (gods). Of these 'bisimbi', the nearest to the living include ancestors of those who are presently alive and the most influential and respected of these ancestor spirits are of those men who on earth lived an exemplary life and who died a heroic death.[134] The spiritual hierarchy is also patrifilial, as MacGaffey observes: 'The hierarchy of spirits, thought of as something like a sequence of generations was also a patrifilial sequence (father, sons, grandchildren), on the model of the ideal hierarchy of all local groups, in which each title holder stood in a paternal relationship to his subordinates.' and he quotes Doutreloux:

> From the Supreme Being to man, by way of the intermediary Spirits, extend the relations of Father to Son that structure the society of man.[135]

As the Prophet's son, the present 'Chef Spirituel', Diangienda Kuntima, (and to a lesser extent his brothers, Kisolokele and Kiangani) take their place in the spiritual hierarchy stretching from man towards 'Nzambi a Mpungu'. Diangienda's role is far more than that of an administrative head of the EJCSK and indeed much more than that of a wise spiritual guide (which by all accounts he is). The high respect (even awe) in which he is held by Kimbanguists is explained by their perception of him as forming, while yet visibly and physically present among them, an integral part of the spiritual hierarchy. Their veneration is manifested not merely by their kneeling before him (for that can also express the honour that any son worthy of the name would show towards his father in traditional Kongo society). It is observable rather in the crowd of people who are willing to wait many days for an audience with him at his modest residence in Kinshasa[136] and the manner in which he is spoken of as no ordinary mortal would be.[137] The strong centralized administrative structure of the EJCSK has its spiritual counterpart, for Diangienda is to the Kimbanguist a 'spiritual facilitator', to whom the needy can go for prayer or for blessing, in time of illness, unemployment, or new endeavour. Kimbanguists testify to Diangienda's knowledge of their inmost thoughts, even at distance. His presence is at the 'nsinsani', even if he himself is ill in bed at home. His contact with his father the Prophet is uninterrupted,[138] just as Kimbangu's contact is with Christ, and Christ's is with 'Nzambi a Mpungu'.

When the Kimbanguist speaks of Kimbangu or his sons using the term 'nzambi' (god), it is from within the Kongo (or Bantu) world-view; outside of that world-view such concepts are understood only with difficulty and more often than not misunderstood. Because of the broad tendency of coincidence between cosmology and language, the world-view in question expresses itself most easily in Kikongo and then in Lingala. Expressed or translated into French, such language seems to stick out awkwardly. Asked if it was merely by coincidence that the 'distinctively Kimbanguist' hymns were to be found in Kikongo and Lingala whereas almost without exception the French hymn were 'ecumenical', a spokesman for the 'Bureau Téchnique' admitted with noticeable embarrassment that it was not coincidence and that the 'typically Kimbanguist' hymns were not put into French because 'people in other countries might be offended by the hymns which speak of the Prophet; they might misunderstand the hymns as saying that Kimbangu is God, whereas we know that he is not God but only a small god.[139] You have to become a Kimbanguist, then you will understand; someone on the outside will not understand'.[140] Kimbanguists have to be able to adjust their terminology according to the world-view presupposed by the one they are talking to. In the course of a service, for example, the Kimbanguist will happily say of the three 'mvwala': 'Bino bojali banzambi na biso' (Lingala: You are our gods),[141] or even sing 'Mfumu a Nlongo, yo kaka ojali nzambi na ngai' (Lingala: You alone, 'Chef Spirituel', are my god).[142] But in conversation the Kimbanguist will adjust his terminology for the outsider so as to reserve the epithet 'nzambi' to designate God and even criticise the song quoted for having not passed through the proper control channels.

The Kimbanguist's pluralism is facilitated by areas of approximation between the indigenous and biblical world-views (Supreme God, patrifiliation, multiplicity of spiritual beings, deliverance from evil, need for mediation between lesser and greater). This has permitted ready inter-penetration of the two worlds and of the two it is usually, but not always, the biblical that has proved the dominating element.

One example of the cosmological reorganization under the biblical impact (beside the most important of Christ as Son of God, Lord and Saviour) is the personification of evil within the satanic model — some 43 hymns were noted in this connection, with references to 'Satana', 'nkadiampemba' (the word in Kikongo usually denoting the chief of the spirits of evil),'mianda mia satana' (spirits of Satan). The emphatic renunciation of 'kindoki' (sorcery), too, finds plenty of Scriptural support. Some of the elements of Kimbanguist theology find their legitimation (though not necessarily their origin) in Roman Catholic tradition, as in the case of mediation of the saints. While official Kimbanguist theology acknowledges that Christ is the sole mediator between man and God, conversations and Kimbanguist writings agree that the mediation of Tata Simon (and , by extension, that of his three living sons) is desirable. For he forms part of the inner 'royal court' in the immediate presence of Christ, within reach of him as others are not and is therefore well placed for accelerating the process of effective supplication:

> This is not obligatory, given that Christ directly receives all prayer. Nevertheless it is still no less true that Kimbanguists can choose to resort to this possibility... It becomes clear that Simon Kimbangu is the one who supports our prayers before Christ, so that the Lord can answer them as quickly as possible. [143]

Martin, commenting on a prayer offered by the 'Chef Spirituel' at the Prophet's Mausoleum at Nkamba, concludes:

> 'The prayer, addressed to God and Christ, turns to Simon Kimbangu: for he is risen from the dead and is with Christ... African spirituality and consequently worship knows that man on earth is too small and too sinful to approach the great King. Simon Kimbangu is not the Saviour, he is God's envoy (ntumwa) and remains the go-between, not unlike the saints in the Catholic Church. [144]

There exists, therefore, parallel to the sociological pluralism which MacGaffey identified as 'customary and bureaucratic', a complex theological pluralism which (on account of its two principal components) might be termed 'indigenous and Biblical'. The twin elements of the theological pluralism, like those if its sociological counterpart, cannot be simplistically distanced from each other by labelling one 'old' and the other 'modern', as if the mere passage of time will gradually see the one fade in favour of the other. Nor should it be assumed that for the Kimbanguist the two are incompatible in such a way as to compel him to belong either to a so-called non-official, Kimbangu-centric majority, or to a so-called Christo-centric reformist circle of the present leaders (eg. Asch's dichotomy of 'le kimbanguism des Kimbanguistes' and 'le kimbanguisme official'. [146] On the contrary, the two perceptions are co-existing and 'organically related' and the Kimbanguist finds it quite possible to be able to slip, as the need arises, from one perception to the other and back again. He does, however, readily acknowledge the difficulty of outsiders to do the same.

Whether the Kimbanguist Church, with its increasingly international aspirations will be able to maintain this sort of pluralism is open to question. Its membership of the World Council of Churches, its constant desire to contribute its spiritual perception at conferences and in writing, its need for wider acceptance and recognition — all these might encourage readjustment of Kimbanguist views concerning the identity of the founder. On the other hand, the centenary year (1987) of the Prophet's birth seems set to emphasize (by its celebrations, speeches, testimonies, etc.) the distinctiveness of the ECJSK and thus encourage a heightened rather than a modified perception of Simon Kimbangu. [146]

2. Ecstasy and Pain

A striking characteristic of the Kimbanguist hymns is their mixture of joy and anguish. Many hymns express gladness, thankfulness, praise. Even more express suffering and vulnerability. The 'Christ/ Kimbangu-event' is revealed in the hymns as being at the root of both.

The Kimbanguist singer exults in the knowledge that Christ's love went as far as the Cross, 'Jesus our Saviour loves us truly; he gave his life as a sacrifice on the Cross'[147] 'Jesus on the Cross died for our liberty' [148] 'in Him we have forgiveness;'[149] 'we have received salvation in the One you have sent, in Jesus our Chief'.[150] Infectiously joyful Christmas songs thank the Father for sending the Saviour or thank the Saviour for coming to be born in Bethlehem; such hymns are sung not only at Christmas but on any happy occasion.[151] The triumph of Christ over death by the resurrection is further cause for happiness. Such sentiments would be entirely in place in any other Christian hymnbook and are a reminder of two of the tethers of the Kimbanguist Church, namely, its historical Protestant origins and the central role of the Bible. Celebrating the Gospel-event which is the focal point common to all Christianity, it is not surprising that many of the hymns of the EJCSK bear close textual resemblance to Christian hymns from other countries and continents.

While this shared Christian heritage forms an essential part of the total Kimbanguist picture, there are other ingredients which are more distinctively Kimbanguist. As we have seen above, the Kimbangu event is an important additional impulse for joy, for all that Jesus did is 'brought near' in both time and place in the events that surround the historic person of Simon Kimbangu. Within the Kimbanguist perception, the healing power of God was visibly seen in and around Nkamba as Kimbangu(whom many still remember) raised the dead, brought sight to the blind and made the lame to walk. A sense of wonder and delight that God acted thus, 'in our very midst', comes through several of the hymns:

> The tidings of God have been heard
> > Here in the country of Africa,
> The Prophet of God has appeared
> > Here in the country of Africa.[152]

or again:

> I am thanking God greatly in my heart
> > For He has given us the Saviour on earth,
> I am thanking Jesus greatly in my heart
> > For He has given us the Prophet on earth.[153]

Some hymns reflect the colonial situation of the 1920s when this great revelation of the love of God in and through a humble Black gave a sense of vindication in an unfair world: 'The cause of the Blacks will soon be judged, now and for all peoples.'[154] As Heintze-Flad points out,[155] many hymns express joy that God Himself has rehabilitated the entire Black race, granting to it a Prophet whose equal is hard to find amongst other peoples. In so doing, God has deliberately bypassed the powerful and privileged and set Africa ahead of others. In words which recall God's astonishing choice of 'Bethlehem, Ephratha, though small among the clans of Judah' as the place of messianic promise and fulfilment (Micah 5:2, Mt. 2:6), Africa is chosen in preference over others, with a new privilege and a new responsibility:

> Land where the prophet died in the cell,
>
> (Land where) for thirty years he triumphed on earth,
>
> Africa of the Blacks, you have been placed at the head!
>
> Up! Show the light to the world![156]

or again:

> Who would have thought that we would be recognised
>
> as an honourable race
>
> by the nations which surpassed us?[157]

Sung and listened to in the utmost solemnity, the hymns effectively communicate deep, collective convictions:

> Today, joy knows no bounds,
>
> Who could have imagined that Father God would remember the Blacks?
>
> Yet today, Father God has brought us back into His heart,
>
> Be exalted, God, our God![158]

Against the background of colonial oppression and suffering, the benefits of God's 'remembering the Blacks' are understood not only in spiritual terms (forgiveness, healing, etc.) but also in social status and even material blessings:

> Let me praise Tata Kimbangu for the great work he has done
>
> for me; he has made me into a 'somebody' (lit. a great

person); I am able to sit alongside the great. (see Appendix
V, B 3 ii)

As for riches and prosperity, Kimbanguist hymns reveal the same diversity of opinion on the subject that is to be found in the rest of Christendom. Some hymns look upon wealth as an evil obstacle hindering the Christian on the heavenward journey:

Abandon the riches (kimvwama) of this world, that you
might be holy on the day of judgment,[159]

or again,

Woe to those who acquire riches on earth! You will not find
a place in heaven.[160]

Others, however, see rescue from poverty into wealth as part of what the prophet has accomplished for his followers:

He who gives life has come, let us love one another; he has
brought us all that we desire... Tata Simon has come, let us
love one another; he has brought us riches (kimvwama), we
shall not be afflicted eternally. Tata Simon has come![161]

In a sermon at one of the big central Sunday services, the preacher asked the rhetorical question

If today we can see a young Zairian girl driving a big
Mercedes limousine, isn't this astonishing? Who has done
this for us? Is it not Kimbangu?[162]

However, of far greater importance than material possessions is political independence and freedom and racial equality and rehabilitation. The fact of the near coincidence of the official recogniton of the EJCSK with the termination of the colonial rule and the gaining of national independence is not lost on the Kimbanguist. Significantly, the important speech given by the 'Directeur de Cabinet', Bena-Silu, on the occasion of the dedication of the enormous church at Nkamba-Jerusalem in 1981 was entitled 'Simon Kimbangu libère et réhabilite la race noire'. It was published as a duplicated document and is often quoted in Kimbanguist literature.[163] In it Bena-Silu views the special contribution of the Prophet in terms of liberation and revelation of the Black:

Kimbangu's desire and struggle was that over the entire surface of the globe the Negro should be recognised as a full member of the human family and no longer as a human sub-species... It led the Negro to recognise his own values and above all to struggle resolutely to liberate himself from the slavery in which the Whiteman holds him... Kimbangu was condemned to death so that the world might also have black political leaders, black ministers, black governors, black scientists. His prophecy that 'the White will become the Black and the Black will become the White' has become a reality.[164]

Statements like these would have been taken by the colonial régime in the nervous pre-independence era as substantiating evidence in their accusations that Kimbanguism was subversive and xenophobic. However, several hymns insist that (whatever God for His part was choosing to bring about) the duty of the Kimbanguist was to love and bless their oppressors. A hymn which Heintze-Flad dates '1960 or before' alludes to the taking of Jericho by God's ancient people of promise and exhorts the Kimbanguist:

Surround the city today for the first time,
Do not lay a hand on anything;
By marching and by the sound of the trumpet,
Leave room for God to act,
By flutes and by accordions, but not
by the sword which spills blood.
... one day it will come about.[165]

The recurring theme of vindication and rehabilitation of the Black continues to the present day to be a powerful element in the overall Kimbanguist perception of the Kimbangu event in history. With the role of the Prophet and of his church widening to embrace land and conditions beyond the confines of the BaKongo and Zaïre, it is believed that his message is for all the downtrodden whatever their country and whatever their colour. For, as in the Old Testament, God's election privileges are designed not to breed complacency but responsibility towards others. The year 1987 marked the official centenary of the birth of the Prophet and significantly the theme chosen for the celebrations was 'Libération de l'homme opprimé' a theme which will assist international acceptance of Kimbanguism, providing, as it does an echo to the liberation theology which once was particularly associated with Latin America, but which increasingly (not least through the publications and activities of the WCC) has been internationalized.

And yet, alongside the ecstasy and triumph is the pain. For the prophet was arrested, tried and sentenced to death and those who identify with him share his rejection. Suffering (Lingala and Kikongo: 'mpasi') is a major theme in the hymns, Kimbangu's own hardships the pattern and inspiration of those of his followers: 'The apostle of Jesus was whipped, chained, harmed, carried off... soldiers, hold fast, do not weaken'.[166] The early Kimbanguists, deported up-river to be separated for decades from their own tribe and language[167] were suffering not for crimes of theft, robbery or insurrection, but for faithfulness to God and his prophet:

For having preached the name of Christ, they were taken afar,
  exiled far from their country, put in chains,
For no other crime than having proclaimed the name of God,
  put to death for no other crime than believing in Christ...[168]

Is it not the message of Jesus that we believed?
  and the world has set about persecuting us.
Haven't we received our white masters and the world is oppressing us?
  We have loved our white masters and we have become martyrs.[169]

Some of the early (1920s) hymns are moving in their pathos as calamity follows calamity and hope is all but gone:

We suffer deeply here at our place; we become ill, our tears flow,

Come to our aid, Holy Spirit, come, come, come to help us!
Famine is raging amongst us; do not lead us into temptation!

Come to our aid; there are many conflicts in our
country.[170]

The Whites are not imprisoned;
the enemy has taken away our staff (Kikongo:
'mvwala'=Kimbangu?)
All suffering comes upon us;
we are ill, tears are flowing... [171]

Illness, famine but above all persecution and deportation. Asch
estimates that some 3,200 Kimbanguists were deported,[172] but
agrees that, in addition to the men themselves, perhaps ten times the
number of family members were directly affected by these measures,
bringing the figure quite close to the official Kimbanguist number of
37,000.[173]

Many of the hymns are a response to the trials that surrounded them
in those days of bitterness. If one reaction was anger and hatred
towards their persecutors, there is little if any evidence of it in their
hymns. It can be argued that it would have been in their own interest
to eliminate any such hymns as they would be incriminatory evidence.
It can also be argued that anger does not normally express itself in
song but in violent action. The reports of the colonial administration
would, however, tend to support the view that the Kimbanguists
reacted to their hardships in a Christian way and were notable for their
industry and obedience.[174] Their chief recourse was to prayer: *'Even
if suffering comes upon us, let us pray hard to God'*,[175] or again, *'When
a conflict arrives, we resist through our prayers.'*[176] Well over half the
hymns in Category A (Godward) are hymns of petition, pleading
primarily for strength to persevere. A clear source of strength was the
knowledge that Jesus himself shared in their suffering. The empathetic shared-experience of Kimbangu again made Christ's sympathy
seem more real:

All our catechists have been deported because of the name
of Jesus;

   We shall do everything we can so that they will let us
continue.

Jesus, come, help us; when we have to go to the Haut-Congo
(exile) —

   Jesus, you were the first to go. We follow you.[177]

Over one third (37%) of all the hymns under analysis are of the
Category B (mutual) exhortation type. And of the many means of
exhortation, calls to perseverance and steadfastness in trial constitute the major one.

   It is impossible to determine from the collections what the contemporary perception of 'suffering' (mpasi) has become. The Kimbanguist
Church has moved beyond the years of 'clandestinité' and persecution, into the phase of acceptability and even respectability. Indeed, to
some extent the Kimbanguists and the Catholics have exchanged
roles, with the Kimbanguists aligning themselves with the Mobuto
régime,[178] while the Catholics (especially during the 1970s) sounded
the voice of protest against some of the practices of the administration.
The Kimbanguists still sing the old hymns about suffering and new
hymns on the same theme keep appearing. A hymn dating from as
recently as 1983 urges God to intervene as the sufferings of the time
of the Prophet continue down to the present day and persecution by
the 'enemy' is unabated. But despite what the hymn claims, times
have changed for the Kimbanguist and there has occurred a perceptual shift within the familiar Kimbanguist vocabulary of suffering.
While the characteristic vocabulary of 'mpasi' (and its associated
cluster of synonyms) continues to constitute a part of Kimbanguist
hymnology, the perceived meaning of the terms adds to the 'fossilized'
historical meanings more dynamic ones of the present day.

   These latter meanings of 'mpasi' are made more explicit in other, less
poetic, statements such as sermons and prayers and, of course, in
conversations. From these, a picture emerges of 'mpasi' which relates
less to persecution and more to such realities as: the harsh economic

conditions that make life in modern-day Zaïre a daily struggle for survival; the seemingly universal presence of illness,[179] together with its associated tragedies of death and bereavement; and the insidious temptation to moral and social sins. The term 'mpasi' is elastic enough to accommodate without strain all these contemporary dimensions of suffering and this illustrates once more the flexibility of symbolic language and why hymns provide such a resilient means of expressing belief.

3 Hope realized and deferred (eschatology)

Kimbanguism shares with the rest of Christianity the tension between the 'already' and the 'not yet' which results from the Christ event. The Kingdom is already to hand, yet its final 'dénouement' is yet to be. As has already been suggested, the Christ-event in Kimbanguist perception has been re-enacted in Zaïre in the person of the Prophet Kimbangu and there results a sort of double eschatology in which the one overprints the other, but with a slight shift.

Christian hymns through the centuries have found one of their richest themes in the eschatological vision. Kimbanguist hymns likewise are full of imagery and symbols of the last days. The glorious return of Christ is imminent and because Kimbangu's mission was parallel to Christ's, Kimbanguists expect that their Prophet will return with Christ.

Let us get ready to receive the Saviour; He is on the way,

Let us get ready to receive the Saviour; our Prophet arrives.[180]

or again,

You who persist in pleasures, earthly pleasures are fleeting

Do you know the day of Jesus' return? The world will be judged.

Do you know the day of Tata Simon's return? The dead will rise.[181]

Jesus goes before us to prepare a place in the City of Glory,

Friend, get ready to follow the Saviour.

The promised Jerusalem is open, Jesus and His Prophet arrive.[182]

As befits the subject, apocalyptic language features prominently, although many categories of biblical apocalyptic imagery in Revelation are absent (e.g. dragon, adulterous woman, Babylon, plagues, etc.) In company with several other independent African churches,[183] it is the image of the celestial city which is preferred. References abound to the 'Yelusalemi' (Jerusalem), 'mbanza mpa' (new city), 'mbanza zulu' (heavenly city), 'mbanza velela' (holy city) and 'mbanza ya nkembo' (city of glory). As in the case of Christ/Kimbangu, so in the case of the New Jerusalem there is a double dimension. The future heavenly state is 'brought near' temporarily and geographically. The birthplace of the prophet, Nkamba in Bas-Zaïre, is the 'locus terrestri' of the heavenly city. Already in 1962, Masson was writing;

> 'la cité do Seigneur commence, il faut le croire, quelque part
> vers l'embouchure du fleuve Congo,'[184]

but the mystique around Nkamba can be traced back to very early days. As early as April 4th 1922, (scarcely one year after the start of Kimbangu's brief public ministry) the minutes of the colonial District Council for Bas-Congo read:

> At the end of 1922 the natives, including some from French
> Congo, start coming again to Kamba which they call Mbanza
> Jerusalem. They go to pray before the hut of Simon Kim-
> bangu. Thomas Nzoafunda tells them that Simon Kimbangu
> will soon return and that the Whites will no longer come to
> Nkamba because God has blocked their way.[185]

It was as Nsambu came in sight of Nkamba in 1956 that he 'received' his first hymn 'The New Jerusalem is ready' (see above p 160). With its mausoleum (Kimbangu's remains were brought from Shaba to Nkamba in March 1960) and its pool of holy water, Nkamba is the 'holy place "par excellence" for all Kimbanguists... a sort of Mecca'.[186] Thrice-yearly communion services are held there ever since April 6th, 1971, when the first Kimbanguist communion was held, attended by a crowd said to number 350,000.[187] In 1981, to mark the 60th anniversary of Kimbangu's ministry, the huge church was officially opened at

Nkamba, reckoned to be the largest of its kind in Africa and claimed to have a seating capacity of 37,000 (symbolic numerically of those who were deported during the long years of 'clandestinité'). A collection of appropriate hymns was made for the occasion, entitled: 'Nkunga mia programme ya ngiendolo ya ku Yelusalemi' (hymns for the programme of the journey to Jerusalem).

Nkamba expresses for the Kimbanguist heaven on earth. It epitomizes the realized eschatological Kingdom. Of Nkamba the Kimbanguist would say what the Eastern Orthodox would say of the ikons that fill his churches, that it is a point of meeting between heaven and earth.[188] Heintze-Flad agrees by saying of Nkamba:

> It is, so to speak, the meeting place between the Church Millitant here below and the Church Triumphant in heaven',[189]

and just as 'nothing impure will ever inter in' (Rev. 21:27) so those who go to Nkamba on pilgrimage must be prepared to abandon the sins that cling to them:

> In the Holy City... in the presence of the Lord Jesus,
> Leave behind your sins... the Lord is calling you.
> Friends, come on... Let us go to see the glory,
> Leave behind your sins... Yes, the door is open!
> In the Holy City... in the presence of Mama Mwilu!
> She is holy... She is calling you.
> In the Holy City... in the presence of Tata Simon!
> He is holy... He is calling you.
> In the Holy City... in the presence of the three Guides (mvwala)
> They are holy... they are calling you.[190]

Kimbanguists would give differing answers if they were asked whether the hymns which speak of the New Jerusalem are to be understood as referring to Nkamba or to heaven. The question attempts to force from the symbol a distinction it cannot readily accept or provide, as Masson notes:

Here the spiritual dimension and the material dimension,
the eternal dimension and the temporal dimension meet
and mix, as in almost all milleniarisms.[191]

Eschatological aspirations concern the present and the future. Chief among these is the prayer for and hope of purity or holiness. The New Jerusalem is holy itself and destined for the pure, as two of Nsambu's hymns reveal:

Pure City, Holy City, Pure City, Holy City,
The New City is ready,
Lord prepare me so that I arrive;
There I will shine with purity.[192]

Wash me, wash me
May I be purified, my God,
Wash me so that I am clean,
So that in you I can praise the Saviour.

Keep me, Keep me,
Bring me to the holy country
Prepared by our Father,
So that in You I can praise the Saviour.[193]

The purity which characterizes the New Jerusalem and its citizens is God's to give, yet the Kimbanguist can here and now have assurance of this eternal destiny and can have his name 'written in the book' by responding believingly to God's action through His Prophet and by expressing that response by obeying God's commands and by openly belonging to the community which Christ has set up through Simon Kimbangu and which is now led by the 'Chef Spirituel' and his brothers:

I will shake the whole world. Friend, where will you be?
I will reveal heavenly things, I will come for the holy ones,
That they may rejoice in glory.

I will show my glory to your persecutors. Friend, what will

you get?

Let us be obedient towards the 'Mvwala' (the three sons)
and the preachers.'[194]

Great emphasis is laid on conformity to God's commands. Since an
official communiqué in 1985 at least, the Ten Commandments must
be read at a given point during the mid-week and the Sunday services,
Article 10 of the document declaring the Ten Commandments given by
God to Moses are still binding. One of the large banners carried by the
'Bolingo ya '56' choir in their march-past bears the inscription in
Lingala: 'Whoever keeps the whole law yet stumbles at just one point
is guilty of breaking it all' (James 2:10).'[195]

Another eschatological expectation is that Kimbanguism will be the
means of bringing to an end the scandalous divisions of Christianity.
Several Kimbanguists in conversations enquired about differences
between Catholics and Protestants and expressed disapproval about
the dozens of denominations or 'Communautés' in the Zaïrian Protestant Church. They spoke of the EJCSK as being not only free of such
divisions itself,[196] but also uniquely placed to bring to an end the
divisions of others. A hymn in French, sung in majestic slowness as
if heavy with portent, declares:

We are approaching the fulfilment;

We are approaching the reality;

We will be led... by one Lord,

We will be gathered... into one Church,

We will speak... one language.[197]

The EJCSK does not perceive itself as having added yet one more to
the already large number of Christian confessions, but rather as being
the divinely chosen means of bringing harmony and peace ('kimia') to
religious confusion and rivalry.

The Kimbanguist vision has, undoubtedly, its future dimension, but
to a far greater extent than other, 'mainline', churches its eschatology
is realized. The days of promise have come; the Holy City has
descended. In language reminiscent of Jesus' words to His disciples
in Matthew 13:16-17, one hymn proclaims:

This blessing promised to me by the Lord
    should have been experienced by the prophets of old;
This news proclaimed to me by the Lord
    should have been received by kings of former times.

Your eyes are blessed
    which see the time promised by the Lord.
Have you believed? Or are you still unbelieving?
    everything will be fulfilled at this time.[198]

For the Kimbanguist, the last days, even if they have not reached their final apocalyptic climax, have certainly come.

Conclusion

While the EJCSK lives, worships and works primarily in the oral dimensions, as it has from the beginning, its increasing exposure to the world of literary expression comes both from within and from without. There is, within the Kimbanguist Church itself, a determination to articulate its potential contribution to the worldwide Christian Church. Its leadership is becoming increasingly travelled,[199] both attending conferences in other parts of the world and hosting important gatherings in Kinshasa. Its list of books and articles for international readership is growing. The numbers of dissertations and theses produced at the Kimbanguist Faculty of Theology steadily mounts. Meanwhile, from outside, an increasing number of academic research articles focus international attention upon one or other area of Kimbanguist thought and life.

Whether the resultant imposition of literary analytical precision will influence certain areas of plurality which at present are happily accommodated by the flexibility of orality, remains to be seen. It may be that interpenetration of the two will be kept at a minimum by the language factor, with orality expressing itself primarily in Kikongo and Lingala, while French and English remain the languages of literary thought. What seems clear is that the reality of majority beliefs and behaviour is expressed more truly in the oral than in the literary domain.

References

1. W. A. Graham, in Richard C. Martin (ed.), *Approaches to Islam in Religious Studies,* University of Arizona Press, 1985, quoted in the section on 'The Quran as spoken word : an Islamic contribution to the understanding of Scripture', p. 27. I owe this quotation to Fuad Nahdi, in a paper presented to SOAS MA Seminar, London, 26th November, 1985.

2. According to W. J. Ong, of the some 3000 languages currently spoken in the world only 78 have a literature. W. J. Ong, *Orality and Literacy: the technologizing of the word,* Methuen, London and New York, 1982, p. 7.

3. Ong points out that technological advances have, in radio and television, brought about an age of 'second orality' in the literate world. W. J. Ong, op. cit. p. 3.

4. J. Mbiti, 'The Biblical basis in present trends of African theology', in *Bulletin de Théologie Africaine,* Vol. 1, No. 1, 1979, p. 12.

5. S. Asch, *L'Eglise du Prophète Kimbangu; ses origines, à son rôle actuel au Zaïre,* Editions Karthala, Paris, 1983, p. 9 and 326.

6. Diangienda Kuntima, *L'Histoire du Kimbanguisme,* Editions Kimbanguistes, Kinshasa, 1984, p. 9.

7. ibid, p.9.

8. S. Asch, op. cit., Annex 5, pp. 327ff.

9. ibid, Fig. 4, p. 331. It is not clear from the figure at what point

Asch places the dividing line between the 'lettrés' and 'intellectu-els', I have taken it to be between primary and secondary school.

10. eg. Diangienda K, op. cit, Bena-Silu, *Simon Kimbangu libère et réhabilite la race noire,* Editions Kimbanguistes, Kinshasa, 1981; Luntadila, L., *Kimbanguisme, un rayon d'espoir,* Editions CEDI, Kinshasa 1974.

11. cf. Bena-Silu, op. cit. p. 26-27.

12. Diangienda, op. cit. p. 17. states that Kimbangu was born on September 12th, 1887. This is now the officially accepted birth date within the Kimbanguist Church and the centenary cele-brated in 1987 has served to establish it further. However, the alternative date of September 24th, 1889 is to be found in Luntadila *Libération et développement du kimbanguisme, 1921-1960,* Kinshasa, 1971, p. 12 and G. Balandier, *Sociologie actuelle de l'Afrique noire,* P.U.F., Paris, 1955. Cf. W. Ostorf, *Africanische Initiative: das aktive Leiden des Propheten Simon Kimbangu,* Her-bert Lang, Bern and Frankfurt, 1975. Ustorf includes a 30-page chronological summary of Kimbanguist origins, tabulating sources; he cites the Sept, 1889 date of Kimbangu's birth on p.105. Photo posters picturing the Prophet as the founder of the EJCSK are still to be seen with the dates: 1889-1951. Several earlier 'Faculté de Théologie Kimbanguiste' theses and disserta-tions, presumably following Luntadila, have the 1889 date, eg. Nzinga Mansoni 'La vocation du Prophète Simon Kimbangu, à la lumière de la Bible et de l'histoire.' FTK, 1977, p. 28.

13. The details of Kimbangu's training and early ministry are subject to differing opinions. Diangienda writes that Kimbangu was appointed catechist and quotes in his support the Catholic Van Wing, Diangienda, op. cit. p. 18. Others, eg. J. M. Tombu, insist that Kimbangu was disappointed never to have been made a catechist: Diangienda, op. cit. p. 18, n. 14.

14. D. J. McKay, 'Simon Kimbangu and the BMS tradition', in *Journal of Religion in Africa,* Vol. 17, No. 2, 1987, p. 124. Cf. also McKay's 'The once and future Kingdom. Kongo models of renewal in the

church at Ngombe Lutete and in the Kimbanguist Movement',
PhD. Aberdeen, 1986.

15. S. Asch, op. cit. p. 19.

16. ibid, p. 19. The significance of this does not escape Kimbanguist
writers either. cf. Nzinga Mansoni, op. cit. p. 27: 'Les missionnaires ne guérissaient plus les malades... '

17. Diangienda, op. cit. p. 22.

18. S. Asch, op. cit. p. 21; but cf. also the question asked of
Kimbangu at his trial (September, 1921) by De Rossi: 'Lors de
votre séjour aux Huileries du Congo belge, vous étiez en contact,
selon des renseignements en ma possession, avec des groupes
subversifs noirs américains, notament avec Garvey. Qu'en dites-
vous?' in Diangienda, op. cit. p. 98. Kimbangu categorically
denied the charge.

19. Detailed accounts of this incident are given in P. Raymaekers,
*Histoire de Simon Kimbangu, Prophète, d'après les écrivains
Nfinangani et Nzungo, 1921.* BOPR, (Kinshasa, 1971), purport-
edly recounted by Kimbangu himself, pp. 27-28; and Diangienda, op. cit. pp. 29-30. W. Ustorf, op. cit., p. 110, demonstrates
that an early tradition which dates this incident between March
13-18, 1921, is substantially corroborated by the few available
references in contemporary missionary reports.

20. Since 1971, April 6th is marked by the celebration of Holy
Communion (Eucharist). The other two dates for Communion are
October 12th (death of Kimbangu) and December 25th (Christ-
mas).

21. Contemporary administrational despatches include:
Les plantations et élevages de Kitobola connaissent des
désertions en masse: 150 travailleurs sur 200 ont quitté
le travail.*Lettre 360 du 30.5.1921 de A. T. Thysville*
and
Plus de la moitié de la population de son territoire est allé
voir le prophète de Nkamba. Actuellement c'est le tour des
indigènes du Congo français. Tous y portent leurs grands
malades. *Lettre 113 du 31.5.1921*, A.T. Luozi.
Both quotations from R.M. Mithridate: *Histoire de l'Apparition de*

206

Simon Kimbangu. Tome I, Kinshasa, Editions Notre Kongo Dieto R.D.C., stencilled, undated.

22. For excerpts of colonial reports expressing fears, see Asch, op. cit. p. 22.

23. Diangienda, op. cit. pp. 18 and 66 n. 30.

24 ibid, pp. 56-57. The Jesuit press was often scathing:
Ce prétendu prophète noir... cet agitateur révolutonnaire, qui expie maintenant ses méfaits par la prison à perpétuité.
Missions Belge de la Compagnie de Jésus, Vol. 25, 1923, p. 50.

25. Diangienda, op. cit. pp. 43-47. The more sympathetic attitude of most Protestant missionaries towards the emergent Kimbanguist movement was seen by some Catholics to be but further evidence of Protestant doctrinal disarray:
Auprès des missionnaires catholiques la doctrine de Kimbangu ne pouvait trouver de sympathie, elle s'opposait si grossièrement à l'oeuvre et au travail apostoliques de ses prêtres que dès le début elle rencontra chez eux une opposition intransigeante et acharnée... Du côté protestant, la situation fut tout autre. Ce mouvement religieux qui prenait une si grande importance pourrait peut-être se répandre pour le bien de leur religion. Le protestantisme, par son principe même admettait des interprétations laxistes, des compromis plus ou moins réguliers, et permettait par quelques concessions habiles de capter et de diriger la source nouvelle de ferveur religieuse...
Missions Belges de le Compagnie de Jésus, op. cit. p. 52.

26. J. Chomé, *La passion de Simon Kimbangu*, Présence Africaine, Brussels, 1959.

27. Diangienda, op. cit. p.104ff.

28. The secret 'kidouma' alphabet is given in S. Asch, op. cit. p. 36.

29. The Kimbanguists no doubt resented not only Mpadi's paganistic tendencies, but also his rivalistic religious and political pretensions, of which one African author wrote:
Mpadi prit conscience du rôle qu'il était appelé à jouer: diriger 'L' Eglise des Noirs' et libérer les Congolais du joug

colonial. Au cours d'une très grande assemblée tenue dans le territoire de Madimba, Simon-Pierre Mpadi fut désigné à l'unanimité comme le 'Messie Noir', successeur digne et légitime du Prophète Kimbangu alors incarcéré à la prison d'Elizabethville.'
Mbasani Mbami, *L'implantation de l'Armée du Salut au Congo Belge et au Congo Français*, Kinshasa, undated, pp. 8ff.

30. According to M-L. Martin, Kimbangu saw his youngest son during his prison years and appointed him as the spiritual leader, with his two brothers intimately assisting him. (Conversation with M-L. Martin at Lutendele, 21st Feb, 1987) .

31. The historicity of the event at the Baudouin Stadium is questioned by F. Bontinck on the grounds that the Stadium belonged to the Catholics and its use was carefully controlled. It would have been inconceivable for permission to have been granted for a potentially violent incident involving Kimbanguists. (Conversation with F. Bontinck, 2nd Feb, 1987, Scholasticat P. Kongolo, Kinshasa).

32. C'est à partir du moment où l'EJCSK, sous la direction de Joseph Diangienda, s'engage dans des négociations avec l'administration coloniale en vue d'obtenir un statut légal, qui mettrait un terme aux persécutions "pour cause de kimbanguisme" que le contenu idéologique du kimbanguisme officiel est fortement modifié.
S. Asch, op. cit. p. 129.

33. Face à l'administration coloniale, l'EJCSK s'est déclarée apolitique, ce qui lui a permis d'obtenir sa reconnaissance officielle. L'EJCSK a, par la suite, obtenu son admission au COE au prix d'un réformisme favorable au protestantisme international. Enfin, le conservatisme de sa politique vis-à-vis de l'Etat mobutiste a rendu possible l'obtention d'un rang de troisième force religieuse parmi les institution nationales officielles.
S. Asch, 'Contradictions internes d'une institution religieuse', In *Archives de Sciences Sociales des Religions*, No. 52 26 (1) (1981), p. 103.

34. Bena-Silu reported a long session with Asch at Bongolo when she revisited Kinshasa, during which he systematically refuted various details of her book. He also produced a 55-page mimeographed critique of Asch's book, 'A propos de "L'Eglise du Prophète Kimbangu" de Susan Asch, Editions Karthala, 1984. Illustration de falsification de l'histoire et des préjugés', (Direction internationale de l'Eglise Kimbanguiste, Kinshasa, 1984). He personally delivered or sent it to libraries in Europe which had received Asche's book. The critique quotes and refutes 150 of Asch's 'affirmations'. (Conversation with Bena-Silu, 26th Feb, 1987, Bongolo).

35. All three of these documents were originally issued separately, but have been included together in Diangienda's *Histoire*, op. cit. pp. 254-307.

36. W. J. Hollenweger, 'The 'What' and the 'How': Content and communication of the one message', in *Expository Times*, Vol. 86, No. 12, Sept. 1975, p. 357.

37. A Droogers, 'Kimbanguism at the grass roots; beliefs in a local Kimbanguist Church', in *Journal of Religion in Africa*, Vol. II, No. 3, 1980, pp. 188-211. Although his field research concerned the situation in Kisangani back in the 1960s and 1970s, it could equally describe the present popular religious situation of Kimbanguism in Kinshasa.

38. eg. J. Dubois and A. Gourbin, A propos de 'L'essence de la théologie kimbanguiste' in *Telema*, 3:19, (1979) p. 50.
W. Beguin and M-L. Martin, 'Study report on the EJCSK, its present situation and its ecumenical relations', unpublished, 1968.
P. Raymaekers, in *Zaïre*, 13:7, (1959) pp. 675-756.
W. Heintze-Flad, *L'Eglise kimbanguiste, une église qui chante et que prie*, Interuniversitair Instituut voor Missiologie en Oecumenica, (Leiden, 1978), p. 2 and passim.
Biblical scholars have long insisted that the New Testament writers incorporated portions of early Christian hymns, for example: John 1:1-18, Phil. 2: 6-11 and Col. 1: 15-20. Von Allmen makes much of these hymns to argue that poets contributed to the shaping of Christian belief in the early Church before the

theologians. D. Von Allmen, 'Pour une théologie grècque?' in *Flambeau*, February, 1970, No. 25, pp. 2-34. The article has had several important reprints and stimulated much debate.

39. The story can be found for instance in Nsambu T., 'Exposé sur le mobile des chants kimbanguistes' stencilled document, dated: 6.10.1981, Kinshasa.

40. In 1948, Mama Mikala Mandombe, one of the Kimbangu's contemporaries, received a hymn while she was in internal exile at Lowa. Mama Mikala, now very aged, is held in high esteem by the Kimbanguists.

41. Pastor Nsambu Twasilwa (formerly Nsambu André), the current Director of the 'Bureau des Chants Kimbanguistes' in Kinshasa, was born in 1926 near Mbanza-Ngungu in Bas Zaire.

42. Nsambu T, typed autobiographical notes, handed to the author, Kinshasa, February 1987, p. 2.

43. Figure from statistics sheet, 'Bureau des Chants Kimbanguists', Kinshasa, 27.3. 1987.

44. When asked about the widespread belief that missionaries deliberately withheld from the Africans part of God's truth and power, Pastor Nsambu quoted as proof hymn 748 in *Minkungu mia Kintwadi* (Uppsala, 1947): *'The half has not been told'*, a devotional hymn well-known in some Protestant circles in the West, referring to the unimaginable delights of Heaven, but understood by some Africans to be an unguarded admission by missionaries of their duplicity.

45. Independent confirmation of this came in a letter from Rev. A. S. Cox (1st Jan. 1987):
    It was some time between the years 1954-57 while I was serving with the BMS at Kimpese in the Lower Congo that the Rev H. Casebow of Ngombe Lutete arranged for Lucien Fwasi to come for a few days to Kimpese in order that I might transcribe some of his hymn-tunes, with a view to putting some of them into the new edition of the hymn-book *Nkunga Mia Kintwadi*. Fwasi was introduced to the

student population in an assembly in the Church and he spent a most enjoyable time singing and teaching his hymns. Thirteen of his hymns found their way into the hymn-book... There are two unusual moments in these hymns

a) In No. 9 there are words which are intended to be said in between two sung verses. The meaning is a little obscure and seems to point to a 'special revelation' to the composer. I remember Fwasi repeating these words very clearly.

(Cox gives a translation of the words to be spoken:

'That night I was in the holy place of God; I saw the Saviour. He showed me the first miracle; he came to me in the time of coming near, he came to me to save me from evil.' K.G.M.).

b) After the third line of the refrain of No. 27 Fwasi insisted on three beats of complete silence — 'to drive home the meaning of the words',he said.

In a PS, Cox added in his letter:

I have a note from Rev. Casebow against (one hymn) saying that the words could be used in an anti-white crusade, so he advised against using it 'at this juncture'.

46. There exist at the 'Bureau' no fewer than 10 of these reel-to-reel tapes, recorded by Fwasi on both sides. For each of the many hymns, Fwasi sings the four parts one after the other, with apparently no hesitation or uncertainty.

47. Biographical details recounted by Pastor Nsambu and by Pastor Mfoko Ndombala, Fwasi's nephew. Conversations at Bongolo, Kinshasa, 13th Feb, 1987. There are several photos of Fwasi in the 'Bureau', one or two of them taken towards the end of his life, showing Fwasi as an emaciated and obviously terminally ill man.

48. Since 1972 retreats have been a feature of the EJCSK and not only in Kinshasa. The retreats last typically about four days, for much of which fasting will be practised. The time is taken up with personal and group prayer, public confession of sin, Bible study and meditation. The retreats are definitely not recreational but rather concentrated spiritual exercise for those who are serious about their spirituality. Cit Nziama (translation assistant for the

Kimbanguist hymns) confided that he had been on one retreat but had found it almost too demanding and probably would not go on one again. (Conversation, Bongolo, Kinshasa, Feb, 1987).

49. Conversation with Cit Mabika Masala, Bongolo, Kinshasa, 13th Feb, 1987.

50. Conversation with Cit Ndungidi Mfumu a Tezo, Kinshasa, 13th Feb, 1987.

51. Conversation with Cit Nsinsani, 'Chef de Protocole', Kinshasa, 17th Feb, 1987.

52. Wono Kwemba Tshihuisa, 'La théologie kimbanguiste dans les chants captés en 1921', Mémoire de fin d'études, Faculté de Théologie Kimbanguiste, Lutendele, Kinshasa, 1982, p. 9. The 'theological themes' selected for treatment by Wono are: victory, liberation, kingdom and love.

53. Tshibola Dibeya Mudiulay, 'Esquisse d'une théologie kimbanguiste autour des cantiques captés entre 1956 et 1960', Mémoire de fin d'études, Faculté de Théologie Kimbanguiste, Lutendele, Kinshasa, 1982, p. 13ff. While providing a little new information, neither this dessertation nor that of Wono (see note 52) were as useful as their titles might suggest. It is beyond the scope of this chapter (and the competence of the author) to comment much on the musical aspects of Kimbanguist hymns. The most striking feature of the hymns is that they seldom share the pronounced rhythm of 'typically African' music. Body-swaying or foot-tapping, even during the liveliest of songs, was conspicuous by its absence. Commenting on Fwasi's hymns, missionary-musicologist A. S. Cox states:

>(His) melodies have not very much of the African folk-tune about them. They are nearer to negro-spirituals. The most typically African characteristic is the use of solo and response (also found in negro spirituals). There are very occasionally little twists of rhythm which are nearer to jazz. Otherwise, many of the tunes would not be out of place in a book of European or American 'spiritual songs' They are not completely pentatonic, but there is certainly no trace of modulation or chromaticism.

(Letter from A. S. Cox 1st Jan, 1987). Another characteristic of present-day Kimbanguist hymn-singing is the whole-hearted adoption of unaccompanied, well-executed, four-part rendition (soprano, alto, baritone, bass) which gives Kimbanguist singing a recognisable (but again rather 'unafrican') style. In a circular letter to all choirs in 1981, Nsambu sought to dispel opposition to this standardization by stating:

En égard à l'épanouissement des activités de l'Eglise à travers le monde, nous avons été amenés d'adapter la mélodie répondant aux principes de chanter. Cette adaptation a suscité pas mal de mécontentements (sic) de la part de certains groupes des Dirigeants qui oublient que l'Eglise doit évoluer au lieu de rester au même niveau. Grâce à la compréension et la clairvoyance de Notre Chef Spirituel nous avons pu quand même surmonter ces difficultés et actuellement la situation s'améliore malgré l'opposition de certains irresponsables qui n'ont rien avoir avec les activités de notre Département.

Letter by Nsambu T., 'Directeur Général des Chants', 'Exposé sur le mobile des chants kimbanguistes', 6th Oct, 1981, p. 4, (copy given to author).

54.   Il ne faut pas oublier que ces chants sont "captés" par des chrétiens sans formation particulière, souvent des culti-vateurs, parfois des enfants, qui ne sont pas censés connaître les fondements de la théologie évangélique... Et surtout, ces chants inspirés par le Saint Esprit à nous les Noirs, sont la manifestation éclatante que Jésus-Christ est réellement notre unique Sauveur et Seigneur à nous les Africains par l'intermédiaire du ministère de notre Papa Simon Kimbangu, ouvertement et avec puissance...
Tshibola D. M., op. cit. p.13ff.

55. Kadi Bingana, 'La confession dans l'Eglise kimbanguiste', Mémoire de fin d'études, Faculté de Théologie Kimbanguiste, (1976) p. 46.

56. Examples of rejected hymns include:
a) a 1959 hymn, *Nzambe utuvene nsambu,* rejected on account of its constantly recurring refrain of meaningless gibberish: '*Faria, faria do!*'
b) one from 1973, *Zimpangi zeti banza Kinshasa zulu dio,* which refers to Kinshasa as heaven.

c) a 1985 Christmas hymn, *E mbandu'eyi ku Betelemi*, which reads: 'Let us now go to Bethlehem to adore the new-born Jesus, let us adore the new-born Tata Mfumu a Mbanza (Kiangani), let us adore the new-born Tata Mfumu a Nlongo (Diangienda).'
d) An undated hymn, *Mfumu Yisu mu Kwiza kena*, which reads: 'The Lord Jesus is coming again to proclaim a competition. Ah! an exam! Ah! an exam!. in which the terminology was deemed to be inappropriate.

57. The term is used in Tshibola, op. cit. p.12.

58. The removal of shoes in deference to Exodus 3:5 marks not only choir rehearsals, but all Kimbanguist meetings.

59. Many of the choir groups rehearse in different corners of the 'Centre d'Accueil' where I was staying during my three weeks with EJCSK. The bounds of the 'Centre' are extensive enough (equivalent to perhaps six football pitches) for half a dozen or more choirs to sing out of doors without disturbing each other. I was able to observe their rehearsals 'incognito' from within my rooms, or as I walked around the grounds. Often my presence was apparently unnoticed; it was clear that their manner of rehearsing was not affected by my being at the 'Centre'. Some groups continued rehearsing into the night, before dispersing and returning considerable distances home.

60. Although accurate counting was quite impossible, the number was estimated by counting those in each Sunday's march-past (approx. 2,750) and reckoning that for every one marcher there were perhaps five who did not march. (Central meetings attended on 8th, 15th and 22nd Feb, 1987).

61. Expressive of the increasing centralization and standardization of the EJCSK, the liturgy for both weekday and Sunday services follows the stipulations laid down in a duplicated document in the name of the 'Chef Spirituel', Diangienda: 'Nouvelle disposition relative au programme cultuel pour l'encadrement spirituel des fidèles', Nkamba/Jérusalem, 29th April 1985.

62. The four sermons heard during the month of February, 1987, followed a somewhat similar pattern in which a text was read, briefly commented upon and then expounded so as to find their fulfilment or parallel within the Kimbangu 'event':

1. 8th Feb, 1987 Kimbanseke. Zechariah 3:1-5. Joshua opposed by Satan. Present-day opposition to the 'Chef Spirituel'. Whereas in former days God's power was at work to raise the dead, now it is diminished because of factional strife within the EJCSK. (Exhortation to submit wholeheartedly).

2. 12th Feb, 1987, Matete. (On the occasion of Kisolokele's birthday) Luke 2:1-20. Birth of Jesus in the obscure village of Bethlehem. Just as many had no idea of who Jesus was, so it was on 12th Feb, 1914, when 'Sa Grandeur' Kisolokele was born. Many still do not realise who he is.

3. 15th Feb, 1987, 'Centre d'Accueil'. (Young woman pastor, Director of Retreats. She preached clearly and unselfconsciously.) Genesis 2-3. Adam and Eve were expelled from the presence of God because of their sin. Today many of us are separated from the three "Tatas" (sons of Kimbangu) by our hidden sins. The only solution is to repent and become obedient.

4. 27th Feb, 1987, 'Centre d'Accueil'. Luke 10 (parable of the Good Samaritan). Brief review of the story. We, too, were mistreated, beaten, relegated, left for dead. God sent His Son. He was shamefully treated and returned to Heaven but He did not give up. He sent us the Comforter, Simon Kimbangu, who rescued us.

63. Remark made by a choir leader at the 'nsinsani' 8th Feb, 1987, Kimbanseke.

64. Determined to take part in the 'nsinsani' marching but unused to the system of making multiple small offerings, I had to withdraw as other marchers, observing my embarrassment in having no more to cast in the bucket after the first circuit, started passing their money to me so that I should have something to offer. (22nd Feb, 1987).

65. Major 'nsinsanis' were held at all three of the Sunday services at which I was present and smaller 'nsinsanis' took place at each of the special evening choir receptions in different parts of the town.

66. S. Boka and P. Raymaekers, *250 Chants de l'Eglise de Jésus-Christ sur la Terre par le Prophète Simon Kimbangu*, (EJCSK), I Première Série: 85 chants de Nsambu André. Institut de

Recherches Economiques et Sociales, Université Lovanium, Léopoldville, 1960.

67. W. Heintze-Flad, *L'Eglise kimbanguiste, une église qui chante et
qui prie.* (Les 'chants captés' kimbanguistes, expression authen-
tique de la foi de l'Afrique), Interuniversitair Instituut voor Missiologie en Oecumenica, Leiden, 1978. Pastor Heintze-Flad served
for several years as teacher at the Kimbanguist Faculty of Theology, Lutendele, Kinshasa; his commentary is sympathetic and
non-critical.

68. Field Research methodology. Most of the three weeks of February
7-27th, 1987, were spent in the 'Bureau des Chants Kimbanguistes' at the Bongolo administrational headquarters in Kinshasa,
about 30 minutes walk from the 'Centre d'Accueil'. Pastor
Nsambu Twasilwa, Director of the 'Bureau' gave unstintingly of
his time and assistance. In addition to the help in translation of
hymns given by Cit Nziama, the 'Département des Chants' laid on
a carefully organized programme of evening visits to different parishes in Kimshasa, including Kintambo, Bongolo, Matete, Ngiri-
Ngiri, Lutendele and Kimbanseke. At each of these, local choirs
presented a programme of introductions, speeches and singing.
On several occasions there were opportunities for 'scéances de
travail' (work-shops) in order to learn about the inner workings
of the different parts of the 'Département'. There were also two
'soirées musicales' at the 'Centre d'Accueil', Zone Kasavubu, at
which choirs from all over Kinshasa sang. These activities
afforded opportunities to record, observe, hear and experience
the Kimbanguist sing. Almost inevitably there was someone
present to translate the Kikongo hymns when requested.
Residence in one of the 36 'studios' at the Kimbanguist 'Centre
d'Accueil' permitted daily contact with Kimbanguists who shared
their beliefs and answered questions without any reticence.
Innumerable conversations, mainly in Lingala and French, but
also in Swahili, supplemented the information gleaned from the
hymns, while participation at Sunday and other services set the
hymns in their intended liturgical context. Without the generosity and openness of my Kimbanguist hosts, the field research
would largely have failed.

69. R. Finnegan, *Oral Literature in Africa,* Clarendon Press, (Oxford,
1970), pp. 184-185.

216

70. G. C. Oosthuizen, *The Theology of a South African Messiah*, E. J. Brill, (Leiden/Köln, 1967).

71. eg. on p. 306 of his book *Zulu Zion and Some Swazi Zionists*, Oxford University Press (1976). In his acidic criticism of Oosthuizen, Sundkler seems to have overlooked the fact that he himself had to adjust his own earlier perspective from that of an 'outsider' to that of the Swazis themselves; a shift which he justifies in ch. 9 'An Interpretation', op. cit. pp. 304ff.

72. B. Sundkler, op. cit. p. 186.

73. ibid, p. 190.

74. W. J. Ong, op. cit. ch. 3, *'Some psychodynamics of orality'*, pp. 31ff.

75. ibid, p. 40.

76. ibid, p. 41.

77. ibid, p. 42.

78. ibid, p. 45.

79. Well-loved English hymns are commonly granted a certain poetic licence: for one example among many, Charles Wesley's expression of the Incarnation would go further in the direction of the 'kenosis' than most orthodox theologians would wish, when he writes that Christ *'emptied Himself of all but love...'*

80. At many of the evening visits to choirs referred to in note 68 (above), joyful Christmas hymns were sung, for no other reason than because they captured best a mood of happiness. Seven out of eight hymns sung on the occasion of the birthday of Kisolokele (12th Feb, 1987) were Christmas carols.

81. From the Kikongo hymn: *Nzambi a mpungu totondanga*, Nsambu T., (1957).

82. From the Kikongo hymn: *Amakesa ma ndungidi*, Mukoko J., 1921.

83. From the Kikongo hymn: *Nzambi mvangi a zulu ye ntoto*, Nsambu T., n.d.

84. cf. McKay's PhD thesis, op. cit. which explores the historical and theological background of the Kimbanguist movement.

85. S. Asch, op. cit. pp. 155ff.

86. A. Droogers, op. cit. p. 192.

87. From the Kikongo hymn: *Nsi ya mpa yitusa kubikilua*, Nsambu T., n.d.

88. From the Kikongo hymn: *Nzambi mvangi a zulu ye ntoto*, Nsambu T., n.d.

89. From the Kikongo hymn: *Nsangu za Yisu zimuangane*, Nsambu T., n.d.

90. From the Kikongo hymn: *Butwamana tambula Yisu Mwana Nzambi*, Nsambu T., 1956.

91. From the Kikongo hymn: *Mambu ma Yisu*, Nsambu T., n.d.

92. From the Kikongo hymn: *Lu bantwenia, Iwiza makutakania*, Nsambu T., n.d.

93. From the Kikongo hymn: *Matondo kwa ngeye, Nzambi'ame*, Nsambu T., n.d.

94. From the Kikongo hymn: *O Mfumu watu zola*, Nsambu T., 1956.

95. From the Kikongo hymn: *Zinzila zama zulu zizibuka*, n.d.

96. From the Kikongo hymn: *E ngeye nkundi bu weti landa nkembo*, 1958.

97. From the Kikongo hymn: *Tukubama muna Mvuluzi*, Kunzika P., 1957.

98. From the Kikongo hymn: *Ntumwa Mfumu wafwa vava nza*, Luzolo P., 1957.

99. See note 26, above. It is difficult to know to what extent if any Chome's book has directly influenced Kimbanguist theology. The hymn above (note 98) predates Chome's book. The notion that the sufferings of Kimbangu were 'for us' comes repeatedly in hymns. In conversation, one Kimbanguist distinguished, however, between the atoning sufferings of Christ for sins and the liberating sufferings of Kimbangu.

100. Conversation with F. Bontinck, Kinshasa, 2nd Feb, 1987 and with Professor J. Stengers, London, 27th April, 1987.

101. Diangienda, op. cit. 11. n.1.

102. From the Kikongo hymn: *Kembela! Tukembela*, Nsambu T., 1957.

103. W. MacGaffey, *Modern Kongo Prophets*, Indiana University Press, (1983), p. 140.

104. From the Kikongo hymn: *O Ngunz'a Nzambi ifulukidingi*, Luzolo P., 1957.

105. In his Dip.Th. dissertation, Mfinda Luhunakio lists five Old Testament categories of intercessors (patriarchs, kings, prophets, priests, and angels) and five New Testament categories (Christ, the Holy Spirit, apostles, Christians and saints (sic)). It is the category of 'saint' which particularly interests Mfinda, who finds a parallel between the Roman Catholic doctrine of the mediation of the saints and the Kimbanguist/Bantu conception of the ancestors. Using Bénézet Bujo's article 'Nos ancêtres, ces saints inconnus' (BTA, I: 2 (1979) 105-179) in his support, Mfinda argues that those ancestors particularly who were heroic and virtuous and who were 'in Christ' and remain close to Him, are our intercessors before Christ. 'La théologie de l'intercession dans l'Eglise kimbanguiste', Mémoire de fin d'études, Faculté de Théologie Kimbanguiste, Kinshasa, 1982. cf. Conversation with a choir member, Kinshasa, 11th Feb, 1987:

    If I need forgiveness I will of course go to Christ who suffered for my sins. But I will go *through the Prophet Simon Kimbangu*. It is true that Christ suffered so that we could come direct to God, but (gesturing towards the impressive, walled 'Résidence' within the 'Centre d'Accueil')

I can't just march straight in there with my problem. I must explain my problem to the guard at the gate, who would make sure it reached the important person inside the 'Résidence'.

106. Dialungana Kiangani, *Biuvu ye Mvutu.* (Catechism in Kikongo, Lingala and French), 31 juillet, 1970, Nkamba-Jérusalem, 22: De quel contemporain est Papa Simon Kimbangu? Papa Kimbangu a existé avec Dieu dès le commencement. (Jean 1: 1-2)"
(Question: Whose contemporary is Papa Simon Kimbangu? Answer: Papa Kimbangu existed with God from the beginning.)

107. G. C. Oosthuizen, op. cit. 56.

108. Diangienda, op. cit. 96. The author in a footnote quotes his source as being *Document Secret No. 885, folio No. 4/A du Conseil de Guerre* found in the 'Archives coloniales belges' one month after Independence in July, 1960, but surmises that the larger part of the record of the trial was taken from Congo by the departing colonial authorities.

109. 'Ils ne prient pas Simon Kimbangu; ils prient Dieu. Kimbangu est un envoyé de Dieu.' Lettre 937 du 3.1.1924 de A. T. Thysville, from *Histoire de l'apparition de Simon Kimbangu,* Tome I (1921-1940), Kinshasa, Editions 'Notre Kongo Dieto', R.D.C., undated, duplicated papers.

110. Simon Kimbangu n'est pas à la place du Christ... Simon Kimbangu n'est pas donc un messie noir qui ouvre la porte des cieux (comme par exemple I. Shembe au Zululand) mais plutôt le doigt de Jean-Baptiste pointé vers l'agneau de Dieu qui ôte le péché du monde.
M-L. Martin, Appendice B, *Essai d'interprétation théologique de la vie et de l'enseignement de l'Eglise de Jésus-Christ sur la terre par le Prophète Simon Kimbangu,* in *Actualité du Kimbanguisme, Le monde non-chrétien,* 1968, p. 33.

111. G. C. Oosthuizen, op. cit. Appendix, 157ff.

112. B. G. Sundkler, *Zulu Zion,* op. cit 310ff.

113. T. Ware, *The Orthodox Church*, Penguin, (Harmondsworth, 1963), pp. 40, 214.

114. From the Kikongo hymn: *Nsi ya mpa yitua kubikilwa*. The expression 'visible sign' translates the Kikongo: 'kiamona meso'.

115. From the Kikongo hymn: *Bonokono a zola kwa Nzambi mu bantu vava nza*, Nsambu T., n.d. ('bonokono' has been translated 'reflection', Fr. 'reflet') .

116. See note 90, above.

117. Translated from Kikongo in Boka and Raymaekers, op. cit. *Jésus est le thaumaturge magnifique*, p. 38. The expression in Kikongo is: '*Nsongi waunene wa bimangu*'.

118. From the Kikongo hymn: *Nsangu za Yisu zimwangana*, Nsambu T., n.d.

119. From the Kikongo hymn: *Mu ntemo'e zulu fwete diatila*, Fwasi L., 1959.

120. The ikon can be understood as a window between the viewer and the ultimate object to be perceived. The viewer can either focus his eye *on* the window, or *through* the window on that which the window discloses. cf. George Herbert's hymn:'The man that looks on glass/ on it may stay his eye/ or if he pleases through it pass/ and then the heaven espy.'

121. D. McKay, PhD. thesis, op. cit. p. 345.

122. 'Nsinsani' service, 'Centre d'Accueil', 15th Feb, 1987.

123. Diagienda, op. cit. p. 307.

124. Bena-Silu, op. cit. (note 34) p. 17a (there are two pp. 17), also pp. 18, 21, 24, 25, 26, 44, 46, 48.

125. Nzinga M., *Dip. Th. dissertation*, op. cit. (note 12) p. 91.

126. The one member of the EJCSK who in my hearing unambiguously distinguished between Kimbangu and the Holy Spirit was

Dr M-L. Martin. Her preferred expression is *'the Holy Spirit who worked through (or, who descended upon) Simon Kimbangu."* But the inescapable overall impression was gained that most other Kimbanguists would want to go further than Dr Martin.

127. Two instances of the use of these 'text-clusters' were in conversations with Cit. Wayawa, the keeper of the 'Résidence' at the 'Centre d'Accueil', Kasa-Vubu (7th Feb, 1987) and with the Swahili-speaking goat-herder from Kivu, also at the 'Centre', (7th Feb, 1987). There were several other instances during the three week stay in Kinshasa.

128. The book was shown to me by Pastor Nsambu as evidence for the belief that the Holy Spirit is a man. The section concerned was heavily underlined. The same belief was expressed by Pastor Matondo who works in the 'Résidence, Centre d'Accueil' (Zone Kasa-Vubu), who received his pastoral training at Nkamba.

129. From the Kikongo hymn: *Nzambi'a moyo tukulombele*, author unknown, 1958.

130. From the Kikongo hymn: *Tata Nzambi wasala salu kiandi*, author unknown, 1957.

131. From the Kikongo hymn: *Yave Nzambi bukambokele*, author unknown, 1958.

132. From the Kikongo hymn: *Nzambi'eto utu vana do*, Luzolo P., 1957.

133. From the Kikongo hymn: *Masivi ma Nzambi mbe wamwena mo e?*, Nsimba P., 1959.

134. Conversation with Dr Zola, 'Vice-Doyen' of the Faculté de Théologie Kimbanguiste', Kinshasa, 21st Feb.,1987.

135. W. MacGaffey, *Modern Kongo Prophets: Religion in a plural society*, Indiana University Press, (Bloomington, 1983), p. 129.

136. It is said that Diangienda preferred to remain at his unpretentious home (Rue Monkoto), rather than move into the sumptuous 'Résidence' in the 'Centre d'Accueil', which is now reserved for special audiences and meetings.

137. eg., one evening a member of the Kimbanguist brass band came
to explain about his unemployment predicament and concluded:
This evening I am going to talk about my problem to 'Son
Eminence', indeed, he is here present with us listening to
all we say. I'll ask him to pray to his father (Simon
Kimbangu) about it.
(10th Feb, 1987, 'Centre d'Accueil').

138. Pastor Nsambu communicated to each of the evening choir
gatherings in February, 1987, the 'Chef Spirituel's' recent vision
of his father. The Prophet was sitting dejected (here Nsambu sat
down on the sand, with his head between his hands, to demonstrate). When Diangienda asked his father why he was so sad,
Kimbangu replied: *There is sin in the Church. Tell the people to
repent of their sins.*

139. The hesitation with which the speaker formed his sentence (we
were talking in French) indicated the difficulty of finding the right
words. Not in the same conversation, but on several other occasions (and once by the 'Chef Spirituel' himself), God's words to
Moses were appealed to for biblical legitimation: *See, I have
made you God to Pharaoh.* (Exodus: 7:1).

140. Conversation with members of the 'Bureau Téchnique', Bongolo,
18th Feb, 1987. M-L. Martin likewise insists that only by spiritual
participation and submission to Kimbanguist life, discipline and
worship can a true understanding be gained. M-L. Martin,
'Worship and Spirituality in the Kimbanguist Church', Seminar
given at S.O.A.S., London, 25th Sept, 1974.

141. Words of the officiating pastor at the 73rd birthday celebration
service at Matete (12th Feb, 1987) in honour of Kisolokele,
Kimbangu's eldest son. On the day of his birth, Kisolokele *akiti
lokolo, akomi awa na nse mpo na kosadisa biso* (Lingala, he
(Kisolokele) came down from above to help us here below).

142. Sung by one of the choirs at the Sunday service, 'Centre D'Accueil', Kinshasa, 22nd Feb, 1987.

143. Ceci n'est pas obligatoire, étant donné que Christ reçoit di-
rectement toute prière. Il n'en demeure pas moins vrai
que les Kimbanguistes recourent discrétionnairement à

cette possibilité... Il ressort clairement que Simon Kimbangu est celui-là même qui appuie auprès du Christ nos prières, afin que le Seigneur puisse y donner suite le plus rapidement possible.

Diangienda, op. cit. p. 264. On two occasions, the 'Chef du Cabinet', Bena-Silu, gave exactly the same explanation (April, 1981, when the author was one of a group visiting the EJCSK and February 1987). It may well be that Bena-Silu was one of the (if not the principal) authors of 'La théologie kimbanguiste'. See also above, note 105.

144. M-L. Martin, 'Worship and Spirituality', op. cit. p. 8.

145. S. Asch, op. cit. p. 95.

146. In February, 1987, as part of the centenary year activities, a series of weekly lectures was launched in Kinshasa, under the title: 'Qui est Simon Kimbangu?' Contemporaries of Kimbangu and eye witnesses of miracles and apparitions, gave their testimonies. The author was able to attend two of these lectures.

147. From the Kikongo hymn: *Yisu Mvuluzi mu beto*, Nsambu T., 1956.

148. From the Kikongo hymn: *Tata ku kayengele*, Banimbadio A., 1959.

149. From the Kikongo hymn: *Nu yimbilanga nkunga*, Lusiete P., 1921.

150. From the Kikongo hymn: *Twatambula mvuluzu*, Nsambu T., n.d.

151. For instance at the birthday service for Kisolokele, or frequently even at my visits to the choirs, February, 1987.

152. From the Kikongo hymn: *Nsangu za Nzambi za wakana*, Nsambu T., n.d.

153. From the Kikongo hymn: *Ngina tonda Nzambi ame mu ntina*, n.d.

154. From the Kikongo hymn: *E bankundi mu kiese bakuizilangana*, 1921, quoted in Heintze-Flad, op. cit. p. 35.

155. W. Heintze-Flad, op. cit. p. 37.

224

156. From the Kikongo hymn: *Nsi yafwila Ngunza mu pelezo*, Ntemo K., 1976.

157. Translated from Kikongo in Heintze-Flad, *A cause des pleurs et des prières*, op. cit. p. 21.

158. Sung in Lingala, recorded at Kintambo, Kinshasa, 10th Feb, 1987.

159. From the Kikongo hymn: *Sanisina Mfumu, sanisina*, Babaka Anne, 1957.

160. From the Kikongo hymn: *Ewonga kenumoni ko*, Ndongala, 1957.

161. From the Kikongo hymn: *Tata Simon wayazidi tuzolana*, author unknown, 1972.

162. Sermon in Lingala, 'Centre d'Accueil', 22nd Feb, 1987.

163. Bena-Silu, *Simon Kimbangu libère et réhabilite la race noire*, Editions Kimbanguistes, (Kinshasa, 1981).

164.   Kimbangu voulait et lutta pour que sur la surface du globe, le Nègre fut reconnu comme membre à part entière de la famille humaine et non plus comme une sous-race du genre humain... Il amena le Nègre à prendre conscience de ses propres valeurs et surtout à lutter résolument pour se libérer de l'esclavage dans lequel le maintient l'homme Blanc... Kimbangu avait été condamné à mort pour que le monde ait également des Chefs d'Etats Nègres, des Ministres Nègres, des Gouverneurs Nègres, des hommes de Science Nègres. Sa prophétie 'le Blanc deviendra le Noir et le Noir le Blanc' est devenu une réalité.
Bena-Silu, op. cit. p. 15.

165. Translated from Kikongo, in Heintze-Flad, *Encerclez la ville*, op. cit. p. 19, Kikongo: *Zunge no, ntete lumbu'eki*. Heintze-Flad gives the date as '1960 or before'.

166. From the Kikongo hymn: *Mambu ma Yisu*, Nsambu T., n.d.

167. I owe to Rev H. H. Jenkinson, a missionary to Zaïre in the 1920s, the testimony of an early Kimbanguist deportee in Buta, Haut-Zaïre, André Yengo. According to Yengo, the Belgian officials sought to intimidate the Kimbanguists by telling them they were being sent to cannibalistic tribes who would soon finish them off. (Letter, Jenkinson to Molyneux, July, 1986).

168. Translated from Kikongo, in Boka and Raymaekers, *Pour avoir prêché le nom du Christ*, op. cit. p. 34.

169. ibid, *N'est-ce pas le message de Jésus?* p. 44.

170. Translated from Kikongo in M-L. Martin, *Prophetic Christianity in the Congo* (publication of the Christian Institute of South Africa, 1968, p. 23) *'We who follow our affair'*.

171. ibid, *God made the earth and the heaven*, p. 22.

172. S. Asch, op. cit. p. 41.

173. Diangienda, op. cit. p. 169.

174. Cf. letter, Jenkinson to Molyneux (July, 1986, see note 167, above), relating personal reminiscences of exemplary exiled Kimbanguists such as Yengo in the North-East of Zaïre. Also S. Asch, op. cit. p. 35.

175. From the Kikongo hymn: *Ingeta nkundi sala ngolo*, author unknown, 1957.

176. Translated from Kikongo, *God made the earth and the heaven* in M-L. Martin, *Prophetic Christianity*, from, op. cit. p. 23.

177. ibid, *Come Jesus the redeemer* p. 22.

178. M-L. Martin disputed this statement and cited as an example of the EJCSK's continuing voice of protest the official disapproval expressed about some of the nationalistic excesses of the 1970s, such as enforced dancing at flag-raising ceremonies. (Conversation with Martin, 21st Feb, 1987).

179. Illness was much talked about during February 1987, as all three of the 'mvwalas' (Kimbangu's sons) were ill.

180. From the Kikongo hymn: *Tukubama muna Mvuluzi*, Kunzika P., 1957.

181. From the Kikongo hymn: *E ngeye nkundi bu weti landa nkembo*, author unknown, 1958.

182. From the Kikongo hymn: *O Yisu tekela fulu kele kubika*, Ndala D., 1967.

183. A notable example from Zululand is the sacred place of Ekuphakameni, see B. G. Sundkler, *Zulu Zion*, p. 131ff.

184. J. Masson, 'Simples reflexions sur des chants kimbanguistes', in *Devant les sectes non-chrétiennes*, Louvain, Desclé de Brouvwer, n.d., 1962?

185.   Fin mars 1922, des indigènes parmi lesquels certains du Congo français, recommencement à venir en pélerinage à Nkamba qu'ils appellent Mbanza Jérusalem. Ils vont prier devant la case de Simon Kimbangu. Thomas Nzoafunda leur déclare que Simon Kimbangu va revenir bientôt et que les Blancs ne viendront plus à Nkamba car Dieu leur a barré la route.
P.V. (Minutes) of 4th April, 1922, de CDD/Bas-Congo, in R. B. Mithridate, op. cit. n.d., pp. 9-10. Fr Bontinck's personal library, Scholasticat, Kinshasa.

186. Diangienda K. writes of Nkamba as the: *'lieu saint par excellence pour tous les Kimbanguistes... une espèce de Mecque'*, op. cit. p. 212.

187. ibid, p. 212.

188. T. Ware, op. cit. p. 277.

189. W. Heintze-Flad, writing of Nkamba:
Elle est en quelque sorte le point de rencontre entre l'Eglise combattante ici-bas et l'Eglise triomphante dans les cieux, op. cit. p. 18.

190. Translated from Kikongo, in Heintze-Flad, *Dans la cité sainte*, op. cit. p. 18, Kikongo: *Ku mbanza nlongo, kuna Mfumu Yisu.* Author? 1975.

191. J. Masson, writing of Nkamba:
Ici le plan spirituel et le plan matériel, le plan éternel et le plan temporel se rejoignent et se confondent comme dans presque tous les millénarismes. op. cit. p. 85.

192. Translated from Kikongo, in Boka and Raymaekers, *Cité pure, cité sainte*, op. cit. p. 4.

193. ibid, *Lave-moi, lave-moi,* p. 5.

194. From the Kikongo hymn: *Nzunganisa zula yawonso,* Tusevo J., 1958.

195. Observed at the 'nsinsani' service, at Kimbanseke, Kinshasa, 8th Feb, 1987.

196. In fact, the EJCSK does have its secessionist groups, see MacGaffey's 'historical catalogue of modern prophetism', in *Modern Kongo Prophets*, op. cit. p. 42.

197. Hymn sung in French, recorded February, 1987: Nous approchons de l'accomplissement / Nous approchons de la réalité / Nous serons conduits ... par un Seigneur / Nous serons groupés ... dans une seule Eglise, / Nous parlerons ... une seule langue.

198. From the Kikongo hymn: *Ma nsambu'ema mansila Mfumu,* Banimbadio A., 1959.

Appendix I

Two hymns from 1921

Amakesa ma ndungidi
   Nu vwat'e nwaninwa
Kwa Yisu nu sambulwa
   Nu vwat'e nwaninwa

Soldiers of righteousness
   Put on (your) armour,
That you may be blessed by Jesus;
   Put on your armour.

Mwanda osa kunu sambula
   Muna moko ma Mvuluzi
Mbeni osa kuku finama
   Kanu kitakesanga

The Spirit will bless you
   In the hands of the Saviour,
The enemy will draw near to you
   To trouble you.

Nu talak'o Mvuluzi,
   Ndion'okunu sundisa
Muna vita yina wau,
   Nu vwat'e nwaninwa

Look only to the Saviour,
   The One who will cause you to
                overcome
In this war which is going on now.
   Put your armour on.

Nu samba kwa Nzambi'o Se
   Ndiona wanu yekwele
Yisu Klisto wa Mvuluzi
   Nu vwat'e nwaninwa

Pray to the Father God,
   He who gave up His Son for you,
Jesus Christ the Saviour,
   Put your armour on.

Yisu wa i yekwele
   Ka komwa vana nti
Menga mandi ma solele
   Muna kutu kianzisa

Jesus gave Himself up,
   He was nailed to the tree;
His blood dropped down,
   That we might be cleansed.

Mukoko Jean

230

O Nzambi o zenga nkanu	God gives judgment
Muna wantu a nsiona	To the orphans,
Ndion'o dilanga i kekonka	The one who is weeping He protects,
O Nzambi wazola a sumuki	God loved sinners.

O Nzambi inzodia nsiona	God loves the orphans,
Kwa ndiona wina yo mpasi	(He goes) to the suffering one,
Muna wa u ka didila	For that (one) He wept,
Oku nyandalang'aka mpe	And He will save them.

O Nzambi wa nzodi a nsiona	God is the lover of the orphan,
Oyandalanga mosi vana bena	He comforts one among them,
O mvwala Yisu yatololwa	The staff Jesus was broken,
Kansi wavumbul'aka yo.	But He raised it up.

Kana vo wantu akangua	Although people were bound
Kansi Nzambi kekangwanga ko	But God is not bound,
Kadi Nzambi wasengoka	For God was revealed
Kwa yeto wanti ava nzo.	To us people on earth.

Kimbangu Simon

Appendix II: Tonic Solfa Transposition

(for translation, see Appendix V, A4)

Titre: Vuvu Kiame mu nge nzanbl'ame

Groupe: Vuvu ye Lukuikilu

Refrain

II Vuvu kiame mu ngeye Yisu
Mu Mambu ma Moyo mawa Nsonga
Kana vimpi yovo bela
Ngina siandama kuame ye mbaninu:

III Tata Kimbangu Mwanda velela
nge waveno, konko biya bia ntoto
do kunsisi ko bukotesa
ba nlongo baku ku mbanza velela:

Capté par: Luneko – 1985

Appendix III

Table of contents of hymns collection intended for publication
Ndandani za mi Nkunga

1.	Nzambi Tata	God The Father	No. of Hymns
1.	Nsemono	Creation	2
2.	Nkembelolu' andi	His glory	28
3.	Zola kwandi	His love	34
4.	Ngolo zandi	His power	4

2.	Nzambi Mwana	God The Son	
5.	Luwutuku (Noël)	His birth	20
6.	Luvuluzu lwandi	His work of salvation	45
7.	Salu kiandi	His ministry	16
8.	Mvukululu'a sumuki	Call to sinners	15
9.	Luviluku lwa ntima	Conviction	84
10.	Nkabu ye zizila	Courage and perseverance	28
11.	Vuvu ye lukwilu	Hope and joy	31
12.	Kivungudi	Shepherd	6
13.	Ngang'a wuka	Healer	2
14.	Mpasi ye mfuntu	Suffering	27
15.	Lufwa ye lufukulu	Death and Resurrection	31
16.	Nsilu a Yisu	His promise (Return)	2
17.	Ntumwa za Mfumu	His messengers	2

Appendix IV

Bureau des Chants Kimbanguistes
Bongolo, Kinshasa

Statistique des Cantiques, (Chants Captés) 1986

Mois	J	F	M	A	M	J	J	A	S	O	N	D	tot
Catégorie													
Louange	7	5	10	6	1	10	17	3	9	17	4	5	94
Prière	10	8	7	5	7	12	3	5	6	8	0	5	76
Noël	0	0	0	0	0	0	0	0	0	8	15	26	49
Exhortation	8	5	5	5	3	0	15	6	4	2	5	0	58
Langue													
Anglais	0	0	2	0	1	0	2	0	0	0	0	0	5
Swahili	1	0	0	0	2	0	3	0	0	0	1	0	7
Français	3	4	0	5	4	7	6	4	6	8	5	10	62
Lingala	10	4	12	7	1	8	15	6	7	12	10	15	107
Kikongo	11	10	8	4	3	7	9	4	6	15	8	11	96
Total:	25	18	22	16	11	22	35	14	19	35	24	36	277

Le Chef du Bureau Téchnique,
Kinshasa,

27.02.1987

Appendix V

Type Hymns

Category A: 'Godward'

A1. Praise

i). Tata ku kayengele
        tukutonda beni
Buwatuvana nsadisi
        kaza fwila vana nti

Father, in the highest heaven
        We worship You,
For having given us a Helper,
        Who died on the tree.

ref: Tonda, tonda!
Tonda, tonda!
Tukutonda, Aleluya
Tonda ngeye Mvuluzi
Buwatuvana nsadisi
Wena yeto na de

Praise you! Praise you!
We praise you, Hallelujah,
Praise you, Saviour,
For giving us a Helper
Who is with us forever.

Banimbadio Albert, 1959

A2. Confession

i). Twakala kweto mimbangiki,
   Tata, tukiyekudi kwa nge,
Twakala kweto minkwamisi,
   Tata, tukiyekudi kwa nge.

We were persecutors,
Father, we cast ourselves on You,
 We were oppressors,
Father, we cast ourselves on You.

ref: Mfumu Yisu do utuwila
     E Tata tukiyekudi kwa nge

O Jesus, hear us!
O Father we cast ourselves on
                 You.

Twakala kweto minyekudi, Tata, etc.   We were traitors, Father, etc.
Twakala kweto mimfundisi, Tata, etc. We were condemners, Father,
etc.,

Twakala kweto minlevudi, Tata, etc., We were revilers, Father, etc.,
Twakala kweto mimvwezi, Tata, etc., We were despisers, Father, etc.

Twalembwa zaya nge Nzambi, Tata, We did not know you, O God,
etc.,   Father, etc.,
Twalembwa zaya nge Yisu, Tata, etc., We did not know you, O Jesus,
Father, etc.,

Twalembwa zaya nge Mwanda, Tata, We did not know you, O Spirit,
etc.,   Father, etc.,
Twavweza beni nzil'aku, Tata, etc., We did not follow your way,
Father, etc.

Mandiangu Henri, 1959

ii). Nkolo Nzambi na biso   Lord, our God, (Chef Spirituel),
(Mfumu a Nlongo)   Have pity on us, we are
yokela biso mawa tonyokwami   oppressed,
Bolamo nyonso ejali na yo   All goodness belongs to You,
kimia na mokili ejali na yo.   The world's peace depends
on You.

Adamu na Eva bajali pene na yo   Adam and Eve are beside You,
bajali kojila basenga bolimbisi   They are waiting to ask
mpo ete lisumu ya mokili esila   forgiveness,
mokili mojua kimia na yo,   So that the world's sin might
Njambe   end,
that it might have Your
peace, O God.

Ee, Tata, ee! Ee, Nkolo, ee!   Oh, Father! Oh, Lord!
lakisa bolingo na yo na Adamu   Teach Adam and Eve Your
na Eva   love,
Ee, ee! ndenge nini, Tata,   Oh, oh! Why are You hidden,
obombani?   Father?
ee, ee! biso bakila moya lolenge   Oh, oh! We human beings
no yo   are Your image,
Ee, Tata, ee! Ee, Nkolo, ee!   Oh, Father! Oh, Lord!
sadisa Adamu na Eva bayeba   Help Adam and Eve to
mabe na bango   know their evil.

moto na moto na mokili
            ayeba
mabe na ye akosalaka
Ee, ee! ndenge nini, Tata,
            obombani?
Biso bana na yo,
Ee, ee! biso bakila moya
            lolenge na yo.

May each person on earth
    know the evil he commits,
Oh, oh! Why are You hidden,
            Father?
    We Your children,
Oh, oh! We human beings
            are Your image.

A3. Petition

i). E. Nzambi twik'e
            Mwand'avelela
Wavunzuna mavangu meto
            x2

O God, send us the Holy Spirit
To take away our transgres-
            sions x2

E Yisu twik'e Mwand'avelela
Wavunzuna mavangu meto
            x2

O Jesus, send us the Holy Spirit
To take away our transgres-
            sions x2

Tata Simon wutu
            finamang'owau
Twa tambulang'o Mwand'avelela
            x2

Tata Simon, draw near to us
That we might receive the Holy
            Spirit x2

Nsambu Twasilwa, 1957

A4. Response

i). Vuvu kiame, Mungu Nzam-
            bi'ame
O mu mambu maku mawa
            nsonga
kana mpasi, yovo wete,
    ngina siandama kwame ye
            mbaninu

In You I put my hope, my God,

    for all You have taught me;

whether in suffering, or in joy,
    I will persevere to the end.

ref: Ngina lama, a ngina lama,
    ngina lama ngeye Yisu
            mwana Nzambi
    Ngina lama, a ngina lama,
    mpasi vo ya koteswa
            mu yaku'enzo

I will follow, I will follow,
    I will follow You, Jesus Son of
God.
    I will follow, I will follow,
    so that You will open your
home to me.
    I will follow, I will follow,

Ngina lama, a ngina lama,
mpasi vo ya kembela mu
nzo a di Se
O O nkembo wa ngitukulu
kansongele
weta kembelanga baveledi
mu yaku'ensi.

Vuvu kiame, mu ngeye Yisu
Mu mambu ma moyo
mawa nsonga
Kana vimpi yovo bela
ngina siandama kwame ye
mbaninu

Tata Kimbangu, Mwanda
velela
nge waveno konko biya bia
ntoto
do kunsisi ko bukotesa
ba nlonga baku ku
mbanza velela

that I may rejoice in the
Father's house.
He has shown me an aston-
ishing glory
sung by the holy ones in
Your land.

In You I put my hope, Jesus,
in the living words which
You showed me,
Whether in health or in illness
I will persevere to the end.

Father Kimbangu, Holy
Spirit,
To you have been given the
four corners of the ground
(earth),
Do not leave me when you
bring in
your sacred ones to the Holy
City.

Luneko, 1985

Type B. 'Mutual'

B1. *Exhortation*

i). Se tunwana yay'evita
Yisu kieto nwanina
A makesa mwamu vita
Ke numoni wonga ko

ref: Se tunwana, se tunwana,
x2
Se nutadi Yisu telamene
Osa kuna sundisa

Se tunwana yay' evita
Yisu weto ntanini

We want to fight,
Jesus is our armour,
Fighters,
Do not fear this battle.

We want to fight, we want
to fight, x2
Look, Jesus stands
To give us the victory.

We want to fight,
Jesus our deliverer,

A makesa nwamu vita
  Ke numona wonga ko

Fighters,
  Do not fear this battle.

Se tunwana yay'evita
  Yisu osa kutu sundisa
A makesa awamu vita
  Ke nuyoyi nkutu ko

We want to fight,
  Jesus will give us the victory,
Fighters,
  Do not be discouraged.

Nsambu André, 1956

B2 *Instruction*

i). ref: Kwiza ke kwiza Aleluya
    Engwe yandi wukwiza
                tutalanga

He is coming, Hallelujah!
    Yes, we await He who is
                coming.

Yisu wa samuna se kavutuka
Engwe yandi wukwiza
            tutalanga

Jesus has said He will return,
    Yes, we await He who is
                coming.

Lumbu kika kwiza kizeyi kio
                    ko,
    Engwe yandi etc.

When He will come I do not
                    know,
    Yes, etc.

Wu kwiza mu ngonda Aleluya
    Engwe, etc.

I do not know the month of
                His coming,
    Yes , etc.

Lumbu kika kwiza ye ntoto
                nikuka
    Engwe, etc.

When He comes the world will
                be shaken,
    Yes, etc.

Lumbu kika kwiza mafwe
                mefuluka
    Engwe, etc.

When He comes the dead will
                rise,
    Yes, etc.

Wukwiza mu nsungi Aleluya
    Engwe, etc.

I do not know the time of His
                coming,
    Yes, etc.

?, 1956

B3. Affirmation and testimony

i). O Yave mvungudi ame
   kikondwa nkutu ko
O kumfila va fulu kia vundilu
   kikondwa nkutu ko

Jehovah is my shepherd
   I lack nothing,
He leads me to heavenly rest,
   I lack nothing.

O Yisu nlundi ame
   Kikondwa, etc.
oku ntalanga fuku yo muini
   Kikondwa, etc.

Jesus is my protector,
   I lack nothing,
He watches over me night
                           and day,
   I lack nothing.

O Ntumwa nsongi'ame
   kikondwa, etc.
mu nzila Nzambi yavelela
   kikondwa, etc.

The Prophet (Sent One) is my
                           guide
   I lack nothing,
On the holy way of God,
   I lack nothing.
      Ntangu Alphonse, 1958

ii). Likambo likoteli ngai na
                           motema
   oyo nakomeli lelo moto
                           monene
   nakoki koloba, nakoki kobi-
                           angama
      o bisikia minene
   nakomi solo moto na bonsomi
   uta nabimelaki o libulu
                           monene
Tika nasepela, nakumisa
   Nzambi na lola
Tika nasepela, nayembela
                Yesu Mobikisi
   Nasanzola Tata Kimbangu
                mosala monene
asaleli ngai, solo
   akumisi ngai lelo moto
                           monene
a! elikia ejalaki te, ndeko,
   misala nakomi kosala na
                bato minene

A matter has entered my heart,
   namely, today I have become
                           important,
I am able to speak, I am able to
                           be called
   to important places,
Truly, I have become a free
                           person
   since I came out of the deep
                           hole.
Let me rejoice and exalt the
                God of heaven,
   Let me rejoice and sing to
                Saviour Jesus,
I'll praise Tata Kimbangu for
                the great work
that he did for me, truly
He has established me today as
                someone big.
Oh, friend! there was no hope,
I can now do important
                people's work.
      (author and date unknown)

Type C. 'Outward'

i). Nzunganisa zula yawonso
    Nkundi kweyi siwa kadila
                x2

I will shake the whole world
    My friend, where will you be?
                x2

Solo: Songa, nsonga ma zulu
    vava mvav'aveledi
mu nkembo bakembela

I will reveal heavenly things,
    I will seek the holy ones
So that they may rejoice in glory.

Mbwene ntemo kw'aveledi
Ngeye kweyi siwa kadila x2

I saw the light of the holy ones
    Where will you be?   x2

Solo: Mfumu wavanga ma
               lunungu
Ye wunungisang'aveledi
Kiese ye nlemvo biena yau

God created what is just
    He causes the righteous to
              triumph,
They have joy and forgiveness.

Nsonga nkembo kw'atovoki
Ngeye nkiama weti vingila

I will reveal my glory to the
              weary,
What are you waiting for?

Solo: Ntama yafilwa vava nza
    bisinsu masivi yanusonga
weyi nulembi kwikidilanga

Long ago I was sent into the
              world,
    I showed you signs and
              miracles,
Why is it you do not believe?

Nsonga kiese kwa baluvwe-
              zanga
ngeye nkundi nki siwa
              tambula

I will reveal my power to the
              persecutors,
What will you receive?

Solo: Tulanda nsilu twasilulu
    tulemvokila Mvwala
              minlongi mpe
twa veleleswa

Let us follow the promise that
              was made,
    Let us obey the 'Mvwala' and
              the preachers,
That we might be made holy.
          Tusevo Joseph, 1958

244

D. 'Others'

ex: Christmas (Lingala)

i). Banzelo o likolo bayembeli
                         Nkolo
     ozana, ozana.
     Ozana, Mwana ya Davidi.

ref: Ee Tata Nzambi totondi yo
     na ndeng'otindeli biso
                         Mobikisi
     Banzelo o likolo bayembeli ye
     Ozana, Mwana ya Davidi

The angels on high sing to the
Lord,
     Hosanna! Hosanna!
Hosanna! Son of David!

     O Father God we praise You
     For the way you sent us the
Saviour,
     The angels on high sing
praise to Him
     Hosanna! Son of David!

Gbala, n.d.

Chapter Four
In Search of a Theology to Live By

'Gospel and Culture Seminars': an experiment in
contextual theologizing in North-East Zaïre

On paper at least, the 'Communauté Evangélique au Centre de l'Afrique' (CECA) and its founding society, the Africa Inland Mission, have reason to be encouraged with the progress of evangelization and consolidation in North Eastern Zaïre.

Background

When the Mission entered the country in 1912,[1] it was one further step towards the fulfilment of the vision of its founder, Rev Peter Cameron Scott,[2] to establish a chain of stations from Mombasa on Kenya's coast to the Tchad. The initial party was compelled by almost insurmountable difficulties[3] to modify their plan to push straight on westwards to the Azande tribe. Instead they made a temporary base at Kasengu near Mahagi Port on Lake Albert (now Lake Mobutu).[4] It was almost a year and a half later that a small party reached Dungu in Azande territory and established a station. Before this moment,

> there was not one Protestant mission station between Lake Albert and Lake Chad, a country occupied by millions of natives.[5]

Inevitably, what leadership there was in those early years was almost entirely expatriate and the work laboured under the then common problems of geographical remoteness[6] and sickness among its missionary personnel.[7] Gradually new stations were opened, more missionary personnel arrived, churches were started and developed and national workers emerged and were trained.

CECA now occupies a crescent-shaped territory lying NW-SE stretching about 450 miles from Assa near the frontier with the Central African Republic to Mwenda on the foothills of Mt Ruwenzori near the Uganda border (see map, Appendix I). For administration purposes the territory is divided into seven 'Districts', which in turn are sub-divided into 'Sections' and further into 'Paroisses' (local churches). Local churches in the CECA region number almost 600 and they vary considerably, ranging from tiny mud-and-thatch shelters in which perhaps a dozen gather for worship in remote rural areas, to very large permanent buildings scarcely able to contain the hundreds attending Sunday services. The CECA Church has inherited and perpetuated a generally 'low-church', non-conformist' style, with a minimum of ritual, vestments, set prayers, etc. but with a strongly centralized organization. Local church hierarchy descends from pastor to elders to deacons and deaconesses.

In all CECA churches, the Sunday service is the high-point of the week. It lasts well over an hour and sometimes (on special occasions such as a baptismal service, or Christmas) for many hours. The early stages of the service are taken up with singing as the worshippers arrive. The congregation unite in singing Swahili translations of Western hymns set to Western tunes. Some possess their own Swahili hymn-book, but many know the hymns by heart and usually the leader calls out the first line of each verse and directs the tempo. Trumpets (and more recently, guitars) provide accompaniment. Indigenous instruments, such as harps, drums and rattles, are used in some areas. An increasingly large part of the service is taken up with small choral groups of children, women, or students, who compose their own songs and set them to African tunes and rhythm. Usually these songs will relate a Bible incident with an application, or will exhort the listeners to Christian obedience. Often the teaching of these songs is too vague and general to be arresting or penetrating. Prayers are offered by the leader of worship or by a member of the congregation, man or woman. Although the role of women in the CECA Church is not prominent (women are not ordained to the pastoral ministry) it is important in terms of evangelism and practical compassion.

In true 'low-church' tradition, the sermon is the climax of the Sunday service. Clearly, the style, skill and degree of contextualization of preaching vary enormously, but almost without exception, sermons are based on the explanation and application of the Bible. Only in very few churches is the preaching of a consecutive, expository nature, working systematically through an entire book or epistle of the Bible. More frequently sermons are non-sequential, expounding a Bible text or addressing a biblical topic (such as 'faith' or 'the final judgment'). The pastor of the local church is usually responsible for the preaching, but in urban churches (eg. in Bunia) or in the larger rural centres (eg. 'mission stations' where there are schools, hospitals and Bible Schools) different pastors and missionaries take turns in preaching, which again militates against consecutive teaching with its cumulative impact.

It is not CECA practice to have Sunday evening services. Instead, members will frequently meet in homes or around fires to sing hymns and pray. Many local churches also have a daily early morning prayer meeting in the church building and there is usually a weekday evening prayer meeting, which includes a brief meditation by the pastor or one of the elders and opportunity for all to take part in extemporary prayer.

Membership of the church and participation at monthly communion celebration is by confession of faith in Christ and by believers baptism. Baptism, which is by immersion, usually takes place in a nearby stream or river as very few church buildings have a baptistry. It is conferred only after the candidate has completed a period (at least six months) of baptismal classes for basic doctrinal instruction; he/she must be able to answer catechism questions to the satisfaction of the pastor and/or elders of the local church. Church leaders have sometimes expressed disquiet that eligibility for baptism seems to depend more on cognition (ie, knowing the right answers) than upon evidences of a changed life (such as behaviour, spirituality, etc.). Church discipline is actively exercised, most frequently for irregularities such as drunkenness or immorality. The offender is excluded from participation in communion until he/she demonstrates a change of heart and behaviour. Registered (communicant) members of the CECA number over 150,000.[8] The very large majority of these are from non-professional, subsistence sectors of society, although in a town like Bunia the number of salaried members is much higher. Systematic, evangelistic campaigns organized each year by the national Church both to areas within the CECA region and beyond Zaïre into Sudan and Kenya, add many new converts each year.[9]

Against a general gradual decline in the number of missionaries sent to the Third World from the West, the Africa Inland Mission has seen its total active missionary numbers rise to a current 624, of whom 81 are currently serving in Zaïre (see Appendix II). They are increasingly concentrated in the more technical fields of medicine and higher education.[10] The CECA/AIM shared with most of the other Church bodies in Zaïre the anguish of the bloody 1964 Rebellion and with all the other Church bodies in Zaïre the tensions of readjustment when, by governmental decree, the CECA became autonomous from the AIM.[11] Good relations between the two bodies were such, however, that when in 1973 foreign mission societies were allowed no longer to exist as such in Zaïre, the AIM had little difficulty in accepting to continue in Zaïre at the invitation, and under the direction, of the national CECA Church.[12] Advances in medical and educational work have paralleled these developments in the Church, with the building of 4 CECA hospitals and 29 dispensaries and whereas before Independence there were 11 primary schools and 2 secondary, there are now 134 primary and 20 secondary.[13]

'Loci' of theological reflection in Zaïre

From the earliest years, most (if not all) of the missionary personnel saw the wisdom and importance of developing a strong national church.[14] Basic Bible training and, later, higher-level theological education was seen to be an essential aspect in leadership preparation. This education has taken place over the years in a number of different 'loci'. Initially, the well-proven residential Bible School (of which there are many hundreds in Africa) represented almost the only deliberate attempt at Christian leadership training. More recently, these have been joined by other less formal, more innovative methods which have sought to target other sectors of the CECA membership. Together, these loci of leadership training have come to be considered the points at which theological 'reflection' takes place. For it is here that time and place are deliberately set aside to learn and think about the Christian faith and its outworkings in Zaïre. The various different processes display a considerable variety of methodology and educational level. However, they all share a style which can broadly be termed 'instructional'. They are outlined below in order to provide the background against which the 'Gospel and Culture Seminars' which form the subject of this chapter may be viewed, as a radically different alternative.

1. Bible Schools

Training specialist national leaders to assume responsibility for the spiritual well-being and extension of the Church in Zaïre was one obvious means of ensuring the health of the national church. Currently serving the 571 local churches are some 2,572 evangelists and catechists and 496 pastors.[15] The training of such men takes place in the 10 CECA Bible Schools of different levels.

Before Independence in 1960, the Bible School at Aba was the only one in CECA and it served the entire church body. It was moved from Aba to Blukwa and then to Adi where it became a training school for pastors. Following the Rebellion, not only did the need for training leaders increase with the growing numbers in the Church, but the increasing difficulties of travel led the CECA Administrative Council to decide that each of the seven 'Districts' should have its own Bible

School. In addition, there is one intermediate-level Bible Institute in French at Aungba and the higher-level Bunia Theological Seminary which provides Dip.Th and BA-level courses.

There is thus a three-tier system of Bible and theological training reflecting both the widely differing levels of academic attainment of candidates and the diverse needs of rural and urban churches. Candidates are either chosen by their local district as being suitable for training, or they themselves ask to be sent to Bible School. Either way, they need the official backing of their local church and 'Section', for it is these latter who will be required to support the student and his wife financially through their years of training and to appoint them as pastors and evangelists within their area after the completion of their training. The Bunia Theological Seminary, for instance, turns down several candidates each year who, while meeting financial and academic requirements for admission, do not have the written recommendation and pledged support of their church bodies.

Table 1[16]
Bible and Theological Institutions (1985)

School	Language	Staff			Students		
		Zairian	Expat	tot.	Men	Women	tot.
Level 1							
Adi	Bangala	2	3	5	?	?	?
Banda	Pazande	2	1	3	?	?	?
Chyekele	Swahili	7	-	7	35	26	61
Linga	Swahili	7	-	7	43	47	90
Napopo	Pazande	3	2	5	12	33	45
Oicha	Swahili	4	1	5	40	38	78
Todro	Bangala	6	-	6	44	45	89
Level 2							
Aungba	French	4	1	5	42	35	77
Level 3							
Bunia	French	5	3	8	40	33	73
		40	11	51	256	257	513

Emphasis within the Level 1 Bible Schools' programme is upon Bible knowledge and practical skills of evangelism and preaching. The curriculum in these schools is largely standardized and, reflecting the programme of the original, missionary-staffed Bible School at Aba, displays a range of subjects which would be similar to that of many Western Bible Schools. Undoubtedly the teaching staff, of whom the large majority are Zaïrian, attempt consciously or unconsciously to adapt their teaching to the African context. However, the predominant pedagogical method is that of teacher-pupil transferral of knowledge. At this Level 1, which represents the majority of CECA theological institutions, this transmission would be by teachers dictating their notes, or writing them on the blackboard for the students to copy verbatim. The method is laborious and provides little time for discussion given the overloaded curriculum, but with few if any text books or duplicated hand-outs (given the financial and material circumstances), there is little alternative. At Levels 2 and 3 there would be more opportunity for discussion and personal study, but even here the patterns of rote learning familiar to generations of Zaïrian school pupils die slowly and are reinforced by examination systems which encourage the exact reproducing of the teachers' course-content.

The Bunia Theological Seminary is situated within CECA territory, but CECA is just one of five church bodies in Zaïre's North and East who jointly administer the college.[17] Together, they have provided a theological training centre of a standard and scope which none of them would have been able to provide alone. Already back in the 1950s before Independence, the need was perceived by certain missionaries and nationals for higher-level theological training as the growing Church in Zaïre moved towards maturity. First plans were made and a constitution drawn up in 1957. In 1961 the first students were admitted to the new school at Banjwade, near Kisangani.[18] For lack of suitably qualified candidates the first class of only three men was admitted for a 'Cours Moyen' on a lower level.[19] The Simba Rebellion (1964-66), particularly ferocious in the Kisangani (Stanleyville) area, scattered staff and students. The school relocated briefly at Linga near the Uganda border, before settling permanently in 1967 at its present location in Bunia. In 1976 the Seminary conformed with national standards for Diploma-level programmes by admitting only those who have successfully completed their State secondary education and in 1986 a degree programme was added to the Diploma course for those capable of going further. Students from all over the country and sometimes beyond Zaïre, attend the Seminary.

In a number of ways, the Bunia Theological Seminary has sought consciously to match the training it provides with the real requirements of the churches who send the students. At the annual Board Meetings, the church delegates are reminded that the Seminary does not exist so as to self-perpetuate, but rather to serve the churches. The Board members are encouraged to comment about the training programme and to suggest how it might more effectively meet the needs of the supporting churches. The 'raison d'être' of the college thus is firmly rooted in the needs and aspirations of the Zaïrian churches. At the beginning of each academic year the staff and students are introduced to the congregation of Bunia's largest CECA church in order to underline to both Seminary and Church the links that unite the two. The graduation service at the close of the academic year takes place not at the Seminary, but again in the large CECA Church, for the same reason. Academic education is not permitted to exclude practical training; students are required to participate in weekend ministry in church or church-related activities: preaching, teaching, prison and hospital chaplaincy, children's meetings, etc. In addition, a probationary month at the end of their second year at the Seminary provides students with opportunity to return to their churches in order to work alongside more senior pastors, becoming acquainted with the demands of the work. Both the churches which organize the probationary month and the students who fulfil the assignments are required to submit a detailed report which further guides the Seminary staff as to possible ministry gifts of the students. Upon completing the three-year course at Bunia the students return to the churches that sent them. The sending church thus assigns the graduate to his function, but it will be guided in this assignment by the recommendation of the Seminary staff who by that time will usually have a clear idea of the strengths and weaknesses of the students concerned.

The large majority of those who have graduated from the Seminary are actively involved in church or para-church work (see *Table 2*).

Table 2[20]
Present Occupations of Bunia Graduates

Ministry	No.	% of total
Bible teaching	43	37
Religion in schools	16	14
Pastor	8	7
Administration	9	8
Evangelism	5	4
Chaplain	11	9
Translation	3	3
TEE	1	1
Christian Education	2	2
Further studies	7	6
Radio	1	1
Other	2	2
No information	9	8
total	117	100

Beyond being sensitive to the stated needs of the churches, the Seminary attempts to relate its training and education to the African social and cultural context. Expatriate missionary teachers are required to do at least one year in church work, acquainting themselves with the African scene before being allowed to teach at the Seminary. One missionary teacher chose to spend a year living in a remote village with his family in an attempt to penetrate the life-style and world-view of at least one African tribe and thereby make his teaching and preaching more pertinent.[21]

The official Course Description includes such excerpts as:

(Dogmatic Theology)... to learn to apply Christian Doctrine to social, religious and political problems, thus enabling us to make a critique of the message we preach.

(Ethics)... relationship between Christian ethics and African ethics.

(African Sociology)... Africa is to a large extent 'evangelized' but the problem of the Christian faith taking root still remains. Study of African philosophy, sociology and culture will help the theologian or pastor to adapt his message better. The task is first to know and understand the people who receive the Biblical message.[22]

While not ignoring the practical and spiritual dimensions of training, the Bunia Seminary is committed to academic excellence. Its admission and graduation conditions are rigorously applied and those graduates who continue their studies elsewhere achieve results that commend both themselves and the Bunia Seminary.[23]

A self-evaluation in 1983-84, critically examining in detail all the administrational and educational dimensions of the Seminary[24] revealed, however, that teachers have tended to be prisoners to a style of teaching which overloads the teacher while it does little to stimulate active reflection on the part of the students. The average class-load of a full-time teacher was $12^1/2$ class-hours (= $10^1/2$ clock hours) per week (the maximum in 1984 was 15 class hours = $12^1/2$ clock hours). For most of those hours, the teacher lectures the students, who take copious notes. The large number of hours and the lecture style of his teaching mean that the teacher (who also has multiple extra-curricular responsibilities) has little time to prepare his courses adequately. More important, the didactic style produces in the student an attitude of passive receptivity which exercises the memory more than it does powers of reflection and discovery. Observed as a model by the student during his three years in the Seminary classroom (not to mention his many preceding years in primary and secondary education), it also reinforces in him a probable future style of teaching, thus perpetuating reflection deficiencies in the Church.[25]

The new degree programme, launched in 1986, is designed (according to its written objectives) to

> train researchers competent in the exegesis of Old and New
> Testaments in order to respond biblically to contemporary
> problems in the African Church.[26]

The first intake of seven students represented three different church bodies, though the large majority were from the CECA church. Six of the seven students completed their diploma studies at the Seminary. The seventh graduated from the Protestant Faculty of Theology in Kinshasa. After completion of their diploma-level studies, four of the seven were chaplains and teachers of Religion in secondary schools (one of these had several years in Bible translation), the three others taught in Bible Schools.[27] It is perhaps to be expected that a theological college jointly sponsored by five church bodies all of which are of evangelical persuasion, should choose to specialize in Biblical Studies. A large part of the curriculum is taken up with exegesis of the Old and New Testaments, but it is clear from the recommendations of the commission which drew up detailed plans for the degree course that much more is intended than the transmission of information as an end in itself. The guiding principles recommended by the Commission envisage attitudes and skills, more than mere factual content:

> to maintain a spirit of research and to provide methods and
> tools for research... to give students opportunity to prepare
> and present talks and take part in discussions... field
> experience, exposure to and research in traditional ele-
> ments of oral societies... knowledge of contemporary theol-
> ogy and contextualization...[28]

In speaking of objectives, the Commission recognized that the graduates would eventually have (like all other graduates of Bible Schools) administrational, teaching, or pastoral appointments in the Church, but that they would, at the same time,

> be available for biblical research into problems confronting
> the Church and also be competent to write and have
> published a range of literature.[29]

In a way in which theological education in Zaïre generally and CECA in particular has so far failed largely to do, the degree programme will attempt to provide the skills necessary for responding to the open-ended agenda of interpenetration of the biblical and cultural horizons in contemporary Africa. However, with only about 1% of the total CECA Bible School population enrolled in the degree course, it represents merely the very tip of the apex of the theological training pyramid and that furthest removed from the grassroots church life.

2. Pastors' retreats

Students graduating from any of CECA's Bible Schools will have amassed a considerable baggage of Bible knowledge and associated skills of preaching and counselling. Once in the work, however, there is very little to provide on-going intellectual and spiritual stimulation. It is not uncommon for pastors and evangelists to have been in the work for over twenty years with no additional in-service training. Many of the more rural pastors can read neither English nor French and apart from their Bible and hymn-book, possess almost no reference or devotional literature to provide their ministry with fresh insights. What meetings there are on a regional basis are often almost exclusively Church councils, concerned with administration, finance and church problems. The concept of vacational or sabbatical breaks, taken now for granted in the West, is still rare or unknown. The consequences upon the ministry of Church workers are almost inevitable: fatigue, discouragement and staleness.

Occasional one- or two-day seminars for pastors and evangelists have been organised, but with no personnel officially appointed for the task and no over-all stragegy or planning, these have been exceptional, one-off attempts to meet the need.[30] The need for some form of 'recyclage' (refresher course) for Church personnel had often been discussed, but all suitable personnel have been fully committed with existing (mainly Bible-teaching) ministries.

In an AIM Theological Commission 'workshop' in Nairobi in 1985, Zaïrian delegates underlined once again the critical need for pastors and other Church workers to be given some sort of in-service assistance. They commissioned one of the delegates, English AIM missionary Rev D. Richardson, to present to the next Administrative Council of CECA, Zaïre, the urgent need for one or more competent people to be set aside for the specific task of helping the pastors. The Council considered the proposal and decided that Rev Richardson himself was the only possible candidate for the task, suitable on account of his long experience in Zaïre (his parents were among the early missionaries into the country and he was born at Adi) and because of his recognized abilities in preaching and teaching.[31] Realistically, it is probably true also that Richardson was chosen because his appointment would not involve the CECA in any additional financial burden on the annual budget. He was consequently released from responsibilities at the Adi Bible School in order to devote himself to the new appointment.

Richardson was not given a detailed job-description, but was simply asked to explore means of helping pastors and do what was necessary. Meetings were held with church leaders in a number of areas and with local church councils and on the basis of their recommendations, a tentative programme was drawn up. One of the reservations initially expressed by local church leaders was the problem of housing and feeding a number of visitors for the duration of even a short retreat.[32] It was thus decided to commence with gatherings lasting a mere two days, the minimum possible to make worthwhile the travel to and from the meeting. Richardson emphasizes that the courses are not for concentrated reflection or even instruction, but rather for mutual edification and spiritual refreshment. The meetings are thus called 'retreats' rather than seminars and prayer occupies a large part of the programme.

Attendance is restricted to pastors and their wives, plus leaders of the women's work. Richardson reports a lot of requests to broaden the scope and attendance of the retreats, but has decided on the advice of the Church leaders to restrict the gatherings to manageable proportions. Initial reservations, however, about the duration of the retreats soon gave way to enthusiasm and a decision to extend the

258

retreats to three days. Typically, the day's programme commences at 8am with a short period of prayer in which all will participate. Richardson will then give an hour's exposition from the Bible (usually Colossians), which is designed not only to edify and instruct the delegates, but also to serve as a model:

> One of the greatest lacks in the Zaïre Church is of consistent Bible exposition. Pastors are not expounding the Word. Most of these men supervise several churches and, with special meetings (ordinations, etc.) and district committees, they have a roving ministry and no congregation has the benefit of regular teaching. As a result, very few know how to expound a book. They are so enthusiastic about being taught a book like Colossians and our prayer is that they will get a vision for doing the same... We feel too that these retreats inspire them to do their own study, and we put great emphasis upon this.[33]

The Epistle to the Colossians was Richardson's own choice, but it was prompted by a remark by one of the pastors who expressed alarm at the invasion of cults and sects in his area.[34] The Bible exposition session is followed by a time of prayer informed and guided by the passage expounded. After a mid-morning break there will be a second exposition from Colossians.[35] The men and the women then separate, with Richardson's sister Joyce joining the women for prayer.[36] The afternoons are occupied with a discussion session entitled 'Sickness and Remedy' (Bangala: Malari mpe dawa). The first topic (sickness) has usually been about 'Prayer-life, personal and church'. After a few preliminary remarks from Richardson, the session is thrown open for discussion on why the prayer life of the Church is so dead and what can be done about it. The other topic is that of 'youth'. The issue is of vital concern to the delegates, not only because the Church often fails to retain adolescents, but also for personal and family reasons, as almost all the representatives at the retreats have one or more children who have rebelled against the Christian faith. Richardson reports that in these sessions, the delegates 'really open up' and that discussion is very animated.

Within the first year of his appointment, Richardson and his sister have sought systematically to hold retreats at each 'Section' of the Aru and Aba 'Districts' (see Table 2). To accompany the retreats, a 16-page duplicated booklet on Colossians was produced by the Richardsons. A small charge was to be made, but this was waived when Richardson discovered at Adja that many of the pastor-delegates had received no pay for 10 months or a year. The intention is to produce similar booklets on Galatians, Ephesians and Philippians and to get the series of four printed at the CECA press as one volume on public sale throughout CECA. For many years the CECA committee for Bible Schools (Comité d'Enseignement Biblique) has lamented the lack of inexpensive literature available in local languages and adapted to the Zaïrian context. The Committee has repeatedly appealed for Zaïrian and missionary Bible School personnel to write even the most modest booklets of this sort, but the usual problems of lack of time and lack of funds have thwarted all efforts.

Table 3[37]
Pastors' retreats, 1986-87

Centre	men	women	totals
Adi	33	23	56
Adja	16	37	53
Ondolea	19	27	46
Telea	15	20	35
Lanza	9	15	24
Abedju	17	21	38
Aungba	22	23	45
Todro*			68
Aba*			52
Faradje*			13

*Projected at time of correspondence, with expected attendance.

The new ministry among pastors has been warmly received. Those Zaïrian church leaders who strongly opposed the Richardsons being withdrawn from their work at the Adi Bible School in which they were considered indispensable are now enthusiastic about their new assignment. Richardson himself, feeling that he and his sister are 'unfitted' because of their culture and failure to understand specifically African problems, laments the fact that CECA's Administrative Council is not yet ready to appoint a Zaïrian to help (or rather, to direct) this ministry, but recognizes that to be suitable, the person would have to have good theological training and also command the respect of the older pastors.[38] The few who fulfil these conditions are all 'sucked into administration'.[39]

Despite Richardson's reservations, however, the retreats are doing something for CECA's in-service pastors which was not being done before. Response from the delegates indicates that the retreats are meeting a felt need within the Church. Pastors are appealing for the length of the retreats to be extended and for similar retreats to be held for catechists, who have far less resources even than the pastors. There are indications, too, that the retreats are having positive repercussions, at least among some of the delegates. At Lanza, for example, a group of delegates stayed up all night on the last day of the recreat to discuss how the prayer life of their local churches could be changed in the light of their discussions during the retreat.[40] It is, however, only the small beginning of an attempt to meet the in-service needs of the hundreds of local church leaders throughout CECA. Beyond the Aba-Aru 'Districts' are seven others, including the vast Zandeland District, where the population is sparse and distances such that it is difficult and costly to organize conferences or retreats. Even if the Richardsons were able to cover the northern half of CECA territory, they do not possess a working knowledge of Swahili, spoken in the remaining, southern half.

While instruction and reflection undoubtedly take place, the primary objective of these retreats is devotional edification and mutual encouragement for under-resourced church workers. As such they will probably contribute valuably to the spiritual refreshment of hundreds of men and women serving the CECA Church who, with very little to encourage or stimulate them, labour to build up the local churches that are under their care.

3. 'Women of the Good News'

The rapidly growing women's movement in Zaïre 'Women of the Good News'[42] (WGN) is one of the most active and vigorous organizations in the CECA area. It provides Christian women, long denied a role of ministry and leadership in the Zaïrian Church, with important instruction, leadership and ministry opportunities.

The origins of WGN in Zaïre can be traced back to the early 1960s when Pastor Elia Giringara and his wife Rebeka sought refuge from the Simba Rebellion by moving across the border into neighbouring Central African Republic. There Rebeka witnessed the activities of an evangelistic women's movement, an initiative of Grace Brethren missionaries. She determined that something similar was needed back in her native Zaïre, but it was only in 1970 that Rebeka was able to bring her vision to fruition. In that year an American AIM missionary couple, Lyman and Virginia Jones, returned to Banda in the far N-E of CECA territory and Rebeka and Mrs Jones were soon co-operating closely with one another. According to Jones,

> (Rebeka) was the one who envisioned this programme for the
> women in her church. She wanted the programme in the
> local language, and she wanted it to involve the preparation
> of women leadership.[43]

The movement thus began in the Zande district of the CECA in 1970, with the Pazande name 'Ade Wene Pangbanga' (Women of the Good News). Since then, it has spread to other districts of the CECA to such an extent that it now numbers between 20,000 and 30,000 women.[44] The WGN has succeeded, as few other movements have done[45] in crossing mission and Church-body boundaries: in 1985 there were an estimated 300 churches associated with Grace Ministries which had WGN groups attached to them and the movement was increasingly becoming accepted in churches associated with the 'Communauté des Eglises Baptistes au KivuZaïre Est' and with the 'Communauté des Assemblées de Dieu au Zaïre.[46]

Undoubtedly part of the success of the WGN is that it has been allowed to develop within CECA as an indigenous church-women's movement, without patterns being imposed from overseas. A few expatriate missionary personnel are actively involved in WGN, but increasingly they have been replaced in the key positions by nationals and remain as 'technicians' in an advisory or facilitatory role. Details vary from place to place, but broadly, the activities of WGN include a characteristic range of religious and social activities. Once a week, the women meet for Bible study and prayer. In Bunia, this meeting takes place in the early morning (6.00-7.30am) before the busy round of work in the fields or in the market begins. Included in the devotional Bible study will be Scripture memorization, a feature of the WGN. Prayer requests (concerning family, health, or financial needs) will be shared, as will answers to the prayers of preceding weeks. Frequently in the large Bunia group, the meeting will divide for prayer into pairs so as to encourage even the most timid and inexperienced to partici- pate in whichever language is preferred.[47] The emphasis upon member participation is further encouraged by the dividing of the whole Bunia group into ten work and witness sub-groups, each responsible in turn for the organizing and leading of the meeting. In this way elitism (where everything is done by the professional few for the passive many) is avoided.

The sense of opportunity for active ministry is without question part of the attractiveness of the movement to women. Women customarily have been excluded from positions of leadership and active ministry in many African churches. The WGN has provided them with openings for responsibility and service within a parachurch organization which, far from being threatening to the male leaders of the Church, has been welcomed as a valuable additional dimension to the churches' vitality. Pastors sometimes lament the lack of comparable zeal on the part of the men in the Church. Tucker[48] relates the appreciation of Pastor

Kysando of Beni for the local group of WGN members who are responsible for a large part of his church's outward ministry. For apart from the in-church weekly devotional meeting, the Beni women, like other WGN members elsewhere, are actively involved in various sorts of outreach. Some of these are directly evangelistic (seeking to persuade other women to accept the Christian message), or pastoral (visiting other women who once were members of the Church but who have lost interest). Other ministries express the Gospel in action, as members visit the sick in hospital, provide firewood, food and comfort for the weak and elderly or for women in prison and even contribute financially towards special needs (such as tuition fees for local church members in training at Bible School).[49]

Regional conferences are organized within the broad linguistic areas represented in the CECA territory, namely, 'Swahili-land' (to the south), 'Bangala-land' (to the north) and 'Zande-land' (to the north-west). However, representatives from other areas are also present at each conference. Choice of venue is dictated by facilities of feeding and accommodating a large number as regional conferences can vary in attendance from 50 to 2,000.[50] The WGN leadership plans the programme of these conferences and several of the leaders (including usually a woman missionary) are responsible for preaching and teaching. The emphasis at these conferences is on practical Christian living, or on a major Christian doctrine such as Christ's return.[51]

Leadership training was part of the original vision of Rebeka and it continues to be an objective in the activities of WGN. Seminars for leaders of the WGN lasting from two to five days permit the delegates to go through the 40 lessons of the latest WGN manual. To date (1987) there have been four or five WGN manuals each with some 40 lessons, and include: 'Women of the Goods News' (outlining the organization and aims of the movement), 'Ten Rules of the WGN' (with each 'rule' developed over four lessons), 'Women of the Bible' and 'Our Daily Conduct'. While the manuals are not mere translations of material used in the West, the authors are missionary rather than Zaïrian, although probably national women were consulted on some of them.[52]

The manual 'Our Daily Conduct' was based on a Scripture Union publication 'Our Daily Walk'. The books place much emphasis upon Bible teaching and each lesson has a number of Scripture references. There is thus considerable uniformity throughout CECA of the basic material, but the lessons are designed so as to allow local adaptation and leaders are encouraged to apply the teaching in a way which will be relevant to local issues.[53] At the leadership training seminars, the use of the manual is demonstrated to the regional delegates who then return to their districts and reproduce the seminar at a more local level so that those local leaders can return to their rural churches to teach the lessons to the WGN group, in the weekly Bible Study meeting. In this way, a uniform but flexible programme is adopted throughout the extent of CECA.

Although the Grace Brethren missionaries in Central African Republic originally developed the women's movement there with the newly emerging middle and upper class women of that country in mind,[54] a striking characteristic of the movement in Zaïre is its appeal to all economic and social classes of women, both in urban and rural areas. The movement has granted women a new identity and sense of belonging. To join the WGN a woman does not have to be a baptized church member, nor does she have to belong to a monogamous marriage (though both of these conditions would pertain for a WGN leader), but she should consider herself to be a Christian,[55] attend three consecutive weekday meetings and be willing to join in the witnessing and other activities.[56] While regular financial contribution is encouraged, this 'cotisation' is not a condition of membership, since some of the women live in extreme poverty. The meetings themselves have their own character: they start by the leader shouting: *'Let us teach...'* and the members respond with *'...the Good News!'* The leader repeats *'Let us teach...'* and the members shout back, *'...to everyone!'* Then in unison they all cry out: *'We, the women of the Good News!'*[57]

Conscious group identity comes not only from attending the weekly meeting, but also from participating in street marches and the wearing of distinctive yellow wrap-round dresses and headscarves. Such elements contribute to a visible 'identity' and this is emphasized at the big regional conferences which are for the women and by the women. In contemporary Zaïrian society, while women have a certain economic independence (woman easily predominate as both buyers and sellers at the market) they are largely marginalized in other domains of decision-making. The WGN provides the women with opportunities to be liberated from their constraints within the private domestic domain and to cross into the public domain of leadership and authority[58] — a transfer which perhaps only a political career would otherwise afford.[59] While this is an attractive feature for the women, it is sometimes viewed askance by husbands.[60]

According to Tucker, the new-found liberty and responsibility among women has, in places, led to tensions within the Church, with women leaders of the WGN asking for office space in the church office building. Some Zaïrians have expressed resentment at the 'emergence' of women and their subsequent loss of passive submission to their husbands.[61] In CECA the sensitive question of remuneration of WGN officials has recently surfaced, with the 'Coordinatrice' and 'Vice-Président' receiving a fixed salary, while at District level remuneration is decided by the local District Church Council. At present these salaries are provided by funds collected within the WGN. Dix claims[62] that within the CECA area there is little if any evidence of male disquiet towards the WGN; while the movement provides the women with an identity of their own, it has not created a church within a church. There does exist a sort of low-level church discipline within the WGN, but it reinforces rather than replaces full church discipline; for instance, it is accepted within the movement that only those women who are communicant members of the Church (ie, not under any sort of church discipline), are eligible to wear the yellow 'uniform'.

Church leaders of CECA are generally enthusiastic about the contribution of the WGN to church and community life, an there is little doubt that the movement has permitted Christian women a greater spiritual and social maturity than would have been the case otherwise. Undoubtedly, the emphasis of the movement is upon biblical instruction and practical evangelistic and compassionate ministry. Much less time, if any, is spent on group reflection on theological questions or on key issues of cultural values and practices. If such reflection does take place, Dix suggests, it happens when women meet informally at each other's homes or around the fires in the evening.[63]

4. Theological Education by Extension

Theological Education by Extension (TEE) traces its origins to an experimental project in 1962 in Guatemala.[64] It has rapidly spread to other countries as an innovative alternative to residential, centralized theological education.

In the CECA area, TEE has a relatively recent history, having been introduced in early 1974.[65] For an initial period, duplicated materials were produced locally by missionaries M. Southard and E. Kuhnle. Later, it was co-ordinated by AIM missionary Rev D. Langford, who quickly set about training a Zairian[66] to assume responsibility, with Langford remaining as assistant-coordinator.

In keeping with the TEE principle, students who enrol for theological education by extension remain where they are and in their existing occupations rather than moving to a residential theological institution or Bible School. Instead, they are linked to local 'centres' each of which has a leader responsible for guiding the students and organizing weekly seminars relating to the studies. The movement in CECA currently has 142 of these centres, each responsible for between eight and fifteen students, so that in all there are approximately 1,500 students enrolled in TEE.[67] All but nine of the 39 'sections' of CECA have TEE centres.

Historically, TEE has sometimes been promoted forcefully by its proponents as a radical solution to the inherent weaknesses of traditional patterns of theological education. One of the founding members of the TEE movement, F. R. Kinsler, insists that the residential theological school system is long overdue for criticism. Such schools strive to become 'exalted' communities of theological reflection and spiritual formation but:

> some have suggested that our seminaries and Bible institutes are not even appropriate places in which to carry out theological education. They may in fact damage, thwart and stifle the churches' natural capacity to grow and develop their own leaders and carry out a dynamic ministry to their own members and to society. The movement called Theological Education by Extension has come on the horizon at this particular moment of history as an alternative model to the traditional schools of the past 150 years.[68]

Kinsler goes on to list what he sees to be some of the built-in weaknesses of established theological education: it attracts young, inexperienced candidates who are then dislocated from their social setting and excluded from the normal processes of leadership selection and experience; it produces a salaried, prestigious and professional stratum which the church finds difficult to support financially; it induces superiority complexes in the tiny minority who can benefit from it and inferiority complexes in the large majority who cannot; it relies largely on the lecture method which does little to stimulate the reflective capacity of the student.[69] Kinsler concludes:

> The extension approach to theological education can and does break these patterns of ecclesiastical and theological dependence. It reverses the elitist tendency of the ministry. It recognises and values and elevates local leadership in a process of contextualization.[70]

Advocates of residential, centralized theological education have been quick to come to the defence of the more traditional patterns of Bible teaching: central, residential institution permits a concentration of highly qualified staff and better resources (library, etc.) than would otherwise be possible; the prolonged 2 or 3-year period of teacher-student acquaintance allows more carefully attuned nurturing than weekly 1 or 2-hour seminars; sharing life and study with other students from different ethnic and denominational backgrounds is an enriching and broadening experience in itself. Within CECA, however, the two processes exist side by side, both officially approved by the CECA Administrative Council and there is no apparent friction between the two.

Currently TEE in CECA operates on two levels; the first for those who have a background of primary education in the languages of Swahili and Bangala, the second for those beyond. While the former level is that at which the typical weekly extension system functions, the higher (French) level is as yet compelled to operate for concentrated periods in the two centres of Aungba and Bunia where adequately qualified instructors are readily found. The very large majority of TEE students are registered at the lower level.

Crucial in the TEE methodology are the programmed texts and the weekly seminars. Each student purchases his programmed text book[71] on the subject of his choice.[72] The manual acts as 'teacher', guiding the student step by step through the material, prompting, correcting and reinforcing as the need arises. The student is entirely responsible for organizing his own timetable but will be expected to complete five lessons of the manual within a week (one a day), in time for the next group seminar. Upon successful completion of the 10-week course, the student receives an attestation and is free to commence another course.

The weekly seminars at the centre last typically two or three hours and provide opportunity for all the students in that locality to review the week's chapter and to discuss it in the light of their daily ministry. Each centre has its leader whose task it is to help the students to maximize their benefit from the lesson by discussing problems encountered during study and by prompting the students to explore the contextual implications of what they have learned. The advocates of the extension movement would argue, probably correctly, that the TEE student is thus more powerfully motivated than his residential counterpart who seeks to acquire information in the artificial context of a classroom. Not only so, but contextualization of the material comes more easily, since learning takes place against a background of real everyday life and ministry.[73]

Most of the CECA TEE leaders are local pastors who have themselves been through Bible training and who bring to the counselling
session a wealth of experience. The pastor is incidentally stimulated
and helped by having to cover the same ground as the students and
by the cross-fertilization of ideas in discussion. Four-day training
seminars for TEE leaders, with a view to developing skills in tutoring
and counselling, have been held at (among other places) Aba, Adja,
Bedu, Oicha, Blukwa, Chyekele, Bogoro, Ara, Linga and Beni, as well
as in several Bible Schools from which, it is hoped, future leaders for
TEE may emerge. Follow-up seminars for further instruction have
been held in several of these centres, as have 'inspections', in which
top TEE personnel visit the centres personally in order to ensure that
full functioning conditions are met.[74]

Two TEE personnel receive salaries, the Co-ordinator and the
Secretary. Their salaries are met partly by the CECA annual budget
and partly from overseas funds. In an effort to become less dependent
upon external funds, TEE has purchased a small flour milling
machine,[75] the proceeds from which are ploughed back into the work.
In the same year, a motorbike was purchased for TEE, to enable the
Co-ordinator or his assistant to visit the centres. While the overhead
costs of running the TEE initiative are but a small fraction of those of
a residential Bible Institute or seminary, it is clear from the annual
reports that funding is a major problem.

That both TEE and residential theological training happily co-exist
in CECA might be partly because the TEE co-ordinating personnel
belong to both 'camps'; Southard was producing basic programmed
texts while he was director of Bunia Seminary, Langford was part-time
professor at the Bunia Seminary whilst at the same time co-ordinator
of TEE, and both of the Zaïrians who succeeded him as co-ordinator
received their theological training at the Seminary. It was debated in
Seminary staff meetings whether it would not be a good thing for TEE
to be a department of the Seminary. Beside this reason, however, both
'sides' recognize that neither system on its own can fully meet the total
theological needs of the Church. TEE in CECA seeks to cater for the

many who wish to gain some sort of theological education (either for the full-time ministry or not), but who cannot leave their homes or places of work to move to a residential theological institution for two or three years. Their reasons might be family (eg. children in crucial stages of education, elderly parents needing help, etc.) or professional (eg. wish to continue in business or secular education rather than train for a full-time career in the Church). TEE recognises that Christian ministry involves many more in the Church than the few who train in Bible Schools and seeks to equip them for their contribution.

Well over twice as many are enrolled in TEE as there are in the CECA residential institutions, but the most important contribution of TEE is related not to numbers but to the sort of person being reached. The extension movement in CECA is placing theological and Bible training within reach of many who probably will never become salaried 'Church-workers' but who nevertheless perform a variety of important church-related ministries: Sunday School teachers, choir leaders, youth workers and members of the Women of the Good News.[76] TEE is thus strengthening the infrastructure of the Church, a sector largely neglected in the traditional emphasis upon the 'élite' conveyed by the more prestigious residential schools. According to the Co-ordinator:

> the reports we receive during our visits to the (TEE) centres
> or from the centre leaders indicate that those doing the
> courses are growing spiritually and are becoming more
> mature in their faith and the quality of their work is
> improving.[77]

With limited manuals available, priority is still being granted to those (listed above) who have a ministry in some way directly linked to the Church. Others, such as Christian businessmen, merchants, medical workers and teachers, currently accounting for a mere 1%[78] of all those enrolled on extension courses, will gradually become a more important TEE student category in years ahead. Such ones, usually totally absent among those trained in Bible-teaching institutions, will undoubtedly strengthen the vast lay sector of the Church.

Theoretically, 24 courses of TEE are equal to two years of Bible Institute, 48 courses equal 4 years.[79] To date no one has completed the entire 24 courses, let alone the 48; indeed, there are not yet this number of courses available. The most courses that have been completed by a student to date is 18. It is still early to know whether TEE, for all its contribution will be seen in the eyes of the Zaïrian Church to have the same standing as traditional residential institutions of theological training, or whether it will always be considered to be a poor-man's option, a second-class alternative. However, irrespective of whether Zaïrian perception will grant TEE an equality-status alongside residential training, the Church in CECA cannot but be significantly strengthened by the extension movement.

Inadequacies

The CECA Church is thus more fortunate than many Zaïrian church bodies in having a variety of initiatives for strengthening church life and the needs of the Church might appear to be catered for at every level. Yet the CECA Church shares with many other African Christian communities weaknesses which disturb not only some of the expatriate missionaries working there but also many African leaders who discerningly see beyond the numerical strength of the Church to its inner frailty. A missionary from Africa (working with a different Church) reported to the International Missionary Council in Willingen in 1952:

> African Christians, it is suggested, live on two irreconcilable levels. They are members of a Church... as such they subscribe to a statement of faith. But below the system of conscious beliefs are deeply embedded traditions and customs, implying quite a different interpretation of the universe and the world of spirit from the Christian interpretation. In the crises of life — birth, marriage, death, the 'customary' matters more than the Christian; the Church is at those moments an alien thing.[80]

Many African Christian thinkers would admit the problem of the 'two levels' and explain it as a consequence of a Christianity which has been imported from the West and therefore does not fit the African context and world-view. Eboussi Boulaga laments the rigid, authoritarian presentation of Christianity by the West that left no room for African contribution, only unthinking acceptance:

> Everything is 'for' the new converts, never 'by'... (This results in) dictated understanding, evidence acquired by proxy or substitute, conformity to the system of unconditional acceptance...[81]

He does not wonder, therefore, that damaging contradictions set in:

> When the neophyte tires of salvation (ie. the Western Christianity package) and begins to long for healing and physical and moral wholeness... suddenly the ancient piety (ie. traditional African religion) is the essential thing again... But this reappropriation is always accompanied by a sense of shame. It is always clandestine, for it is contraband. Now the neophyte will lead twin lives, a cloven life, a life in twain.[82]

African Christian converts have accepted from the hands of the missionaries the 'package', but have found that its parameters do not coincide with those of their total needs; it meets some of these needs, but in places leaves wide gaps. Increasingly, African Christian thinkers such as Mbiti are warning of the inadequacy of a merely 'received' theology:

> Let it be said once and for all as loudly as technology can make it, that *imported Christianity will never, never quench the spiritual thirst of African peoples.*[83] (italics his)

While African writers disagree on the details of the remedy they envisage, they are agreed that it needs to be more than superficial. Kwesi Dickson expresses it with admirable clarity:

> To speak of the process of doing theology in Africa as indigenizing or translating Christian theology is to misunderstand the nature of the theological task facing the Church in Africa; this task consists not primarily in thinking

through the theological deposit from the West — it consists
in thinking through faith in Christ.[84]

Others emphasize the urgent need to release the Christian gospel
from the theoretical hairsplitting of the West to engage the pressing
practical problems of real life in Africa:

> The context of Western theology is scientific empiricism. Its
> modern roots can also be traced to the intellectualism and
> scholasticism of the Renaissance... Western theology em-
> phasizes the intellectual and theoretical, (whereas) our faith
> must confront the issues of the day.[85]

Camerounian theologian, Engelbert Mveng, agrees:

> For us in Africa, theology isn't a scholarly exercise of
> pedantic words and enigmatic formulas. For us, theology
> belongs rather to the totality of our religious experience, to
> the sum-total of our life.[86]

In Zaïre, four aspects of the theological process combine to harden
or 'set' these observed inadequacies, making them more likely to
perpetuate themselves in coming years and push a solution yet
further out of reach. Firstly, the teachers, the agents of theological
instruction, whether expatriate or national, tend to be locked into a
self-reproductive cycle that does not address in detail some of the vital
issues that lie deepest in the minds of the African students. Admittedly
in recent years the trend towards national staff has been accelerating.
Of the 43 teachers in CECA Bible Schools today, for instance, only
eight are expatriate. However, the national teachers often do little
more than repeat what they themselves received from missionary
teachers; the cycle is hardly affected. Secondly, the curriculum is
often modelled on Western patterns and in the often overcrowded programme of studies there just is not room to 'get sidetracked'. Thirdly,
library facilities, where they exist, are stocked with books from Europe
and America. Theological literature by Africans and in African languages is almost non-existent; where there are books in Swahili or
Lingala they are almost always translated from English and French.[87]

Finally, the pedagogical methodology in both primary and secondary schools (and which is carried over into Bible Schools) favours learning by rote rather than by reflection and the emphasis upon content memorization militates against a questioning, investigative approach to understanding.

The 'Gospel and Culture Seminars'

It is against this background that the 1983 experimental 'Gospel and Culture Seminars' should be seen. Involving a select number of Church leaders in the CECA territory, the seminars were brought about by American missionary, John Gration.[88] Fifteen years of service as a missionary in Zaïre and Kenya, followed by active participation in the 1974 Congress on World Evangelism in Lausanne[89] and in the Willowbank Consultation on the Gospel and Culture in 1978,[90] permitted a combination of practical experience and theoretical reflexion. Looking back over his years as missionary teacher in Zaïre, Gration reflected:

> I recognized that I had delivered many pre-packaged boxes of biblical 'truth' to my Zaïrian students. Although the content was biblical, it did not speak to many issues, crucial to the Zaïrian Church, of which I was only dimly aware. Furthermore, the delivery system fostered a mentality of theological dependency that matched the colonial context.[91]

Reviewing his previous ministry with a deepening understanding of the implications of contextualization for missions and churches, Gration had a sense of 'unpaid debt' to the Zaïrian Church.[92] He returned briefly to Zaïre in 1981 and again (this time at the formal invitation of the CECA Church) in 1983 and 1984 to meet with CECA Church leaders, some of them his former students. The overall aim was to encourage an active and dynamic interaction between the context of culture and the text of Scripture.[93] Gration determined from the beginning that the process to be employed would have to be different from his usual. In a preparatory letter to Zaïre missionary

David Langford who helped to set up the seminars, Gration wrote:
> I am a lecturer by nature... but at all costs we must avoid the
> lecture method... it is rather a consultation in which every-
> one invited is expected to make significant contributions.[94]

Reporting after the event, Gration explained that the method used, far from providing all the answers,
> does not bring anything but questions. It is my conviction,
> however, that there are times when asking the right ques-
> tions is more important than providing the 'right' answers,
> especially to questions that no-one is really asking.[95]

Indeed, it is clear from Gration's preparatory correspondence that the process or method of the project was much more important than its content as such:
> While the end product is very important, the process itself
> is crucial and lies at the heart of the learning experience...
> We must be terribly careful that we ourselves provide a
> perfect model in this regard and in no way set the agenda...
> what we are really interested in is starting a process.[96]

Gration's article in *Missiology* anticipates accusations that he, as an expatriate, was inevitably manipulating or imposing the agenda, but he insists that his role was simply one of 'active dialogue' in which there is both receiving and offering of mutual help and correction.[97]

Since the process was a dynamic one, Gration was concerned to limit the numbers in the seminars to no more than 18, so as to encourage free discussion and corporate reflection.[98] As regards the delegates themselves, the missionary presence was discouraged in an attempt to permit the most uninhibited exchange of opinion possible among the Africans themselves. During his preliminary visit to Zaïre in 1981, certain African leaders had confided in Gration that some of the subjects he was touching on were never discussed with mission-aries 'because they would laugh at us',[99] their minds having been conditioned by the scientific and secular worldview of the West. The delegates were therefore (with one or two exceptions) Zaïrians, chosen by the Church itself as being in key, influential positions.[100] Reflecting

Gration's conviction that theology is not the 'exclusive domain of an erudite elite'[101], the first of the two seminars in 1983 was at Rethy for pastors who had had basic Bible School training but little else. It was in Swahili, with 16 participants. Following it, another seminar was held in the town of Bunia. Conducted in French, it brought together a total of 17 Church administrators and teachers in Bible Schools, Theological College and secondary schools. All of the latter group had had post-secondary education at Theological College or University and almost without exception were pastors.

Since the overall aim of the seminars was to permit a fruitful interaction between gospel and culture, it was important that the delegates should be aware of the meaning of the two constituent elements. The first question to be asked at the seminars was 'What is the gospel?' Especially at the Swahili seminar, there was astonishment that such an elementary question even needed to be asked. The 'cascade of clichés'[102] that resulted confirmed what Gration had anticipated when, months earlier, he had written to Langford:

> I rather expect that we will not get very full-orbed answers
> to the first question. A simple verse or two will probably
> explain it all. To my mind, this is probably the reason why
> very little ethnotheology has developed. We have not begun
> to explore all the dimensions of the gospel.[103]

Almost as if they were in a catechism class, the delegates repeated what they had retained from their own training. To encourage reflection, Gration assumed the position of

> one who was not antagonistic to the gospel, but who was
> totally ignorant of its special, technical vocabular.[104]

Seeking to lead the delegates in the Swahili seminar beyond set answers, they were asked to explain what it was in the Christian message that had attracted them and in what sense it qualified as 'habari njema' (Swahili: good news). In the French seminar the same process of probing familiar terminology to deliver its real-life meaning led one delegate (a seminary teacher) to protest that instead of keeping to the original objective of defining the gospel, the seminar was 'getting into theological matters'.[105] The question was then discussed as to whether theology could be avoided in a discussion of the gospel, although it was agreed that technical language could be.

In both seminars it soon became evident that the term 'gospel' so easily used by the delegates in their preaching and teaching, in fact embraced a great deal. Exploring together why the Christian message could be considered 'good news', the delegates began to unearth new dimensions of the meaning of the gospel. The 'good news' presupposed a lot of 'bad news' (human disobedience, a broken law, alienation from God, divine judgment, etc.), and, as a result, 'salvation' (Swahili: 'wokovu', French 'salut') implied far more than 'a forensic justification';[106] it was also 'a release from the bondage of sin in its various manifestations.'[107] Gration was to write later:

> As the excitement produced by the discovery of the richness
> of this simple term 'gospel' became evident, I only wished
> that I had used this approach twenty-five years earlier.[108]

Having established at least partially what was meant by the 'gospel', the next task was to consider 'culture'. Gration had anticipated[109] that some delegates would experience difficulty in distancing themselves from and thereby objectifying their culture. From his own understanding of culture as 'the total lifeway of a people'[110], Gration sought by discussion and illustration to guide the delegates to a perception of the various elements of 'culture'. As a conceptual tool, Gration proposed a role-play in which a Zaïrian would seek to explain to (for instance) a Senegalese the local way of life. Another idea for facilitating the conceptualization of 'culture' was for the delegates to contrast what they thought was 'particularly African' with what they considered to be 'European'; 'anything to help bring out the heart and essence of African culture'.[111]

Of greater difficulty than understanding the distinctiveness of customs and institutions, was the concept of 'worldview' and values. Gration's task here was helped by a 'propitiously timed' thunderstorm which made it difficult for the delegates to hear one another but which provided a helpful key to understanding:

> I immediately asked if everyone in the town heard the

thunder and saw the lightning. The answer was a unanimous affirmative. I then asked if these phenomena meant the same thing to everyone in this cosmopolitan town. This time there was a unanimous negative. I asked what different meanings were attached to them. Diverse and intriguing explanations, differing from tribe to tribe, were shared. This became a natural bridge to a fuller understanding of the significance of worldview in the life of a people. Worldview was thus graphically seen as the perception of the 'system' by which the world operates.[112]

With a clearer understanding of the meaning of 'gospel' and 'culture', the seminars were ready to move into the third phase, namely, the interaction of the two. The larger group subdivided into small 'buzz groups' to discuss the areas in which, according to the delegates, the gospel had touched and transformed African culture.

It was this stage of the discussions that compelled Gration to contrast the Swahili and the French seminars. The French group were more analytical and perceptive, *'more reluctant to be as positive or absolute'*[113] in their affirmations. The Swahili group, on the other hand, were less able to engage in reasoning dialogue or interaction, preferring rather to launch into 'sermonettes'.[114] One evidence of this, according to Gration, was in the discussions on tribalism. While both groups insisted that the gospel had transformed this issue, the French group voiced unease that tribalism was still active in the Church beneath the surface.[115] These observed differences were confirmed by the author's own field research in January, 1987.[116] Higher level education (rather than any inherent differences in the languages) may be the major factor for providing the developed skills of reflection and reasoning that were evident in the participants of the French seminar. If, as Kalilombe insists, a 'higher level' facilitator is needed for grassroots theologizing,[117] one of his skills would have to be to control and prompt group interaction so as to rescue discussion from 'set piece' monologues and stimulate dynamic cross fertilization of ideas.

Among the reasons advanced by the Swahili group as to why the gospel was 'good news' to their people were: the promise of eternal life, the ability to approach God without fear and the hope of heaven instead of the prospect of eternal judgment.[118] Gration conjectures that these answers possibly reflected the orientation of early gospel preaching. Discussing further their comments, the delegates repeatedly implied that the gospel brought release from fear — the fear of spirits, of death and of misfortune.[119] The French group, for their part, declared that the gospel had satisfied the need for forgiveness which was deeply rooted in pre-Christian African thinking. Power over evil spirits was cited as another profound influence of the gospel.[120]

On the surface, the answers given as to the impact of the Christian message seemed satisfactory enough to the delegates. However, the next question was the negative corollary of the foregoing and was designed to lead to the heart of the purpose of the seminars, namely, to expose deliberately those areas of the African context which remain untouched by the gospel. While this could be considered the most important stage of the seminars, it was also the most sensitive and could easily have been construed as yet another judgmental exercise by a Westerner, imperiously sure of his own attainments and censorious of those of others. Gration therefore was careful to introduce the session by illustrating from his own experience of life in the USA facets of national, ecclesiastical and personal life which he recognised were not transformed by the gospel. This was:

> In order both to illustrate what was specifically meant by these three areas and to indicate my own vulnerabilities both as American citizen and churchman... We missionaries have known very little of what it means to be vulnerable in front of our African brethren. We represent still a powerful, dominant political force. The affluence of our Western churches represents tremendous power in and of itself even where it is not overtly used. In maintaining a strong 'testimony' before our African brethren they have all too often seen too little of our real selves that struggle, that hurt and that grapple with issues where there are sometimes more

questions than easy answers. Westerners tend to maintain a façade of triumphalism that papers over real needs and hurts that we share in common not only with humanity but in a special way with our national brethren.[121]

All that preceded was preparation for this part of the seminar, for it was at this point that the Church began really to bring the gospel face to face with the real world of the African context. Subdivided into three small groups for about 1¹/2 hours,[122] the delegates listed issues of vital concern to Africans which (in their opinion) had not really been exposed to the gospel. The three lists were then conflated by the reunited plenary group. In the case of the French seminar, this list, 'the Church's unfinished agenda' comprised no less than 29 topics.[123] Not all of the issues were directly 'cultural'; some of them related to Church practice but were understood by at least some of the delegates as urgently needing fresh examination.

The delegates were then asked why these issues had not been previously discussed with missionaries. In his field notes, Gration lists eight reasons suggested by the delegates which may be conflated as follows: The missionaries did not encourage dialogue; they remained apart from the Africans (the notes do not clarify whether this 'apartness' referred to the location of their homes or to their attitudes; perhaps both). They were better educated and felt that the Africans were ignorant; thus, the missionaries' word was considered to be final and non-negotiable (one delegate explained: *'our fathers received their word as the final authority, not to be discussed'*). As a result, Africans expressed to the missionary not their real beliefs and feelings, but rather what they thought the missionary wanted to hear. The missionary attitude was that Africa was *'the dark Continent'* and that everything African was *'diabolical'*. The Belgian notion of the *'évolué'* as describing those Africans who imitated the Belgian way of life and thought, was reinforced by a parallel missionary concept of the *'spiritual évolué'* — the African Christian who reflected the missionary way of thinking and acting. One delegate even insisted that the only reason why the consultations had taken place was because Gration had proposed it — had the seminars been proposed by one of them, questions would have been asked about the motives for wanting to discuss such matters.[124] For all these reasons (in the opinion of the delegates) such issues had not been deliberately brought into the open and not only were missionaries largely unaware of their existence, but, more serious, the questions were largely excluded from what was considered to be the appropriate agenda of the African Church associated with the missionaries.

So as to reduce the immediate task before the seminar to manageable proportions, the delegates were asked to select the three most pressing issues from the list of 29. At the insistence of the delegates themselves this was done by secret ballot. They chose: fetishism, beliefs in dreams and visions, and tribalism. The issue that Gration himself secretly hoped would be chosen in fact lost by one vote.[125] Each of the three groups chose a topic that was particularly relevant to their region[126] and a basic process of reflection was suggested: First, the problem the group had chosen was to be defined and clarified. Second, the group would go to the Bible and seek out as much relevant data on the subject as they could find, using the limited tools of concordances and Bible indexes that were at their disposal. Again the differences between the Swahili and French seminars became apparent:

> Especially for the Swahili group this kind of dialogue between the Bible and life situations was a new experience...
> The group, composed largely of men with pastoral responsibilities, inclined to be far more sermonic.[127]

The French group were guided as to their methodology by René Padilla's article *Hermeneutics and Culture, a theological perspective*,[128] each delegate having received a copy before the seminar began. The method proposed by the author reflects the view that Scripture is authoritative for faith and practice, a conviction shared by AIM missionaries[129] and by the CECA Church.[130] The article argues that the hermeneutical task requires an understanding not only of Scripture (attained, Padilla insists, by the *'historico-grammatical'*

282

approach), but also of the context or *'current concrete situation'*. Part of the reason, Padilla maintains, that the gospel has a

> foreign sound, or no sound at all, in relation to many of the dreams and anxieties, problems and questions, values and customs of people

is that Western missionaries have rightly insisted on the first aspect of the hermeneutical task, but wrongly ignored the second.[131] The clearer the understanding of real issues in culture, the better the questions brought to Scripture. Padilla thus proposes a *'hermeneutical spiral'* in which a deeper understanding of Scripture permits a greater understanding of the receptor culture, which in turn reveals new dimensions of the biblical message. The dynamic interplay between receptor culture and Scripture strives *'for a merging of our own horizons with those of Scripture'*.[132] Padilla ends his article:

> The urgent need everywhere is for a new reading of the Gospel *from within* each particular historical situation, under the guidance of the Holy Spirit. The contextualization of the Gospel will not consist of an adaptation of an existing theology to a particular culture... It can only be the result of a new, open-ended reading of Scripture with a hermeneutic in which Gospel and culture become mutually engaged in a dialogue whose purpose is to place the church under the lordship of Jesus Christ in its historical situation.[133]

Inevitably, the results of the discussions were incomplete, but it was the process rather than the product which excited both the Zaïrian delegates and Gration himself:

> I had faithfully delivered the 'product' over 15 years of teaching, often to realise that some of the boxes had remained unopened or at best their contents only partially used. In this new situation, Africans would pose their own questions, discover their own answers and fill their own boxes. In a word, they would be theologizing. The result would be an aspect of theology that would be pastoral in nature, for they were wrestling with issues right out of the

Christian community. My excitement was matched only by theirs... Scripture assumed a new relevancy as it not only provided answers to questions that were being asked but itself raised questions.[134]

While the Swahili groups ended up with no written statement (Gration had to distil the essence of what the groups discussed and note key phrases on the blackboard), the French groups were able to present their thinking more incisively and systematically and each produced a 'working paper'. In the plenary discussion that followed Gration could note that

> again and again, it was obvious that the Africans were breaking new ground in their thinking. The barriers between African culture and biblical truth were gradually being broken down.[135]

During the evaluation session towards the close of the French seminar one of the delegates expressed the dangers of including certain subjects in the Church's agenda:

> Young people will applaud and clap their hands when they see us even mentioning some of the things we have discussed here (fetishism, etc.)... but they will be looking at them through another window... these ideas can easily be distorted and perverted.[136]

The remark betrays the fear on the part of some Church leaders that the very discussion of certain practices will be construed by some as implying a change of attitude by the Church authorities which will be exploited by some and become the cause of disorder and confusion in the Church.

The Swahili and French seminars ended differently as to proposed future action. At the former, it fell to Gration to raise the question of follow-on from the seminar. It was agreed by the delegates that all that had been discussed should be shared with the local churches, although Gration was sceptical as to how much (if at all) the method of dialogue would be reproduced.[137] As for the French seminar, the delegates lamented that most seminars were 'one-offs' and insisted that this consultation should not share a similar fate. Concrete proposals from the delegates included: 1) special commissions could guide the CECA's Administrative Council in their decisions on key issues affecting Church policy (eg. marriage customs); 2) co-ordinators were chosen to reproduce the same style of seminars with others in three regions of CECA territory; 3) cells representative of the three sub-groups should continue to meet in their regions (centred on Rethy, Aungba and Bunia respectively) with a view to producing a written document each, firstly for initial discussion and interaction, then to be published for the benefit of the whole CECA Church.[138]

Gration returned home from his seminars in Zaïre in 1983 enthusiastic about the fresh ground that had been covered by the seminars, yet uneasy on two counts. First, he was unconvinced that the process had gone far enough towards being all that contextualization should be in terms of

> grappling with the religious, social, political and economic issues and dynamics of a society in a specific context.[139]

While feeling that the seminars had been more than an exercise of backward-looking 'indigenization',[140] he sensed that they could have and should have gone further:

> I see in contextualization an active, dynamic, at times even aggressive posture on the part of the church vis-à-vis its societal context... meaning that the church not only applies Scripture to its total life and context, not only engages in dialogue and interaction with its world, but at the propitious moment actively, and dare I say even on occasion militantly, confronts its world... Something of this exciting mandate I sensed lacked in our seminars.[141]

Indeed, the list of topics chosen by the delegates reflects little, if any, political awareness, although perhaps 'corruption', 'injustice' and 'fear of speaking out against evil' point in that direction. One possible reason for this might be the traditional (though changing) evangelical attitude of non-involvement in politics conveyed by missionaries.

Another explanation might be the danger with which any critical interference in politics is fraught in Mobutu's Zaïre. Secondly, Gration also feared that the seminars, instead of signalling the start of an ongoing process, would be considered merely an end in themselves.

Meanwhile, the delegates, having returned to their respective regions and occupations, set to work on the topic that each group had agreed to address. The general procedure for all three groups was for the topic to be sub-divided between the members, so that each would work separately and with appropriate research on one aspect of the subject.[142] In time, each member would read the draft of his part to the whole group for discussion and modification.[143]

Gration returned to Zaïre the year following (1984) in order to hold a follow-up seminar in Bunia with the same (French-speaking) participants. He found that the three sub-groups had continued to meet and had prepared a document each on their topic. The papers were read to the plenary group who responded to them; modifications in style and content were suggested and additional relevant material, both biblical and cultural, was recommended for inclusion, with the plan to prepare a revised edition for possible printing.[144] Over the following months, two groups produced revised editions of their documents incorporating the recommendations made in the plenary group. Summaries of these and of the unrevised third document follow.

The Documents

Document 1. *The Gospel and African Beliefs*[145]

The subtitle of this document specifies: *'The case of Rethy and its surrounding area'* in order to make clear that the group were concerned to reflect not just as Africans or even Zaïrians, but as members of the Lendu and Hema tribes situated in a defined geographical locality. These two Nilotic tribes are distinct but related, sharing a common language, Kilendu, and both are engaged chiefly in cattle rearing on the grassland plains to the west of Lake Mobutu.[146] Two of the group had a background in secondary teaching, while the third had seven years experience in Bible School education.[147]

The group chose to widen the scope of their topic from the narrow confines of the subject selected at the Bunia seminar (beliefs concerning dreams and visions) to include other persistent African traditional beliefs. Then, in order to narrow down the potentially very wide field of study and provide it with a structure, the group chose to look at those beliefs that surround four phases of major concern to Zaïrians: childhood, adult life, death and the after-life. With regard to the multiplicity of traditional beliefs surrounding these, the document poses the rhetorical quetsion:

> Is it necessary to hold that all these beliefs are false (as some evangelicals would have)? Or all true (as some pagans would hold)?

In order to answer the question, each area of investigation describes the traditional beliefs, then alternative modern (medical) viewpoints and finally any specifically Christian position.

The document establishes that birth and childhood are of paramount importance to the African life-view, ensuring as they do family perpetuation, prestige and potential economic advantage.[148] It illustrates the measures that some parents take in the traditional society to safeguard their offspring from illness and death by citing a case during the 1978 cholera epidemic when a pastor, entering the home of a bereaved family, found the corpse of the child wrapped around with charms in the form of shells, leopards' teeth and pieces of animal skins. The authors, drawing on their interviews with Zaïrian and expatriate medical staff at Rethy Hospital, refer next to modern medicine, with its vaccinations and regular rural health clinics, that provide 'scientific protection'. The authors insist that even this medical protection, however, is not foolproof and above and beyond both charms and modern medicine is God, who has shown himself concerned about health and powerful to restore and sustain it. The document then puts forward the biblical teaching of God's care for His people and the specific example of the little child Samuel whose mother dedicated him to God instead of having recourse to charms.[149]

As for adult life, the document lists and discusses at least five areas of major concern to Africans where traditional beliefs cluster thickly: illness, accident, failure, sterility and dreams and visions. In all these, the document maintains, the African traditionally looks beyond the particular event or incident to the underlying cause for nothing can happen, especially anything of misfortune, in and of itself.[150] Behind the calamity there must be an evil spell, or a malevolent spirit, or an offended ancestor and it is against these that the African traditionally must protect himself.[151] For each of the five areas, the authors give typical traditional responses which reflect the widespread belief in sinister (supernatural) causes. For example:

1 Illness: 'all illness is suspect and prolonged sickness is presumed to be from an evil spell...'

2. Accident: ' Why was that person at the roadside crushed by a vehicle? Is it not because he was punished by a sorceror or evil spirit? Can it be simply the chauffeur's fault? '

3. Failure: 'How is it that I am not intelligent at school while my friends are always successful? Could it be because there are some in my clan or village who are against me?'

4. Infertility: 'infertility results from a curse by relatives, following a marriage of which they disapprove...'

5. Dreams and visions: 'Traditional Africans take some dreams seriously, especially if their dreams agree with ideas current in their society...'[152]

The document does not seek to explain away these things from a scientific point of view. Indeed, there are instances where the reality of these malevolent causes are readily allowed. For instance:

It must, however, be recognized that certain alchemistic products such as 'rutanga', 'kisege' (comparable to electrocution), 'uu', or 'tsuu' (small scabs or spots) are indeed produced by malicious individuals in order to harm people. Evils such as these do not yield to dispensary medicines ... And we are aware of the fact that evil spirits can also intervene to cause accidents.[153]

However, the writers do suggest other, 'neutral' explanations which could (and in their opinion, should) be considered. For example, having discussed the traditional beliefs about the causes of accidents, the authors continue:

> Often, the inquest establishes that the cause of the accident was that the driver was drunk, or he did not obey the highway code, or there was a mechanical failure.[154]

Having discussed illness and sterility with a qualified (Christian) doctor at Rethy, the group explain how modern medicine can treat many cases yet maintain there are others of a frankly supernatural origin which can be effectively countered only on the supernatural level:

> It (modern medicine) can calm physical and psychical disorders, but it admits its inability when it is confronted by supernatural causes, those due to evil spirits and sorcerors.[155]

The document next examines the subject of dreams and visions, emphasizing (as other students of African religion have done[156]) the importance of the subject:

> For the African, the dream is never accidental; it always has a role to play. It can give information on the future, or communicate to the living the wishes of the dead.[157]

Modern psychological and medical explanations of dreams are given. Then the question of divine revelation is taken up and dreams and visions are emphatically included (along with nature, conscience, the Bible and fellow Christians) as being among the means God uses for communicating His will to men. The section concludes with a warning from the Bible itself (I John 4:1) about the need to discern, or 'test the spirits' in a world where 'false prophets are everywhere'.

For each of the areas listed, the document seeks biblical examples of how God is supreme, able either to overrule in protection and healing or, when he sees fit, to use each for his own wise purposes and the good of the person in question.[158] The supernatural realm, therefore, is freely admitted, but within that realm God is shown to be in control and worthy of entire trust.

The ambivalent attitude in traditional African thinking towards death as something inevitable but unthinkable is acknowledged in the document: *'L'homme sait qu'il mourra, mais il n'accepte pas la mort.'*[159] Never sure of the moment of his death nor the agent by whom it will come, the (traditional) African *'surrounds himself with protective objects'.*[160] In connection with the subject of death, the document discusses the belief in ancestors expressed by the Senegalese writer Birago Diop, *'les morts ne sont pas morts...'* and cites examples of local burial customs:

> The African believes that the deceased continues to live in the vicinity... The ceremonies... aim to safeguard the peace and life-force of the family and clan and to permit, amongst other things, the spirit of the departed to find peace and rest in the world of ancestors, the 'after-life'. Otherwise the spirit will be condemned to wander 'outside' and this will involve the entire clan running the risks of failed harvest, infertility, failure, frequent illness in the family and numerous family deaths.[161]

One of the group had done his Diploma thesis at the Bunia Seminary on the burial practices of his tribe and had researched the whole question thoroughly.[162] The authors again (while not denying all the traditional explanations for death) list possible other causes: foolishness, ignorance, infection, accidents, suicide and murder. The document, however, in contrast to much African theological opinion which appeals for a christianization of existing African concepts of the *'living dead'*[163] finds no room for the traditional African view that ancestors return to partake unseen in clanish life, quoting in its support several verses of the Bible[164] and prefers to explain the apparent reappearance of ancestors by demonic activity.[165] In considering the question of the after-life, the *'village of the dead'*,[166] the general validity of the traditional belief in the hereafter (that death is not the end of existence) is endorsed. In the opinion of the document, it is the traditional African belief in the ready access of 'the living dead' to the present world which provokes the dread and fear lying behind a host of rites and taboos. While Roman Catholic teaching and practice would encourage prayers for the dead and the mediation of saints on behalf of the living,[167] the authors are emphatic that according to the Bible this ready intercourse with the deceased does not exist[168] and consequently, the African Christian has no need to fear the anger or displeasure of his ancestors. So Christians can attend the funeral ceremonies for the dead, but only to express their sympathy for, and solidarity with, the bereaved.

The paper concludes by returning to the original question as to whether all traditional beliefs are wrong or whether they are all right. It insists to its readers that the aim of the paper was not to repudiate all traditional beliefs, but rather to clarify them and then see where the Christian should stand with respect to each. Another aim was to ascertain whether the African should respect his traditions more than the will of God, thereby coming under the judgment that Christ reserved for the Pharisees:

You have a fine way of setting aside the commands of God

in order to observe your own traditions! (Mark 7:9)

What is found to be not in conflict with the revealed will of God is, however, permissible and good.

Document 2: *Fetishism and Healing*[169]

It is recognized in the CECA Church that fetish-related problems are particularly marked in the Aungba region.[170] It was not surprising therefore that at the Bunia seminar the topic chosen by the four members of the Aungba group[171] was that of fetishism. They subsequently elected to include in their study the allied realm of healing. While inevitably the subject chosen by the Aungba region's delegates overlaps in places with the preceding study, its field of investigation is narrowed to these two major questions, both of them of concern to Africans generally and Zaïrians in particular.

The document makes it clear from the beginning that its study of fetishism concerns all the wider field of occult power-manipulation. Its

origins are sought and located with the help of many biblical references primarily in Satan, whose existence as the personification and
source of evil is assumed, not argued. However, man himself because
of his estrangement from God and his replacement of God by objects
of his own making also is responsible; examples from the Old and New
Testament as well as from traditional African society are quoted.[172]
Further, it is demonstrated that repeatedly the Israelites were con-
taminated by occult influences, primarily through marriage alliances
with the pagan nations that surrounded them and the parallel with the
present-day Zaïrian Church is drawn:

> It is exactly the same with some Christians today. They
> disobey and wander from the law of God in establishing
> relations with pagans through marriage.[173]

Again, many biblical references point to the consistent and severe
judgment of God upon such practices, especially with regard to His
people. Biblical examples (Elijah, Josiah, the martyrs of Revelation 14)
and cited to demonstrate that compromise is not inevitable.

Reasons for the use of fetishes are sought and listed: to protect from
the power of evil spirits, to expose a sorcerer or evildoer, to defend
against or seek revenge against another person, to procure success in
natural or personal realms (harvest, fishing, hunting, childbirth,
wealth, studies, etc) and to recover health.[174] According to the
authors these are but some of many reasons.

A distinction is made by the authors between the simple fetish-user
and the sorcerers.[175] The latter are the 'priests of fetishism' and are
feared and despised everywhere in Africa. The authors list the tribal
names for sorcerer: 'adjoga' (Alur), 'adroa' (Lugbara).[176] 'muraguzi'
(Hema), 'ndruba' (Lendu). They may, say the authors, be easily
recognized: bizarre clothing, unkempt appearance and life-style,
terrifying voice and strange gestures.[177]

Having clarified fetishism (albeit very superficially),[178] the document then proceeds to consider its encounter with the Christian
Gospel. The central purpose of the Gospel is stated: the forgiveness of
the sinner through the sacrifice of Christ, through whom also the

sinner receives power to live a new life both inwardly and outwardly: *'He completely transforms the heart, the character, and the deeds of a man.'*[179] Significantly, instead of banishing the sorcerer from their Christian worldview, the group are able to situate him or explain his existence and activity:

> The Gospel affirms that all creation is the work of God; everything visible, everything invisible, all was created by him and for him and therefore owe him honour. Astrologists, magicians, diviners, necromancers, spirits, soothsayers, sorcerers, all are the creatures of God. All should offer him worship in sincerity and faithfulness to his glory. Why do some become sorcerers? Because of their foolishness, says the Apostle Paul in Romans 1:22.[180]

In the understanding of the group, therefore, the sorcerers too, perverse as they may be, can be placed within an integrated universe whose centre is God; they do not have to be passed over in silence as having no place in reality, nor do they have to be relegated to a second, non-Christian universe. And, argues the document, if this is so, then they are within the reach not only of the judgment of God, but also of His mercy:

> Despite their attachment to fetishes, the Gospel, by its power, has transformed many such people and continues to this day to do so in our churches. In the regions of Aba and Aru especially and elsewhere in the CECA territory, there are men and women sorcerers who have been touched and transformed by the gospel.[181]

The section closes with a strong statement of the incompatibility of the gospel and fetishism.[182]

The document next turns its attention to healing. It notes that traditional healing continues to be practised widely even where modern medicine is available. It is often more immediately effective, and sometimes less expensive. Although the Gospel *'stifled'*[183] such practices, the document claims that they are on the increase again. The ingredients of traditional healing are listed as including: roots, bark, leaves, flowers, certain fruits, seeds, excrement, feathers, blood, bones of certain animals, soil, ashes, locally made salt, water, stones, and fire. The paper states that some of these are useful under certain conditions and if they are used *'without superstition or rites'*.[184]

The disadvantages of traditional medicine are listed: lack of hygiene, arbitrary dosage, uncertain diagnosis, difficulty in long term conservation of medicines, secrecy surrounding practice, exorbitant charges by some healers. Christians are warned about these risks. But the document puts its Christian readers on guard against the greater danger of the fetisher-healers who use, in addition to their natural medicines, supernatural powers. It is probably because of the close association between much traditional healing and occult spiritual powers that the two subjects were linked together for study by the same group.

The document concludes with a summary which attempts to distinguish clearly between what is acceptable for the African Christian in the light of biblical teaching and what is not. Detailing no fewer than 8 biblical examples (mainly from the Old Testament),[185] the document is intended to leave the reader in no uncertainty as to the absolute opposition of God to all expressions of fetishism since it is a form of idolatry and, anyway, the Christian does not need to have recourse to it as the power of God available to him is greater than that of fetishism.

For traditional medicine, however, a less clear-cut conclusion is drawn:

> Wisdom is called for. Nothing need prevent its use, as long
> as it is used wisely and for the glory of God.[186]

Christians are urged to develop non-Western methods of healing, and to *'teach positively on the subject, using the Word of God.'*[187]

Document 3. *Tribalism*[188]

The Seminar members constituting the Bunia group were easily the most numerous of the three groups.[189] Appropriately, since the group of eight members represented no fewer than five different tribes, it was decided at the Seminar that theirs would be the topic of tribalism. The group produced both the longest[190] and the most academic document of the three.

After a preliminary section outlining the major ethnological and linguistic categories of the African continent, the authors go on to examine the strengths and possible dangers of tribal consciousness. On the positive side can be listed tribal solidarity, shown especially at times of burial, marriage, hospitality and (formerly) war. Tribal identity also preserves customs and traditions which would otherwise be lost. However, the document argues that there are more disadvantages than advantages and shows how tribalism easily and frequently expresses itself in egocentrism that compels the individual to push himself and those of his clan or tribe forward at the expense of others. It blinds the offender to his own faults and those of his fellows. It sacrifices competence in the interests of favouritism, it dissembles the truth where it might be prejudicial to 'the group', it breeds pride and therefore jealousy, and because it is suspicious of others, seeks to surround itself with only those closest related and most trusted.[191]

The document seeks to identify the 'door' through which these tribalist tendencies entered the Christian Church and places the blame on the early missionaries and their choice of the first collaborators. On any given mission station in a multi-tribal region, the missionary chose the first pastor and/or the first house helper from the dominant tribal group. It was from this same dominant tribe that candidates were chosen for secondary, technical and Bible schools and the process has continued ever since by imitation.[192] The paper unfearingly insists that the CECA itself (particularly in its upper echelons) is full of tribalist tendencies and lists examples while not revealing names: favouritism in appointment of personnel, biased church discipline, preferential selection for grants for further study, and partiality in promotion.[193]

With the contemporary reality of tribalist tendencies both inside and outside the Church clarified, the document then seeks to establish what the Bible has to say on the subject. At first view, the Bible could even be thought to promote tribalism since it was God, according to the Bible, who chose one tribe Israel, to be his own people. The document argues, however, that this preferential election of the Jews was never intended by God to be an end in itself, but always a means to an end, namely, the bringing of blessing to all the nations of the world, (Genesis 12:1ff). If God insisted that His tribe be distinct and separate from others, it was so that the light might shine undimmed from the one to the many. Everything the people of God did should come within the boundaries of 'holy' and the detailed sacred laws and the 'Holiness Code' in the Pentateuch spell out what that holiness means:

> not a collection of moral virtues, but a total belonging to God,
> a complete consecration to God. The life of the people of God
> cannot be divided into religious acts and secular acts.
> Everything is sacred, even questions of food and drink. With
> regard to the distinction to be observed between clean and
> unclean animals, one reads repeatedly in the Old Testa-
> ment: *You must be holy, for I the Lord am holy.'* The
> Christian life cannot be other than a thorough-going belong-
> ing to God, otherwise it is a lie.[194]

God's sovereign decision to use one tribe to reach the many is accomplished in Christ, through whom present-day believers become the posterity of Abraham and partakers of the blessing that was his. Several New Testament references are quoted to support the point that present day Gentile (and therefore Zaïrian) believers are, by their faith, recipients of the divine blessing promised through Abraham:

> So is proved the impartial attitude of God, so different from
> our human clanishness and prejudices; despite a diversity
> of cultures, of nations, of tribes and of social classes, God
> forms a united and harmonious people in Christ.[195]

However, while tribalism is nowhere condoned in the Bible, it is seen in the mistaken pride of the Jews in being the chosen people of God and being the trustees of the Law. While Jesus might have had every cause to share the prejudices of tribalism (being a Jew of Davidic descent and of the royal tribe of Judah) he chose instead to live as a servant. He was sensitive to the needs of non-Jews, even if he understood his first responsibility to be towards his own race. At the end, he specifically commissioned his followers to go into the entire world and preach the Gospel to every tribe and nation. A few weeks later, on the day of Pentecost, they had opportunity to proclaim the message to hundreds in Jerusalem from many different parts of the world and many non-Jews believed the news about Jesus and the Kingdom.[196]

The document admits that even in New Testament times tribalism reared its head. The Hellenistic widows were discriminated against (Acts 6) and even the Apostle Peter had his prejudices about what (and who) was 'clean' and 'unclean' (Acts 10) and on one occasion gave in to hypocrisy under pressure from the Judaistic Christians from Jerusalem (Galatians 2). Each time, however, the error was exposed and dealt with. The New Testament writers are shown to be of one mind on the question:

> Paul follows the example of James in not ceasing to remind
> Christians of the doctrine of their unity within the 'ekklesia'
> (Church)... Being sons and daughters of the same Father, all
> barriers fall. It is the love of God that binds them together.
> So tribalism should give place to brotherly love... This love
> that the believer receives from God knows no racial, ethnic,
> or tribal barrier.[197]

The document ends with an expression of hope that the readers, as children of God, will be compelled and provoked by it into examining their daily living.

The three documents are unequal in depth of analysis, but seem to share certain characteristics. Firstly, all three deal with areas of ethical or cultural concern which are central to African thought and life and yet which are rarely dealt with in normal Bible school or seminary curriculum. They go part way towards facilitating an encounter between Christianity and African world-views. Secondly, there is no doubt that each group was at pains to test everything by the norms of the Christian Scriptures as they understand them. Areas which normally are reserved for a separate conceptual compartment (hence the 'two levels') have been deliberately brought within the circle of the biblical worldview and examined there.

The investigations may have proved rewarding for the participants themselves who brought their draft documents to the second seminar in 1984 where they were read and amended and two of the documents were rewritten accordingly, but the plan to use the documents for the benefit of the entire Church did not succeed. For want of follow-through and capital,[198] the documents were not printed and remain in the files of their group leaders. Not only so, but the plan to hold replica seminars at the different centres never came to anything. To all appearances and indeed to Gration himself,[199] it seemed that the bold experiment was of limited impact and its effects very circumscribed.

With a view to exploring at a deeper level the effects (if any) of the seminars, a period of field-research was undertaken. Correspondence with participants in the seminars confirmed that the twin objectives of further locally-organized seminars and the publishing of the three documents had encountered discouraging problems. The aim of the field work was to investigate participant response to the methodology used in the seminars and to establish to what extent, if at all, the process used then had had any ongoing results in other directions. The basic method of field research was personal interview using a questionnaire (see Appendix III).[200]

Some 2^1/$_2$ years had elapsed since the last seminar had been held. In a sense, this distance aided the objective of the research as it provided adequate time for participants to reflect upon and put into practice what had taken place in the seminars. However, it did also constitute a problem, insofar as detailed memories of the discussions were beginning to fade, although the majority evidenced little difficulty in answering the questions.

Participants' appraisal

1. The Seminars

In an attempt to assist the delegates to recall to mind the methodology and content of the seminars, the questionnaire asked the participant to give his appreciation of the meetings in fairly general terms.[201] The almost unanimously positive response to the question was probably predictable, given that the interviewer was a missionary.[202]

Of greater interest (because less predictable) were the different reasons advanced to substantiate their enthusiastic appraisal. The admired feature most frequently stated (56%) was that the seminars encouraged the delegates to be discerningly critical of their world instead of simply letting things be. A variety of actual expressions was used: 'to judge for oneself',[203] 'to understand the old ways which persist even today, some of which are good', 'to distinguish between the good and the evil', 'think for ourselves', 'discovery (as opposed to being told) permits deeper understanding', 'helped to re-appraise some of the good things that missionaries had rejected offhand; some were bad, but some were good', 'the seminars opened our eyes to discern', 'helped us to acknowledge the mistakes of the past.' Whatever the actual wording used, most of the delegates seemed to agree that the seminars, by their methodology, had stimulated a sifting or distinguishing of the diverse elements of behaviour and thinking characterizing their religious and cultural situation. One participant saw in the process a means to deeper maturity; instead of remaining with a passive, receptor attitude the delegates found themselves developing an active, enquiring approach.

Of the remaining reasons given for the positive assessment of the seminars, the most important (26%) was that real, burning issues came to the surface for consideration. One Bunia pastor emphasized that the issues discussed were major controversies, urgently needing the attention of the Church. All the other four participants who expressed the same conviction were members of the Swahili seminar, and three of these explained that the seminars came at a time when the issue of tribal burial practices (matanga) was causing major concern in the Church, with Christians participating in pagan ceremonies without discerning the danger. Other minor reasons for approval of the method adopted at the seminars included: the 'exceptional' openness and frankness of discussion, the 'multi-departmental approach' which brought together for a single task leaders of different departments of the Church[204] and, finally, since the seminar did not depend upon the teaching of someone from 'outside' but rather upon a method that the delegates now possessed, the discussions could be self-perpetuating.

2. Gration's role

In an attempt to establish to what extent the 'success' of the seminars depended upon the personal contribution of Gration, the delegates were asked to comment on what they perceived to be his role, and, separately, whether they felt he was personally qualified in some special way. In answer to the first question, the most frequent answer (56%) stated that Gration simply asked questions. Most of those who gave this answer specified further that this was in contrast to the lecture method, in which the speaker transmits information to passive hearers. Almost a half (47%) of the delegates also gave the opinion that Gration's role was to 'activate' the delegates: he *'stimulated discussion instead of passive listening'*, *'he didn't teach; it was we who did the discussing'*, *'he oriented us, rather than imposed his ideas on us'*, *'he guided the debate'*, etc. One delegate stated that Gration's contribution to the seminar was to provide *'a formula which facilitated discernment'*,[205] but that *'he let people talk'*. It was this non-self imposing aspect of the methodology that the delegates most appreciated as contributing to the fruitfulness of the discussions. Referring to the list of 29 topics that the French seminar delegates produced, one participant stated:

> If, instead, Gration had listed in a lecture the areas of weakness which he observed in the CECA Church and if, by

coincidence, his list comprised exactly the same items that we came up with, we would not have accepted it.[206]

Asked as to the personal qualities that made Gration a good one to lead such seminars,[207] one delegate stated that age (and thereby respect) was important. Another felt that Gration's academic training helped him to know the right questions to ask (although his rusty French, according to another, was not an asset), while several believed that years of experience in Africa were important. It was clear, however, that these qualifications were not nearly as important in the eyes of the delegates as manner. Over half (56%) of the delegates specifically chose to mention Gration's 'vulnerability';[208] '*he accepted criticisms about missionaries*', '*acknowledged his weaknesses*', '*admitted his errors*', '*not oversure of himself, someone who is overconfident would not succeed*', '*often his questions bounced back on him, but he wasn't offended; he was there to repair*', '*honest*', '*open*', '*humble*'. These qualities in turn enabled the delegates to lower their own defensive barriers and be open and honest. Several stated that in addition Gration had the right motives: he was not there as a judge or critic, but as a '*brother*', '*one who was suffering alongside us*', '*wanting to put right errors of the past*', '*caring*'. Again, this created a spirit of trust which made it easier for the participants to be open with him and with others, rather than defensive and self-justifying. Gration was not the only missionary known to the delegates to possess these traits, but the fact that such qualities were so conspicuous would seem to indicate that they are not perceived by the delegates to be general or even common among missionary personnel.

Follow-on from the Seminars
1. Replication of the Gospel and Culture Seminars

The seminar participants stated that apart from the discussions on their designated subjects with a view to producing the three documents, they had not had similar seminars in their own areas. The questionnaire did not ask them the reasons for this, but several volunteered the information: '*too busy*', '*practical problems of transport', 'lack of financial means', 'co-ordination problems'*[209] and *'preoccupation with administrational matters within the Church'*.

Of the two seminar groups, it was the Swahili delegates who understood it to be their responsibility to report back to the churches that they represented:

i. The 'pasteur responsable' of the Rethy area[210] and member of the Swahili seminar, saw it as his duty to convey to the pastors and elders of the local churches under his auspices something of what the seminar had covered — especially since the issue of burial practices (matanga) was causing widespread confusion among Christians at the time. Minutes of by-gone Rethy Church Councils witness the recurrent concern which traditional 'matanga' customs cause the church and its leaders.[211] The major problem concerned with mourning customs is the 'enlèvement de deuil' (literally, 'lifting of mourning'), a second ceremony held some months (sometimes even years) after the decease and burial of a clan member. The practice is common among several Zaïrian tribes.[212] While exceptions cannot be ruled out,[213] the custom is generally observed out of fear of ancestral spirits.[214] The traditional conception is expressed by Nkongolo wa Mbiye:

> Our fathers, mothers, and brothers are still members of our family... If you neglect your fathers and mothers who have died, the spirits will turn their back on you. Of such an evil-hearted egoist the spirits declare: 'This one doesn't know his parents any more; he has forgotten us. So now, we also will forget him.'[215]

Consequently, the custom is frequently observed of taking a portion of soil from the grave and an item of clothing from the deceased to bury nearer to home and of placing eating utensils beside the grave for the hungry returning spirit. Some church members similarly wish to observe the traditional customs out of fear of ancestral spirits; the others perform certain duties, not from fear of the spirits, but from the desire to express their respect for the departed by honouring their memory. Church Council minutes in the past have simply outlawed the customs for Christians, with little or no evidence of tackling the underlying thinking from a theological standpoint. One Council minute states: 'We forbid the Church to bury earth or clothing after a funeral, or to walk in front of the corpse, or to place a plate and fork. All this is lies (Swahili: 'uwongo'). For this is not Church practice.'[216] The Rethy pastor visited all 14 of the local churches within his oversight,[217] explaining to elders and pastors what had been done at the seminar and discussing particularly the question of 'matanga'.

ii. The current CECA director of radio spoke of a seminar of about 15 pastors and elders held towards the end of 1984 at Bogoro. In the seminar, he sought to reproduce what he himself had participated in several months previously, but adapted it to a lower educational level. The delegates considered the culture of which they were part and especially those aspects of it that the Gospel had not yet touched such as marriage, and funeral and burial practices. Discussion established distinctions between practices which were not in conflict with their understanding of Scripture and others that were.[218]

While it was obvious that very little of an organized seminar nature (apart from the above examples) had taken place following Gration's visits, the questionnaire sought to probe further in order to ascertain whether in the delegates' individual ministries the seminars and their methodology had exerted an influence. While the large majority of the participants are pastors, their particular occupations may be summarized as follows:

Bible and theological teaching	7
CECA administration	4
pastors in local churches	4
chaplains in secondary schools	2
evangelism	1
co-ordinator Christian Education	1
editor of CECA publishing house	1
director of CECA printing	1
radio programme producer	1
co-ordinator TEE (see 21ff.)	1

23

The questionnaire asked:

> Have the seminars influenced your ministry in any of the following areas: preaching, Bible teaching, hymn composition, seminars for youth, elders, deacons, etc, publication, others ?

Participants were asked to furnish concrete examples in their answers.

2. Preaching

Several participants indicated that they had already been in the habit of contextualizing their preaching and were not aware that they had changed their practices becuase of the seminars. One admitted frankly that certain issues, such as tribalism, were so 'hot' that he felt it wiser to steer away from them in preaching.[219] Over half of the seminar-participants responded positively with examples of sermon subjects or applications more oriented towards the real African world as a result of their discussions in 1983 and 1984. Examples include:

i Death and the hereafter

a) The Legal Representative of the CECA (French seminar) was invited to preach on the occasion of the funeral of the father of the Commissaire Sous-Régional (Bunia's leading political figure). He preached in the open air in front of the Commissaire's residence in Bunia and in the presence of a very large crowd. The sermon sought to explain the Biblical view of what happens at death and was based on Psalm 23, with special emphasis on v. 3a, *'He* (God, as opposed to spirits) *restores my soul'.*[220]

b) Rethy's leading pastor (Swahili seminar) sought to address the question of death and the hearafter in a sermon which was based on Jesus' words to the dying thief: *'Today you will be with me in paradise'* (Luke 23: 43). From the text he taught that Scripture leaves no room for ancestor activity, and that the repentant criminal had nothing to fear beyond death. He further illustrated the error of pagan burial rites and the placating of spirits by citing the example of David who spent seven days and nights praying and fasting to save his child's life but when he realised that it was dead, knew he could do nothing more for it:

> Now that he is dead, why should I fast? Can I bring him back again? I will go to him, but he will not return to me. (2 Samuel 12: 23).[221]

ii. Tribalism

a) A Bible Institute teacher (French seminar) preached a sermon at the CECA centre of Linga,[222] where tribal tension has for several years hindered harmony and progress in church work, he chose as his text for the Sunday service I Corinthians 12: 13[223] and in the application spoke of Christian unity in a context of tribal conflict.[224]

b) The leading pastor of CECA station Linga (Swahili seminar) was among the hundreds that converged on Bogoro[225] for the funeral of a well-known pastor/evangelist in 1986. Because of tribal tension in the area, the women from one village refused to partake of the meal which had been prepared by the women of the deceased pastor's village, lest it had been poisoned in a spirit of revenge. The interviewee chose to preach on the subject of tribalism and Christian unity and later persuaded the women to eat together so as to put the message preached into action.[226]

iii. Fetishism (protective witchcraft)

a) In a sermon at the CAFEZA centre of Lolwa,[227] the same pastor as in ii.a) (above) sought to counsel the newly-converted by deliberately discussing some of the real-life features of village life which would severely test the new believers, such as fetishism and pagan dances.[228]

b) Another Rethy pastor (Swahili seminar) stated that he was seeking to make his preaching more penetrating both inside the church and by the graveside. At one service, preaching about witch-craft and faith, he testified that when three of his own children were gravely sick one after the other, a family member urged him to consult the 'nganga kisi', but he refused, quoting Philippians 1:20-21:

I eagerly expect and hope that I will in no way be ashamed,
but will have sufficient courage so that now as always Christ
will be exalted in my body, whether by life or by death. For
to me, to live is Christ and to die is gain.[229]

iv. Sorcery (destructive witchraft)[230]

a) A seminary teacher (French seminar) related a recent fireside
sermon and discussion that took place at Bogoro on the occasion of
a funeral of a Sunday School teacher. The wife of the deceased, shortly
before his death, had a vivid dream in which she saw a woman
approaching, armed with a large stick. She woke to find that her
sleeping husband had a woven grass string around his throat and
concluded that it was the work of the woman she had recognized in her
dream. Alarmed, they woke the rest of the village, but the woman
strenuously denied the accusations which the couple made against
her. The following night, the man found a second string like the first,
inside his bed. Convinced of the inevitability of his doom, he committed suicide.[231] At the public 'palabre' the woman eventually admitted
she had conspired with two other men to kill the deceased. Her added
confession that she had tried to kill the elder brother of the interviewee
'on several occasions', but had never been able to, gave the intended
victim opportunity in the fireside discussion to explain that a truly
committed Christian need fear nothing from sorcery.[232]

v. Sermon illustrations from traditional culture

a) One of Rethy's pastors (Swahili seminar), in his capacity as
'Inspecteur de finance' for the Church, endeavoured to educate local
church congregations to be better stewards not only of their money,
but also of their other forms of wealth. To illustrate his point and
enable his hearers to relate to it, he reminded them how their
predecessors offered all manner of things to their 'miungu' (Swahili:
gods): samples of their crops, libations, choice parts of animals they
had killed, etc. To an even greater extent, they should recognize that
the true God has claims not merely on their money, but rather on all

that they possess. (With much of the rural population involved in subsistence farming, the pastor was attempting to encourage his church-goers that not only monetary offerings but also gifts of livestock, poultry, vegetables and grain would all help in providing for those who serve the churches).[233]

b) The elderly Honorary President of CECA (Swahili seminar) related a sermon he was invited to preach at the burial of Chief Uchama of Anbake, north of Lake Mobutu. In his sermon he contrasted the inevitably transitory nature of human chieftainship with the permanence of Christ's: *'Jesus Christ is the same yesterday and today and forever.'* (Hebrews 13:8)[234]

3. Teaching

Of the seven involved in Bible teaching or theological education, six gave examples of how they felt the seminar methodology had helped in their classroom ministry. Only one, a Seminary teacher, specified that he had not been consciously helped in his teaching by the meetings.[235]

i. Teaching methodology

The Coordinator of Theological Education by Extension (French Seminar) spoke of the 142 centres in the CECA region at each of which an average of between eight and fifteen students meet once a week to discuss the questions in their programmed texts (for discussion of TEE, see above, pp. 262ff). The TEE system, with its less formal approach to teaching, favours discussion rather than lecture for its weekly meetings, and this was reinforced for the co-ordinator by the methodology used in the Gospel and Culture seminars. A workshop was held in order to initiate all group leaders in the skills of stimulating reflection and discussion about the daily realities of Zaïrian life, in an attempt to root the teaching firmly in the soil of the local context.[236]

ii. Homiletics

In his preaching classes, a teacher at Linga Bible Institute favoured the 'problem-solution' method of sermon preparation. A problem of contemporary Zaïrian society, such as polygamy, was chosen for consideration by the class and led to a 'vif débat'. Then a student was designated to prepare a sermon addressing the problem and proposing a Christian (biblical) solution. Other examples of problems included: corruption, discouragement, sorcery, immorality, divorce, juvenile delinquency and the generation gap. Sermons were delivered first to fellow students for further discussion before being used in local churches.[237]

iii. Theology

a) The official Bunia Seminary curriculum[238] stipulates that the subject of Biblical Anthropology should cover

man, his original nature, the image of God, the Fall, sin, Satan, and the angels.

The Seminary teacher responsible for Systematic Theology (French seminar), regularly goes beyond the stated limits of the subject in order to discuss in depth the question of evil spirits which he perceives to be of major importance in the society from which the students come and to which they will be ministering.[239]

b) The Oicha[240] Bible Institute director (French seminar), responsible for some of the theology classes in his institution, chooses to probe not only orthodox definitions of, for instance, 'faith' and 'prayer', but also what these things really mean in everyday life and typical crises of the Zaïrian situation. In his interview he cited the example of a 'case study' discussion in class about a church member being treated in hospital and praying for healing while also secretly contacting a 'nganga kisi' because he suspects that he is the victim of sorcery. The class then discussed his actions, motives and fears and their relation to faith and prayer.[241]

iv. Practical Theology.

a) Every year as part of their practical training, Bunia Seminary 2nd-year students complete a month-long apprenticeship with an experienced pastor in a local church, being exposed to a wide variety of activities (preaching, committees, counselling, youth groups, etc).

The Seminary teacher (French seminar), designated to counsel the students before they set off for their practical 'stage', also chooses to discuss with them as a group after their return and includes suitable issues in his 3rd-year Ethics course. Two examples of such issues were cited:

1. In the Adi-Abedju area near the frontier with Sudan it is customary for the brothers of a deceased to pay the maternal uncles as *'compensation for lost benefits'*; if they fail to do so, they can be cursed. What should the Christian attitude be towards such family obligations?

2. In the Oicha region, fashion dictates that girls should plait their hair; the Church, however, forbids the practice. Is it the girls who should change their ways, or the Church its rules?[242]

b   Another Seminary teacher (French seminar), responsible for the course on Christian Home, not only includes the wives of the men in his course, but integrates them fully in the discussions by dropping French in favour of Swahili.[243] The course is designed not only to help the student couples themselves in a society where marital and sexual questions are seldom discussed openly, but also to address questions that they will be having to deal with in their practical church ministry upon leaving the Seminary. The Seminary has from its inception emphasized that the training it provides is intended to equip the wives of the students for ministry alongside their husbands. Thus among the questions covered is that of 'trial marriages', increasingly common among Zaïre's young people. Underlying reasons are sought for the apparent turning from both traditional and Church weddings, including: reluctance of long-term commitment, fear of the shame of the marriage not lasting, the desire to ascertain fertility before life-long commitment to a partner and the unreasonable bride-price demands that are made. The interviewee stated that the course was always a most lively and enjoyable one and that when the reasons were carefully sought behind certain traditional practices and attitudes, then appropriate guiding principles from the Bible were not difficult to discover.[244]

4. *Hymns*

The generally scant response to this question from the participants revealed that few of the leaders of CECA have yet realised how important hymns are in both expressing and influencing belief patterns. Most of those interviewed expressed that they either lacked the time or the gifts to involve themselves in choirs. Yet the importance of choir groups in current church liturgy is indicated not only by the number of groups (the Rethy Section alone has about 30 choir groups),[245] but also by the proportion of time given to them in regular church services.

i. Of all the participants questioned, it was the leading pastor at Rethy who spoke most enthusiastically about the role of choirs in communicating the Christian message. In his own Rethy region, most of the 30 choral groups are regularly involved in the Sunday worship services. At the central Sunday morning service lasting two hours, just over half the total time was taken by choral groups singing, some of them accompanied by locally-made harps of different sizes. The interviewee was eagerly anticipating a forthcoming seminar at Rethy, intended in part for choir leaders and members.[246]

ii. The Rethy Christian Education Seminar, 4th-8th February, 1987. One of the four days was designated for instructing and exhorting choir members. The duplicated hand-out intended for the delegates (two sides of closely typed foolscap paper) represents probably the most serious attempt to impress upon the choir members the purpose and importance of their contribution. It was prepared by the CECA Department of Christian Education in Bunia, intended not only for the Rethy seminar, but for others in different regions of CECA territory. Liberally supported in its various guidelines by Bible references, the document establishes that the personal life-style of the singer must in no way contradict what he sings about. The various objectives of any choir are listed (praise, worship, repentance, comfort, prayer, edification, etc.) and the delegates are solemnly reminded that no song should be devoid of teaching or meaning.[247] The rightness of all and any instruments for choir purposes is affirmed (supported by the reference to the exhaustive list in Psalm 150 and by Psalm 33 which, with its mention of harps and lyres, would be particularly appropriate for the Rethy area), but it is emphasized that they should never just be played for their own sake, nor should they ever drown the words. Further, the rhythm should be moderate so as to avoid causing some to tap their feet or move their bodies in an unseemly way.[248] Beyond this, the document does not directly address the sensitive question of dance; CECA policy is to discourage it as too close to practices which it considers to be incompatible with Christian behaviour.[249] Sundry details as to posture, dress[250] and gestures are added in the document, as well as exhortations about personal conduct. While the document does mention in the briefest possible way that choirs may have a role of comforting the sad and paying *courtesy visits*, it surprisingly does not explore at all the possible role of choirs or hymns in the work and witness of the Church outside of services, at birth celebrations, weddings, times of drought or harvest, funerals, etc.[251]

iii. The Co-ordinator of Christian Education (French Seminar) reported that during the one year of 1984 there were no fewer than 46 marriage ceremonies in the church at Aru-Ania. Songs were specially composed to be sung at some of those weddings, with the express purpose of conveying Christian teaching on the subject of marriage.[252]

5. Seminars

While, as we have seen, the three regional groups as such did not organize seminars in their areas, several individuals who had participated in the seminars have sought to lead seminars on given subjects:

i. Aungba[253] seminars on fetishism. The Bible School director of Aungba (French seminar) held a series of monthly seminars, first for church members of the immediate locality and then for wider participation by leaders of different church organizations in the whole Aungba 'District'. Both seminars were on fetishism and included both talks and lively discussions. A duplicated handout was prepared for the latter seminar.[254]

ii. The current Administrative Secretary for CECA (formerly teacher at Rethy secondary school, French seminar) and co-author of the document 'The Gospel and African Beliefs', led a seminar for pastors in his area of Rethy in 1984, in which he sought to reproduce the non-lecture method of stimulating reflection. It concerned some of the areas covered in the document. This in turn led to being invited by the CECA Co-ordination d'Education department to lead a series of seminars for primary and secondary directors[255] on the general subject of syncretism in the Church. The seminars took place at important CECA centres of Rethy, Kasengu and Watsa. In 1986 he was further invited by the Church to hold seminars in two widely separated centres of Beni[256] and Djugu.[257] In these latter two, the delegates themselves discussed and then listed what they felt to be the *'illnesses'* of the Church. One of the striking things to emerge from the exercise was that while there was some duplication of items, the two lists were far from identical. The Beni group placed as their priority the evils of sorcery and fear of spirits, while the delegates at Djugu (situated as it is in an area interpenetration of the Bahema, Walendu and Alur tribes) placed 'tribalism' and 'fear of speaking out' as the most important weaknesses in the Church. The interviewee stated that the contrast between the two lists had shown him that people's needs were not the same everywhere and that preachers and teachers needed to understand this fact if they were to have a message that penetrated by meeting real needs. The participants of the two seminars, having identified the various ills of the Church on the one day, returned the next day to search together for *'remedies'*.[258]

iii. Two Bunia pastors (French seminar) reported on an experiment in the five local churches in and around the town of Bunia. In an attempt to encourage active reflection about burial practices (an area in which the leading pastors considered there was compromise or, at best, lack of discernment on the part of church members), a list of typical activities was sent to each local church. These included the wearing of a straw in the hair by the (male) mourners, the sounding of car horns 50 metres from the cemetry and the washing of hands after the return from the cemetry. The local church elders were asked to discuss why these practices were observed and whether the reasons advanced were compatible with Christian belief. At a subsequent meeting, the delegate(s) reported on their discussions, where it became evident that while some traditions were incompatible with Christian belief (for instance because of the implicit fear of ancestral and other spirits), other practices were positively good, while still others were not wrong in themselves, but meaningless and serving no useful purpose. It was then urged by the leading pastors that sermons should then be preached on the subject to share with the church members the conclusions arrived at.[259]

iv. The Oicha Bible Institute director (French Seminar) conducted a seminar (talk followed by discussion) on the subject of fetishism at Oicha. The day following the seminar, a youth came to him and declared that he had sensed during the seminar that all that the director had said was aimed at him, as he possessed and used an aphrodisiac powder. He wanted the pastor to witness his throwing away of the powder as a determined break with his former practices. The director, however, insisted rather that the youth take the powder back to the one who had provided him with it, so that his renunciation of the powder might (hopefully) have a positive influence on the supplier.[260]

v. The director of 'Editions CECA' (French seminar) was invited by the organizers of the 'Ligue pour la lecture de la Bible'[261] to hold seminars on the subject of tribalism for a youth camp at the CECA centre of Linga. Over the years Linga has shared with Rethy the tribal tensions which have been the cause of serious difficulties in the Church. Between 70 and 80 campers were present, drawn from all over the CECA territory.[262]

vi. The same director spoke of weekly seminars held at Rethy and regularly (and, by all accounts, eagerly) attended by between 50 and 80 young people, mainly from the secondary school. A speaker is proposed for a subject of current importance in society; examples included sex and marriage, bride-price, the home. The 'exposé' is followed by an open discussion after which the speaker will attempt to summarize what was discussed and suggest biblical principles which might guide thought on the subject. Those who attend do so of their own volition as the seminars are not an obligatory part of the school curriculum.[263]

6. Writing and Publishing

As would be expected, it was the delegates of the French seminar that were the more concerned about the importance of exercising an influence through publishing. At the close of the 1984 seminar in Bunia, it was agreed that each of the three groups should amend their documents in the light of comments and criticisms by the plenary group. The intention was that the revised documents would be printed, although Gration's field notes record that at least one delegate, aware of the realities of limited means within the country, suggested that printing would depend upon outside funds (from Gration or someone else). The three documents, as has already been stated, have not been published, for a variety of reasons (see p. 244 above).

However, apart from the three documents, certain publishing has taken place in line with the interests of the seminar:

i. 'Cheka na Fikiri' (Swahili: Laugh and Ponder). A small monthly foolscap paper, produced at Rethy, aimed at a wide rather than an intellectual readership, with an emphasis upon light-hearted but thought-provoking articles, seeking to penetrate key areas of thought and behaviour. The producer, one of the participants at the French seminars, had had training in literature and communications in Nairobi.[264] Sales were encouraged by the offer of a monthly prize for correct answers to a quiz. A promising initiative was brought to an end after an article (illustrated by, but not written by the producer) provoked a storm of protest. It was entitled 'Sheria za dawa' (Swahili: The laws of medicine) and targetted corruption and bribery in hospitals (eg. monetary incentives for proper treatment, etc.). Although their own hospital was not mentioned by name, medical personnel at the Rethy Hospital had little doubt that the accusations were levelled against them and that it was the personal work of the producer. They reacted violently, insisting that the producer retract the article. Their behaviour was so threatening that the producer had to send his wife to another hospital for the birth of their child. Publication of the sheet ceased soon after, subsumed by the magazine 'Tujenge'.[265]

ii. 'Tujenge' (Swahili: Let's build). This biannual magazine was launched towards the end of 1984 as the official Editions CECA publication, aimed generally at 15 to 35-year-olds. On the back cover of the magazine the objectives of both Editions CECA and of the magazine 'Tujenge' were listed,[266] the former including the aim: '*To penetrate structures of Zaïrian belief and culture with the living truth of God's word*', and the latter that of: '*addressing difficult questions of our time in the light of the word of God*', both goals coinciding exactly with those of the seminars. The magazine was on an altogether more ambitious scale than the leaflet 'Cheka na Fikiri', comprising about 20 pages of letters to the editor, news items of current interest, topical articles and cartoon and/or photo stories. It was published simultaneously in French and Swahili and French and Lingala. The chief editor of the magazine was the same as for 'Cheka na Fikiri'.

The magazine sought to be faithful to its stated objectives by addressing important issues in society and in the church, including abortion, drink, marriage, divorce, polygamy and corruption.[267] Vol. 1, No. 2, for instance, chose the subject of fashion among young people and the dangers accompanying an obsessive attitude towards it. Illustrated by several photos and with examples with which any young person in Zaïre could readily identify, its appeal would have been considerable. A photo comic-strip story dealt light-heartedly but thought-provokingly with attitudes towards marriage among young people. Finally, an article presented both sides of the question of whether or not the CECA should break from its traditional past and adopt an episcopal system, quoting proponents and opponents, some of them highly-placed in the Church. At a time when the issue was causing tension in the CECA, the article sparked strong reaction in the leadership of the Church. After just two numbers, publication of the magazine was ordered to be suspended by the Administrative Council on the grounds that it was not the correct forum for sensitive Church issues to be discussed.[268] Later, at a journalism seminar in 1986, advisors from Nairobi suggested that (in addition to the other reasons) 'Tujenge' had been too ambitious from the start and that the producers would have been wiser to start with something more modest and gradually expand as their readership stabilized and grew. The first issue had 1,900 printed, the second 1,000.[269] The Director of 'Editions CECA' is convinced that 'Tujenge' has only temporarily halted production and predicts that it will one day recommence.

iii. One of the authors of the Rethy document on 'Gospel and African Beliefs' prepared a substantial article on syncretism (the fruit, in part, of his seminars on the subject, see p 257). The article was too long to be published in 'Tujenge' and may be published as a separate booklet in its own right.[270]

iv. Writers Clubs. While there was no formal link between the Gospel and Culture Seminars and the recently established Writers Clubs, both initiatives share a similar spirit and vision. Missionary David Langford, who was involved in both the seminars and the Clubs states:

> The 'philosophy' of the Writers Clubs is to develop Zaïrian writers who can address Zaïrian needs and problems.[271]

There was partial overlap in the delegates at the two initiatives.

Delegates who were at the two Gospel and Culture Seminars and who worked on the three documents saw a strategic relationship between their work and the 'Editions CECA' printing and publishing house. According to Kwany,

> right from the first seminar, the participants hoped that Editions CECA would be the outlet of the seminar. The reason why Bura Thenga was chosen to be the executive co-ordinator of the follow-on from the seminars was that he was (then) the only one working in the editorial bureau of the Press.'[272]

Two journalism seminars were organized at Rethy. Delegates to the first (3rd-6th October, 1983) were chosen by Bura and Langford, with recommendations from others at Blukwa and Bunia. Selection was guided partly by the participants' recognized ability (or promise) in the area of communication and partly in terms of centres which would later serve as nuclei for eventual working together. The centres in mind at the time were: Aungba, Rethy, Blukwa, Bunia and Oicha. It was Kwany (by then chosen to be director of the 'Editions CECA' who was responsible for selection of participants at the second journalism seminar (1st-3rd July, 1986). Fewer were invited to the second seminar in an effort to keep costs down; of the twelve who attended, five had taken part in the first seminar and had demonstrated their enthusiasm by having done some writing. For both seminars, journalism experts were invited from Kenya: Haron Wachira, then assistant editor of Step magazine attended both seminars and he was joined for the second seminar by Tim Stafford.[273]

At the close of the second seminar, the participants themselves suggested a list of some 39 topics of vital concern or interest to Zaïrians.[274] Many of the topics suggested were identical to those proposed at the Gospel and Culture Seminars. Each delegate left with a copy of the list, which had below it certain remarks from the seminar leaders concerning the prioritization and categorization of the topics and also advice concerning establishing clearly before writing the 'target readership' (youth, church workers, etc.)

About six weeks after the second seminar, Kwany sent out a letter to all those who had attended, informing them that they constituted the new 'Clubs d'Ecrivains', that they could associate others who shared the basic aim of the initiative and urging them to get to work without further delay. The letter included simple guidelines: the clubs should meet together once a month for sessions no shorter than 3 hours in order to read, discuss and critique each others articles. Each club should choose a leader who would be responsible for calling the meetings and for constantly encouraging the members to write. Each member was sent a copy of the objectives of the 'Editions CECA' and they were reminded that their articles should correspond with these objectives, the most pertinent of which would be No. 4:

Help believers to deepen their spiritual life

a) by penetrating the structures of beliefs and customs of Zaïrians,

b) by seeking to correct social evils (such as corruption, immorality, polygamy, drunkenness, etc.)

c) by providing tools for the ministry of pastors.[275]

The articles deemed best by each group were to be returned to Rethy for possible printing.[276]

By July 1987, there were four such Clubs functioning more or less regularly: Napopo, Aungba, Rethy and Bunia, with two others (Blukwa and Oicha) seeking to become established. From the work of these Clubs has come a modest publication 'Cahiers d'Auteurs' as an outlet for the articles written. The 'Cahier' is a three-page double-sided duplicated document, stapled together in one corner. The selection and editing of the articles has been entirely Kwany's work. Articles include: a true story of a schoolgirl pregnancy, abortion and death; a two-part article taking a critical look at pastors' attitudes and lifestyles; another on the folly of smoking; one by Kwany himself entitled 'One baboon mocks another';[277] one on the use of time; another by a Zaïrian doctor at Nyankunde on marital fidelity.

The Clubs are still in their early days and it is impossible to know at present if they will continue and grow or otherwise, although with a Director of 'Editions CECA' who has considerable organising skill and has benefited from further technical skills training in Nairobi, the outlook is promising. Of considerable importance is the fact that of the seven contributors of the articles in the first two issues, only two are pastors. The opportunity for lay Christians (school teachers, doctors, administrators) to contribute to the spiritual and reflective life of the Church represents an encouraging departure from the monopoly held to date by ecclesiastical 'professionals'.

7. Other

i. Radio

The recently appointed Director of Radio for CECA (French seminar) has been set aside in order to prepare programmes for transmission from the local national radio station, CANDIP.[278] The multi-language transmissions from the station are listened to by many hundreds of thousands in N-E Zaïre (as far away as Kisangani, 700kms to the west) for entertainment, agricultural, educational and medical information, as well as for national and international news. The CECA is accorded two half-hourly religious broadcasts each week. The director of CECA radio programmes, Seminary-trained and for several years co-ordinator of evangelism, seeks to produce programmes adapted to the Zaïrian scene, not only by addressing some of the issues of contemporary society, but also by taking as his starting point for the Christian message any national events on the calender (eg. 30th June, Independence Day... freedom... search for liberation... freedom in Christ; January 1, New Year's Day... joy of new beginnings... new birth in Christ, etc). The interviewee explained how Gration's seminars had only served to underline and clarify previous insights, acquired in Nairobi and Kinshasa, years before. [279]

ii. Cassettes

Two of the French Seminar participants[280] are actively working on exploring the use of cassettes for evangelism and Christian teaching. Although the project is still in a pioneer stage, the experiment proceeds on the basis that the oral method of teaching/learning is closer to traditional African ways than the literary and residential methods imported from the West. Cassette programmes in the trade languages of Swahili and Lingala (or Bangala) and perhaps even in local tribal languages, would seek to teach groups gathered informally in the shade of a tree or around the fire in the evening. The cassette of 'real life' drama stories portraying typical ethical or religious predicaments could be interrupted by the pastor/evangelist to give time for listeners to suggest what might happen next, or what they themselves would do in the given crises, and why. The recording could then be resumed, with heightened interest on the part of the listeners, and the cassette would end with appropriate biblical principles to guide a Christian seeking to lead a consistent Christian life in the contemporary (Zaïrian and village) community.[281] The two initiators of the method expect that the process will facilitate an integrated thought-behaviour pattern. In contrast, the method of knowledge-acquisition which characterizes residential theological institutions (artificial, classroom context and emphasis on success in examinations) can easily result in an accumulation of factual, cerebral theory divorced from the issues of the real world (cf. the 'two levels', pp. 269ff).

Conclusion

Superficially, the seminars appear to have fallen short of their goals. Three years after the second seminar one of the three documents has still not been revised following the discussions in plenary session, (May, 1984) and none of the documents has been printed in any form. The three groups have not continued to meet as such to explore other issues and the entire group-reflection process has virtually ceased. The reasons for this lack of success would include the following:

a) Loss of co-ordination. For various reasons the co-ordinator chosen by the delegates in 1984 no longer exercises that role. No successor was appointed. Without the prodding and encouragement of a co-ordinator, delegates quickly became fully reabsorbed in their usual heavy round of immediate duties.[282]

b) Practical and financial problems. The 1984 seminar in Bunia raised the unavoidable practical questions of transport, feeding and materials, each with accompanying financial implications. The decisions made then displayed a continuing dependence upon external funding (with its accompanying negative implications on 'ownership') but even this was hampered by departure from Zaïre of expatriate personnel.[283]

c) Ecclesiastical problems. Several delegates expressed awareness of the sensitivity of the Church hierarchy to certain issues. One of the factors is the difficulty of sifting and selecting elements of the cultural complex. Culture may be compared with a web in which strands are not only many and varied, but also interconnected in such a way that it is impossible to pull one free without affecting the others.[284] For this reason, many church leaders would prefer to make a clean break with certain practices simply because they are part of the traditional scene which they feel is already too compromised. Early undiscerning missionary attitudes, rightly castigated by many African thinkers as dismissing whole areas of traditional African life as evil, now reappear among African church leaders themselves. Paradoxically, it is often missionary thinkers who are the most radical in their concern for contextualization. A distinct problem which was cited by more than one delegate was that new preoccupations within the church (for instance, the episcopacy issue) had distracted the participants from the areas discussed by the seminars.

For these reasons, the seminar process foundered, at least temporarily. However, closer examination would suggest that at a deeper level more has been achieved. Despite apparent lack of success of stated aims, the seminars have created or given fresh impetus to the delegates' concern to engage the real social, cultural and religious issues of life in Zaïre with the Christian gospel. As individuals, many of the delegates have readjusted their preaching and teaching to be more pertinent to the concerns and ways of thinking of their hearers and students. That the seminars have had these positive results may be attributed to certain factors:

a) Delegate calibre. Gration himself was encouraged with the maturity of reflection of the Zaïrian delegates, especially those of the French seminar. In 1984 he had conducted two similar seminars in Kenya (at Kapsabet and Machakos) which he sensed were not as fruitful. A possible reason for the deeper discernment of the Zaïrian delegates could be due to the fact that, bereft of expatriate help during the troubled years of 1964-67, the African leadership of the Church in Zaïre was compelled to stand on its own in a way which the Kenyan church has not known.[285] Of the two seminars, it was the French one where, in Gration's opinion, reflection was more penetrating. Further education (secondary and university) permitted the French seminar delegates to conceptualize, analyse and express themselves in a way which was apparently denied the members of the Swahili seminar. This does not deny the profitability of the Swahili seminars; it does imply that the two levels proceed at different speeds and according to different dynamics.

b) Gration's role as 'facilitator'. Interviews with the participants made it clear that they perceived Gration's role to have been crucial to the success of the initiative (see pp. 299ff). While none ruled out that another missionary or national leader could help in such seminars in future, it was made clear that for such a one to succeed, he would need a comparable combination of humility (vulnerability), sensitivity and wisdom. These qualities were perceived to be of greater importance than age or experience, although these too helped. Only in a setting of transparent honestly could there be a true sharing of attitudes, prejudices and failings; a facilitator whose attitudes and manner failed to portray and encourage such frankness could not be expected to succeed. This is the 'one small point' isolated by Barrett as having too often been absent in Western missions — 'love as listening, sharing, sympathizing and sensitive understanding in depth between equals'.[286]

c) Seminar methodology. The large majority of the delegates readily recalled and appreciated the methodology of the seminars as being one that permitted and prompted them to do the talking, reflecting and problem solving. This was in contrast to many seminars where the delegates do little more than passively absorb new information. Of importance to the success of the methodology is the choice by the facilitator of key questions which, far from dictating the course and outcome of the seminar simply permit the delegates to establish their own priorities. In the particular case of the Zaïre seminars, the key questions were: 'How has the Gospel touched and changed African culture' and perhaps more penetrating still, 'What areas of African culture has the Gospel not transformed?'[287] The process is thus open-ended, as opposed to closed (as in the case of content-transmission), and as such requires and encourages a certain maturity on the part of the participant. One Swahili seminar delegate proposed that the methodology should be used far more in theological education at all levels; for lack of mature discernment the present system of theological education has produced church leaders who are dogmatic about what they have learned but unsure of anything beyond ('pastors who know all and who dislike questions and who mistrust research and initiative').[288]

d) Issue-consciousness. The seminars took place at a time when various problems were 'outcropping' in the CECA scene, particularly those of burial practices and tribalism. The delegates were aware that certain issues were threatening the life and health of the Church. The seminars, therefore, were not mere academic exercises, but a genuine urgent grappling with critical questions. The seminar methodology of delegate agenda-setting was flexible enough for the real issues to be located and discussed. In a tranquil church situation it is unlikely that the discussions would be as productive.

It should not be assumed that the methodology can only succeed in centralised meetings with all the implied expense of transport, feeding and accommodation. Nor should it be perceived as an alternative to residential theological and Bible School practice; the latter would be made more effective if it incorporated the former, that, is, instead of the teacher relying exclusively on the lecture method of content-transmission, due place should be given to student participation, personal research and group discovery.[289] Clearly, certain theological subjects lend themselves more to discussion than others, while disciplines such as biblical languages and Church History still of necessity demand a larger proportion of content transmission. Theological curriculum should not only address but also be informed by the socio-cultural milieu in which the education takes place to ensure it is answering questions that are really being asked.

If, as Dickson says, the quest for African Christian Theology is 'To bring faith in Christ to bear upon the African life-experience[290] then discursive theological reflection such as that done in and since the Gospel and Culture seminars is an important means to that end. By deliberately pursuing an integrated Christian understanding of real-life issues where there is no discrepancy between belief and behaviour, the seminar delegates were looking for and discovering a theology to live by.

References

1. A preliminary 'scouting' trip into North-Eastern Congo had been made 18 months earlier, in 1910, by Messrs Stauffacher and Gribble. The first party to settle in the Congo was led by C. E. Hurlburt (appointed General Director of the Mission in 1897, missionary in Africa from 1901 to 1925) and consisted of Dr Florence Newberry, John and Florence Stauffacher and two sons, Mr and Mrs Haas and baby and Miss Harland. They landed at Mahagi Port (on the shores of Lake Albert) on 20th April, 1912. Historical details in: K. Richardson, *Garden of Miracles; the story of the Africa Inland Mission*, AIM, London, 1968. C. E. Hurlburt's own description of the arrival in Congo is in *Hearing and Doing* (magazine of the AIM, Vol. 17, No. 2, 1912, - archives AIM, 2 Vorley Rd., Archway, London). Also of historical interest but in popular style, M. S. Grimes, *Life out of Death, the story of the Africa Inland Mission*, AIM, 1917.

2. Peter Cameron Scott, Founder of the Africa Inland Mission. Born in Glasgow, 7th March, 1867. Emigrated with his parents to Philadelphia, USA. After two critical spiritual experiences, Scott dedicated himself totally to God's service, entering the New York Missionary Training College. Feeling the divine call to serve in Africa to be too persistent and urgent, he did not complete his 3-year training. His first attempt to reach the interior of the Continent was from the west, landing at Banana on the mouth of the Congo River, in January, 1891. Only months after arriving he was compelled to bury his own brother John who had joined him and soon after he himself was evacuated from the country unconscious. During a convalescent period based in Scotland,

Scott visited Westminster Abbey and, as he knelt beside the tomb of David Livingstone, he received a 'vision' of missionary stations reaching across Africa from the East. Scott returned to the United States, where a committee was formed to plan towards the fulfilment of the vision. The first party of eight left America in August, 1895 and eventually arrived in Zanzibar in October. The coastal areas of Kenya were already occupied by other missions such as the Church Missionary Society, the German Lutheran Mission and the Methodist Mission. Scott, however, made his ambition that of St. Paul:

> to preach the Gospel where Christ was not known, so that
> I would not be building on someone else's foundation.
> (Rom. 15:20).

Within less than one year, Scott had opened three stations, travelled 2,600 miles on foot, built six houses, planted gardens, tended the sick and tended to correspondence as well as keeping a diary. Barely a year after landing in Kenya, Scott contracted blackwater fever and died, 4th December, 1896, aged only 29. cf: K. Richardson, op. cit. pp. 21-36, T. H. Cope, *The Africa Inland Mission in Kenya. Aspects of its history*, 1895-1945, M. Phil thesis, London Bible College, 1979, pp. 13-16. Also: C. S. Miller, *The Unlocked Door — the life of Peter Cameron Scott*, Parry Jackman Ltd., London, 1955.

3. The difficulties related primarily to the mistrust or hostility of the people of the area, inter-tribal warfare, uncooperative porters, thieving which no precautions seem to have been able to thwart, storms which demolished the missionaries' accommodation, and illness. cf. S. Stirton, *Changing Scenes among the Alur*, AIM n.d., 4-6 and K. Richardson, op. cit. pp. 138ff.

4. The original party were forced to relocate their first settlement from lakeside Mahagi Port to Kasengu in the hills overlooking the lake, the relocation compelled primarily by

> illness, due in large part to our sixteen days' sojourn on the unhealthful lake shore'; letter by Florence A. Newberry, in 'Hearing and Doing', Vol. 17, No. 3, (July-September, 1912) p. 10.

5. Letter from J. Stauffacher, quoted in K. Richardson, op. cit. p. 143.

6. The direct distance on the map between Kasengu and Dungu is about 300 kms (almost 200 mls), but this cannot convey the difficulty of the terrain that had to be crossed and the problems of travel. For instance, Richardson (op. cit. p. 142) writes that the initial party that travelled from Kasengu to Dungu
found themselves only two or three days away from Kasengu after two weeks of travel.

7. The hazards of illness in the early years of missionary endeavour are so well known as to hardly require examples: Miss Newberry reported that most of the initial Congo party had suffered from 'serious illness', and 'Mr. Haas nearly succombed to that dread disease hemoglobinuria' (blackwater fever) (letter, Hearing and Doing, July-September, 1913, p. 10), and in a later letter:
Hardly one of us has escaped from the ravages of the most deadly foe of the health of the missionary in Africa — malaria... (ibid, November 1913, p. 15).
The August 1913 edition of Hearing and Doing announced the death of missionary Frank Millen, who had barely started his work in Africa. Similarly, the May 1914 edition of the same magazine reports the death of missionary Tom Hannay; he sailed for Africa immediately after getting married in July, 1913, the telegram announcing his death arrived in the United States on 9th February, 1914.

8. Statistics for CECA, in letter from Etsea Ang'apoza, Legal Representative of CECA, 7th Sept, 1987:

Catechists	1,790
Evangelists	782
Deacons	1,889
Deaconesses	2,316
Pastors	496
Communicant members	155,302
Non-communicant members	54,649

9. Statistics of CECA evangelistic campaigns (Jan, 1983-June, 1987) in letter from Atido Kunde Dong, dated 3rd Aug, 1987, including an up to date report just submitted to the CECA Administrative Office, dated 14th July, 1987. In the 4^1/2 years covered by the report, 21 evangelistic projects had been

completed (some involving as many as 70 team members), including four to Kenya, two to areas covered by Church bodies other than CECA (at their invitation) and four to secondary schools in CECA. Not all the campaigns had returned statistics, but for the 18 that did, an estimated total 816,138 people heard the preaching, 149,231 conversions were registered and 18,648 indicated their intention to return to Church fellowship. The report realistically prefaces these amazing statistics with the caution:

NB, ceci c'est la constatation humaine; c'est Dieu seul qui connait LE VRAI RESULTAT (capitals in original).

10. Table of AIM missionary occupations for Zaïre, 1987. Statistics furnished by AIM International, 17th June, 1987. Not included are missionaries temporarily home on furlough.

occupation	no.	percent	occupation	no.	percent
medical	19	23.5	homemaker	3	3.7
theol. educ.	15	18.5	developmt.	3	3.7
secondary ed.	11	13.6	church ed.	2	2.5
missionary ed.	11	13.6	TEE	1	1.2
church work	10	12.3	translation	1	1.2
field admin.	3	3.7	other	2	2.5
			total	77	100%

11. The readjustment was less traumatic than for some other Missions because by the time the presidential decree was made, the CECA/AIM field constitution had already been rewritten so as to place

the whole government of the Church into the hands of the Congolese. K. Richardson, op. cit. p. 246.

12. The decree in 1973 (14th February) that effectively terminated the independent existence of missionary societies in Zaïre came at a time of heightened nationalistic feeling and the sensitivity (and often stress) in Church/Mission relations is clearly seen in contemporary writings, both missionary and national; cf. Makanzu M, *L'histoire de l'E.C.Z.*, Kinshasa, n.d., but written in 1972 with the 1973 decree appended. In his 'CECA Report' to the International Council of Africa Inland Mission, Nairobi, 9th May, 1985, CECA Legal Representative Etsea Ang'apoza can look back

positively on the events:

> In 1973, God didn't want the two organizations (ie. CECA and AIM) to work back to back but rather hand in hand. Accordingly, the two were joined and were recognized to have but one legal identity under the present name C.E.C.A. The Council became one and the missionaries are working under the direction of the Administrative Council.

13. Statistics from Etsea Ang'apoza, 'CECA Report' op. cit. p. 2.

14. While this may have been the case with regard to the strictly 'spiritual' (ie. Church) domain, missionaries were less unanimous about the desirability of 'secular' education and training for the Africans. cf. Makanzu, op. cit. pp. 11-12. Cope, M. Phil thesis, op. cit. ch. 3, explores the reasons for the missionary reluctance in providing education for the Africans. Missionaries generally believed that their vocation was to evangelism and church-planting. If schools were started, it was largely because they proved to be a very fruitful means to gain converts (p. 45). The pre-war years saw increasing pressure for education being put on the Mission by Africans (p. 145), but this pressure was resisted, particularly, according to Cope, by the American side of the Mission (p. 147). However, at the end of World War II there was change in the American Home Council of the AIM and with it a more positive attitude towards secular education as a corollary to evangelism and medical work (p. 152).

15. see above, note 8.

16. Source: Etsea A., 'CECA Report', op. cit. p. 3.

17. The five Zaïrian Church bodies and their associated missionary societies responsible for the Bunia Theological Seminary are:
    1. Communauté Nation du Christ en Afrique (CNCA) Unevangelized Fields Mission (UFM), (the UFM ceased working as a Mission in Zaïre in 1978, although several UFM personnel continue working in Zaïre under the auspices of other missions),
    2. Communauté Evangélique au Centre de l'Afrique (CECA)/ Africa Inland Mission (AIM),

3. Communauté des Eglises Baptistes au Zaïre Est (CEBZE)/ Conservative Baptist Foreign Missions Society (CBFMS),

4. Communauté Evangélique du Christ au Coeur de l'Afrique (CECCA)/ Worldwide Evangelization Crusade (WEC),

5. Communauté des Frères Evangéliques au Zaire (CAFEZA)/ Christian Mission in Many Lands (CMML).

18. Banjwade, is centrally situated in the territory formerly served by the Unevangelized Fields Mission, one of the two original Missions involved in the creation of the higher-level seminary.

19. It is an indication that the vision of the founders of the Banjwade Bible Institute (to develop indigenous Church leadership) was not illusory that one of the three first students, Dr. Marini Bodho, has since become President of the CECA Church and Vice-President of the national Protestant Church, the 'Eglise du Christ du Zaire'.

20. Source: 'Self-Evaluation Report', Bunia Theological Seminary, 1985, p. 5 and letter from Acting Director, Alo Dradebo, 2nd Sept, 1987.

21. AIM missionary David Langford and family; they lived among the BaHema at Lonyo, one hour's drive north of Bunia.

22. 'Course Description', Bunia Theological Seminary, 1982.

23. For example, the Academic Secretary of the Kinshasa Protestant Faculty of Theology wrote to the director of the Bunia Seminary in 1982 expressing congratulations to Bunia on the results of the Faculty entrance examination for 1982-83, at which the candidates from Bunia had excelled themselves. One of those candidates went on to do doctoral studies in Belgium. Two years later the same Academic Secretary wrote again about another Bunia graduate who had finished the year at the Kinshasa Faculty as top student.

24. The Seminary's self-evaluation was carried out in partial fulfilment of requirements for accreditation under the Acrediting Council for Theological Education in Africa (ACTEA) — a body related to the Association of Evangelicals in Africa and Madagascar (AEAM).

25. ACTEA recommendations were that the Seminary take determined steps to reduce the number of classroom (lecture) hours and to increase the number of hours for self-directed learning such as library research and project assignments.

26. Minutes of Commission for Degree Programme, Bunia Theological Seminary, 2nd and 25th Jan, 1985, p. 1.

27. Information provided by Interim Director of Bunia Theological Seminary, Alo Dradebo, 18th Aug, 1987.

28. Minutes of Commission for Degree Programme, 2nd and 25th Jan, 1985, p. 1.

29. ibid, p. 1.

30. An example would be the 2-day seminars for pastors and deacons held at Bunia and Chyekele (40 mls from Bunia) in 1979 and again in 1980. A team of three national and expatriate pastors met with groups of about 20 and 30 men respectively in the two places, for sessions of expository devotional teaching, methods of Bible study and discussions led by the Zaïrian team member about 'ills in the Church', in which the delegates themselves identified weaknesses in Church life and then proposed solutions. The team submitted a report to CECA Administrative Council of 1980, in which they enthused about the reception the pastors had given the seminars, but expressed their regret that their multiple responsibilities prevented them from attempting to repeat such seminars in the future. The report urged the Council to release one or two CECA personnel for such ministry throughout CECA. The Council accepted the report, but felt unable at the time to make the suggested appointments.

31. Of Richardson, one Zaïrian pastor has remarked:
    God has given you the long claws of a mother hen, to scratch deeply and uncover the insects for us to eat.
    Letter to the author from D. Richardson, 7th Aug, 1987.

32. Travel costs are assumed by Richardson, but he allows the host-church to contribute his food and accommodation costs. In some of the larger gatherings the churches have also contributed to his travel costs.

33. Letter from Richardson to author, 7th Aug, 1987.

34. Included among the sects present in North-East Zaïre are: Jehovah's Witnesses, (and a related group, Kitawala), Branhamists, the 'Good God' sect (Swahili: Mungu Mwema, Lingala: Nzambi Malamu), Colossians is recognized to have been written against a background of religious pluralism. The emphasis on the centrality of Christ was considered by Richardson to present the surest remedy for a similar pluralistic situation in the Zaïrian context:
    I tell them that the first question to ask about the other teaching (ie, of the sect in question) is: 'what do they say about the person and work of Christ?'
    Letter from Richardson to author, 7th Aug, 1987.

35. Initially, the second exposition was in the afternoon, but it became evident that the delegates were fighting drowsiness; they themselves requested that the two exposition sessions be in the morning when they would be at their most alert and that the afternoons be reserved for discussion sessions.

36. According to Richardson, the women are much freer in prayer if they can meet on their own, apart from the men; *their prayer times are enthusiastic and non-stop.* Letter to author, 7th Aug, 1987.

37. Source: Richardson, Letter to author, 7th Aug, 1987.

38. Many of the older pastors understandably feel uncomfortable with a youthful, self-confident graduate of a theological seminary, brimming with neat solutions to all the Church's complex ills.

39. Richardson, Letter to author, 7th Aug, 1987.

40. ibid.

41. The emphasis, in Richardson's own words, is:
    coming apart to meet with the Lord and have prayer together in a 'non-council', 'non-committee' atmosphere.
    Letter to author, 7th Aug, 1987.

42. Swahili: 'Wanawake wa Habari Njema'; Lingala/Bangala: 'Basi na Nsango Malamo'.

43. V. Jones, 'Women in the Zaïre Church', *Inland Africa*, Summer, 1981, quoted in Tucker R., 'African women's movement finds massive response', *Evangelical Missions Quarterly*, 22: 3, July, 1986, p. 284.

44. V. Jones, in 'A sketch of the Women of the Good News', unpublished paper, May, 1985, suggests that the number exceeds 30,000 (quoted in Tucker R., op. cit. p. 284). Alene Dix ventures a more cautious estimate of 20-25,000. Conversation with A. Dix, London, 14th Aug, 1987.

45. Exceptions would include: 'La Ligue pour la Lecture de la Bible' (a worldwide Bible-reading and youth movement, known in Britain as Scripture Union) and 'Gideon's International' (a lay and businessman's organization for the free distribution of New Testaments). Although rivalry between the different Protestant Church-bodies is largely a thing of the past, there is still relatively little inter-Church co-operation, partly because the Church-bodies work within clearly defined geographical areas.

46. The CEBK is the Zaïrian Church-body associated with the Conservative Baptist Foreign Mission Society (CBFMS); it has its headquarters in Boma, Kivu. The CADEZA Church is the Zaïrian Church-body associated with the Assemblies of God and is based in Isiro, Haut-Zaïre.

47. While Bunia is set squarely in the Swahili-speaking region of Zaïre, it is a cosmopolitan centre, attracting people from many different commercial-language and tribal-language zones.

48. R. Tucker, 'African women's movement finds massive response', *Evangelical Missions Quarterly* : 3rd July, 1986, p.286.

49. R. Tucker was told of women's contribution to a local student's Bible school tuition fees by Pastor Kysando of Beni, 'African women's movement', op. cit. p. 286.

50. A. Dix related that at Todro in the north of CECA territory, there were 2,350 women officially registered for the February, 1978 conference, while at the Sunday service, taken and addressed by

the women but attended also by the men, the numbers were about 5,000. Conversation with A. Dix, London, 14th Aug, 1987.

51. A. Dix, conversation, London, 14th Aug, 1987.

52. A. Dix, communication by tape, received 29th Sept, 1987.

53. ibid.

54. Tucker, op. cit. p. 285.

55. Within CECA 'being a Christian' would be understood to mean not simply church-attendance but a personal faith-commitment to Christ as Saviour and a desire to live according to His example and teaching.

56. Consecutive attendance and participation is ideal, but a certain flexibility is allowed, given the African woman's frequent duties of hospitality to visitors and care for sick family members.

57. R. Tucker, op. cit. p. 288. Correspondence with A. Dix confirms that this is the pattern for most of CECA. Tape received 29th Sept, 1987.

58. cf. M. S. Rosaldo, ed., *Women, Culture, and Society: a theoretical overview*, Stanford University Press, 1974, p. 3, who says:
    A universal asymetry of the sexes has developed from the association of women with the maternal role and associated duties, this is regarded as the private domain and of men with those activities and roles taking place outside this sphere in the public domain.
    My attention was drawn to the above work by Sarah Taylor's paper presented to the MA Seminar, SOAS, Feb. 10. 1986: 'The relationship between women's religious roles in Yoruba Orisa worship and their authority in the public domain'. In her paper, Taylor speaks of a comparable (though in detail very different) transference by women from the private to the public domain by means of initiation into the 'Orisa' cults in Yoruba society.

59. Zaïre has actively encouraged the 'libération de la femme' and there are currently several women in prominent political positions.

60. Tucker, op. cit. p. 289, relates a WGN skit in which a man rebuffs WGN members who request that his wife joins them in the movement, saying that her joining would *'make her smarter than me'*.

61. Tucker, op. cit. p. 288, quotes an American missionary's conversation with her students, one of whom told her: *'If I treated my wife as a friend, she wouldn't respect me.'*

62. A. Dix, tape received 29th Sept, 1987.

63. A. Dix, conversation, London, 14th Aug, 1987 and tape, 29th Sept, 1987.

64. An account of the origins of the extension movement is anthologized in R. D. Winter, *Theological Education by Extension*, William Carey Library, South Pasadena, 1969 and a report of the first international workshop on the subject held at Armenia, Colombia, is to be found in the same publication, pp. 148-178.

65. Probably the initial trigger was a seminar held at Bunia, 24th-27th Aug, 1973, addressed by Dr P. White on the subject of TEE, and attended by about 35 missionary and expatriate delegates from several church bodies in the North and East of Zaïre.

66. Initially, Lomago Kali, who then left for further theological studies and then returned to direct CECA's 'Département de l'Enseignement Biblique'; Kana Muruo took over from Lomago and is currently TEE Co-ordinator.

67. Information supplied by Co-ordinator of TEE, Kana Muruo, conversation, Bunia, 21st Jan, 1987.

68. F. R. Kinsler, 'Extension: an alternative model for theological education', in *Learning in Context: the search for innovative patterns in theological education*, Theological Education Fund, New Life Press, Bromley, 1973, pp. 27-28.

69. ibid, pp. 30ff.

70. ibid, p. 31.

336

71. Manuals cost about $2 to produce and the students are asked
    to pay approximately 70p = $1 each. The price per volume was
    almost halved by having the books printed at the mission press
    at Kijabe, near Nairobi, instead of in the West. Annual TEE
    Report, 1982-83, submitted to CECA by Rev D. Langford, then
    TEE Co-ordinator. Despite the very low, subsidized cost of the
    TEE manuals, the annual reports frequently mention the price
    as a reason why many are excluded from benefiting from TEE.

72. TEE courses existing in Swahili and Bangala:
    1. Talking with God (prayer)
    2. Bringing people to Jesus (evangelization)
    3. New Testament Survey — Part I
    4. The Pastor and his Work
    5. Old Testament Survey — Part I
    6. Seven Letters to the Churches
    7. Old Testament Survey — Part IV
    8. New Testament Survey — Part II
    9. Effective Bible Teaching
    10. Life of Christ — Part I
    11. Life of Christ — Part II
    12. Acts of the Apostles — Part I
    13. Acts of the Apostles — Part II
    14. Christian Family Life
    15. Old Testament Survey — Part II
    16. Old Testament Survey — Part III
    17. Genesis — Part I
    18. Genesis — Part II
    19. Bible Study Methods
    20. I Thessalonians
    TEE courses in French:
    1. Old Testament
    2. Introduction to the New Testament
    3. Introduction to the Bible (Hermeneutics)
    4. New Testament Church
    5. The Apostolic Age
    6. Doctrine (theology for everyday life).

73. TEE methodology, however, cannot guarantee freedom from
    making some of the same mistakes that characterize most
    residential theological schools. Even Kinsler himself admits:

It would be dishonest to pretend that the extension movement has broken with all that is domesticating and
irrelevant in theological education. There is, in fact, some
evidence that the extension approach is being used to
indoctrinate and control more efficiently and widely than
ever before... op. cit. p. 37.

74. For instance, the Annual TEE Report for 1984-85 states that the
centres of Oicha, Adi, Bogoro, Blukwa, Lona and Djugu had been
inspected.

75. Stated in the Annual Report for 1984-85, 30th May, 1985.

76. List furnished by Kana Muruo, letter 19th October, 1987.

77. ibid.

78. ibid.

79. ibid.

80. Quoted in Ram Desai, *Christianity in Africa as seen by Africans*,
Denver, 1962, p. 125. cf. Bishop P. Kalilombe, referring to the
'fateful dichotomy' occurring when theology is reduced to a
marginal role as the Word of God is excluded from certain real-
life areas:
> Thus life is split. The 'religious' areas are accepted as
> being under God's influence and judgment, while the rest
> of human life, the profane is, for all practical purposes,
> outside God's Kingdom.
'Doing theology at the grassroots: a challenge for professional
theologians.' Part I, *AFER*, Vol. 27, No. 3, 1985, pp. 150-151.

81. Eboussi Boulage, *Christianity without Fetishes*, Orbis, New
York, 1984, p. 24.

82. ibid, p. 9.

83. J. Mbiti, PACLA Conference lecture, 1976, reviewed by T. Tienou,
'Christianity and African Culture' in *Evangelical Review of
Theology*, Vol. 3, No. 2, p. 198.

84. Kwesi Dickson, *Theology in Africa*, Orbis, New York, 1984, p. 8.

85. B. Simbo, *Evangelical Review of Theology*, 1983, Vol. 7, No. 1, pp. 30-31.

86. E. Mveng, editorial article in *Bulletin de Théologie Africaine*, Vol. 1, 1979, p. 6.

87. The relevant statistics for the Bunia Theological Seminary library, for instance, are as follows:

total number of library books:		4,600
books on African theology	25	
books on African philosophy	20	
books on African religions	8	
books on African Church	106	
total on African religious context	159	ie. 3.5%
total in African languages	22	ie. 0.5%

source: letter from Librarian, Ndagijimana B., 12th May, 1987.

88. John Gration, born 25th May, 1926, in Princeton, N. J., USA. (PhD, New York University). AIM missionary in Zaïre 1953-64, first in schools and with local churches, then (for 6 years) in theological education and church work. From 1964 to 1967 he worked in Kenya as principal of a Bible school. In 1967 Gration returned to the US to be Associate Home Director and Candidate Secretary for the AIM. Since 1975 he has been Professor of Missions at Wheaton College Graduate School and is currently Department Chairperson.

89. Lausanne International Congress on World Evangelisation, July, 1974. Organized by the Billy Graham Evangelistic Association, the Congress was a major meeting of evangelical leaders of the world. It convened 2,430 delegates and 570 observers for 10 days. Over 150 nations were represented. It was considered by many to be a historic landmark for giving fresh impetus to world mission and for giving a more fully-orbed understanding of evangelism as addressing the whole (ie, social and material as well as spiritual) needs of man. It resulted in a 15-point 'Lausanne Covenant'.

90. Willowbank Consultation. As one of the many projects to carry further the processes set in motion at the 1974 Lausanne Congress, the Lausanne Committee's Theology and Education Group convened a consultation on the general topic of transcultural communication of the Christian Gospel. It took place 6th-13th January, 1978, at Willowbank, Somerset Bridge, Bermuda. The Consultation convened 33 theologians, anthropologists, linguists, missionaries and pastors from all six continents. The resulting 'Willowbank Report' includes chapters on culture, revelation, conversion, Church and ethics, each chapter ending with questions for discussion. *Lausanne Occasional Papers, No. 2, The Willowbank Report — Gospel and Culture*, Lausanne Committee for World Evangelization, Wheaton, 1978.

91. J. Gration, 'Willowbank to Zaïre', in *Missiology*, July, 1984, p. 297.

92. ibid, p. 297. Gration adds:
    Through my deepening understanding of what contextualization was saying to missions and churches alike, it was as if the Word of the Lord was coming to me a 'second time' as it did to Jonah (3: 1). I had no choice but to return to the Church in Zaire with this new 'word'. (p. 297).

93. Gration to Dr Richard Anderson, AIM International General Secretary, 12th June, 1984, ie. upon completion of the second seminar. Quoted with permission.

94. Gration to D. Langford dated 26th Feb, 1983, prior to the first Gospel and Culture Seminar. Photocopied by author at Rethy, Jan, 1987.

95. Gration to Anderson, 12th June, 1984.

96. Gration to Langford, 26th Feb, 1983.

97. J. Gration, 'Willowbank to Zaïre', op. cit. p. 298.

98. It appears from Gration's correspondence with Langford that he was helped in his preparatory thinking by his associate, Dr Lois McKinney. Gration to Langford, 26th Feb, 1983.

99. Gration to Anderson, 12th June, 1984.

100. Gration emphasizes that the choice of delegates was by the Zaïrian Church in 'Willowbank to Zaïre', op. cit. p. 299:
    The participants, by the way, were chosen by the Church. Though I led each seminar, there was never any question as to ownership.
    D. Langford specifies that *a small organizing commitee* decided who should be invited to participate, D. Langord, 'Report concerning the consultation on the Gospel and African culture', prepared for the Theological Study Committee of AIM, 1984. Report photocopied, Rethy, Jan, 1987.

101. J. Gration, 'Willowbank to Zaïre', op. cit. p. 298, cf. P. Kalilombe:
    The main challenge that confronts professional theologians when they attempt to do theology with ordinary people comes from the fact that their training has cut them off from the community. The seminary, theological college or university programmes are geared towards the production of professionals who may theologise about or for the people, but really not with them. (Italics his).
    P. Kalilombe, 'Doing theology at grass-roots, in *AFER*, Vol. 27, No. 4, 1985, p. 236.

102. J. Gration, 'Willowbank' op. cit. p. 298.

103. Gration to Langford, 26th Feb, 1973.

104. 'Willowbank to Zaïre', op. cit. p. 299.

105. ibid, p. 299.

106. Gration uses the expression *forensic justification* in the article to summarize what is the predominant pauline conception of salvation, re-emphasized by the Reformation and the one most widely shared by evangelicals. He points out in the article that the technical term was avoided in the seminars, however.

107. 'Willowbank to Zaïre', op. cit. p. 299.

108. ibid, p. 299.

109. cf. Gration to Langford, 26th Feb, 1983:
    This may be difficult for those who have never learned to

take an objective look at their own culture.'

110. Gration takes the definition from C. Kluckhohn, *Mirror for Man, the relationship of anthropology to modern life*, New York, McGraw Hill, 1949, p. 17.

111. The ideas are suggested in Gration to Langford, 26th Feb. 1983. It is not clear in the literature whether these ideas were actually used in the seminars.

112. 'Willowbank to Zaïre', op. cit. p. 300.

113. ibid, p. 300.

114. Gration's field notes, June 16, 1983, photocopy received 15th June, 1986.

115. 'Willowbank to Zaïre', op. cit. p. 300,

116. My personal field research in the Rethy area in January, 1987 encountered the same problem. Questions which required but a brief answer elicited an almost verbatim reproduction of a by-gone sermon or conversation.

117. Conversation with Bishop Patrick Kalilombe, Selly Oak Colleges, Birmingham, 24th April, 1986. Kalilombe discusses the role of the 'facilitator' in his article, op. cit. p. 229ff.

118. 'Willowbank to Zaïre', p. 301.

119. ibid, p. 301.

120. ibid, p. 301.

121. Gration to Anderson, 12th Jan, 1984.

122. Gration's field notes, June, 1983, p. 7.

123. The expression *The Church's unfinished agenda* is used by Gration in 'Willowbank to Zaïre', p. 301. In fact, Gration speaks in 'Willowbank' of 28 items, but in his field notes he lists 29 (two No. 28s) from the French group. The Swahili group proposed 13

342

issues. In both cases, the lists represent issues which, in the delegates' opinion, need fresh, critical examination. The two lists are here conflated; for sake of completeness, all 42 items are listed, although some of the issues obviously overlap:

Issues common to both groups:
tribalism
marriage, bride-price
fetishism
ancestor practices
fear of speaking out (against evil)
stewardship of money/possessions
sorcery

Swahili group only:

lovelessness
nominalism
paganization of Christian practices
false teaching
purses untouched (= stewardship?)
error (= false teaching?)

French group only:
adultery
drunkenness
corruption
fashion
chief enthronement
name of God
attitude to commerce
taboos
injustice
rites and ceremonies
sex
attitudes to illness
attitudes on 'honour'
social conformity
paternalism
inferiority/superiority
accumulation of jobs
by one person
baptismal practices
church discipline
totems
dreams.

124. Gration's field notes, p. 7.— the thought was probably that if one leader proposed, for instance, a seminar on tribalism he would be misunderstood as wanting a forum for accusing others of tribalism.

125. Judging by a margin comment in his field notes, p. 9, the issue with the most votes was 'tribalism', then 'fetishism', then 'dreams and visions'. 'Ancestor practices' was just out-voted.

126. Letter from Alo Dradebo, member of the Bunia group, to Molyneux, 5th Dec, 1985.

127. Gration, 'Willowbank to Zaïre', p. 303.

128. R. Padilla, 'Hermeneutics and Culture, a theological perspective', in *Down to Earth*, ed. J. R. W. Stott and R. Coote, Hodder and Stoughton, London, 1980, pp. 63-78.

129. cf. AIM Doctrinal Basis (with which AIM missionaries must agree):
   The divine, verbal inspiration, infallibility, and inerrancy of the Scriptures of the Old and New Testaments as originally given and their absolute and final authority in all matters of faith and conduct.
   (Section 5 of Article III (Doctrine) in AIM Constitution, ratified May, 1986).

130. CECA Doctrinal Basis (April, 1959):
   Article 5. L'inspiration pléniaire divine et l'infaillibilité des Ecritures de l'Ancien et du Nouveau Testament dans leur forme originale et leur autorité absolute et définitive en tout ce qui concerne la foi et la conduite.

131. R. Padilla, op. cit. p. 77. Kalilombe agrees:
   The matter which should spark off theologizing is the life experience of the persons and communities involved: the total life, with its many facets, aspects, and dimensions, op. cit. p. 150.

132. ibid, p. 77.

133. ibid, p. 78.

134. Gration, 'Willowbank to Zaïre', p. 303. On the last point (that Scripture not only answers questions posed by the contemporary situation but itself in turn raises questions) Gration and Padilla agree. A hermeneutic in which the agenda is set by contemporary cultural issues alone is incomplete. cf. R. Padilla:
   The hermeneutic task is not limited in dealing with the questions raised within the historical context; it must also communicate the questions that the Word of God poses to the situation. Only when the whole situation is placed under the Word of judgment and grace is the interpretive process complete.

135. Gration, 'Willowbank to Zaïre', p. 304.

136. ibid, p. 306.

137. ibid, p. 306.

138. ibid, pp. 304-305.

139. The definitition of contextualization is that of C. Taber, 'Contextualization: Indigenization and/or Transformation', in *The Gospel and Islam*, D. McCurry (ed.), MARC, 1979, pp. 144, 146.

140. Gration here alludes to Shoki Coe, one of the first to introduce the term 'contextualization' into the missiological debate, who states that the *'backward look'* is one essential characteristic of indigenization that distinguishes it from contextualization. cf. S. Coe, 'In search of renewal in theological education', in *Theological Education*, Vol. 9, No. 4, 1973, p. 240. The debate on contextualization has produced a very extensive literature. For the discussion about terminology, cf, among others: J. O. Buswell III, 'Contextualization: Is it only another word for indigenization?', in *Evangelical Missions Quarterly*, Jan. 1978, pp. 13-20; F. R. Kinsler, 'Mission and Context: The current debate about contextualization', in *Evangelical Missions Quarterly*, Jan, 1978; C. Taber, 'Contextualization: Indigenization and/or transformation?', Lausanne Committee for World Evangelization, the North American Conference on Muslim Evangelization, October, 1978; B. Fleming, *Contextualization of Theology*, William Carey Library, Pasadena, (1980); R. Gehman, 'Guidelines in Contextualization', in *East Africa Journal of Evangelical Theology*, Vol. 2, No. 1, 1983, pp. 24-36; S. Kaplan, 'The Africanization of Missionary Christianity: History and Typology', in *Journal of Religion in Africa*, Vol. 16, No. 3, 1986, pp. 167-186.

141. Gration, 'Willowbank to Zaïre', pp. 307-308.

142. For instance, Amula, a Rethy group member, spoke of a consultation with doctors serving at the Rethy Hospital, as part of their group's research into modern medical opinion. Conversation, Rethy, 22nd Jan, 1987.

143. Conversations with Amula, Bura and Kwany, Zaïre, January, 1987.

144. Gration to Anderson, 12th Jan, 1984.

145. Unpublished manuscript, 'Evangile et croyances africaines — cas de Rethy et ses environs', (revised) 1984. Unless otherwise stated, all excerpts quoted in this section are from this document.

146. For situation of ethnic groups: O. Boone, *Les Peuplades du Congo-Belge*, Tervuren, Belgium, (1935), pp. 64-65, and pp. 95-97. For discussion on language classification: A. N. Tucker, and M. A. Bryan in *Linguistic Survey of the Northern Bantu Borderland*, Vol. I, Part III, Oxford University Press, London, (1956) p. 68.

147. The Rethy group consisted of:

Name (yr. of birth)	tribe	occupation
Bura Thenga (1945)	Hema	sch. teacher, editor
Amula Djang'etambe (1955)	Lendu	sch. teacher, chaplain
Bura Ngaba (1955)	Lendu	Bible school teacher

148. Dans le concept traditional africain, les enfants constituent une sécurité familiale face à l'agression extérieure. Aussi sont-ils au sein d'une famille un potentiel économique. Les enfants font encore le prestige ou la valeur d'un couple dans notre société traditionnelle. Un homme sans progéniture meurt sans suite. Mais un fils assure la perpetuité paternelle ainsi que clanique. p. 1.

149. La Bible nous présente Dieu, le Tout-Puissant, comme le parfait protecteur des enfants face aux différents dangers qui les guètent. p.2.

150. Concerning the quest for the cause:
Toujours, l'Africain se demande: 'Pourquoi suis-je tombé malade? Pourquoi... l'échec? Pourquoi suis-je stérile? Pourquoi ai-je connu cet accident? Pourquoi? Pourquoi? Pourquoi? p. 2.

151. This African perception has been widely noted and commented on, both by non-African and African writers: cf. E.

Evans-Pritchard, 'Witchcraft (mangu) amongst the Azande',
Sudan Notes and records, Vol. 12, 1929, pp. 163-249, excerpts
in Max Marwick (ed), *Witchcraft and Sorcery*, Penguin Books,
1970, including:
It is strange at first to live amongst the Zande and to listen
to their naïve explanation of misfortunes with the most
obvious origin as products of witchcraft
(p. 31). cf. also J. Mbiti:
African peoples feel and believe that all the various ills,
misfortunes, sicknesses, accidents, tragedies, sorrows,
dangers and unhappy mysteries which they encounter or
experience, are caused by the use of this mystical power
in the hands of a sorcerer, witch, or wizard.
in *African Religions and Philosophy*, Heinemann, London, 1975,
p. 200. Also, T. O. Beidelman, 'Witchcraft in Ukaguru', in *Witchcraft and Sorcery in East Africa*, Middleton and Winter (eds.),
Routledge and Kegan Paul, London, (1963):
Kaguru believe most misfortunes, however small, are due
to witchcraft. Most illness, death, miscarriages, sterility,
difficult childbirths, poor crops, sickly livestock and
poultry, loss of articles, bad luck in hunting and sometimes even lack of rain, are caused by witches.
pp. 93-64.

152. pp. 2-5.

153. p. 3.

154. p. 3. The traditional African, of course, would not deny these
scientific reasons, but see them as inadequate and go on to
ask *'Yes, but why me rather than him? Why here rather than
there?'*

155. p. 3.

156. Among an abundant literature on dreams and visions in Africa:
E. G. Parrinder, *African Traditional Religion*, Sheldon Press,
London, Third Edition (1974), pp. 27, 61, 131, 135; B. G.
Sundkler, *Bara Bukoba*, C. Hurst, London (1980), ch. 4 'On
dreams and faith', pp. 98-112; K. Laman, *The Kongo III*, Studia
Ethnographica Upsaliensa. XII, Lund, Sweden, 1962, pp. 7-13.

157. cf. J. Mbiti, *African Religions and Philosophy*, op. cit. p. 81, 235;

E. E. Evans-Pritchard, *Nuer Religion*, Oxford (1956), pp. 161-162.

158. For example, the document insists that infertility may be explained by the will of God and quotes Isaiah 54:1 to support the contention that God may have in mind for the childless parents something better, namely, *'faith-sons'* or *'spiritual children'*, (ie. people brought to faith). pp. 4-5.

159. p. 6.

160. p. 6.

161. ibid, Amula gives the French names for these ceremonies: 'enlèvement de deuil' (lifting of mourning) and 'retrait de deuil' (withdrawal of mourning).

162. Amula Djang'etambe, Diploma of Theology dissertation, 'Etude ethno-pastorale sur la pratique de l'enlèvement de deuil chez les Walendu-Watsi (dans le Zone de Mahagi)', Bunia Theological Seminary, 1982.

163. On the christianization of ancestor beliefs, cf: B. Bujo, 'Nos ancêtres, ces saints inconnus', in *Bulletin de Théologie Africaine*, Vol. 1, No. 2, 1979, pp. 166-178; C. Nyamiti, 'New theological approach and new vision of the Church in Africa', in *Revue Africaine de Théologie*, Vol. 2, No. 3, 1978, pp. 33-54; F. Kabasele, 'Le Christ comme Ancêtre et Aîné', in F. Kabasele, J. Dore and R. Luneau, *Chemins de la Christologie Africaine*, Desclée, Paris, 1986, p. 127ff.

164. Jeremiah 22: 10, 2 Samuel 12: 23, Ecclesiastes 9: 5-6, 10.

165. La Bible n'ignore pas l'existence des anges déchus, lesquels sont toujours en action dans cet univers (Ephésiens 6: 12). Ils pourraient se déguiser en esprits des morts, pour séduire les vivants. C'est alors que l'on a la vision des fantômes ou des revenants, dits, 'esprits des morts' . p. 7.

166. *Village des morts' ou monde des ancêtres.* p. 7.

167. For appeal to Roman Catholic dogma for support for African

concepts of 'free access' between the living and the departed, see ch. 3 above, p. 178ff.

168. *'La Bible nie le fait que les morts reviennent parmi les vivants.'* For biblical references to support their contention, see note 164, above.

169. Unpublished manuscript, 'Le fétishisme et la guérison à la lumière de l'Evangile'. Unless otherwise stated, all quotations in this section from this document.

170. The author remembers remarks made by Bunia Seminary student Ayibho (formerly chaplain at Aungba secondary school) and by Pastor Uchanda (Aungba Bible Institute director), both emphasizing the prevalence of activities related to sorcery and fetishism in the Aungba region and in the early 1980s prayer was requested among the missionary personnel for the serious situation in the Aungba region and its secondary school because of similar reasons.

171. The Aungba group consisted of:

Name (year of birth)	Tribe	Occupation
Ofeni Kanda	Logo	Bib.Sch. teacher, pastor
Uchanda Unen	Alur	Sec. sch. chpl, Bib. sch. tchr
Atido Kunde	Alur	Co-ordinator evangelism
Angu-andia Gonde	Lugbara	Sec. sch. tchr, Christn. Ed.

Aungba itself is set squarely in Alur territory (lang: Dho Aluur); Lugbara territory adjoins it to the north (lang: Lugbara); the Logo tribe occupy a large territory considerably further north again, centred on the town of Faradje (lang: Logo-ti). cf. O. Boone, op. cit.. pp. 16-18, pp. 254-256 and pp. 251-252 resp. and A. N. Tucker and M. A. Bryan, op. cit. pp. 90 and 94, pp. 92-94 and pp. 91 and 114, resp.

172. Egyptians (Exodus 7, 8), Canaanites (Deuteronomy 7, 8, 20), Assyrians (Nahum 3), Babylonians (Daniel 1, 2), Greeks (Acts 17), then:

Nos ancêtrê sont aussi à l'origine du fétishisme car ils considéraient comme sacrées certaines choses: les montagnes, les forêts, les arbres, les animaux, les chutes d'eau, les tombes et certaines plantes. p. 2.

173. p. 2.

174. Cf. discussion of use of fetishes in E. E. Evans Pritchard, *Nuer Religion*, op. cit. p. 101, where fetishes among the Nuer appear to have more agressive uses than those discussed by the document's authors.

175. The same general distinctions are made in E. G. Parrinder, *African Tradional religion*, pp. 116ff. cf. *'Magic is offensive as well as protective.'* p. 116.

176. Middleton, in discussing such practitioners in Lugbara religion, speaks rather of *'ba enyanya beri'* (people with poison), J. Middleton, 'Witchcraft and Sorcery in Lugbara', in Middleton and Winter (eds.) *Witchcraft and sorcery in East Africa*, op. cit. p. 264.

177. p. 3.

178. The document sets out to address fetishism which it defines as
   L'adoration d'un matériel auquel on attribue des pouvoirs surnaturels,
   but rather loosely includes under the same definition such distinct occult phenomena as astrology, spells, magic, divination, necromancy, foretelling, spiritism, idolatry and sorcery. p. 2.

179. ibid, p. 2.

180. ibid, p. 4. The Bible passage referred to by the authors, Rom. 1: 22-23, says: Although they claimed to be wise, they became fools and exchanged the glory of the immortal God for images made to look like mortal man and birds and animals and reptiles.

181. ibid, p. 4. Aba and Aru are specially mentioned presumably because the former (in Logo and Kakwa territory) is particularly known to Ofeni and the latter (in Lugbara territory) is familiar to Angu-andia.

182. Il n'y a aucune place pour le fétichisme dans l'Evangile. S'il y a des gens qui le font, qu'ils sachent que c'est une inspiration purement diabolique qui lutte contre l'Evangile. ibid, p. 4.

183. The fact that the authors say *'stifled'* rather than *'stifles'* implies that they do not mean that the Gospel 'per se' opposes traditional healing, but rather that the historical presentation of the Gospel (by missionaries and subsequent African Christian leaders) rejected it.

184. At this point in the document there is a marginal correction, probably made at the time of the second seminar in 1984. Where the original stated: *'These elements are useful on condition etc.'*, the amendment reads: *'Certain of these elements are useful on condition etc'*, and specifically excludes 'bones' and 'excrement'.

185. 1. Idolatry of the Israelites reproved by the prophets (Jer. 14: 12-16, Is. 42: 17-22, Ezek. 6: 1-7, Hos. 13: 1-9).
    2. Saul consulting the witch of Endor (I Sam. 28 and 31).
    3. Solomon's disastrous consultation of pagan gods (I Kings 11: 4ff).
    4. The idolatry of Jeroboam which led eventually to exile. (II Kings 15 and 17).
    5. The idolatry of King Nebuchadnezzar resulting in madness (Dan. 3-5).
    6. Pharaoh hardened by the trickery of his magicians (Exod. 7, 8, 12 and 14).
    7. Idolatry listed among the sins which separate man from God (II Cor. 5: 11 and ch. 8. (sic) — I Corinthians in both cases is surely meant).
    8. Idolatry excludes from the Kingdom of God (Eph. 5: 5).

186. Rien ne peut être un ostacle pour son exercice si on l'emploie sagement et pour la gloire de Dieu. p. 6.

187. Donner un bon enseignement pour hausser sa valeur à la lumière de la Bible. p. 6.

188. Unpublished document, 'Le tribalisme'. Unless otherwise stated, all quotations in this section taken from this document.

189. The Bunia group consisted of:

Name (year of birth)	Tribe	Occupation
Djawotto Kisa (1945)	Alur	Seminary teacher
Kana Muruo (1945)	Kakwa	TEE co-ordinator

Okuonzi Amandru (1935)	Lugbara	Finance advisor
Sumbuso Bamaraki (1956)	Hema	Seminary teacher
Ufoyuru Kpathi (1941)	Alur	Evangelism co-ordin. radio
Alo Dradebo (1941)	Lugbara	Seminary teacher
Kwany Londoni (1943)	Lendu	Educ. co-ord. CECA Press

For Alur and Lugbara, see above, note 171; for Hema and Lendu, see above, note 147; the Kakwa territory sits astride the Zaire-Sudan border, to the north and east respectively of the Lugbara and Logo, (lang: Kakwa). Details in O. Boone, op. cit. pp. 242-244 and A. N. Tucker and M. A. Bryan, op. cit. p. 91.

190. The respective lengths of the documents:
     'Tribalisme' — 25 pp., (one-and-a-half spaced)
     'Evangile et croyances africaines' — 8 pp., (single spaced)
     'Fétishisme et guérison' — 6 pp., (single spaced)

191. pp. 6-9.

192. p. 13.

193. pp. 10-12.

194. p. 19.

195. p. 19.

196. p. 22.

197. p. 24.

198. The co-ordination problems referred to were created because the one chosen by the delegates to be responsible for liaising between the groups was compelled by personal problems to relinquish his post. The financial problems arise when a central-ised meeting is proposed: distances are such that transport is costly, communication difficult and feeding and housing expen-sive. The Aungba group never produced a revised document, partly because two of the three members moved from Aungba: Uchanda went to Kinshasa for further education, Anguandia

was called to Bunia to co-ordinate the Christian Education Department.

199. Gration repeatedly expressed misgiving in letters as to the 'success' of the process:

> Maybe deep down I am fearing (and to this I must admit) that you will really find very little as a result of the seminars... I fear that the byproduct (namely the three excellent papers that were produced, of which you have copies) have alas become for the most part the product. As you known, I intended it otherwise and wanted the reproduction process to be the main product of my seminars. This unfortunately has not taken place.

(Letter to the author, 21st Aug, 1986). Or again:

> I fear that not much has happened in terms of follow-up or implementation, or what is a special concern to me, the replication of the seminars.

Letter to the author, 12th Feb, 1987.

200. Field research methodology. Field research was undertaken in the CECA area of North-East Zaire 16th-28th January. Prior contact by letter with the participants was considered but rejected on the grounds that the letters might exert pressure on them to undertake projects that would not otherwise have taken place. The research was divided into two distinct periods:

a) *Rethy area, 16th-21st January.* The objective was to contact and interview as many participants as possible at the Swahili seminar held at Rethy in 1983. The use of time was maximised by the help of Rethy-based AIM missionary, Revd D. Langford, who had been instrumental in setting up the seminars in 1983 and 1984 and who helped in locating the participants for interviews, although he did not share in the interviewing. Gration's field notes (photocopy in author's possession) indicate that 16 men took some sort of part in the Swahili seminar, but that their attendance was 'intermittent'. Of the 16, seven were interviewed, the others either being away from home and unattainable or deemed to have had minimal involvement in the seminars. Interviews were conducted in Swahili. While most were located in and around Rethy itself, three others were found in their home villages in Linga and Huu, some 40 kms from Rethy.

b) *Bunia area, 21st-28th January,* Gration's notes indicate that 17 men took part in the Bunia (French) seminar (with D. Langford, the only missionary participant, the number came to 18). Since I taught at the Bunia Seminary 1978-1984, all the participants are personally known to me. The majority were to be located in and around the town of Bunia. Eleven interviews were held in and around Bunia. One participant agreed to travel by truck from Oicha, 170 kms from Bunia for his interview. Another was later interviewed in Kinshasa where he was receiving further theological education. Five other participants were unavailable, being away on further study in Kinshasa, Bangui, Nairobi and USA. They were sent the questionnaire to complete and return. Four have done so. In this way, all but one of the 17 Zaïrian delegates have been included personally in this analysis. Interviews were always done individually and lasted an average of $1^1/2$ hours, permitting participants to enlarge unhurriedly on their answers. At the end of both periods of investigation, group meetings were held to permit cross-fertilization of ideas.

Swahili seminar delegates interviewed: Buchu, Ukelo, Groche, Laleni, Djaldero, Balonge, Lainya.

French seminar delegates interviewed: Bura Thenga, Kana Muruo, Amula Djang'etambe, Okuonzi Amandru, Etsea Ang'apoza, Bura Ngaba, Sumbuso Bamaraki, Ufoyuru Kpathi, Alo Dradebo, Kile Kpala, Kwany Zaabu (at Rethy), Uchanda Unen (in Kinshasa).

French seminar delegates who responded by questionnaire: Ofeni Kanda (Todro), Djawotto Kisa (USA), Atido Kunde Dong' (Isiro), Angu-andia Gonde (Nairobi).

201. See Question 12 on questionnaire. To assist recall, the participants were often asked to remember where the seminars were held, how many fellow-delegates there were, what the major theme was, etc.

202. One delegate, Pastor Ofeni Kanda, who filled in a questionnaire but was not interviewed because of distance from Bunia, stated that since he was unable to get to the second seminar (1984) he was not in a position to comment on the usefulness of the initiative. Indeed, the interviews were far more productive than the questionnaires, which tended to elicit only an essential minimum of information and sometimes not even that.

203. The actual expression used was *'faire l'autocritique'* (judge oneself), but the context indicated that what was meant was 'judge *for* oneself' instead of simply having to accept someone else's opinion.

204. Thus going at least part way towards the desirable *'interdisciplinarity'* that Kalilombe discusses, op. cit. p. 150.

205. The remark was made by Seminary teacher, Pastor Sumbuso Bamaraki, interviewed 24th Jan, 1987, in Bunia.

206. Remark made by Oicha Bible School director, Pastor Kile Kpala, interviewed 25th Jan, 1987, in Bunia.

207. See Question 14 on questionnaire.

208. *'Vulnerability'* is the word that Gration himself chose (see p. XX) as being of basic importance. The delegates did not use the word, but clearly meant the same thing.

209. See note 198, above.

210. Pastor Laleni Ugentho, head-pastor of Rethy Section, interviewed 17th Jan, 1987, in Rethy.

211. Pastor Laleni furnished details of minutes of bygone Rethy Church Councils where the question of 'matanga' was raised: 29th Sept, 1982, 14th-17th Dec, 1982, 28th Nov, 1983, 25th-28th June, 1984, 15th Aug, 1986.

212. cf. Amula D., Dissertation, op. cit. p. 16, cites as examples of tribes that practice the 'enlèvement de deuil' the BaKongo, the Alur, the Lugbara. E. E. Evans-Pritchard describes something very similar which he terms the 'mortuary ceremony' designed to *'clear the debt'*, it is performed four to six months after burial. *Nuer Religion*, op. cit. p. 146ff.

213. Amula (Dissertation, op. cit. p. 16) states that the Lugbara tribe observe the practice for reasons other than the fear of spirits (does not specify), but that this is an exception to the rule.

214. Examples to substantiate this are given in Amula, op. cit. pp. 33ff.

215. Amula quotes from Nkongolo wa Mbiye, 'Le culte des esprits', Kinshasa, Centre d'Etudes Pastorales, 1974, pp. 16-17, in his 'Dissertation', op. cit.

216. Minutes of Rethy Section Council, 28th Nov, 1983, para 2. The minute also refers the reader back to a similar decision in 1977. It is clear that the problem is a perennial one.

217. The 14 local churches in the Rethy region visited by Pastor Laleni were: Baidjo, Goika, Kwandroma, Djubate, Budza, Lokpa, R'kpa, Nola, Kokpa, Tsangu, Bwaa, Nalepu, Zali, Rethy. Conversation with Laleni, 17th Jan, 1987, at Rethy.

218. Conversation with Pastor Ufoyuru, 22nd Jan, 1987, in Bunia.

219. Remark made by Pastor Kana Muruo, Bunia, 22nd Jan, 1987.

220. Conversation with Pastor Etsea Ang'apoza, Legal Representation and Vice-President of CECA, in Bunia, 21st Jan, 1987.

221. Conversation with Pastor Laleni Ugentho, 17th Jan, 1987, in Rethy.

222. Linga, CECA centre, not far from Rethy and about 120 miles from Bunia.

223. I. Cor. 12: 13, 'For we were all baptized by one Spirit into one body — whether Jews or Greeks, slave or free — and we were all given the one Spirit to drink.'

224. The sermon in question was preached 12th Dec, 1985. Conversation with Pastor Bura Ngaba, 24th Jan, 1987, in Bunia.

225. CECA centre Bogoro, 25 kms east of Bunia, overlooking Lake Mobutu.

226. Conversation with Pastor Buchu, 19th Jan, 1987, in Linga.

227. Lolwa, CAFEZA (Brethren) centre, about 120 kms west of Bunia on the road to Kisangani.

228. Conversation with Pastor Bura Ngaba, 24th Jan, 1987, in Bunia.

229. Conversation with Pastor Lainya Ngadyuwa, 18th Jan, 1987, in Rethy.

230. For distinction between 'good' and 'bad' magic, cf. J. M. Mbiti, *African Religions and Philosophy*, op. cit. pp. 198ff.

231. For the widely acknowledged power of fear, cf. G. W. B. Hunting-ford:
    A spell is effective through fear because the victim be-lieves that the 'ponindet' (sorcerer) has the power to do him harm.
    'Nandi witchcraft', in *Witchcraft and sorcery in East Africa*, op. cit. pp. 178-179.

232. Conversation with Pastor Sumbuso Bamaraki, 24th Jan, 1987, in Bunia. For Christian protection from the harm by evil spirits, cf. J. Mbiti, *African Religions and Philosophy*, op. cit. p. 86.

233. Conversation with Pastor Djaldero, 17th Jan, 1987, in Rethy.

234. Conversation with Pastor Balonge, Hon President of CECA, 17th Jan, 1987, in Rethy.

235. Letter from Pastor Djawotto Kisa, completing PhD studies in USA. He insisted that before the recommendations made at the seminars could be put into effect there should be concensus of opinion in CECA; without this official approbation, pastors who acted on what the documents suggested could be *'subject to church discipline and even banishment'*. (Letter to author, of 12th June, 1987). While other participants expressed the possible dangers of contextualized theology encouraging syncretism, Pastor Djawotto was the only one to state openly that the main danger was from opposition by the leadership of CECA. For discussion of Theological Education by Extension (TEE) and its development in CECA, see above, pp. 266ff.

236. Conversation with TEE coordinator for CECA, Pastor Kana Muruo, 21st Jan, 1987.

237. Conversation with Pastor Bura Ngaba, 24th Jan, 1987, in Bunia.

238. ISTB *Série Programme d'Etudes — Introduction,* (Révision, 1978) p. 2.

239. Conversation with Pastor Alo Dradebo, 27th Jan, 1987, in Bunia.

240. Oicha, CECA centre near the town of Beni, mainly Nande tribe; about 170 kms south of Bunia.

241. Conversation with Pastor Kile Kpala, 25th Jan, 1987, in Bunia.

242. Conversation with Pastor Alo Dradebo, 27th Jan, 1987, in Bunia. Pastor Alo did not elaborate on the answers to the problems discussed.

243. While all the courses at Diploma and BA level are in French, the courses for the wives are provided in both Swahili and French.

244. Conversation with Pastor Sumbuso Bamaraki, 24th Jan, 1987, in Bunia. The reasons for polygamy and Christian answers for the problem, are also discussed. The CECA's position on polygamy would probably not be as sympathetic as that of E. Hillman, *Polygamy reconsidered: African plural marriage and the Christian churches,* Orbis Books, Maryknoll, New York, 1975, cf. also, J. Yego, 'Polygamy and the African Church', in *East Africa Journal of Evangelical Theology,* Vol. 3, No. 1, 1984, pp. 60-84. Yego stands within the CECA tradition, but his article reflects the complexity and sensitivity of the question of polygamy in Africa. Also J. Mbiti, *African Religions and Philosophy,* op. cit. 142-145. Mbiti sets out reasons for polygamy, while abstaining from judgment as to '*right or wrong, good or bad'.*

245. According to Pastor Laleni, each of the choral groups has its 'composer'.

246. Conversation with Pastor Laleni, 17th Jan, 1987, in Rethy.

247. The document reads:
Wimbo isiwe bila mafundisho! Usitunge wimbo isiyo na maana kwa kanisa (Doctrine Evangélique).
(Swahili: A hymn must not be without teaching! Do not compose a hymn that has no meaning for the Church (Evangelical Doctrine.)

248. It is not uncommon in the CECA churches to see members tapping their feet in rhythm with the music; in Kimbanguist services (from observation in the Kinshasa churches) this is strikingly absent.

249. Dance is one area where biblical precedent (for instance King David's example in 2 Samuel 6: 14 and even the command in Psalm 150: 4, a psalm that is quoted in the document to support the use of local instruments) is not followed because the cultural associations are considered to be too compromising.

250. The document permits the use of choir robes; the symbolic colours are given as: white = holiness, glory; blue = heaven; yellow = riches, blessing.

251. Unpublished duplicated document produced by the 'Département de l'Education Chrétienne', CECA, Bunia, n.d.

252. Questionnaire reply from Angu-Andia, Co-ordinator of CECA's 'Département de l'Education Chrétienne', 15th Aug, 1987.

253. Aungba, CECA centre about 200 kms north of Bunia, see also above, note 171.

254. Conversation with Pastor Uchanda Unen, 1st Feb, 1987, in Kinshasa. I have not been able to obtain a copy of the handout, and enquiries at Aungba have failed to locate one. Letter to author from AIM missionary, Ian Campbell, 19th June, 1987.

255. Education was taken over by the State in the 1970s but later returned to private (largely Church) management, although the State determines the curriculum. The CECA, therefore, has 'its' schools and is able to appoint the staff. The directors (and many of the teachers) would be Christians.

256. Beni, pop. 32,000, in North Kivu region, 125 mls south of Bunia and at the very southern tip of CECA territory. The population is almost entirely of the industrious Nande tribe.

257. Djugu, small commercial centre, pop. 8,000 (?), about 50 mls north of Bunia, and near the territorial intersection of the Alur, Lendu and Hema tribes.

258. Conversation with Pastor Amula Djang'etambe, 22nd Jan, 1987.

259. Conversations with Pastors Kana and Okuonzi in Bunia 21st and 23rd Jan, 1987, respectively.

260. Conversation with Pastor Kile Kpala, 25th Jan, 1987, in Bunia.

261. 'Ligue pour la Lecture de la Bible' — an international organisation promoting the daily study of the Bible, known in the UK as Scripture Union.

262. Conversation with Kwany Zaabu, 20th Jan, 1987, in Rethy.

263. idem.

264. Bura Thenga, see above, note 147.

265. Conversation with Bura Thenga, 23rd Jan, 1987, in Bunia.

266. The complete 'Editions CECA' objectives state:
    1. Inviter les gens à être réconciliés avec Christ (évangélisation).
    2. Edifier les croyants dans la foi (croissance chrétienne).
    3. Pénétrer les structures de croyance et coutume zaïroise par la vérité vivante de la larole de Dieu.
    4. Combattre et corriger les maux sociaux (tels que: corruption, immoralité, fraude, cupidité, polygamie, sorcellerie, etc...) sans s'ingérer dans les affaires politiques.
    5. Encourager le développement communautaire.
    6. Alimenter les catéchistes et les pasteurs en outils pour leur ministère.
    7. Faciliter le développement et la distribution de la littérature pour les différents départements de la CECA.
    8. Adresser aux évolués les requêtes d'être disciples.
    9. Développer un sens d'identité dans la CECA (comme par les biographies, l'histoire de la CECA, etc.)
    10. Servir la communauté locale dans ses besoins d'impression.

    The complete 'Tujenge' objectives state:
    1.   Evangéliser les jeunes.
    2.   Aider les jeunes de nos églises: a) à croître dans la foi, b) à affronter les questions difficiles de nos jours à la lumière

de la Parole de Dieu, c) à développer leurs facultés de commu
niquer par écrit aussi.
3. Stimuler une étude sérieuse de la Bible.
4. Encourager l'éducation personnelle et le service personnel.
5. Informer sur les activés de la communauté.

267. Conversation with Cit. Ukelo, who helped with the artwork of some of the articles in 'Tujenge', 18th Jan, 1987, in Rethy.

268. Conversation with Bura Thenga, 23rd Jan, 1987, in Bunia. Also letter from Kwany Londoni, 25th July, 1987.

269. Letter from Kwany Londoni, Director 'Editions CECA', Rethy, 25th July, 1987.

270. Conversation with Amula Djang'etambe, 22nd Jan, 1987, in Bunia.

271. Langford to Molyneux, 12th July, 1987.

272. Kwany Londoni to Molyneux, 25th July, 1987.

273. Langford to Molyneux, 12th July, 1987.

274. List of topics at second journalism seminar, Rethy, 1st-3rd July, 1986, (no attempt has been made to categorize them):

healing	poverty	church finance
death	marriage	offerings
mourning	corruption	mixed marriages
sorcery	betrothal	financial autonomy
wealth	polygamy	the pastorate
evil spells	divorce	immorality
sickness	the home	alcoholism
venereal disease	faith	smoking
illegitimacy	youth	dancing
unmarried mothers	choirs	family devotions
wedding ceremonies	vocation	love
boy-girl relationships	infertility	prayer
preaching and hearing	sex	church administration

275. 'Les Objectifs des Editions CECA', dated 1st July, 1986, in letter from Kwany Londoni, 25th July, 1987.

276. Letter from Kwany to members of Writers Clubs, dated 22nd Aug, 1986.

277. The title is a Lendu proverb 'Nja ngri gbo nja ngri'; as one baboon mocks another for his ridiculously coloured posterior but cannot see his own which is just as ludicrous, so Christians can be critical of others while totally unaware that they have the same faults. The article exploits the African predilection for proverbs as an avenue of communication. Several of the dissertations and theses at the 'Faculté de Théologie Catholique de Kinshasa' concern proverbs.

278. Radio CANDIP (Centre d'Animation et de Diffusion Pédagogiques), set near the College of Education, Bunia.

279. Conversation with Pastor Ufoyuru Kpathy, 22nd Jan, 1987, in Bunia.

280. Pastor Kile Kpala and Rev D. Langford.

281. Conversations with Langford and Kile, 17th Jan, 1987 (Rethy) and 25th Jan,, 1987 (Bunia), respectively.

282. Among the pressures of duties for the Zaïrian Church leader is the struggle (shared with almost all his fellow-citizens) for survival. Salaries are so inadequate that the pastor has to devote a considerable and increasing proportion of his time to cultivation and harvesting. cf. the remark made by Pastor Djaldero (Swahili seminar):
    When I began my work as a pastor, I had my Bible in my
    right hand and the hoe in my left hand. Now I have had
    to put my hoe in my right hand and my Bible in the left.
    Conversation, 17th Jan, 1987.

283. Revd D. Langford left Zaïre for furlough in August, 1984 and the author (latterly seeking to encourage the process, although never directly involved in it) unexpectedly had to leave Zaïre in December, 1984.

284. I owe this suggestive simile (already used in ch. 1) to Dr P. Bowers, course on contextualisation, 7th-18th Jan, 1985, in Nairobi, Kenya.

362

285. Conversation with J. Gration, July, 1984.

286. D. B. Barrett, 'Interdisciplinary theories of religion and African independency', in *African Initiatives in Religion*, (ed. D. B. Barrett) Nairobi, East African Publishing House, 1971, p. 153.

287. Gration wrote in his field notes for the Swahili seminar in Rethy, 1983,
> If one good question is asked (and it elicits a good response) stick with it.

288. The discerning remark was made by Cit. Ukelo, the only participant of the Swahili seminar at Rethy with post-secondary education. At the closing group session at Rethy (18th Jan, 1987) one participant expressed that it would be far better if the Church committees and councils simply made the decisions (on such subjects as burial customs, fetishism, etc.) and then just applied the laws; the church members would know where they stood. Others disagreed, arguing that it is exactly this unthinking passivity among church members which leads to external conformity without inner conviction.

289. The heavy reliance upon lecture method in CECA Bible schools is illustrated by Gration's findings at the Swahili seminar (Rethy, 1983):
> I am tempted to feel that for some of the older men the damage may be permanent and to a measure irreparable. During our last session together we actually discussed the lecture vs. dialogue method. We quickly counted up the number of hours in which they had been lectured or preached to during their two years of Bible school. Then counting all the hours spent in taking exams (a most inadequate form of dialogue and not worthy of the term), we found that they were lectured to about 97% of the time... I am still actively seeking some form of penance for my large part in the creation of this model.

'Willowbank to Zaïre', op. cit. p. 302.

290. K. Dickson, op. cit. p. 8.

363

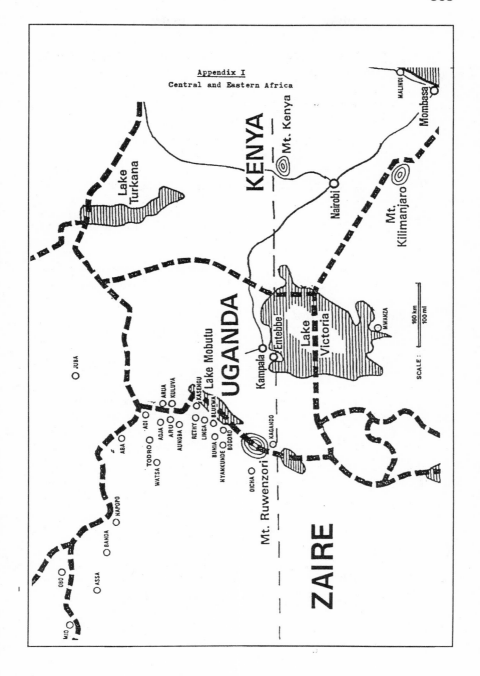

Appendix I
Central and Eastern Africa

APPENDIX II

DISTRIBUTION & STATUS OF AIM PERSONNEL 1956-1986

	1956	1961	1966	1971	1976	1981	1982	1983	1984	1985	1986
Missionaries on the field, by status											
Full term	366	452	363	423	372	387	391	451	481	469	440
Short term	-	-	3	30	48	76	69	91	88	82	84
On loan	-	-	-	-	-	-	-	-	-	-	6
Associate	-	-	10	18	22	47	71	53	65	50	66
Volunteer (9mo-1yr)	-	-	-	-	-	-	-	-	17	27	28
TOTAL	366	452	376	471	442	510	531	595	651	628	624
Missionaries on field, by location											
International office	-	2	-	2	7	7	12	14	18	8	8
Int'l services	-	-	-	-	4	25	25	39	37	46	31
C A R (FEA/CAE)	11	8	14	13	10	13	11	18	16	16	14
Kenya	120	144	185	194	197	207	227	247	299	291	272
Sudan	12	16	-	-	13	29	23	34	29	20	15
Tanzania	71	88	60	57	31	21	20	25	18	25	28
Uganda	24	30	39	29	17	11	11	12	16	18	18
Zaire	124	133	28	108	83	76	74	73	83	81	81
Academies	-	31	40	61	71	85	89	RVA81	85	84	87
USA urban	-	-	-	-	2	5	6	8	9	11	14
Comoro Islands	-	-	-	-	5	11	11	14	15	17	20
Madagscar	-	-	-	-	-	4	2	2	4	2	4
Namibia	-	-	-	-	-	2	2	3	4	5	5

Reunion	-	-	-	-	-	2	3	0	0	0	0
Seychelles	-	-	-	-	-	6	6	9	5	4	3
Lesotho	-	-	-	-	-	-	-	-	-	-	2
Mozambique	-	-	-	-	-	-	-	-	-	-	3
Studying en route	(5)	4	9	7	2	6	9	-	13	10	19
Assignment pending	-	-	-	-	-	-	-	5	0	0	0
FIELD TOTALS	366	452	376	471	442	510	531	595	651	638	624
Missionaries in sending areas											
On furlough	102	86	133	168	161	147	108	104	97	132	166
On home staff:											
Australia	-	2	2	2	2	2	3	4	3	3	3
Canada	-	1	3	5	8	11	10	16	13	13	15
South Africa	-	3	3	2	2	4	4	1	1	1	1
United Kingdom	-	5	6	9	7	12	14	6	12	12	12
United States America	-	-	19	26	30	35	36	41	37	40	58
Missionary appointees	63	33	34	30	48	30	57	88	72	71	94
Retired	8	29	66	76	115	145	146	135	153	139	148
MISSIONARY TOTAL	539	611	642	789	815	896	909	990	1,039	1,049	1,121
Sending Council members											
Australia	2	2	2	2	11	14	11	17	15	16	15
Canada	2	3	6	5	14	15	15	14	17	19	20
South Africa	-	2	-	-	5	9	11	13	13	13	16
United Kingdom	4	4	5	5	13	14	13	14	14	15	11
United States America	19	16	16	18	15	16	12	15	15	15	13
MEMBERS TOTAL	566	638	671	819	873	963	971	1,063	1,113	1,127	1,196

Appendix III

Questionnaire for participants of Gospel and Culture Seminars used during field research, January 1987

1. Noms (en majuscules, svp...

2. Lieu et date de naissance ....

3. Dernière année d'études primaires: ....
   Dernière année d'études secondaires: ....

4. Etudes post-secondaires: ....

5. Postes, avec le nombre d'années (ex. Prof Ecole Bibl., Todro, 3 ans)..

6. Avez-vous participé à la lère Consultation, Bunia, 1983? Oui/Non

7. Avez-vous participé à la 2 ème Consultation, Bunia, 1984? Oui/Non

8. Avez-vous participé aux discussions qui ont suivi les Consultations I et II et qui ont abouti à la rédaction des trois documents? Oui/Non

9. Si votre réponse à la question 8 est Oui, dans quel groupe participiez-vous?:
   1. Evangile et Croyances (Rethy) ....
   2. Fétichisme et Croyances (Aungba) ....
   3. Tribalisme (Bunia)..

10. Depuis la rédaction de ces trois documents, votre groupe a-t-il essayé de continuer ce genre de discussion? Oui/Non

11. Si Oui: 1. Sur le même sujet? ....
             2. Sur un autre sujet Lequel? (lesquels?): ....
             3. Avez-vous essayé d'y associer d'autres gens du milieu(ex. femmes, jeunes, vieux, non-chrétiens, etc) Si Oui, lesquels?: ....

12. Les Consultations, les avez-vous trouveés utiles? Si Oui, précisez ce que vous en avez apprécié: ....

13. Quel était le rôle de Dr Gration dans ces Consultations?
....

14. Pensez-vous que Dr Gration était particulièrement bien placé pour diriger ce type de séminaire à cause de son âge, de son expérience, de sa manière? ou n'importe quel autre mission-naire, visiteur, ou pasteur africain aurait-il pu faire de même? Donnez vos raisons: ....

15. Pensez-vous que d'autres gens de l'Eglise pourraient profiter de ce genre de séminaire? Si Oui, qui?...................................
....

16. Les Consultations, ont-elles influencé les domaines suivantes? (NB, indiquer seulement les domaines où vous constatez que les Consultations vous ont accordé quelque chose de nouveau. Pour chaque réponse, prière de citer des *exemples concrets, avec lieu et date*. Merci):
    a) Votre prédication (ex. choix de sujet, texte, illustrations, ap-plications)? ....
    b) Votre enseignement biblique (ex. aller plus lin que le pro-gramme officiel, aborder les questions que posent les étudiants, etc.)? ....
    c) Composition des chants de circonstance (naissance, mariage, deuil,etc.)? ....
    d) Séminaires des jeunes, des anciens, des diacres, etc.?
....
    e) Publications, articles? ....

f) Autres (ex. radio, camps de la Ligue, etc.)?

....

17. Avez-vous des projets pour l'avenir dans un (ou plusieurs) des domaines cités ci-haut? (Aussi de détails que possible svp.)

....

18. Serait-il souhaitable que Dr Gration revienne pour une Consultation de plus? Si oui, pour quoi faire?

....

Conclusion

A Continuing Odyssey

The initial chapter of this thesis sought to identify and discuss the numerous and diverse factors contributing to the emergence of 'Theologia Africana' as a recognizable phenomenon of the last three decades. While the theological search has been distinct from the political, educational and literary quests in Africa, it nevertheless has shared with these the same basic concern. To some extent at least they have travelled in a similar direction, like leaves borne along by the same current. This 'current' is the common quest for African self-hood or identity. Emerging from long years of colonial experience which allowed the African little pride in his world, African Christianity has sought to find a place where, both in its experience and its understanding (theology), it can 'feel at home'.[1]

The results of this quest are still unfolding. There is, to date, no 'commodity' which one might call 'African Christian Theology'. While there are certain themes which are prominent, such as the reality of the spirit world, the question of ancestors, the meaning of community, wholeness and healing, there is no clear unanimity on these topics and their detailed relation to the Christian Gospel. This thesis, therefore, has been concerned to explore not so much a *product* as a *process*, a quest. What is emerging is not some multi-volume work of theology which will accurately express the theological consensus of Christian thinkers in Nigeria and Tanzania, Botswana and Zaïre. To expect such a product is to suppose that all of Black Africa shares an identical world-view, whereas the reality is one of considerable diversity. In the words of John Mbiti:

> It is all too easy to use the phrase 'African Theology', but to state exactly what that means, or even to show its real nature, is an entirely different issue. And certainly it cannot be expected that such a theology would be uniform through-out the continent of Africa.[2]

The present thesis has been more concerned, therefore, with the varied processes involved in expressing the understanding of faith, rather than with any end-product. The research undertaken and discussed within these chapters has implications in three distinct realms: the first relates to the nature of theology itself, the second to the field of theological education, the third to the question of theological educators in Africa.

'Theology' in Africa

The three case-study chapters which constitute the central body of the thesis illustrate just how varied are the processes that contribute to that quest for religious and theological self-hood. The chapter relating to the Faculty of Catholic Theology in Kinshasa explores one (arguably Black Africa's most prominent) example of theology's academic and literary sector. Characterized by the continuing legacy of scholarly thoroughness inherited from its parent University of Louvain, it has nurtured and attracted a number of erudite African theologians. Their university education and subsequent post-graduate studies in Europe (primarily in Louvain/Leuven or Rome) have equipped them to engage the debate about the nature and methods of theology and to argue for a more positive, integrated theological alternative to the (as they see it) speculative and rationalistic systems of the West. During the 1960s, as we have seen, the Faculty was the arena where the serious debate as to the legitimacy or otherwise of 'African Theology' was staged. That such a debate could take place at all in any meaningful way, pre-supposed a conceptualization and an articulation of African religious and theological understanding.

It was the argument of that chapter that the literary, published nature of the theological task of the Faculty has been integral to its influence and success. The Faculty has not only debated, but it has published those debates and by publishing it has widened the arena and made the debate more important. It has hosted conferences and it has inevitably published the proceedings of the conferences; by doing so it has made the conferences more significant, to be taken more seriously by both speakers and other participants. It set up the 'Centre de Recherches Africaines' as a resource centre for the study of the cultural, religious, linguistic and philosophical heritage with which Christianity is interacting and publishes its findings. The Faculty's unwritten policy (inherited from Louvain): *'on ne croira pas à une recherche qui n'aboutit à une publication'* (no-one will take seriously a piece of research which does not end up published) has resulted in a growing list of serious scientific works as well as the establishing of the Faculty's three major journals (*RAT*, *CRA* and *RPK*). Publication has permitted a literary marketplace for the contributors and emphasized to them and to their readers the significance or 'seriousness' of their research. Undoubtedly, this has made the painstaking labour of research that much more worth the trouble. Had the Faculty not had this emphasis upon publishing, it is unlikely that its importance as a theological research centre would have been recognized except locally.

If African theologians are to succeed in conceptualizing the culturo-religious heritage into which they were born and their own understanding of the Christian Gospel and if they are to communicate credibly that understanding to others outside Africa, it is difficult to see how they can do it except by developing theological skills using scientifically rigorous methods. Mgr Tshibangu, one of Africa's most important contributors to the debate on 'African Theology' would insist:

> Theology is actually a scientific or scholarly act of commitment. Defining it in precise and dynamic terms, we can say that it is 'the science dealing with the divine destiny of

humanity. This science is grounded on God's revelation in Christ' and it is also based on 'deep, thorough-going knowledge of human beings and the factors that condition their lives'. Such knowledge comes to us from philosophy, the human sciences and the basic sciences dealing with the universe.[3]

Publication will carry the results of that sort of theological thinking to the international forum, permitting cross-fertilization of ideas and mutual enrichment.

That the published output from the Faculty has entitled and permitted the FTCK to communicate meaningfully with others in the international academic sector is beyond question. What is more difficult to determine is the extent to which the Faculty engages influentially with the non-intellectual sector, even within its own country of Zaïre. It may be presumed that the many Catholic priests and Church leaders in Zaïre who subscribe to the FTCK's periodicals are influenced in their thinking by what they read. While the theologians inform themselves in their research from what is going on at the 'grassroots', there is little to suggest that their findings return again to those grassroots to affect belief and behaviour. The direction of the debate would seem to be 'up and away' from the oral sector, which in fact represents the large majority of Africa's church members and where dynamics are at work which are very different from those in the literary domain.

It has been one concern of the thesis to argue that although the academic/literary sector is the most recognizably 'theological' in the usual Western sense of the word, theology in the wider meaning as reflection about God and human destiny cannot be confined to this one sector. At different levels of the Christian Church in Africa, African Christians with or without formal educational background are expressing verbally and behaviourally their beliefs about God, Jesus Christ, the Holy Spirit and the spirit world, the Church and how these affect their everyday lives individually and as a community. The chapter on Kimbanguist hymns illustrates just one example of how this unselfconscious, unsystematic expression of belief takes place. The hymns are not for private, intellectual meditation, but rather for repeated singing by choirs and listened to by the hundreds of Kimbanguist faithful gathered for worship. For the worshippers the choir renditions constitute a highlight of the meetings. Whereas in the literary domain an article or book will be 'important' or 'influential' by virtue of its careful background research and well-reasoned argument (and, to some extent, by the stature of the academic journal in which it appears, or of the publishing house), the hymns are 'effective' in their ability to 'excite the heart' and to capture the religious imagination by expressing some aspect of the Kimbanguist identity. In this, a hymn's official approval by the 'Bureau des Chants Kimbanguistes' plays its part, but so also does the technical precision and communicated sincerity of the choir.

Hymns represent but one of the many dimensions of 'oral theology'. Another important element is preaching. To date there have not been many studies made of sermons in the African churches. For the researcher, hymns have the advantage of being learnt by heart by choirs, sung repeatedly and even noted down in choir-members' exercise-books; they are also more popular material for the increasingly ubiquitous tape-recorder. The material is thus readily obtainable for analysis. Sermons, by contrast, are more likely to be 'one-offs' and although many rural churches keep meticulous records of the preacher and his text,[4] they would not, of course, possess copies of the sermons themselves. It is probably for this reason that H. W. Turner's study of preaching in Nigeria's independent churches concerns choice of Bible text rather than sermon content.[5] A researcher would have to spend many months in attendance at several local churches to build up an accurate picture of sermon-content. In addition to sermons, drama is a widely used means of expressing and communicating beliefs. It would share, for the researcher, the same practical difficulties as sermons. Prayers, liturgy and informal fireside conversations, are other elements of unwritten theology, disclosing attitudes and opinions regarding man and his world and their relation to God.

Such elements may not enjoy the privileged status of traditional 'theology' and yet they reflect more closely the real beliefs and attitudes of the great majority in the African Church (as elsewhere). Parratt has correctly insisted about 'oral theology':

> This sort of theology has been regarded as much closer to the
> heart of the Church's spiritual life in Africa as it struggles to
> relate the Christian faith to African experience.[6]

However, because these elements are not the usual ingredients of a theology which at least in the West has come to be an increasingly academic, theoretical subject, their importance is not often recognized, either in the West or in Africa. This thesis seeks to emphasize their proper place within the realm of 'theology'. Indeed, it is precisely because these dimensions are ignored that 'theology' easily becomes an elitist pursuit, out of touch with the majority in the Church with whom it should interact.

The final chapter of the thesis, relating to the Gospel and Culture Seminars in North-East Zaïre, concerns an experiment to encourage just such an interaction. The Seminars were not actually doing 'grassroots theology' for the participants were church leaders with at least some background in Bible School or Theological Seminary. Nevertheless, the methodology was one which sought to ensure that the questions that theological reflection addressed were truly pertinent ones, arising from daily real-life experience of Christians in Zaïre, with its complex overlap of traditional and modern values. Furthermore, the intended direction of the group reflection was not 'up and away' but rather 'to and from' the grassroots. The seminars sought to bring the sum total of life-experience (the context) into the open for discussion and critical appraisal (although in the event, as we observed, directly cultural and religious topics received more attention than political issues). The process involved a deliberate and detailed (but not necessarily technical) understanding of the customs, institutions and values that together make an African who he is and give him a distinct identity. Rather than deny that identity or submerge it as being not the proper material for Christian reflection, the seminars became theological workshops where the different contextual elements were identified, described and critically appraised. This 'standing back and describing' involves a certain distancing of the participant from his context and is an essential part of the process, without which there can be little critical appraisal. Since the delegates shared the evangelical conviction that the biblical revelation is *'the absolute and final authority in all matters of faith and conduct'*, they sought to expose the cultural elements (or at least the three major topics they had time to discuss during the seminar) to what they understood to be the relevant teaching of Scripture. In several cases (for example, tribalism, burial practices, traditional medicine) there was little direct teaching found in Scripture. Closer attention, however, revealed that even where explicit biblical instructions lacked, it was possible to discover principles in the Bible which addressed the underlying moral or spiritual issues.

The findings of the seminars and the documents that resulted from them reflected the approach of critical discernment that the delegates adopted. They sought to avoid the opposing errors of over-eager endorsement of the indigenous socio-cultural heritage on the one hand, and its blanket rejection on the other. Charles Nyamiti (Tanzania) would support such an approach:

> Up to recent times, the general approach among Christians
> towards African religions and cultures tended to be nega-
> tive. A more positive appreciation of African tradition is now
> widespread, but as often happens, this can sometimes go
> to the other extreme. Today one hears much of African
> wisdom, religiosity, philosophy and the like, but little mention
> is made of the deviations in the African cultures. The truth
> lies between these two extremes: each culture and people
> have both their positive and their negative qualities and the
> wise theologian will be able to profit from them both.[7]

Seeking to appraise cultural elements in the light of their understanding of Scripture, the documents, as we have seen, affirm certain traditional African values and behaviour, while rejecting others as incompatible with the Christian Gospel. Such theological reflection is not speculative or abstract; it is practical and situational. It seeks to effect an integrated world where identity is not lost but it is purified by the light of Christ.

The two theologies (oral and literary) need each other, whereas all too often they are mutually out of touch. Where 'oral theology' remains unassisted by critical discernment and hermeneutical skills of biblical interpretation, it is likely to fall prey to certain excesses or weaknesses, especially where a dominant personality is present. De Craemer's study of 'Jamaa'[8] provides one example within Africa and the same can be argued concerning certain beliefs expressed in the 'oral theology' of the Kimbanguists. Certainly Church History outside of Africa provides many examples.

It is also true, however, that academic, literary theology, divorced from the vital life-experience of the vast majority in the Church can become fascinated by the abstract and speculative, debating questions that few are really asking, having little to contribute that is relevant either to its members or to those to whom it should be ministering.

Theological Education in Africa

The recognition of the non-literary sector in theological reflection necessarily has at least two implications for theological education and Church ministry in Africa. Firstly, it indicates the importance of every educational level. Since gaining independence African nations have rightly put much emphasis upon the expansion of tertiary education. The establishing and expanding of university institutions is part of a nation's dignity of non-dependency and constitutes an essential element in national maturity. Theological education in Africa has been caught up in the same drive, rightly believing that it should not get left behind, but should rather be able to provide for the increasing numbers of urban and educated citizens. Numerical growth and academic improvement are often assumed to be the twin barometers of success. The emergence of prestigious residential theological institutions attract funding and personnel. Their 'high profile' attracts candidates from near and far and returns them to their society after three or four years as members of an elite minority. 'Lower-level' Bible Schools suffer by comparison, receiving little encouragement and working under the most difficult conditions. Yet these schools are much nearer to the grassroots community who constitute the large majority of the total membership of the churches and they should be considered important potential workshops where theology is far less removed from everyday life.

Yet whatever the academic level of the Bible or theological schools, they are there to train a (relatively) small minority of the total membership of the churches. The inherent dangers of this 'specialist' training both to the elite themselves and to the rest, have been pointed out by Kinsler:

> It forms in the mind of the pastor complexes which are difficult to surmount: a sense of trying to be something that he is not, of having to justify his role, of attempting to carry out all the functions of the ministry, of being the one who is called and trained and paid to do the job. And it forms in the mind of the members the inverse complexes which are so prevalent: a sense of being less capable than they really are, of not having an essential role, of not possessing the gifts of the ministry, of not being really called — because they are not trained or paid or ordained.[9]

The emphasis in recent decades of the importance of the lay membership of the churches has gone some way towards redressing this imbalance and creating a healthier understanding of church leadership and ministry. Innovative patterns of theological education such as TEE (see pp. 266ff) seek to break from the high-profile patterns of institutionalized theological education and reflect the healthy awareness that ministry within the Church is the prerogative of the many rather than the few. The research into Kimbanguist hymns would suggest that far more could be done to encourage the use of the various means available to the oral sector as avenues of theological education. The acceptance and popularity of hymns and drama as part of the liturgy in most rural and urban churches in Black Africa cannot be questioned.[10] Within the Church, however, these traditional media suffer from two weaknesses. Firstly, such activities are usually more noteworthy for their enthusiasm and style than for their theological content. Church leaders who recognize the potential of hymns and drama could encourage competent personnel in the Church to provide such creativity with theological direction. To this end, music and drama could be included in theological school curricula. Secondly, such activities are almost always restricted to church-service liturgy, whereas their most effective contribution would be out of doors, communicating Christian values in the context of events of central importance to African society. For example, hymns (and even where appropriate, drama) could be commissioned to celebrate a marriage or the birth of a baby, to express grief and also Christian hope by the grave-side, or to contrast corruption and honesty in the market-place.

Judging from both observation and what many have written, traditional patterns of theological education in much of Africa suffer additionally from the fact that the educators are themselves trained in theology but have often received little help in developing pedagogical (or, better, androgogical) skills for communicating their theological knowledge to their students. Peter Savage, while writing primarily with Latin America in mind, describes theoogical education in many other areas of the Third World when he says:

> Few current faculties provide training in education, instruc-
> tional principles and techniques. Many theologians have an
> adequate grasp of their subject but cannot communicate it.
> Many theologians have the subconscious goal of making
> men just like themselves. Instead of producing pastors and
> church planters, they are instead producing maladjusted
> theologians in a pastoral context.[11]

Expatriate theologians who received their own education at universities in the West in which the lecture method predominated, perpetuate similar patterns in Africa. Their national colleagues who studied outside of Africa are sometimes just as conservative in their methods as the expatriates.[12] Both expatriate and national may be unaware that there might be different styles of learning and that teaching methods can and should adjust accordingly.[13] In other words, there must be contextualization not only of the content of theological education, but also in teaching methods. Educationalists would not necessarily argue for the replacement of the lecture method, but underline its limitations when used to the exclusion of other methods. Harrison maintains that the lecture is as effective as other methods for the transmission of information, but it is less effective than more active, participative learning methods in promoting thought, and that it is ineffective in changing attitudes.[14] Yet it is probably true that the lecture method is still the predominant one used in theological institutions in Africa. The students who sit under that methodology during their time at theological school, graduate to become in their turn theological educators and unconsciously reproduce the same patterns of theological education in which the transference of knowledge and its memorization by the students is the accepted norm of theological education. Kornfield, reflecting on Postman and Weingartner's point that students learn what they do (rather than what they hear) asks:

> Now what is it that students do in a classroom? Typically they sit and imbibe information. What they will remember years later is not that information but the method or medium through which it was communicated. And because they will remember what they did, not particularly what was done for them, they will remember very little.[15]

Deliberate attempts at a more contextualized curriculum can go part way towards a more relevant theology, but as long as the methodology remains one of straight instruction it will be self-limiting, ending when the subject matter has been 'covered' or the examination completed and doing little to develop reflective skills in the students for their future years of ministry.

In-course field education undoubtedly does much to break the artificiality of a residential theological education, for it places the student back into the real world of church and society, at least for a month or two. Serving alongside a pastor in his everyday ministry and exposed to as wide a range as possible of all that is involved in the pastoral round of duties, the student is reminded of the practical questions and problems of ordinary people and he is able to benefit from the experience and skills of his senior pastor. However, the periods of practical 'apprenticeship' are brief, often lasting only three or four weeks of the total and representing only a fraction of the total training period.

Educationalists advocate frequent alternation of information and reinforcement-by-doing. Ward[16] has proposed the analogy of a 'split-rail fence', in which one rail represents cognitive input, another parallel to it which represents field experience, connected at frequent and regular intervals by support posts, such as seminars, designed to integrate the two. The analogy suggests the need for students in theological training to interrelate frequently with church and society.

The various elements of the theological scene in Zaïre, whether in residential centres or decentralized cells or in para-church organizations, have this in common — they are primarily *instructional*. They rely heavily upon teacher-to-student transfer of knowledge. It would be wrong to suggest that there is no place for 'content' in Christian theology. The historical dimension of the 'Christ-event', of the Christian Scriptures and of the birth and development of the Christian Church in the world, all produce a certain 'givenness' which simply cannot be ignored. However, as far as Africa is concerned, too often this 'content' has been selected and packaged in the West and its detailed inventory reflects centuries of the West's gradually evolving understanding of the Christian message within the context of Western society and its values. Consequently, many of the constituents of African perceptions of reality have not been addressed by the theological process.[17] As a result, Christianity has been perceived as being alien, a religion of the Whites and the Church a place where any African sense of 'ownership' is low.

The Gospel and Culture Seminars which took place in 1983 and 1984 were notable not because of the new people they involved in the theological process but because they proposed a different approach to 'doing theology'. Their methodology promoted *reflection* rather than additional information. Instead of working to a 'closed curriculum' in which a set 'content' was transmitted to the students by the teacher, the agenda was open-ended. The methodology of discussion rather than lecture shifted the responsibility of reflection from the teacher to the students, from the one to the many, from the expatriate to the nationals themselves. Consequently, the role of the students changed from being passive to being active and their mental process from being one of consuming to one of producing or discovering. 'Discovery' is, in fact, a feature which much so-called theological reflection lacks in the CECA Church and probably in much of Zaïre and Africa. If it is true that whatever a student learns he must learn for himself (no-one can learn it for him), then this sort of participative rather than passive methodology should be encouraged at every level of theological education.

It was argued in the final chapter of the thesis that the methodology of discovery from within the real socio-cultural world of the student, can and should take place within the residential theological institutions and programmes. This will furnish the students with tools of enquiry and reflection which will transform the student's 'theological period' from three (or however many) years to the span of his entire ministry. More than this, however, theology will no longer be made up of a list of esoteric subjects which seem quite alien to the Church in its particular socio-cultural context. For as Dickson has rightly said:

> The Church should be able to recognize itself in the theologian's theology which may have repercussions for the society for which the Church prays.[18]

All too often, as the Church has looked at the theological seminary's curriculum it has recognized little that it can call its own.

In the emphasis upon reflection, however, theological education (especially that which is done with pastoral ministry in mind) cannot afford to forget spirituality. The balance between the training of the mind and the nurture of the spirit constitutes one of the most difficult tasks in any Bible or theological school and the higher the academic level it is for the one to eclipse the other. Perception is not merely intellectual, it is also spiritual. A man who undergoes conversion 'sees things differently' from before. This change, gradual or sudden, cannot be explained away in a reductionist way. The kind of transformation that Saul of Tarsus experienced as recorded in Acts 9 upon encounter with the risen Christ may not occur with the same dramatic intensity for all or even the majority of Christians, but the difference is one of degree rather than nature. Bishop Tshibangu's assertion that it is spiritual renewal which does most to purify and enrich Christian living and that through the work of the Holy Spirit the simple come to an understanding and discernment that surpass those of the learned (see above, p. 124) could be borne out by numberless uneducated village Christians who display an integrated 'from-the-heart' faith that no academic education can bring about. While the 'two conflicting levels' of conception and experience noted and regretted by many African or Africanist authors accurately describes part of reality, it does not tell the whole story. If it be asked how it is that for many Christians in Africa the Gospel has penetrated to the heart and transformed from the centre out, the answer is not to be found only or even primarily in Christian education but rather in depth of spiritual experience which touches the affections and the will. It is one thing to achieve understanding of biblical teaching relating to a certain subject, it is another to interiorize its teachings by willing, wholehearted appropriation. In this respect, retreats for deepening the spiritual life (such as those organized for pastors in the CECA Church) have their undeniable place and provide reflection with an essential dynamic.

It is argued in this thesis that theology can have a wide definition and that understood in this way, it is being done, not only by an elite minority using specialist intellectual and literary skills, but also among a largely oral majority. Theological education does well to recognize the importance of the whole range of theological reflection, and to acknowledge the different dynamics involved in the different types or levels. It will be most effective when it succeeds in interrelating the one to the other and both to the real, perceived needs of the total context.

Theological Educators in Africa

The foregoing has its implications for theological educators in Africa. If theological education in Africa is to move beyond the mere transference of knowledge, then those involved in theological education must be more than lecturers. They must rather be facilitators, stimulating and enabling the process of reflection in such a way that wherever possible it is the students or participants (be they in the classroom, in a seminar, in a church, or around a fire in the evening) who bring their world with its real-life needs and problems to interact with the Gospel. It is very unlikely that the oral sector itself will initiate such a process. Kalilombe argues that in the history of ideas the 'masses' rarely have it within themselves to initiate and carry through projects of socio-economic and political change and that almost always facilitators are needed who are closely in touch both with the 'masses' themselves and also with the sectors the masses would wish to influence. But for this to happen fruitfully, Kalilombe argues, the leaders or specialists need themselves to undergo a 'conversion' of attitude and relationship, as indeed do the non-specialist members of the Church:

> They need to learn to respect the other members of the Church as fellow servants of the Lord and not treat them as mere 'subjects' or clients. For the common members, a conversion is also necessary. They must regain confidence in themselves as full citizens of Christ's Church... they should learn to value and use the special contribution that the leaders and experts bring with them for the common task.[19]

Once these attitudes have been established, Kalilombe believes, the facilitators can begin the process of 'conscientization' by which the ordinary people can be *'helped to see reality'* and can start to understand that *'in God's plan they are corresponsible agents of their own history'*.[20] Those who have written the most about these processes of conscientization of the masses have done so from the viewpoint of liberation theology in Latin America and often from a Marxist analysis of society and its injustices. But the process is valid without the same politico-philosophical assumptions, wherever there are passive majorities dependent on decisions made and handed down from a specialist minority.

The Gospel and Culture Seminars were part of the conscientization process and Gration sought to act as facilitator, awakening an awareness in the delegates that there was theology needing to be done and that they were the ones to do it. Ideally that same process should have self-reproduced in other places and at other levels, with the original participants becoming in turn facilitators. To a limited extent this happened as the follow-up research revealed. Gration's experience was that the process was far harder to achieve with the Swahili-speaking seminar at Rethy in 1983 than at the French-speaking level (see p. 278). Secondary education encourages a questioning mind, and brings about an increasing ability to conceptualize, permitting the student to distance himself from the subject he is studying and look at it from different angles and analyse it. Those who have not benefited from such education are generally happier following directives 'from above'. Thus in a discussion with the Swahili-speaking participants at Rethy during my field-research in 1987, one delegate expressed severe misgivings about the wisdom of letting the members of his local church congregation air their beliefs and questionings:

> Let the decisions rather be made at the top, by the Administrative Council; we will then announce those rules to our church members. Then they'll know exactly where they stand. (Swahili: 'wataogopa', they will fear).[11]

Although some other delegates present sought to convince him that this would likely produce little more than unthinking

(perhaps even hypocritical) conformity, he remained sceptical.[21]

Despite prevailing attitudes which encourage passivity and conformity with little inner understanding, a skilful facilitator well versed
in both the local and biblical 'worlds' can so encourage open expression of inner thought and opinion that when biblical principles are
eventually sought and found, they are perceived to address the
questions directly. This may be part of the vital, first-hand (rather than
mediated) interchange that Dickson refers to in saying:

> It is essential that Africans should be in a position to express
> in a vital way what Christ means to them and to do so in and
> through a cultural medium that makes original thinking
> possible... Christ must be heard to speak to Africans
> direct.[22]

For a theological teacher to be an effective facilitator, he must be in
touch with both 'horizons', the contemporary African one and the
biblical one, permitting and encouraging the interraction of the two.
Most theological teachers in Africa are more or less well trained in the
one world of Biblical knowledge, but are less well-equipped, less aware
in the other world. The expatriate is clearly at a disadvantage in
comparison to his national colleague, for he has little insight into the
ways and values of the nationals and might even feel that there is little
to be gained by trying to penetrate a world which is so different from
his own, or even more regrettably, he might consciously or unconsciously believe it to be inferior to his own and not worth bothering to
understand. Such an expatriate teacher might have some success as
an instructor, conveying information to his students, but he will be
unsuccessful as a facilitator of theological reflection.

The thesis has incidentally provided examples of expatriates who,
in their different ways, revealed attitudes which took seriously the
Bantu world. Tempels' gradual change from an attitude of aloof
paternalism to one of respect and encounter provides what is perhaps
an unusual and even extreme example of seeing as the African sees.
His interest in the people he worked amongst was evident from the

beginning as he collected proverbs, songs and riddles in the Kamina region of South-East Zaïre. After ten years of labour Tempels, according to Smet, *found his way, becoming interested in the (Bantu) man himself*.[23] Tempels recalls how it happened:

> I looked at this man, then, and asked him: 'What is it that you desire above all else? Why do you use magical remedies? What do they mean? How do they operate? [24]

The Franciscan missionary found to his astonishment that at the deeper level the Bantu's aspirations were much his own and that it was the Bantu who helped him discover himself:

> It was a new delight for us both to discover that we were alike, and further, that we were beginning to encounter one another in our very souls.[25]

Tempels was accused in subsequent years of taking the idea of 'encounter' too far, to the point of encouraging deviations which were of discredit to the Jamaa movement that he founded later.[26] This does not, however, invalidate Tempels' genuine quest to understand sympathetically Bantu ontology. Although he was not a fully-trained philosopher, Tempels' knowledge of philosophy was undoubtedly a help in his task, but of greater importance were his long years of patient and sympathetic observation and understanding of Bantu ways of thinking and acting.

In a different way, an honest encounter or interaction of the African world and the Gospel was facilitated by Gration's approach. In this case, it was not so much that Gration himself had penetrated and conceptualized African values and behaviour. His years of experience in Zaïre undoubtedly provided a good background to the discussions, but Gration was self-confessedly only *dimly aware* of many of the crucial issues facing the African Church.[27] Lack of detailed acquired knowledge, however, was not an insurmountable obstacle to Gration, because his objective was not to do the work himself, but simply to ask questions and encourage the participants to seek for possible answers. That the participants were willing to do so was largely, by their own accounts, because Gration helped to create an atmosphere of openness; he acknowledged his own fallibility and that of his own culture and was honestly respectful of the African heritage. This sort of frank discussion about African ways had not taken place before, stated one participant, because *'the missionaries would have laughed'*. And, as has already been remarked, the fact that this aspect of Gration's character was considered so noteworthy by the participants would seem to indicate its relative rarity among expatriate Church workers.

An indigenous facilitator would need just as much openness of character, for his motives in encouraging the exposure of certain controversial issues might be more open to misinterpretation than those of a 'neutral' foreigner. He would obviously have the advantage of closeness to attitudes and values of the African context, but for that very reason he might more quickly jump in with the 'answers' and short-circuit the process of promoting discovery. He would have to exercise even more patience and caution than his expatriate colleague in order to allow participants to verbalize their feelings, beliefs, fears and questionings. As someone with, it may be supposed, a certain theological and biblical training, he would have to resist the temptation to dominate the discussion by his erudition, choosing rather to point the participants themselves towards a discovery of possible answers to their questions. He would guide but not pre-empt the search.

The quest of African Christian Theology is thus complex and open-ended. It represents the task of Africans of both oral and literary sectors to understand their faith from within their 'african-ness' — being faithful both to Christ and to their identity, without denying either.

References

1. The expression *'a place to feel at home'* was first used in this context, to my knowledge, by F. B. Welbourn, in his book on religious independency in Africa, *East African Rebels*, SCM Press, London, 1961, p. 202. The expression subsequently became the title of a book that Welbourn co-authored with B. A. Ogot, *A place to feel at home; a study of two independent churches in Western Kenya*, London, Oxford University Press, 1966. The frequency with which the expression has been used since by other authors implies that it accurately expresses reality. This was confirmed to me during my field research in Kinshasa while talking with a Kimbanguist choir member. In the mid-1950s he had left the Salvation Army to join the still-clandestine Kimbanguist Church, despite the risks. As we walked, he spoke of the delight he experienced when, as a new Kimbanguist, he was able at last to sing hymns which were 'our own' in *'my own language of Kikongo'*. I ventured: *'Lorsque vous êtes devenu Kimbanguiste, alors, vous vouv sentiez 'chez vous' (at home)?'* He stopped in his tracks and exclaimed excitedly: *'Oui, c'est exactement ça! Je me sens maintenant 'chez moi'.* Conversation with member of 'Bolingo 56' Choir', Kinshasa, 11th Feb, 1987.

2. J. S. Mbiti, *New Testament Eschatology in an African Background*, SPCK, London, 1978, p. 185.

3. T. Tshibangu, 'The task and method of theology in Africa,' in Appiah-Kubi and Torres, eds., *African Theology en route*, Orbis Books, Maryknoll, NY, 1979, p. 73.

4. In the author's seven years of experience in the Kisangani area, particularly, it was the practice of the Church Secretary to

note details of every service: date, attendance, preacher, text, response, etc.

5. H. W. Turner, *Profile through Preaching*, Edinburgh, 1965.

6. J. Parratt (ed.), *A Reader in African Christian Theology*, SPCK, London, 1987, pp. 143-144. Parratt recognises the importance of 'oral theology', but mentions it only very briefly in his conclusion.

7. C. Nyamiti, *African Tradition and the Christian God*, Eldoret, Gaba Publications; excerpt quoted in J. Parratt, op. cit. p. 58-59.

8. W. de Craemer, *The Jamaa and the Church*, Oxford University Press, Oxford, 1977.

9. F. R. Kinsler, in *Learning in Context*, op. cit. p. 31.

10. Concerning drama, I am indebted to veteran missionary H. H. Jenkinson for the following account of an indigenous work in the Bopepe region (80 mls north of Kisangani) in 1948:
    The new believers grew in grace and knowledge at a most encouraging rate and the reason was obvious. After a service, instead of rushing home to get a meal, the congregation split up and gathered in shady places, under trees, etc., in study groups of 15 to 20 people, not to criticise the sermon but to digest it. If the message had been based upon, say, a parable, miracle, or scene which could be dramatized, they would act it out spontaneously. Thus their knowledge of the Word of God grew very quickly, and they searched the Scriptures with profit.
    Jenkinson to Molyneux, 1st Dec, 1987.

11. P. Savage, 'Four crises in third world theological education', in *Evangelical Missions Quarterly*, Fall, 1972; p. 30.

12. Dickson quotes with some agreement an English theological educator in Ghana who stated:
    I can see no reason why a black African will necessarily encourage the Africanization of (the Seminary). Many black Africans, particularly black African priests are much more conservative than their white counterparts.
    Dickson, op. cit. p. 212.

13. For instance, Dorothy and Earle Bowen, (teachers at the Nairobi Evangelical Graduate School of Theology), write:

    Our theological students have simply had to adapt themselves to the teaching methods used by the instructors whether they fit their learning styles or not. For the most part, those methods used have been Western, whether or not the teacher was a Westerner.

    According to the Bowens, cognitive styles tests in Nigeria and Kenya (though not necessarily elsewhere in Africa) clearly indicate a preponderence of 'field-dependent' (as opposed to 'field-independent') styles of learning. The Bowens append to their article a list almost 20 contrasting preferences of 'field-dependent' and 'field-independent' styles that might be taken into account by the (theology) teacher. Among the preferences for 'field-dependent' students are: visual orientation (as opposed to auditory), working in groups rather than solitarily and viewing new knowledge with reference to the global totality of life and experience rather than 'for its own sake'. D. and E. Bowen, *Theological Education and Learning Styles in Africa*, in 'Theological News, Incorporating Theological Education Today', vol. 18, No. 1, 1986, pp. 5-9.

14. P. J. Harrison, 'Using the lecture method to best advantage', in *Theological Education Today*, Vol. 9, No. 2, May, 1979.

15. D. Kornfield, 'A working proposal for an alternative model of higher education', in *Theological Education Today*, Vol. 15, No. 3, Sept. 1983. The work Kornfield refers to is, N. Postman and C. Weingartner, *Teaching as a subversive activity*, Dell Publishing, New York, 1969, pp. 17-19.

16. Ted Ward, 'The spilt-rail fence: an analogy for the education of professionals', East Lansing College of Education, Michigan State University, 1969.

17. A notable exception and a striking example of contextualized 'systematic' theology is Donald R. Jacobs' 'Christian Theology in Africa', collated lecture notes given at the Mennonite Theological College. Musoma, Tanzania, in 1963-64. In the preface of the xeroxed copy in my possession, Jacobs explains that the work is

    an experiment in the examination of some problems in Theology assuming the presuppositions of African traditional religion... It is not an attempt to produce a Biblical theology, but simply an honest effort to examine some of the theological problems which perplex the Church in Africa today.

Jacobs organises his material around the central concept of 'power', and each 'lecture' is interspersed with the questions which the students raised and which contributed to the 'excitement and ferment' of the discussions. To my knowledge, the work has not been published.

18. Dickson, op. cit. pp. 205-206.

19. P. A. Kalilombe, 'Doing theology at the grass-roots: a challenge for professional theologians', in *AFER*, Eldoret, Kenya, Vol. 27, No. 4, 1985, p. 233.

20. ibid, p. 234.

21. The exchange took place during the final (group) session of my field-research at Rethy, 18th Jan, 1987.

22. Dickson, op. cit. p. 6.

23. A. J. Smet, 'Le Père Placide Tempels et son oeuvre publiée', in *RAT*, Vol. 1, No. 1, 1977, p. 80.

24. P. Tempels, *Notre Rencontre*, Limete-Leopoldville, p. 36, quoted in Smet, op. cit, p. 80:
     Je regardais donc cet homme en m'adressant à lui: 'Qu'avez-vous? Que vous manque-t-il? Quel homme êtes-vous? Que pensez-vous? Que dèsirez-vous para-dessus tout? Pourquoi vos remèdes magiques? Que signifient-ils?, comment s'opèrent-ils?

25. P. Tempels, ibid, p. 38. Quoted by Smet, op. cit. p. 81:
     Ce fut une nouvelle joie pour nous dfeux de découvrir que nous nous ressemblions et que, de plus en plus, nous commencions à nous rencontrer jusque dans l'âme.

26. The story of the 'Jamaa Movement' is told in de Craemer, The Jamaa and the Church: A bantu Catholic movement in Zaïre', op. cit.

27. J. Gration, 'From Willowbank to Zaïre', op. cit. p. 297.

BIBLIOGRAPHY

Note: The bibligraphy is divided into four on account of the disparate nature of the chapters.

A. General (approximately covering Introduction, Chapter 1 and Conclusion).

Books

Appiah-Kubi K. (ed.), *Libération ou adaptation? — la théologie africaine s'interroge*, Colloque d'Accra, L'Harmattan, Paris, 1979.

Appiah-Kubi K and Torres, S (eds.), *African Theology en route*, New York, Orbis Books, 1979.

Balandier G., *Sociologie actuelle de l'Afrique noire*, Presses Universitaires Françaises, Paris, 1955.

Barrett D. B., *Schism and Renewal in Africa: and analysis of six thousand contemporary religious movements*, Oxford University Press, London, 1968.

Barrett D. B. (ed.), *African Initiatives in Religion*, East African Publishing House, Nairobi, 1971.

Bimwenyi Kweshi, *Discours théologique négro-africain; problème des fondements*, Présence Africaine, Paris, 1981.

Bohannan P., *Africa and the Africans*, The Natural History Press, New York, 1964.

Bontinck F., *Aux Origines de la Philosophie Bantoue; La correspondance Tempels-Hulstaert*, Faculté de Théologie Catholique de Kinshasa, Kinshasa, 1985.

de Craemer W., *The Jamaa and the Church: a Catholic movement in Zaire*, Oxford University Press, Oxford, 1977.

Danquah J. B., *The Akan Doctrine of God*, London, 1944.

Desai R., *Christianity in Africa as seen by Africans*, Denver 1962.

Dickson K and Ellingworth, P., (eds.), *Pour une théologie africaine*, Editions CLE, Yaounde, 1969; *Biblical revelation and African Beliefs*, Lutterworth Press, London and Orbis Nooks, Maryknoll, 1969.

Dillon-Malone C., *The Korsten Basket-Makers; a study of the Masowe Apostles, an indigenous African religious movement*, Manchester University Press, 1978.

Dickson K., *Theology in Africa*, Darton Longman and Todd, London, 1984 (and Orbis Books, Maryknoll, 1984).

Eboussi Boulaga F., *Christianity without Fetishes; an African critique and recapture of Christianity*, trans from French by R. Barr, Orbis Books, Maryknoll, 1984.

Emerson R. and Kilson, M. (eds.), *The Political Awakening of Africa*, Prentice Hall Inc., New Jersey, 1965.

Evans-Pritchard E. E., *Nuer Religion*, Oxford University Press, Oxfordm 1962.

Ferkiss V., *Africa's Search for Identity*, G. Braziller, New York, 1966.

Finnegan R., *Oral Literature in Africa*, Clarendon Press, Oxford, 1970.

Govender S., *Christian Mission and Human Transformation* (Report of Sixth IAMS Conference, Harare), 1985.

Hastings A., *A History of African Christianity, 1960-1975*, Cambridge University Press, Cambridge, 1979.

Hebblethwaite P., *The Runnaway Church*, Collins, London, 1975.

Idowu E. B., *Towards an Indigenous Church*, Oxford University Press, London, 1965.

Idowu E. B., *African Traditional Religion*, SCM, London, 1973.

Jahn J., *A History of Neo-African Literature*, (trans. from German, by O. Coburn and V. Lehrburger), Faber and Faber, London, 1968.

Joppa F. A., *L'engagement des écrivains africains noirs de la langue française*, Editions Naaman, Quebec, 1982.

Kabue B., *L'expérience zaïroise*, Maury, France, 1975.

Kato B., *Theological Pitfalls in Africa*, Evangel Publishing House, Kisumu, 1975.

Kato B., *African Culture and the Christian Faith*, Challenge Publications, Jos, Nigeria, 1976.

Kato B., *Biblical Christianity in Africa*, Africa Christian Press, Achimota, (Ghana), 1985.

Lanternari V., *Religions of the Oppressed*, Knopf, New York, 1963.

Mbiti J., *African Religions and Philosophy*, Heinemann, London, 1969.

Mbiti J., *Concepts of God in Africa*, S.P.C.K., London, 1970.

Mbiti J., *New Testament Eschatology in an African Background*, Oxford University Press, London, 1971.

McSweeney, *Roman Catholicism; the search for relevance*, Blackwell, Oxford, 1980.

Mortimer E., *France and the Africans*, Faber and Faber, London, 1969.

Mulago gwa Cikala, *Un visage africain du christianisme*, Présence Africaine, Paris, 1965.

Mutiso G-C. M., *Socio-Political Thought in African Literature*, Macmillan, London, 1974.

Muzorewa G., The Origins and Development of African Theology, Orbis Books, New York, 1985.

Nordmann-Seiler A., *La littérature néo-africaine*, Presses Universitaires, Françaises, Paris, 1976.

Nkrumah K., *Neo-Colonialism*, Heinemann, London, 1965.

Nyamiti C., *African Tradition and the Christian God*, Gaba Publications, Eldoret, Kenya.

Oladele Taiwe, *An Introduction to West African Literature*, Nelson, London, 1967.

Oliver R. and Fage J. D., *A Short History of Africa*, Penguin African Library, Harmondsworth, 1972.

Parratt J. (ed.), *A Reader in African Christian Theology*, S.P.C.K.,London, 1987.

Des Prêtres Noirs s'interrogent, Les Editions du Cerf, Rencontres 47, Paris, 1956.

Senghor L., *Liberté I, Négritude et humanisme*, Seuil, Paris, 1964.

Shorter A., *African Christian Spirituality*, Geoffrey Chapman, London, 1978.

Tempels P., La philosophie bantoue, edited by Lovanie, Elizabethville, October, 1945. English translation by C. King: *Bantu Philosophy*, Présence Africaine, Paris, 1959.

Tempels P., *Notre Rencontre*, Limete, Kinshasa, 1962.

Turner H. W., *Profile Through Preaching*, Edinburgh, 1965.

Welbourn F. B., *East African Rebels; a study of some independent churches*, SCM Press, London, 1961.

Welbourn F. B. and Ogot B. A., *A Place to Feel at Home; a study of two independent churches in Western Kenya*, Oxford University Press, London, 1966.

Articles

Agbeti J. K., 'African Theology what is it?', in *Presence*, No. 5, 1972.

Appiah-Kubi K., 'Indigenous African Christian Churches: signs of Authenticity', in *Bulletin de Théologie Africaine*, Vol. 1. No. 2, 1979.

Assimeng M., 'Crisis, identity and integration in African religion', in H. Mol (ed.), *Identity and Religion*, 1978.

Balandier G., 'Les mythes politiques de colonisation et de décolonisation en Afrique', in *Cahiers Internationaux de Sociologie*, No. 33, 1962.

Barrett D. B., 'Interdisciplinary theories of religion and African independency', in Barrett (ed.) *African Initiative in Religion*, East African Publishing House, Nairobi, 1971.

Becken H-J., 'The experience of healing in the Church in Africa', in *Contact*, No. 29, 1975, Geneva.

Bediako K., 'Christian tradition and the African God revisited; a process in the exploration of a theological idiom',in Gitari D. and Benson P., *The Living God*, Africa Theological Fraternity, 1986.

Beyerhaus P., 'The encounter with messianic movements in Africa', paper presented at University of Aberdeen, April, 1968. (Centre for new Religious Movements, Birmingham).

Boka di Mpasi, 'A propos des religious populaires d'Afrique subsaharienne'. in *Telema*, June, 1979.

Bowen D. and E., 'Theological Education and learning styles in Africa, in *Theological News incorporating Theological Education Today*, Vol. 18, No.1, 1986.

Buijtenhuijs R., 'Messianisme et nationalisme en Afrique noire', in *African Perspectives*, (Leiden), No. 2, of 1976 (issued 1977).

Bureau R.,   'Sorcellerie et prophétisme en Afrique noire', in *Etudes*, April, 1967.

van Campenhoudt A., 'Séparatisme et pastorale en Afrique noire', in *L'Eglise vivant*, (Louvain), Vol. 22, No. 5, 1970.

Daneel M. L., 'Communication et libération in African independent churches', in *Missionalia*,Vol. 11, No. 2, 1983.

Dozon J-P., 'Les mouvements politico-religieux; syncrétismes, messianismes, néo-traditionalismes', in Augé M. (ed,), *La construction du monde*, F Maspéro, Paris, 1974.

Fashole-Luke E. W., 'Footpaths and signposts to African Theologies', in *Bulletin de Théologie Africaine*, Vol. 3, No. 5, 1981.

Fernandez J., 'African religious movements; types and dynamics}. in *Journal of Modern African Studies*, Vol. 2, No. 4, 1964.

Fisher H.,'Conversion reconsidered', *Africa*, Vol. 43, No. 1. 1971.

Fisher H., 'The Juggernaut's apologia', *Africa*, Vol. 55, Mo. 2, 1985.

Gray R., 'Christianity and religious change in Africa' in *African Affairs*, No. 306:77, 1978.

Harrison P. J., 'Using the lecture methold to best advantage', in *Theological Education Today*, Vol. 9, No. 2, May, 1979.

Hayward V., 'African independent church movements', in *Ecumenical Review*, Vol. 15, No. 2, 1963.

Horton R., 'African Conversion', in *Africa*, Vol. 41, No. 2, 1971.

Horton R., 'On the rationality of conversion', *Africa*, Vol. 45, No. 3, 1975.

Janzen J., 'Vers une phénoménologie de la guérison en Afrique centrale', in *Etudes Congolaises*, Kinshasa, Vol. 12, No. 2. 1969.

Kagame A., 'L'ethno-philosophie des "Bantu"', in Klibansky R. (ed.), *La philosophie contempraine*, Florence, 1971.

Kearns J., 'AFER's index — quite a story!' *African Ecclesiastical Review*, 1984.

Kornfield D., 'A working proposal for an alternative model of higher education', in *Theological Education Today*, Vol. 15, No. 3, Sept, 1983.

Loewen J. H., 'Mission churches, independent churches and felt needs in Africa', in *Missiology*, Vol. 4, No. 4, 1965.

Masamba ma Mpolo, 'Community and Cure; the therapeutics of the traditional religions and the religion of the prophets in Africa', in *Christian and Islamic Contributions towards establishing independent states in Africa south of the Sahara*, Stuttgart, 1979.

Mbiti J., 'Christianity and African Culture', PACLA Conference lecture, 1976, in *Evangelical Review of Theology*, Vol. 3, No. 2, 1979.

Mbiti J., 'Some current concerns of African Theology', in *Expository Times*, Vol. 87.

Mbiti J., 'The Biblical basis in present trends of African Theology', in *Bulletin de Théologie Africaine*, Vol. 1, No. 1. 1979.

Mosothoane E., 'Ancestor cults and communion of Saints', in *Missionalia*, August 1973.

N'Soki K., 'Genèse de l'expression "théologie africaine"', in *Telema*, No. 20, Dec. 1979.

Omoyajowo A. J., 'An African expression of Christianity', in Moore B. (ed.) *Black Theology — the South African Voice*, C. Hurst, London, 1973.

Onibere S. G., 'The phenomenon of African religious independency —

blessing or curse on the Church universal?', in *Africain Theological Journal*, Vol. 10, No. 1, 1981.

Oosterval G., 'Modern messianic movements as a theological and missiological challenge', in *Missionary Studies 2*, (Elkhart), 1973.

Oosthuiszen G. C., 'Causes of religious independentism in Africa', in *Ministry*, Vol. 11, No. 4, 1977.

Pope John-Paul II, *AFER*, Vol. 25, No. 5, 1983.

Pottmeyer, 'Vatican II — 20 years on', in *Pro Mundi Vita*, Bulletin 102, 1985/3.

Ranger T. O., 'Medical science and Pentecost' the dilemma of anglicanism in Africa', in Shiels W. J., (ed.),*The Church and healing*, Blackwell, Oxford, 1982.

Ranger T. O., 'Religious movements and politica in Sub-Saharan Africa', in *African Studies Review*, Vol. 29, No. 2.

'Report of the Second Conference of the Organisation of African Independent Churches', Nairobi, 1982.

Ruch E. A., 'Philosphy of African History', in *African Studies*, (Johannesburg), Vol. 32, No. 2, 1973.

Savage P., 'Four crises in Third World theological education', in *Evangelical Missions Quarterly*, Fall, 1972.

Smet A. J., 'Le Père Placide Tempels et son oeuvre publiée', in *Revue Africaine de Théologie*, Vol. 1, No. 1, 1977.

'Speaking for Ourselves', report by members of African Independent Churches on their pilot study of the history and theology of their churches, Publ. by I.C.T., Braamfontein, South Africa, n.d.

Sprunger A. R. 'The contribution of the African independent churches to a relevant theology for Africa', in Becken H-J., (ed.) *Relevant Theology for Africa*, Durban, 1973.

Turner H. W., 'The place of independent religious movements in the modernization of Africa', in *Journal of Religion in Africa*, Vol. 2, No. 1, 1969.

Turner H. W., 'The approach to Africa's religious movements', in *African Perspective*, No. 2, 1977.

Turner H. W., 'African independent churches and economic development', in *World Development*, Vol. 8, 1980.

Tutu D., 'Théologie africaine et théologie noire; la quête de L'authenticité et la lutte pour la libération', in *Flambeau*, Vol. 49, 1976.

Walls A. F., 'Africa and Christian identity', in *Mission Focus*, Vol. 6, No. 7, 1978.

Ward Ted, 'The split-rail fence; and analogy for the education fo professionals', East Lansing College of Education, Michigan State University, 1969.

Theses

Bediako K., 'Identity and integrity: an enquiry into the nature and problems of theological indigenization in selected early Hellenistic and modern African Christian writers', PhD, Aberdeen University, 1984.

Tienou T., 'The problem of methodology in African Christian Theologies', PhD, Fuller Theological Seminary, School of World Mission, 1984.

B Faculty of Catholic Theology, Kinshasa (Chapter 2)

Abbreviations: FTCK: Faculté de Théologie Catholique de Kinshasa.

Books

Atal D. et al (eds.), *Christianisme et identité africaine*, Actes du Premier Congrès des Biblistes Africains, Missionwissenschaftliches Institut Missio-Aachen, Faculté de Théologie Catholique, Kinshasa, 1980.

404

Bimwenyi Kweshi, *Discours théologique négro-africain; problème des fondements*, Présence Africaine, Paris, 1981.

Bontinck F., *Aux origines de le Philosophie Bantoue; la correspondance Tempels-Hulstaert*, FTCK, Kinshasa, 1985.

Hountondji P. J., *Sur la 'philosophie africaine'; critique de l'éthnophilosophie*, F. Maspéro, Paris, 1977.

Mulago gwa Cikala, *Un visage africain du christianisme*, Paris, 1965.

Des prêtres noirs s'interrogent, Editions du Cerf, Paris, 1956.

Tempels P., *La philosophie bantoue*, Présence Africaine, Paris, 1949; 2nd Edit. 1961; 3rd Edit. 1965.

Yakemtchouk R., *L'Université Lovanium et sa Faculté de Théologie*, Chastre, 1983.

Articles

Abbreviations: *CRA* — Cahiers des Religions Africaines
RAT — Revue Africaine de Théologie

Andrews M. E., 'The Old Testament as Israelite theology and its implications for a New Zealand Theology', in *South East Asia Journal of Theology*, No.17, Issue 2, 1976.

Basinsa N., Review of Hountondji's book, *Sur la 'philosophie africaine'*, in *RAT*, Vol. 3, No. 5, 1979.

Buakasa T., 'Le projet des rites de réconciliation', *CRA*, Vol. 8, No. 16, 1974.

Buetubela B, 'Le produit de la vigne et le vin nouveau', *RAT*, Vol. 8, No. 15, 1984.

'Discours du Pape aux évêques du Zaïre', Kinshasa, 3rd May, 1980', *RAT*, Vol. 4, No. 7, 1980.

Ladrièére J., 'Perspectives sur la philosophie africaine', *RAT*. Vol. 5, No. 10, 1981.

Laleye I-P., Review of work by Diemer, *Symposium on philosophy in the present situation of Africa. RAT,* Vol. 6, No.12, 1982.

Lodewyckx H., 'Philosophie Africaine, origines et perspectives', in *Bijdragen, tijschrift voor filosofie en theologie,* No. 47, 1986.

Malula J., 'L'âme bantoue face à l'Evangile', in *Vivante Afrique,* 1958.

Mampila A., 'Une eucharistie sans pain ni vin? Une question théologique', *RAT,* Vol. 8, No. 15, 1984.

Mbonyikebe S., 'Brèves réflexions sur la conception traditionnelle du péché en Afrique Centrale', *CRA,* Vol. 8, No. 16, 1974.

Mbonyikebe S., 'Faute, péché, pénitence et réconciliation dans les traditions de quelques sociétés en Afrique Centrale', *CRA.* Vol. 14, No. 28, 1980.

Monsengwo P., 'L'exégèse biblique et questions africaines', *RAT,* Vol. 6, No. 12, 1982.

Mulago V., 'Le problème de la théologie africaine à la lumière de Vatican II', in *Renouveau de l'Eglise et Nouvelles Eglises,* Colloque sur la théologie africaine, Kinshasa, 1967.

Mveng E., 'Editorial', *Bulletin de Théologie Africaine* Vol. 1, No. 1, 1979.

Ngimbi-Nseka, 'Théologie et anthropologie transcendentale', *RAT.,*Vol. 3, No. 5, 1979.

Ngimbi-Nseka, 'Esquisse d'une éthique de l'intersubjectivité', *RAT,* Vol. 3, No. 6, 1979.

Ngindu M., 'La Quatrième Semaine Théologique de Kinshasa et la problématique d'une théologie africaine', *CRA,* Vol. 2, No. 4, 1968.

Ngindu M., 'Le propos du recours à l'authenticité et le christianisme au Zaïre', *CRA,* Vol. 8, No. 16, 1974.

Nkeramihigo T., La problématique de la transcendance chez Ricoeur',
RAT, Vol. 5, No. 9, 1981.

Nothomb D., 'Ordonner prêtres des animateurs (mariés) de communauté de base?', RAT, Vol. 7, No. 14, 1983.

Ntedika K., 'Adresse d'ouverture; Religions africaines et christianisme',
CRA, Vol. 11, No. 21, 1977.

Smet A. J., Le Père Placide Tempels et son oeuvre publiée', RAT, Vol.
1, No. 1, 1977.

Tshiamalenga N., 'La vision 'ntu' de l'homme; essai de philosophie
linguistique et anthropologique', CRA, Vol. 7, No. 4,
1973.

Tshiamalenga N., 'La philosophie de la faute dans la tradition luba',
CRA, Vol. 8, No. 16, 1974.

Tshibangu T., Revue du Clergé Africain Vol. 2, No. 4, 1960.

Ukachukwu M., 'The subordination of women in the Church; I Cor. 14:
33b-36 reconsidered', RAT, Vol. 8, No. 16, 1984.

Vanneste A., 'Une faculté de théologie en Afrique?', Revue du Clergé
Africain, May, 1958.

Vanneste A., 'Bilan théologique d'un voyage apostolique', RAT, Vol. 4,
No. 8, 1980.

Vanneste A., 'Une eucharistie sans pain et sans vin?', RAT, Vol. 6, No.
12, 1982.

Vanneste A., 'La théologie africaine; discours de l'épiscopat zairois et
de Jean-Paul II', RAT, Vol. 7, No. 14, 1983.

C. Kimbanguism and Orality (Chapter 3)

Books

Asch S., L'Eglise du Prophète Kimbangu; ses origines, à son rôle actuel
au Zaire, Editions Karthala, Paris, 1983.

Bena-Silu, *Simon Kimbangu libère et réhabilite la race noire*, Editions Kimbanguistes, Kinshasa, 1981.

Boka S. and Raymaekers P., *250 Chants de l'Eglise de Jésus-Christ sur la terre par le Prophète Simon Kimbangu;* Première Série: 85 chants de Nsambu André. Institut de recherches Economiques et Sociales, Université Lovanium, Léopoldville, 1960.

Chomé J., *La passion de Simon Kimbangu*, Présence Africaine, Brussels, 1959.

Dialungana Kiangani, *Biuvu ye Mvutu* (Catechism in Kikongo, Lingala and French), 31st July, 1970, Nkamba-Jérusalem.

Diangienda K., *L'histoire du kimbanguisme,* Editions Kimbanguistes, Kinshasa, 1984.

Finnegan R., *Oral Literature in Africa,* Clarendon Press, Oxford, 1970.

Heintze-Flad W., *L'Eglise kimbanguiste, une église qui chante et qui prie,* Interuniversitair voor Missiologie en Oecumenica, Leiden, 1978.

Luntadila L., *Libération et développement du kimbanguisme,* Kinshasa, 1971.

Luntadila L., *Kimbanguisme, un rayon d'espoir,* Editions CEDI, Kinshasa, 1974.

MacGaffey W., *Modern Kongo Prophets: Religion in a plural society,* Indiana University Press, Bloomington, 1983.

Martin R. C., (ed.), *Approaches to Islam in Religious Studies,* University of Arizona Press, 1985.

Martin M-L., *Simon Kimbangu, un prophète et son église,* Editions du Soc, Lausanne, 1981.

Ong W. J., *Orality and Literacy; the technologizing of the word,* Methuen, London and New York, 1982.

Oosthuizen G. C., *The Theology of a South African messiah*. E. J. Brill, Leiden / Köln, 1967.

Raymaekers P., *Histoire de Simon Kimbangu, Prophète, d'après les écrivains Nfinangani et Nzungu, 1921*, B.O.P.R., Kinshasa, 1971.

Sundkler B. G. M., *Bantu Prophets in Southern Africa*, Lutterworth Press, London, 1948 (rev. ed. 1961).

Sundkler B. G. M., *Zulu Zion and Some Swazi Zionists*, Oxford University Press, 1976.

Sundkler B. G. M., *Bara Bukoba*, C. Hurst, London, 1980.

Ustorf W., *Africanische Initiative: das aktive Leiden des Propheten Simon Kimbangu*, Herbert Lang, Bern and Frankfurt, 1975.

Ware T., *The Orthodox Church*, Penguin, Harmondsworth, 1963.

Articles

Asch S., 'Contradictions internes d'une institution religieuse', in *Archives de Sciences Sociales de Religions*, No. 52. 26 (1), 1981.

Droogers A., 'Kimbanguism at the grassroots; beliefs in a local Kimbanguist Church', in *Journal of Religion in Africa*, Vol. 11, No. 3, 1980.

Dubois J. and Gourbin A., 'A propos de L'essence de la théologie kimbanguiste', in *Telema*, Vol. 3, No. 19, 1979.

Hollenweger W., 'The "What" and the "How"; Content and communication of the one message', in *Expository Times*, Vol. 86, No. 12, 1975.

Martin M-L., 'Essai d'interprétation théologique de la vie et de l'enseignement de L'Eglise de Jésus Christ sur la terre par le Prophète Simon K!mbangu', in *Le monde non-chrétien* 1968.

Masson J., 'Simple réflexions sur des chants kimbanguistes', in *Devant les sectes non-chrétiennes*, Desclée de Brouwer, Louvain.

Mbasani Mbambi, 'L'implantation de l'Armée du Salut au Congo-Belge et au Congo-Français', Kinshasa, n.d. (Fr. Bontinck's library).

Raymaekers P., in *Zaïre*, (Brussels), 13th July, 1959, pp. 675-756.

Theses and Dissertations

Kadu B., 'La confession dans l'Eglise kimbanguiste', Mémoire de fin d'études, Faculté de Théologie Kimbanguiste, 1976.

MacKay D. M., 'The once and future kingdom. Kongo models of renewal in the church at Ngombe Lutete and in the Kimbanguist movement', PhD., Aberdeen University, 1986.

Mfinda Luhunakio, 'La théologie d'intercession dans l'Eglise kimbanguiste', *Mémoire de fin d'études*, Faculté de Théologie Kimbanguiste, Kinshasa, 1982.

Wono K. T., 'La théologie kimbanguiste dans les chants captés en 1921', *Mémoire de fin d'études*, Faculté de Théologie Kimbanguiste, Kinshasa, 1982.

Tshibola D. M., 'Esquisse d'une théologie klmbanguiste autour des cantiques captés entre 1956 et 1960', *Mémoire de fin d'études*, Faculté de Théologie Kimbanguiste, 1982.

Unpublished Documents

Beguin W. and Martin M-L., 'Study report on the EJCSK, its present situation and its ecumenical relations', unpublished, 1968. (In Study Centre for New Religious Movements, Selly Oak Colleges, Birmingham.)

Bena-Silu, 'A propos de l'Eglise du Prophète Kimbangu' de Susan Asch; illustration de falsification de l'histoire et des préjugés', Direction internationale de l'Eglise

Kimbanguiste, Kinshasa, 1984. Copy sent to Molyneux by author, June, 1987.

Diangienda K., 'Nouvelle disposition relative au programme cultuel pour l'encadrement spirituel des fidèles', Nkamba-Jérusalem, 29th April, 1985. Copy given to Molyneux by Nsambu, Kinshasa, February, 1987.

Mithridate R. B., 'Histoire de l'apparition de Simon Kimbangu, Tome I', Editions Notre Kongo Dieto, R.D.C., stencilled, n.d. (in Fr Bontinck's Library, Kinshasa.) The document contains the text of many council minutes and letters written by Belgian colonial officials in the early 1920s.

Nsambu T., 'Exposé sur le mobile des chants kimbanguistes'; stencilled document, Kinshasa, dated 6th October, 1981. Copy given to Molyneux by Nsambu, February, 1987, Kinshasa.

Nsambu T., Autobiographical notes, typed, dated 10th February, 1987. Copy given to Molyneux, February, 1987, Kinshasa.

D. Theological Education, Contextualisation, etc. (Chapter 4)

Books

Boone O., Les peuplades du Congo-Belge, Tervuren, Belgium, 1935.

Dickson K., Theology in Africa, Darton Longman and Todd, London, 1984 and Orbis Books, Maryknoll, 1984.

Fleming B., Contextualization of Theology, William Carey Library, Pasadena, 1980.

Grimes M. S., Life out of Death; the story of the Africa Inland Mission, AIM, 1917.

Hillman E., Polygamy reconsidered: African plural marriage and the Christian churches, Orbis Books, Maryknoll, 1975.

Kluckhohn C., Mirror for Man; the relationship of anthropolgy to modern life, McGraw Hill, New York, 1949.

Laman K., *The Kongo III*, Studia Ethnographica Upsaliensa, XII, Lund, Sweden, 1962.

Makanzu M., *L'Histoire de l'ECZ*, Kinshasa, n.d. (1972/3?)

Mbiti J., *African Religions and Philosophy*, Heinemann, London, 1969.

Middleton and Winter (eds.), *Witchcraft and Sorcery in East Africa*, Routledge and Kegan Paul, London, 1963.

Miller C. S., *The Unlocked Door* — *The life of Peter Cameron Scott.*, Parry Jackman Ltd., London. 1955.

Parrinder E. G., *African Traditional Religion*, Sheldon Press, London, 1974.

Richardson K., *Garden of Miracles: the story of the Africa Inland Mission*, AIM, London, 1968.

Rosaldo M. Z., *Women, Culture and Society; a theoretical overview*, Stanford University Press, 1974.

Stirton S., *Changing Scenes among the Alur*, AIM, n.d.

Sundkler B. G. M., *Bara Bukoba*, C. Hurst, London, 1980.

Tucker A. N. and Bryan M. A., *Linguistic Survey of the Northern Bantu Borderland*, Vol. I, Part III, Oxford University Press, London, 1956.

Warwick M. (ed.), *Witchcraft and Sorcery*, Penguin Books, Harmondsworth, 1970.

The Willowbank Report; Gospel and Culture; Lausanne Occasional Papers No. 2, Lausanne Committee for World Evangelization, Wheaton, 1978.

Winter R. D., *Theological Education by Extension*, William Carey Library, South Pasadena.

Articles

Bujo B., 'Nos ancêtres, ces saints inconnus', *Bulletin de Théologie Africaine*, Vol. 1, No. 2, 1979.

Buswell III J. O., 'Contextualization; Is it just another word for indigenization?', in *Evangelical Missions Quarterly*, Jan, 1978.

Coe S., 'In search of renewal in theological education', in *Theological Education*, Vol. 9, No. 4, 1973.

Gehman R., Guidelines in contextualization', in *East Africa Journal of Evangelical Theology*, Vol. 2, No. 1, 1983.

Gration J., 'Willowbank to Zaïre', in *Missiology*, July, 1984.

Harrison P. J., 'Using the lecture method to best advantage', in *Theological Education Today*, Vol. 9, No. 2, 1979.

Hurlburt C. E., 'Arrival in Congo', in *Hearing and Doing*, (former magazine of the Africa Inland Mission), Vol.17, No. 2, 1912. (AIM archives, Archway, London.)

Jones V., 'Women in the Zaïre Church', *Inland Africa* (current magazine of Africa Inland Mission), Summer 1981. (AIM archives, Archway, London.)

Kabasele F., Le Christ comme ancêtre et aîné', in Kabasele F., Dore J. and Luneau R., *Chemins de la christologie africaine*, Desclée, Paris, 1986.

Kalilombe P., 'Doing theology at grassroots; a challenge for Professional theologians', Parts I and II, *African Ecclesiastical Review*, Vol. 27, No. 3 and 4, 1985.

Kaplan S., 'The Africanization of missionary Christianity; History and Typology', in *Journal of Religion in Africa*, Vol. 16, No. 3, 1986.

Kinsler F. R., 'Mission and context; the current debate about contextualization', *Evangelical Missions Quarterly*, January, 1978.

Kinsler F. R., 'Extension; an alternative model for theological education', in *Learning in Context: the search for innovative
patterns in theological education* Theological Education
Fund, New Life Press, Bromley, 1973.

Newberry F. A., Letters published in *Hearing and Doing* (former
magazine of Africa Inland Mission): Vol. 17, No. 3, 1912;
Vol. 18, No. 3, 1913, Vol. 18, No. 4, 1913. (Archives of
AIM, Archway, London.)

Nyamiti C., 'New theological approach and new vision of the Church
in Africa', in *Revue Africaine de Théologie*, Vol. 2, No. 3,
1978.

Padilla R., 'Hermeneutics and Culture, a theological perspective', in
Stott J. R. W. and Coote R., *Down to Earth*, Hodder and
Stoughton, London, 1980.

Simbo B., 'An African critique of Western theology', in *Evangelical
Missions Quarterly*, Vol. 7, No. 1, 1983.

Taber C., 'Contextualization: Indigenization and/or Transformtion?'
in McCurry D. (ed.), *The Gospel and Islam*, MARC,
1979.

Tucker R., 'African women's movement finds massive response', in
Evangelical Missions Quarterly, Vol. 22, No. 3, 1986.

The Willowbank Report — Gospel and Culture, Lausanne Committee
for World Evangelization, Wheaton, 1978. (Reprinted in
Stott and Coote (eds.), *Down to Earth; Studies in Christianity and Culture*, Hodder and Stoughton, London, 1980.)

Yego J., 'Polygamy and the African Church', in *East Africa Journal of
Evangelical Theology*, Vol. 3, No. 1, 1984.

Unpublished material

Africa Inland Mission: a) Doctrinal Basis (from AIM Constitution,
Article III, Section 5, ratified May 1986. Provided by AIM,
Archway, London.

b) Minutes of AIM International Council, Nairobi, 6-10th May, 1985.

c) Statistics of missionary personnel and occupations. Provided by AIM, Archway, London.

Bunia Theological Seminary (Institut Supérieur Théologique de Bunia):

a) Minutes of Commission for Degree Programme 2nd and 25th August, 1987. Bunia.

b) Course Description, 1982. Bunia.

c) Course Programme, (revised, 1978). Bunia.

d) cf, Self-Evaluation Report 1984-85. Bunia.

Communauté Evangélique au Centre de l'Afrique (Bunia):

a) CECA Doctrinal Statement (from Constitution, April, 1959).

b) Editions CECA. Objectives (1st July, 1986), Rethy. Copy sent by Kwany L., 25th July, 1987.

c) Manuscripts (copies received from Bura T., Rethy):
   a) Document 1 — 'Evangile et Croyances Africaines' (produced by Rethy group),
   b) Document 2 — 'Fétishisme et guérison' (produced by Aungba group),

   c) Document 3 — 'Tribalisme' (produced by Bunia group),

d) Report on evangelization, (1983-1987), submitted by Atido K. to CECA Office, 14th July, 1987. Copy sent to Molyneux, August, 1987.

e) Stencilled document, undated, produced by the CECA Department of Christian Education, on Seminars held at

Rethy, February 1987, on Choirs, Christian Home, Sunday School, Leadership. Procured at Rethy, January 1987.

f) Theological Education by Extension (TEE) Annual Reports: 1982-83; 83-84; 84-85; 85-86; 86-87. Copies supplied by Kana M., 19th October, 1987.

g) 'Tujenge' objectives (printed on back cover of the 'Tujenge' magazine). Rethy.

Sources

The following are the more important of the non-literary sources used in this thesis:

Faculty of Catholic Theology, Kinshasa

Atal sa Angang, b. in Bandundu, 1934. Professor of New Testament FTCK. Conversation concerning 'African Theology' and hermeneutics, at the Faculty, 4th February, 1987.

Mudiji Malamba, b. 1941. Professor of Metaphysics and Contemporary Philosophy FTCK. Conversation at FTCK on philosophy programme.

Mulago gwa Cikala, b. in Birawa (Kivu, Zaïre) in 1924. Studied in Zaïre, Rwanda and Rome. He was a principal contributor to the seminal work: *Des prêtres noirs s'interrogent*. After several periods of pastoral office, he joined the FTCK, the Faculty's first African teacher. In 1966 he was appointed Director of the 'Centre d'Etudes des Religions Africaines' and of its related journal, *Cahiers des Religions Africaines*. Author of several books and numerous articles relating to 'African Theology'. Lengthy conversation, at Mulago's résidence, Kinshasa, 1st Feb, 1987.

Tshibantgu Tshishuku, b. 1933 in Shaba, (Zaïre). While still a student at the Theology Faculty in 1960, opposed Vanneste in the debate on 'African Theology'. Author of, among other works, *Théologie positive et théologie spéculative* and of numerous articles. Made Bishop in 1970. Rector of National University of Zaïre, 1971-1981. Conversation, résidence Cardinal Malula, Limete, Kinshasa, 2nd February, 1987.

Alfred Vanneste, b. 12th Aug, 1922, Courtrai, Belgium. Professor of Dogmatic Theology at FTCK. Dean of FTCK 1957-1971; Assistant Dean 1978-1985. Author of many articles on African Theology. Numerous conversations in his Kinshasa home, 28th Jan,-6th Feb, 1987.

Kimbanguists

Bena-Silu, Director of the 'Cabinet du Chef Spirituel' and one of the leaders of the EJCSK. Conversation on theological and administrational matters. Bongolo, Kinshasa, 26th Feb, 1987.

Mapeka ma Kisonga, Director of the 'Bureau Téchnique', Bongolo, where 'inspired' hymns are processed. With his colleagues, answered many questions during a work session at Bongolo, 18th Feb, 1987.

Mabika Masala, Unfailingly cheerful Secretary of the 'Département des Chants', Bongolo, Kinshasa and himself a receiver of 'inspired hymns'. Accompanied me on several of the choir visits. Interviewed (Bongolo) 13th Feb, 1987.

Marie-Louise Martin, Dean of the Kimbanguist Faculty of Theology at Lutendele, Kinshasa (soon to leave there to devote herself to theological education by extension among Kimbanguist leaders). Correspondence on several occasions. Arranged informative visit to the Faculty, 21st-22nd Feb, 1987. Many conversations about historical and theological matters relating to the Kimbanguists.

Mfoko Ndombala, Fwasi's nephew, now a Kimbanguist pastor. In conversation at Bongolo, 16th Feb, 1987, he related much about his famous uncle.

Nziama, Kimbanguist bank employee in Kinshasa, made redundant just before my arrival, and thus able to spend every day working with me on the translation of hymns from Kikongo into French, February, 1987.

Nsambu Twasilwa, Director of the 'Département des Chants', Bongolo, Kinshasa. His friendliness and knowledge of the story of Kimbanguist hymns from the beginning and his co-operation in making available archive material, proved to be of invaluable assistance. After Mista Fwasi, the most prolific 'receiver' of 'inspired hymns'.

Gospel and Culture Seminars, CECA

a) Members of the French-speaking Seminars

Alo Dradebo, b.1941. Graduate of Bunia Theological Seminary, Kinshasa Protestant Faculty of Theology and University of Geneva. Assistant Director of Bunia Seminary. Interviewed 26th Jan, 1987.

Amula Djang'etambe, b.1955. Graduate of Bunia Theological Seminary. Chaplain and secondary school teacher at Rethy. Recently appointed as Administrative Secretary of CECA. Highly articulate member of the 'Rethy Group'. Interviewed 22nd Jan, 1987.

Angu-Andia Gonde, b. 1944. Bunia Theological Seminary Graduate. Secondary school teacher 7 yrs. Assistant Co-ordinator of Christian Education, CECA, 7 yrs. Absent for interview; questionnaire returned July, 1987.

Atido Kunde-Dong', b. 1935. Eight years of service as Co-ordinator of Evangelism, CECA. Absent for Interview; questionnaire returned July, 1987.

Bura Ngaba, b. 1955. Bunia Theological Seminary graduate. Seven years as Bible School teacher. Interviewed Bunia, 24th Jan, 1987.

Bura Thenga, b.1945. Post-secondary studies in Nairobi in communications, journalism, etc. School teacher for many years, then Chief Editor at 'Editions CECA', Rethy. Interviewed in Bunia, 23rd Jan, 1987.

Djawotto Kisa, b.1945. MTh. at Vaux, Paris. Pastor in Bunia 1979-1986 and part-time teacher of Old Testament at Bunia Theological Seminary 1979-1986. Currently completing PhD studies (USA). Absent for interview; questionnaire returned June, 1987.

Etsea Ang'apoza, b. 1935. Post-secondary studies at Vaux, Paris. Currently Legal Representative of CECA. Interviewed Bunia, 21st Jan, 1987.

Kana Muruo, b. 1945. Graduate of Bunia Theological Seminary. Teacher in Primary and Secondary schools. Since 1982 Co-ordinator of Theological Education by Extension (TEE). Interviewed in Bunia, 21st Jan, 1987.

Kile Kpala, b. 1935. Bunia Theological Seminary graduate. Some 20 years in secondary and Bible School teaching, the last 4 years as Director of Oicha Bible School. Colourful and enthusiastic. Interviewed 25th Jan, 1987.

Kwany Zaabu, b.1943. Following post-secondary education in mathematics/technology, spent many years as teacher. director and Education Co-ordinator for CECA secondary schools. Currently Director of 'Editions CECA' based in Rethy, where interviewed, 20th Jan, 1987.

Okuonzi Amandru, b.1935. Graduate of Bunia Theological Seminary and for many years its Administrative Secretary. A man of many gifts and shrewd perception. Interviewed 23rd Jan, 1987, Bunia.

Sumbuso Bamaraki, b.1956. Bunia Theological Seminary graduate, further studies in Bangui, CAR. Currently Academic Secretary, Bunia Theological Seminary. Interviewed Bunia, 24th Jan, 1987.

Uchanda Unen, b.1938. Bunia Theological Seminary graduate. Thirteen years in Bible School teaching, eight as Director of

Aungba Bible School. Currently doing further studies in Kinshasa's Protestant Faculty of Theology, where I interviewed him, 1st Feb, 1987.

Ufoyuru Kpathi, b. 1941. Bunia Theological Seminary Graduate. Served as chaplain (4 yrs.), Bible School teacher (4 yrs.), Evangelism Co-ordinator (4 yrs.) and currently Director of Radio Programmes CECA. Interviewed 22nd Jan, 1987.

b) Members of the Swahili-speaking seminar, Rethy

Balonge, b. 1916. Honorary President of CECA. Interviewed at Rethy, 17th Jan, 1987.

Buchu, Head Pastor, Linga. Pastor since 1962. Interviewed at Linga, 17th Jan, 1987.

Djaldero, b. 1928. Pastor since 1964. Interviewed at Rethy, 17th Jan, 1987.

Groche, b. 1942. Pastor for 20 years. Interviewed at Rethy, 17th Jan, 1987.

Lainya Ngadyuwa, b. 1945. Pastor for over 20 years. Not a participant of the Rethy Seminars, but one who heard the report of the Seminar and who shared their findings with the elders of his church. Interviewed at Rethy, 18th Jan, 1987.

Laleni, Loquacious and energetic head pastor at Rethy. Interviewed 18th Jan, 1987.

Ukelo, b. 1952. Attended some but not all of the Seminar sessions. Secondary school teaching (4 yrs.); currently engaged in Bible translation into the Alur language.

c) Others

John Gration American AIM missionary 1953-64 in secondary and Bible teaching. Sometime Associate Home Director and Candidate Secretary for AIM (USA). Since 1975 Professor of Missions at Wheaton College Graduate School. Initiator of the 'Gospel and Culture Seminars' (ch. 4). Frequent correspondence since 1985. I am indebted to him for photocopies of relevant letters, field notes, etc.

David Langford, Helped Gration set up the 'Gospel and Culture Seminars'. Was of great assistance in enabling me to contact the Swahili-speaking participants in the Rethy and Linga areas for interviewing. Frequent correspondence. Currently researching innovative methods of theological education in the CECA area, such as use of tape-recordings. For several years a colleague at the Bunia Theological Seminary; now based at Rethy.

DATE DUE